Political Parties and Linkage

Political Parties and Linkage

A Comparative Perspective

Edited by Kay Lawson

New Haven and London
Yale University Press

Designed by James J. Johnson
and set in Monophoto Times New Roman type by
Asco Trade Typesetting Ltd., Hong Kong.
Printed in the United States of America by
The Vail-Ballou Press, Binghamton, N.Y.

Library of Congress Cataloging in Publication Data

Main entry under title:

Political parties and linkage.

  Includes index.
  1. Political parties—Addresses, essays,
lectures. I. Lawson, Kay.
JF2011.P57   324.2′04   79–26751
ISBN 0–300–02331–6

10 9 8 7 6 5 4 3 2 1

Contents

PART I

Introduction

1.

Political Parties and Linkage

KAY LAWSON

Political parties can be put to almost any political or
governmental purpose. They can articulate interests, aggregate interests,
recruit leaders, make government policy, transmit policy decisions to
the people, carry out policy, adjudicate disputes, and educate or coerce
entire peoples. Of course, other institutions, public and private, also
perform these functions. But what distinguishes parties from all the rest
is their emphasis on linkage. Parties are seen, both by their members
and by others, as agencies for forging links between citizens and policymakers. Their raison d'être is to create a substantive connection between
rulers and ruled. As Giovanni Sartori has pointed out, this does not
mean that party members are not self-seeking: "The existence of parties
by no means eliminates selfish and unscrupulous motivations. The power-
seeking drives of politicians remain constant."[1] Nevertheless, "even if
the party politician is motivated by crude self-interest, his behavior must
depart—if the constraints of the system are operative—from the motiva-
tion. . . . Parties are instrumental to collective benefits, to an end that
is not merely the private benefit of the contestants. Parties link people
to a government."[2]

However, although there seems to be general agreement that such
is the purpose of parties, there is in the literature on parties very little
systematic effort to determine what it means, in toto, for parties to link

The author wishes to thank Heinz Eulau and Kenneth Janda for their careful
review of this introductory essay and useful suggestions for its improvement.

1. Giovanni Sartori, *Parties and Party Systems: A Framework for Analysis* (London: Cambridge University Press, 1976), p. 25.
2. Ibid.

3

citizens to government. Studies of the linkage roles of particular parties are manifold, and indeed much of the existing literature on parties could be subsumed under various linkage-related subtopics, for example, parties and voter alignments, parties and leadership recruitment, party discipline in legislative bodies, and so on.[3] But the very concept of linkage implies a series of connections, a chain of relationships. In order to understand the role of parties in linking citizens to governments, we must begin to solder together the disparate elements, connect the connections, and, in short, begin to formulate a theory of party linkage.

In undertaking this task, it is useful to be able to refer to a body of studies that are focused directly, not implicitly, on the question of parties and linkage in specific settings. Exploring the contributions of multiple case studies dealing with the same topic but drawing their conclusions from entirely different sets of data is often a powerful means of bringing out the theoretical dimensions of that topic while keeping the discussion firmly rooted in reality. It is also an excellent way to uncover some of the lacunae in the conceptual framework conventionally employed for the study of that topic. The studies in this volume provide such a body of work relative to the topic of parties and linkage. They also make clear the need for further development of the theory of party linkage and, at the same time, provide, singly and in combination, many of the conceptual tools needed to take that next step. This introductory essay will address the task of theory building, which these essays make both imperative and possible.

One of the conceptual problems that the essays, in combination, make clear is a general lack of agreement about what exactly is meant by the term "linkage" in the study of politics. The first task must be, therefore, to try to bring the many usages of the term into a single context. Once political linkage has been defined, the function of parties in the linkage process can be determined—that is, the linkage roles that parties may and sometimes do take unto themselves can be identified. Close consideration of the fifteen studies published in this volume permits elucidation of four forms of linkage in which political parties are frequently key participants.

Having profited by considering the implications of these studies in

3. For examples, see Seymour M. Lipset and Stein Rokkan, *Party Systems and Voter Alignments: Cross-National Perspectives* (New York: The Free Press, 1967); Lester G. Seligman et al., *Patterns of Recruitment* (Chicago: Rand McNally, 1974); R. T. McKenzie, *British Political Parties* (New York: St. Martin's Press, 1955).

combination, we will then be in a position to consider what they have to tell us one by one. The second part of this essay will undertake this task, grouping the essays according to the four forms of political linkage in which parties are most commonly active. As will be hinted at in this discussion, and made amply clear in the individual essays, these studies are richly informative about how parties really do—or do not—fulfill linkage roles. In the third section of this introduction the implications of the essays will once again be considered in combination, first, to advance the development of the theory of party linkage and, second, to evaluate the role of political parties in democratic government. The concluding comments will thus move us from the effort to build systematic theory to a yet more challenging endeavor, the task of relating these findings and their implications to normative theory: Do political parties really help us with the tasks of building democracy? If not, could they? What role *should* parties play in linking citizens to states? And, finally, are there any rational grounds for expecting that parties will, either now or in the future, play such a role?

Linkage: Meanings and Non-Meanings

What does linkage mean? In the abstract the question is not too difficult to answer: linkage means a series of links, and a "link" is a connection, usually with a connotation of interaction: the elements linked behave differently *because* they are linked.

However, when we turn to the uses of the concept of linkage in studies of politics and government, a variety of more complex distinctions must be made. In particular, three questions must be answered: What are the units that are being linked, which units instigate the linkage relationship, and what are the processes by which linkage is established?

THE UNITS BEING LINKED

The concept of linkage has been employed to study interconnections among all levels of government. As James N. Rosenau has pointed out, the concept of linkage lends itself to all forms of "across-system" study, that is, to efforts to "specify how and under what conditions political behavior at one level of aggregation affects political behavior at another level."[4] The analyst of linkage is always ready "to ignore long-standing

4. James N. Rosenau, "Theorizing across Systems: Linkage Politics Revisited," in Jonathan Wilkenfeld, ed., *Conflict Behavior and Linkage Politics* (New York: David McKay, 1973), p. 25.

5

conceptual boundaries and think anew about interaction across different levels of aggregation," is "not content to presume that the properties that are lawful at the level of aggregation that interests him can be adequately explained by holding other levels constant . . . [but] is impelled to expand his explanatory net beyond the dynamics operative at the level" of his dependent variables.[5]

Rosenau makes it clear that for him the term "system" can be applied to any level of political life—local, national, or international— and he specifically sanctions the widest possible interpretation: "Depending on the perspective of the analyst, of course, a virtually endless number of levels can be used as the basis for inquiry."[6] However, in practice Rosenau and his associates have been most concerned with the relationships between a *nation's* internal affairs and developments in the *international* arena. Indeed, the subtitle of *Linkage Politics* (edited by Rosenau) is *Essays on the Convergence of National and International Systems*, and the subconcepts Rosenau has used (interdependence, penetration, intervention, emulation, integration, and adaptation) are all employed to help explain the nature of national-international "convergences" (although several have obvious applicability to intranation linkages as well).[7] Focusing on these units of study leads to thoughtful analysis of such topics as "External Factors in Latin American Politics," "Superpolities," "Externalizing System Stress," and so on but clearly takes us only a few of the many steps necessary to develop a comprehensive theory of linkage.[8]

Furthermore, although Rosenau has noted the possibilities for wider uses of the linkage concept, he himself makes no use of it in a subsequent work in which his topic is closely related to the form of intrasystem linkage explored in this volume. In *Citizenship between Elections*, Rosenau investigates the reasons some members of the attentive

5. Ibid., pp. 26–30.
6. Ibid., p. 26.
7. James N. Rosenau, ed., *Linkage Politics* (New York: The Free Press, 1969); see also Rosenau, op. cit., pp. 30–42.
8. See Douglas A. Chalmers, "Developing on the Periphery: External Factors in Latin American Politics," and Bernard C. Cohen, "National-International Linkages: Superpolities," in Rosenau, *Linkage Politics*, op. cit., pp. 67–93 and 125–46 respectively, and Leo A. Hazlewood, "Externalizing System Stress: International Conflict as Adaptive Behavior," in Wilkenfeld, op. cit., pp. 107–23. See also Rosenau's introduction to *Linkage Politics*.

6

fraction of the polity are mobilizable while others are not, and the behavioral differences between these two groups.[9] Although he is discussing the interaction between these kinds of citizens and political leaders, he never seizes upon the seemingly obvious opportunity to fit this study into the wider perspective of linkage studies.[10]

On the other hand, others focusing on relationships between intrasystem units have made free (in some cases, it will be argued below, *too* free) usage of the term "linkage." For V. O. Key, linkage refers to "the interconnections between mass opinion and public decision"—his units of analysis are thus individual citizens (aggregated in polls and election results or operating independently via written or personal contact with officialdom), intermediate collectivities (parties, pressure groups), and "governments."[11] Norman Luttbeg has edited a volume of essays "considering the linkage between public opinion and public policy." And Susan Welch and John Comer have coedited a book of readings on public opinion in which the last section is devoted to "elections and parties as linkages."[12]

In these and numerous other studies of American politics, there seems to have been an automatic and often unthinking agreement that the units of analysis summoned up by the word "linkage" would necessarily be those designated by Key. In a nod to more recent developments, participation in protest demonstrations has sometimes been added to the list of acts of aggregated citizenship (i.e., in addition to voting and replying to pollsters), but the units of analysis remain the same: citizens, intermediate groups, governments.[13] Some of the studies have been limited to one link in this participatory chain (e.g., "The Missing Links

9. James N. Rosenau, *Citizenship between Elections* (New York: The Free Press, 1974).

10. He does discuss the probable impact of worldwide interdependence on patterns of citizenship in one chapter, but there too no direct reference is made to the concepts developed in his earlier work. (Ibid., pp. 21–88.)

11. V. O. Key, *Public Opinion and American Democracy* (New York: Knopf, 1964), pp. 409–558.

12. Norman R. Luttbeg, ed., *Public Opinion and Public Policy Models of Political Linkage*, rev. ed. (Homewood, Ill.: Dorsey Press, 1974), and "Assessing the Influence of Public Opinion, An Overview: Elections and Parties as Linkages," part 6, in Susan Welch and John Comer, eds., *Public Opinion* (Palo Alto, Calit.: Mayfield Publishing, 1975), pp. 409–531.

13. Michael Lipsky, "Protest as a Political Resource," in Welch and Comer, op. cit., pp. 478–503.

in Legislative Politics: Attentive Constituents"), others have dealt with
a limited number of links (as in Heinz Eulau and Kenneth Prewitt's
study of linkage processes in urban governments), and still others have
attempted to cover the whole spectrum of intrasystem participatory
linkage (e.g., chapters 16 to 21 in the work by V. O. Key previously
cited).[14] But in no case known to this author has any effort been made to
relate such studies of intrasystem participatory linkage to the kinds of
linkage studied by Rosenau and associates. Although both kinds of
studies (national-international convergences and intrasystem participatory connections) clearly deal with the "levels of aggregation" contained in the Rosenau schema, no one appears to have noted that a *body*
of linkage-oriented study, across all levels, is in fact emerging. Strange
to say, those studying linkage have somehow divided into two camps,
unlinked.

THE UNITS THAT INSTIGATE LINKAGE

Once it is accepted that linkages may be found among all manner of
political units, the second, related question must be confronted: Which
unit instigates the link? On which side of the link, at which of the levels
linked, is the instigation of linkage found? Some of the greatest difficulties in the development of the concept of linkage to date have to
do with the failure to make the answer to this question clear.

The confusion has arisen in large part because of the tendency
of some scholars to use the concept far more figuratively than others.
"Linkage" has often been used as a metaphor for democracy and even as
a synonym for representation. How may citizens be represented in the
making of policy? By engaging in acts by which they link themselves to
decision makers, that is, by articulating their interests, by helping to
recruit nominees, by campaigning, by voting for one candidate rather
than another, by maintaining contact with those elected. So suggests
the metaphor.

Furthermore, the confusion stimulated by this figurative usage is
exacerbated by the fact that the metaphor is not one, but two, removes
from reality. First, linkage is taken to mean only acts of citizenship, of

14. C. R. Boynton et al., "The Missing Links in Legislative Politics: Attentive
Constituents," *Journal of Politics* 31, no. 3 (August 1969): 700–21; Heinz Eulau and Kenneth
Prewitt, *Labyrinths of Democracy: Adaptations, Linkages, Representation, and Policies in
Urban Politics* (New York: Bobbs-Merrill, 1973); Key, op. cit.

participation in politics (as in the Key model); and second, acts of participation in politics are synonymous with acts of representation. How can the damage be undone?

Heinz Eulau and Kenneth Prewitt have taken an important step forward in their study of the relationship between citizens and local councilmen,[15] although they continue to use linkage as a synonym for participatory politics. According to them, "linkage" is a matter of citizen activity in constitutive processes (leadership recruitment, campaigning, and elections) and in petitioning processes (by organized groups). These are, of course, the very stuff of political participation.[16] But Eulau and Prewitt do make amply and usefully clear that although participation is likely to stimulate representation, it cannot be used as its equivalent. For them, the essence of representation is responsiveness by elected officials: the instigative units are on the other side of the link.

In a later work, which Eulau coauthors with Paul Karps, responsiveness is broken down into four elements: policy responsiveness, service responsiveness (providing particularized benefits), allocation responsiveness (providing more generalized "pork barrel" benefits), and symbolic responsiveness (projecting a nonsubstantive image of responsiveness). The ideal representative is seen as someone who acts in the interests of those represented, who is "responsive" in all these senses of the term, but who reserves the right to use his own judgment: "As he occupies a superior position in the relationship [between himself and the mass] by virtue of his 'elevation,' one should expect him not merely to be reactive but to take the initiative."[17] This update of the Burkean model of representation not only usefully separates the concept from participation but also makes clear (albeit inadvertently) that both representation and participation are, in fact, forms of linkage between citizens and states. In the former linkage is instigated by government officials, in the latter by citizens and citizen organizations.[18]

15. Eulau and Prewitt, op. cit.
16. See, for example, Sidney Verba and Norman H. Nie, *Participation in America: Political Democracy and Social Equality* (New York: Harper & Row, 1972), or Lester Milbrath and M. L. Goel, *Political Participation*, 2nd ed. (Chicago: Rand McNally, 1977).
17. Heinz Eulau and Paul D. Karps, "The Puzzle of Representation: Specifying Components of Responsiveness," *Legislative Studies Quarterly* 2, no. 3 (August 1977): 249.
18. Which does not mean that officials' representative acts, as defined by Eulau and Prewitt, may not be inspired by citizens' participatory acts (and vice versa).

9

In sum, not only does the concept of linkage permit us to investigate the relationships among a "virtually endless number of levels"; it also alerts us to the wide variety of relationships possible between the units concerned. Where the units under consideration are citizens and governments, it is important to ask whether citizens or governments—or both— are instigating the linkages observed.

THE PROCESSES BY WHICH LINKAGE IS ESTABLISHED

Once the units to be studied have been determined and those which are instigative have been identified, the key question can be confronted: *How* is linkage established? By what acts are connections made between the units under consideration? What are the processes of linkage?[19]

For Rosenau, two basic processes are at work in creating linkage relationships: penetrative and reactive. A "penetrative process occurs when members of one polity serve as participants in the political process of another."[20] More frequently, he suggests, the process is reactive, meaning that there are responses in one unit to actions taken in the other unit, without movement of actors across boundaries. (A third process cited by Rosenau is "emulative," but this, as he points out, is a subcategory of reactive; it is established when the response in the second unit takes essentially the same form as the action in the first unit.)[21]

Rosenau also gives us some language for locating instigative units in the linkage process, borrowing the terms "input" and "output" from the language of systems theory. In systems theory, "output" refers to the flow of policy and the implementing processes produced by decision makers at least partly in response to the "input" of support and demands from the populace and organized groups.[22] But Rosenau, concentrating on the linkages between nation-states, has put these terms to new use. Now the output of one nation becomes (sometimes) the input for another nation's policy processes either directly or by influencing the international system to which the second nation's policymakers must respond. The notion of reciprocal causation is accommodated by Rosenau by the term "fused linkage," which "arises out of the possibility that certain

19. The term "process" is used in its most elementary sense: "a particular method of getting something done."
20. Rosenau, *Linkage Politics*, op. cit., p. 46.
21. Ibid.
22. David Easton, *A Systems Analysis of Political Life* (New York: John Wiley & Sons, 1965).

outputs and inputs continuously reinforce each other and are thus best viewed as forming a reciprocal relationship."[23]

A similar effort to adapt the language of systems theory to questions relevant to linkage has been made by Lester Milbrath and M. L. Goel. Their concern is to keep the "focus on the individual as he relates *to* the system"; therefore, they use the terms "inputs" and "outtakes": "An input is something a citizen does to try to influence official decisions. In contrast, an outtake is something that an individual takes from the system."[24]

These efforts to name the processes of linkage are useful, as several authors in this volume demonstrate, but the nomenclature remains at a very high level of abstraction. To understand more about particular penetrative or reactive processes, further distinctions must be made. Thus, when we turn to the question of the links between citizens and their governments, we might make the following distinctions:

Linkage by penetration:
    a. governments locate their agents openly or covertly in citizen organizations;
    b. citizens place some of their members in government (via electoral processes or via acts of revolution, thus establishing a new government altogether).
Linkage by reaction:
    a. governments engage in acts of representative response to citizen views on policy;
    b. governments engage in acts of coercion to which citizens must perforce respond;
    c. governments and citizens exchange rewards for votes.

Four comments should be made about the above list. First, it is not exhaustive, merely illustrative. Second, it does not exclude the possibility that several different linkage processes may be coexistent; indeed, such a pattern is the more common one. Third, such a list, in fact, combines all three aspects of the meaning of linkage: we are specifying units of study, instigative units, and processes. Fourth, we have moved much closer to a framework of analysis useful for studying the role of political parties in the work of linkage politics and for considering the ways in which the essays in this volume elucidate that work.

23. Rosenau, *Linkage Politics*, op. cit., p. 45.
24. Milbrath and Goel, op. cit., pp. 9–10.

Parties and Linkage: The Authors' Contributions

The question of the relationship between the work of the editor and the work of contributors is a linkage problem in itself. Rosenau's definition of "fused linkage" comes back to mind: "Certain outputs and inputs continuously reinforce each other and are thus best viewed as forming a reciprocal relationship." In this case the editor began with an interest in linkage politics in the more limited sense of the term as employed by V. O. Key, and wondered what other investigators, studying political parties on all the continents of the world, might make of the term in applying it to their work in the field. Each author was therefore simply asked to write about parties and linkage, defining his or her terms and providing an analysis of a particular case, based at least in part on fieldwork in the nation under study. The result is a collection of studies that are (a) all focused on the same topic and (b) richly suggestive of a variety of ways to name and study the components of that topic. So richly suggestive, in fact, that it has proved possible to set forth the preceding analytical framework, and then, returning to the individual studies, to locate them in the overall context of the study of linkage politics.

In the first place, the units of study in this volume are, for the most part, intrasystem units: the focus is on how parties help (or hinder) the creation of links between *citizens* and *governments*. However, in two studies an effort is made to demonstrate the links between specific external systems and specific internal groups of a particular system.[25] There is thus no bias against the view that linkage relationships may be found at all levels of aggregation; however, it is to be expected that when the subject is the role of political parties in establishing linkage, the bulk of the analysis will fall within particular systems.

Second, it is interesting to note that in most of these studies the instigative units are the governments. In seven of the fifteen studies (see parts III and V), the focus is on roles parties may play in the acts undertaken by governments to link themselves to their citizens. Three studies consider cases in which linkage is reciprocal (votes for favors), but the emphasis here is on governments as the more significant actors (see part IV). And in the five remaining studies, which consider how citizens may establish links with their governments, only two consider

---

25. See the essay in this volume by Tom Truman and that by William Martin and Karen Hopkins.

acts of grass-roots citizenship; the remaining three consider whether parties have placed leaders in power who are agents of participatory politics (one suggests they have not; the other two conclude with a mixed assessment).

Third, the studies demonstrate that parties are involved not only in penetrative linkage processes (recruiting citizens and helping them secure sufficient votes in electoral competition to become members of the government) but also in reactive processes: parties may help governments link themselves to citizens by providing responsive and effective leadership, by serving as the channels through which governments and citizens exchange rewards for votes, and by serving as the channels through which more coercive governments make the unilateral demands to which citizens must respond.

As has already been hinted, the organization of this volume has been shaped, first, by the authors' treatment of the second variable: *instigative units.* Part II includes studies that treat the political party as the vehicle that helps citizens become the instigators of linkage; parts III, IV, and V include studies that treat political parties as agents assisting governments to be the instigators of linkage, or at least more significant in this regard than citizens in situations where interaction is reciprocal. A second consideration, which distinguishes parts III, IV, and V from each other, has been to ask *by what process* do political parties facilitate linkage. Here the key question has been not linkage by penetration versus linkage by reaction but rather the five more substantive distinctions made *under* those two broader categories (see page 11). Two of these have been combined: studies of linkage formed when parties assist governments by accommodating members of those governments as members of their own organizations (a form of penetrative linkage) are grouped with studies of linkage formed when parties serve as the channels for the transmission of coercive government policy to which citizens must perforce respond (a form of linkage by reaction) to produce the category of *directive linkage.* Thus, the net result of applying the larger analytical framework of linkage politics to the studies produced for this volume has been the discovery of four forms of linkage in which political parties play dynamic roles in linking citizens to states. These four forms of linkage by party are as follows:

Participatory linkage: linkage by political parties that serve as agencies through which citizens can participate in government.

Policy-responsive linkage: linkage by political parties that serve as

13

agencies for ensuring that government officials will be responsive to the views of rank-and-file voters.

Linkage by reward: linkage by political parties that act primarily as channels for the exchange of votes for favors.[26]

Directive linkage: linkage by political parties that are used by governments as aids to maintain coercive control over their subjects.

Not all of the studies fit with comparable ease into the above categories, particularly those that deal with compound linkage processes, but on the whole, the typology seems to work; because it was derived *from* the studies, this is no major accomplishment—the real test must be its applicability to other studies in the future. In any case, the following consideration of individual cases may make clearer the fit between the preceding theoretical discussion and the data explored by the contributors.

Participatory linkage. Five studies explore the capacity of parties to transmit citizen views to decision-making processes. Two of these investigate the proposition that a key way in which parties perform as this kind of transmission belt is by recruiting socioeconomic peers of their support groups for positions of power in party and government: for example, a workers' party must recognize that only workers know what workers want and will remain committed, once in leadership roles, to transforming their wishes into government policy. But both studies find that in the cases examined there is little tendency for such parties to choose such leaders, and that party leaders are consistently of higher socioeconomic background than party followers. Roland Cayrol and Jérôme Jaffré document the French Socialists' choice of bourgeois leadership and the party's tendency to opt for *societal linkage* over *preferential linkage* (i.e., for representing the entire French population in its social composition rather than merely the workers, who would seem to be the first and foremost objects of its electoral appeal). They suggest that should the steadily gaining and rhetorically ever more radical Socialists take power in a future election, the party leaders' class background may prove more meaningful than either their campaign rhetoric or the views of the majority of their supporters.

---

26. Note that this category collapses the Eulau and Karps categories of service responsiveness and allocation responsiveness and, further, treats such responsiveness not as a form of unilateral representativeness but as a two-way exchange between unequal partners.

However, Michael A. Marsh, who examines the leadership, support base, and degree of radicalism of eight European Social Democratic parties and finds a similar discrepancy between leaders' and followers' social-class standings, goes on to suggest that the importance of this variable for participatory linkage may be overrated. He finds no relationships between leaders' social class and the policy stances of elected representatives, nor between socially appropriate leadership recruitment and a party's capacity to mobilize working-class support.

A third study here focuses on the quality of leaders as well, but from a different perspective. Young Whan Kihl begins with the assumption that a party's elected leadership must have positive attitudes toward popular participation in the nation's political processes in order for citizens to have any hope of access via party to those processes. His queries to ruling and opposition party elites in South Korea examined their views on a people's capacity to rule themselves and their beliefs regarding decentralization and local autonomy. His mixed findings produce a mixed assessment; however, despite the unstable nature of South Korean politics, even those responses that are only weakly oriented toward democratic values give some hope for the future establishment of links between citizen and state.

Dwaine Marvick's longitudinal study of party activists in Los Angeles takes a different approach to the question of participatory linkage. For Marvick, party activists constitute a key link in the chain of party-created links between citizen views and government policy. To function effectively as such links, party activists must (1) offer, via their respective parties, meaningful alternatives to the voters and (2) be responsive to changing voter opinion. In one of the few unreservedly positive assessments to be found in the volume, Marvick demonstrates that activists in the two major American parties are, at least in the Los Angeles area, well matched in strength and well differentiated ideologically (thus able to offer meaningful alternatives) and able and willing to shift their own issue stances in response to shifting voter preference patterns.

Tom Truman is also more concerned with grass-roots participatory linkage, as he looks at the interaction between specific Australian groups and the Australian Labor party. Truman demonstrates not only the effectiveness of these groups in influencing the ALP; he goes further and shows how these groups themselves have been influenced by specific international events to change the nature of the input they make in Australia's political process. With this incorporation of reference to external factors, Truman tends to adhere more closely to the Rosenau analytical framework than any other author in the book.

Policy-responsive linkage. Four of the essays in this volume consider the conditions that must obtain in order for elected party representatives to exercise control over decision-making processes in such a way as to maximize the impact of the views of their followers. One such condition, especially in multiparty politics, is the capacity of leaders of *different* parties to interact positively and cooperatively with each other and with government officials so that policy of *any* type can be decided upon and effectively executed. Two studies consider this condition. Samuel J. Eldersveld explores the ability of Dutch M.P.'s to work within the framework of the Netherlands' consociational system. He measures the impact of interaction with the M.P.'s on the attitudes of Dutch civil servants and vice versa. In a generally positive assessment, he discovers that the more contact civil servants have with M.P.'s, the greater their sympathy for *political* perspectives, and he finds both groups generally supportive of accommodation and compromise regardless of levels of intergroup contact.

William Martin and Karen Hopkins look at the question of across-party accommodation with respect to an even less well-known party system, that of Finland. Rooting their analysis in a careful historical study, they point out the utility of external dangers—in this case, the perennial threat of Russian domination—in producing a spirit of internal accommodation in an otherwise deeply fragmented state.

Neither Eldersveld nor Martin and Hopkins takes up the second half of the problem, however: granted that such postelectoral accommodation is often necessary for *any* policy to be enacted, can it be achieved without a loss of responsiveness on policy issues to the party's own supporters? A. H. Somjee, shifting the analysis to the level of local politics in India, suggests that the answer must be no. Although across-party accommodations among the political leadership of the town of Anand are both common and productive of more stable and productive governmental processes than would otherwise be possible, they are made at the expense of the party's role as linkage agent between citizen and state: as new and less partisan alliances evolve for problem-solving purposes, campaign promises are set aside and party loyalties are strained or set aside. Like Eldersveld and Martin and Hopkins, Somjee does not find this process reprehensible, given the positive results it has for effective government. However, all three studies suggest that the role of parties in establishing policy-responsive linkage in multiparty systems is severely limited.

The fourth study that properly fits in this category takes up the topic from a very different perspective. Frances Hill, studying linkage possibilities in African party-states, asks not whether different parties' elected representatives can or should cooperate effectively on the making of policy after the hostilities of electoral battle have faded away but rather whether or not they *have* any effective policymaking role to play. She argues that parties are able to play such a role only where legislatures retain effective control of policy—the legislative process provides the means and the arena for aggregating partisan demands; where effective power has shifted, as is the case in most African party-states, to the agencies of the administration, then no such role is possible. "A legislature cumulates precisely where an administration fragments," she states. It is no accident of history that the earliest parties began as external representations of legislative factions, carrying the job of *cumulating* out into expanded electorates in pursuit of popular majorities translatable into legislative majorities. But the symbiosis between party and parliament is broken when parliaments decline and administrative rule becomes the order of the day. Then linkage responsibilities tend to shift to interest groups, specialized and fragmented, each dealing with the appropriate agency in a specialized and fragmented network of administrative government. Hill, whose fieldwork was in Tanzania, traces the process in African systems in general.

Linkage by reward. Three studies consider the tendency of some parties to abandon efforts to provide avenues for participatory or policy-responsive linkage and to engage instead in a much more pragmatic relationship with their supporters: votes for favors. Robert Leonardi makes clear how the Italian Christian Democratic party has developed and used its control over patronage (especially jobs) to accomplish two ends, the maintenance of voter loyalty and party domination of all branches and agencies of the government. That party's capacity to survive, despite the severity of Italy's current economic and social problems, as well as the government's apparent incapacity to find and apply useful solutions, may be explained in large part by the success of this form of linkage. Leonardi's study thus suggests the *costs*, in public services as well as in democratic processes, when links are formed by payoffs. The same moral may be drawn from Steffen Schmidt's interpretation of Colombian clientelism. Local power brokers, *gamonales*, deliver the votes of their community in exchange for access to national party leadership. When clever and sufficiently flexible, these local notables may ensure some material return for their clients' blindly delivered votes, but linkage in the sense of popular control over national policymarking remains nonexistent.

Joel Barkan and John Okumu give point to Frances Hill's comments regarding the decline of meaningful party activity in African parliaments and provide the third example of linkage by reward. They show how parties have so declined in Kenya that their elected representatives, the Kenyan M.P.'s, seek reelection far less as party loyalists than as individual purveyors of government services to their constituencies. Parties may thus be not only reduced to linkage by favors but supplanted altogether where that kind of linkage becomes the norm.

Directive linkage. Governments intent on mobilizing populations in the pursuit of goals determined exclusively by system leaders, whether on their own or on the nation's behalf, often employ parties as agencies of manipulation and control, not as agencies of participation or response.

Focusing on the Partido Revolucionario Institucional (PRI) of Mexico, John Corbett explains the manipulative party's need for a strong local presence as necessary to limit the operation of opposition parties, promote political socialization, and ensure compliance with national directives. He finds three directive linkage techniques are employed: symbol saturation, organizational penetration (controlling local institutions), and recruitment centralization. Their combined efficacy is sufficient to maintain the PRI securely in power but not sufficient to reduce the high abstention voting rate in national elections.

It is to be expected that an essay on USSR party politics will be illustrative of directive linkage, but Ronald Hill's essay on Soviet linkage processes nevertheless contains a few surprises. Hill does not take for granted the manipulative qualities of the Communist Party of the Soviet Union (CPSU). He traces how the party sets guidelines, to be discussed and comprehended by the local party and then transmitted, by its members, into the soviets and thus into the state implementation process. But he also shows how the deputies in the soviets serve to funnel popular demands and worries into the party processes, and how communications directly from citizens to the party are taken seriously. The net result is thus directive linkage mixed with a stronger element of policy-responsive linkage (albeit within a carefully limited framework) than is often acknowledged by Western observers.

The tendency to combine directive linkage with other linkage processes is also illustrated by Thomas Turner's study of the government's use of the single party in Zaire. Describing the party's involvement in the development of chieftaincy policy in that nation, Turner shows how the state used the party apparatus for directive purposes by incorporating the chiefs into the party hierarchy, but then found its reforms backfiring as the new structures permitted more "effervescent" party politics, that is, the threat of participatory linkage. The next step, as he shows, was for the government to "give in" to those chiefs who were resisting the new policy because to do so (a) eliminated the threat of participatory linkage and (b) offered a new opportunity for linkage by reward (favors to the chiefs), and *thereby* permitted the restoration of directive-linkage patterns. Such an analysis, besides showing how tortuous a path may be followed in developing linkage processes in a new state, also makes clear how closely related linkage by reward may be to directive linkage, a point we will return to below.

Implications

What hypotheses might be drawn from the studies in this volume regarding the role of parties in linkage politics? The following list may be suggestive. The names following each hypothesis identify the study or studies from which it was drawn. In some cases, the studies cited have documented the truth of the hypothesis for the particular instance; in others, the hypothesis is deduced from what appears to be the underlying assumption of the study cited.

1. Parties that make their electoral appeal to workers do not choose socioeconomic peers of workers as their leaders (Cayrol and Jaffré; Marsh).
   1a. When the elected leaders of workers' parties are of higher social-class background than the members, the policy stances of the party will be less oriented to the interests of those members than would be the case if leaders and members were socioeconomic peers (Cayrol and Jaffré).
   1b. When the elected leaders of workers' parties are of higher social-class background than the members, the policy stances of the party will be neither more nor less oriented to the interests of those members than would be the case if leaders and members were socioeconomic peers (Marsh).
   1c. Social-class backgrounds of the elected leadership of workers' parties have no relationship to such parties' capacity to mobilize working-class support (Marsh).
2. Parties that select leaders supportive of participatory values will

serve more effectively as agencies to maximize the capacity of citizens to influence governments (Kihl).

3. Competitive parties that offer meaningful alternatives to voters will serve more effectively as agencies to maximize the capacity of citizens to influence governments (Marvick).

    3a. Where party activists in competing parties are well matched in strength, the parties are more likely to offer meaningful alternatives to voters (Marvick).

    3b. Where party activists in competing parties are well differentiated ideologically, the parties are more likely to offer meaningful alternatives to voters (Marvick).

4. Competitive parties that are capable of changing issue stances in response to shifting voter preferences will serve more effectively as agencies to maximize the capacity of citizens to influence governments (Marvick).

    4a. Where party activists in competing parties are capable of changing issue stances in response to shifting voter preferences, the parties as a whole will be capable of making comparable changes (Marvick).

5. The stronger a domestic group's links to a foreign organization or nation, the more it will respond to international events that are of significance to that external entity by changing the quality and/or quantity of its linkage with domestic parties (Truman).

6. The more contacts elected party representatives have with administration officials, the greater the potential for accommodation and compromise across party boundaries (Eldersveld).

7. The greater the threat of external dangers to a system, the greater the potential for accommodation and compromise across party boundaries among elected party representatives (Martin and Hopkins).

8. The greater the accommodation and compromise across party boundaries, the more elected party representatives depart from campaign promises to voters (Somjee).

9. The weaker the parliament in decision-making processes, the less capable parties will be of placing in office leaders who will be responsive to citizens' views (F. Hill; Barkan and Okumu).

10. The greater a party's control over patronage appointments, the more likely its voters will remain loyal (Leonardi).

    10a. Hypothesis 10 holds even where voters are seriously disappointed in policy responses (Leonardi).

11. The greater a party's capacity to distribute material rewards of any kind, the more likely its voters will remain loyal (Schmidt).

12. The greater a party's capacity to exchange material rewards for votes, the less likely it will serve as an agency for participatory linkage (Schmidt; Leonardi).

13. The less capable a party is of forging participatory or responsive

links between citizens and governments, the more likely it is to be replaced by other agents capable of linking governments to citizens by the distribution of favors (Barkan and Okumu).

14. The more capable a party is of supporting and controlling strong local organizations, the more capable the party is of serving the government as an agency of directive linkage (Corbett).

   14a. The greater the symbol saturation in the local community by a national party, the stronger will be the party's local organization (Corbett).

   14b. The more agents of the national party control local institutions, the stronger will be the party's own local organizations (Corbett).

   14c. The more recruitment procedures for local party posts are centralized at the party's central headquarters, the stronger will be the party's control over its local organizations (Corbett).

15. Permitting a measure of policy-responsive linkage enhances the capacity of a party to function as an agency for directive linkage of state to citizenry (R. Hill).

16. When directive-linkage processes threaten to "deteriorate" into participatory linkage, governments may employ parties as channels for substituting linkage by reward, thereby restrengthening directive-linkage relationships (Turner).

A wide range of comments could be made about these twenty-six hypotheses and subhypotheses. Some have been explored in other studies, some are merely speculative, many suggest possibilities for further research, and many suggest alternative hypotheses equally likely to improve our understanding of how parties do in fact function as agencies of linkage. Given the limitations of space, and returning to the kinds of questions that first prompted the collection of these studies, we will simply try to answer the following: What do they suggest is the role of parties as agencies of democracy, that is, as agencies that help citizens influence the processes of government (by *any* of the forms of linkage noted)?

Most of the conclusions are negative. Parties cannot ensure that citizens' views will influence policymaking processes by choosing as leaders the socioeconomic peers of those citizens. If the elected representatives of parties are capable of influencing policy processes at all, they probably do so at the expense of participatory linkage: learning to function cooperatively with leaders of other parties may well mean learning to forget commitments to the voters. When parties demand that governments serve citizen interests, they may, in fact, be facilitating foreign influence over a nation's internal policy processes, not necessarily to the benefit of its citizens. Especially (but not exclusively) in developing nations, the party's natural arena for bringing citizen preferences to bear, the legislature, has itself lost all influence over policy processes. Parties do better in serving as channels for the exchange of votes for favors, but the favors come at very high cost: loss of influence over broader policy questions (which, of course, may contain the seeds for far greater material returns than the petty rewards of clientelism) and/or acquiescence in the maintenance of predominantly directive-linkage relationships. And permitting minimal policy-responsive linkage is itself, in some cases, a governmental technique for maintaining directive linkage via party.

But perhaps now is a good time to stop and ask one of the more important questions in political research: *So what?* Presumably there may be agreement that citizens should have the means to influence policy processes, but why must *parties* provide that means? If parties have been reduced to "keeper of the seal" (the party label) in developed nations, and to the rudimentary organization necessary for "the institutionalization of participation *from above*" in developing nations, it may mean only that other organizations have replaced parties as agencies of democratic linkage. Why be so concerned about parties?

However, a quick glance around the globe is likely to suggest that the hope that other agencies are performing linkage functions more satisfactorily is not well founded. Shall democratic linkage be entrusted to the one-way communications of the public media? Are organizations composed of the loyalists of a single candidate/savior/demagogue likely to do the job? Pollsters can find out "what voters want" on given questions on given days, but how are such wishes to be enforced? Single-interest pressure groups often succeed in blocking policy contrary to their interests and even occasionally in having policy made supportive to their interests, but is this "flawed pluralism" really what is meant by popular sovereignty?[27] And it need scarcely be asked if panicky responses of governments to acts of terrorism, or even to lesser forms of popular protest, are a sufficient substitute.

Nevertheless, it may still be argued that expecting parties to serve as agencies of democratic linkage is naïve and unrealistic. What, after all, would such a party look like? Would it have, perhaps, the following characteristics?

27. The term is Carol Greenwald's, in her *Group Power* (New York: Praeger, 1977), p. 341.

1. Those active in the local party are aware of and responsive to the sentiments of less active but supportive rank-and-file members of the party.

2. The local party meets frequently, elects leadership democratically, discusses issues, votes on policy stances, sends instructed delegates to higher, intermediate levels of party organization, and chooses (by majority election) its own candidates for local offices.

3. Intermediate party organizations follow the same pattern as local parties, sending instructed delegates to central headquarters.

4. The central party office is composed of elected representatives from intermediate levels, who set national party policy and choose party candidates for national office in accord with majority decisions, plus an administrative apparatus whose services (research; fund raising; preparation of party leaflets, posters, and publications; training in campaign techniques) are fairly distributed among all levels of the party.

5. Party issue stances (at all levels) are adopted with adequate attention to electoral feasibility, that is, the party is committed to winning a sufficient number of positions of power to have a meaningful impact on policy.

6. Party campaigns are substantive, issue-oriented, educative, honest, and always based on the party program.

7. Party candidates (at all levels) are chosen on the basis of their loyalty to the party program and are renominated only if such loyalty has been amply demonstrated (in or out of office). Personalistic politics are grounds for expulsion.

8. Elected party representatives work to transform the party program into public policy to the maximum extent consistent with the maintenance of effective and stable government.

9. Party leaders actively resist all efforts to transform the party into a channel for the exchanges of rewards for votes or into an agency of directive linkage.

If those engaged in the quest for parties as agents of democratic linkage answer, "Yes, something like that," they must expect the following rejoinders: Where may such selfless paragons to staff the parties of the world be found? Parties were created out of a blend of public and private *interests*. They are agencies for the acquisition of power, not selfless political versions of the Red Cross, to whom citizens may go crying in time of need. Parties *claim* to serve as agencies of linkage because that is one way to maintain legitimacy, to capture the votes, which are their currency in the markets of power. To the extent that they ever operate in a fashion to enhance citizen control of government, they do so because citizens have made it clear that only thus are their votes to be secured. The responsibility for making and keeping parties useful intermediaries can never rest more than partially with the more idealistic of their own activists and leaders. In the final analysis, only an informed and assertive citizenry can compel parties—or any other organization—to adopt the structures and practices necessary to aggregate their interests; to recruit responsible, electable, and effective leadership; and to transform reasoned wishes into public policy. The question of how to find such a citizenry is, happily, not the subject of this book.

PART II

Participatory Linkage

2.

Party Linkages in France: Socialist Leaders, Followers, and Voters

ROLAND CAYROL AND
JÉRÔME JAFFRÉ

One of the main objectives of political parties in pluralist systems is the development of a solid and durable linkage between the party's electorate and the policymakers. As in the interrelational networks between citizens and government, parties are expected to represent the social composition of those who mandate them and to respond politically to the demands of their electorate.

This problem is particularly crucial in the case of opposition parties that have been kept out of government for a long time. They have to change their image as minority parties and develop their credibility as a majority party. In order to acquire power they are obliged to gather the maximum amount of support. In the European countries governed for decades by conservatives, the left-wing parties are now rediscovering the advantage of the "catch-all party," to use Otto Kirchheimer's expression.[1] This is the case, for instance, for the Communist party in Italy and the Socialist party in France.

These political organizations are trying to eliminate the image of a party that neglects the specific problems of the upper and middle classes. Enlisting voters who belong not only to the working class but to all

1. Otto Kirchheimer, "The Transformation of the Western European Party Systems," in Joseph La Palombara and Myron Weiner, eds., *Political Parties and Development* (Princeton: Princeton University Press, 1966), pp. 177–200.

social strata has become one of the major preoccupations governing their tactics and their propaganda. The goal is to develop an organization in all levels of society. This is the purpose of the kind of linkage that shall be called *societal linkage*: its aim is to make the structures of the electorate as a whole coincide with those of the party voters.

Another problem of linkage is the coexistence in structured parties, at various levels of organization, of members, active militants, leaders (who are often paid party workers), and those who are elected. This shall be called *intrapartisan linkage*. The main difficulty here is to preserve a minimum amount of homogeneity between the various levels of party structure. This issue has often been discussed within left-wing parties, where the social background of the rank and file may differ significantly from that of the leadership. Inequalities in education and professional training exist, and the skills required of party executives often give the advantage to those who are better qualified in these respects. When leaders are recruited predominantly from a single, higher social level, intrapartisan linkage is threatened.

A third aspect, *preferential linkage*, is related particularly to parties calling themselves Socialist. These organizations center their activities on popular classes; they fight for emancipation of the working class and the underprivileged groups in capitalist societies. Here the problem of linkage takes on a twofold aspect: To what extent do they really have their roots in the working class (and in particular, to what extent do they attract working-class votes?) and to what extent does the party organize the representation of the working class in their executive bodies?

It is necessary to mention a contradiction encountered by all European Socialist parties: the impossibility of having the party electorate correspond to the overall social structure of, *and* simultaneously giving pride of place to, the working class. *Societal linkage* can bring about a weakening of *intrapartisan linkage* and even more of *preferential linkage* with the working class.

To deal with these problems on the basis of empirical data, the example of the French Socialist party will be investigated. The goal of the Socialist party (PS) is to become the majority party. Since it renewed its leadership in 1971—when Francois Mitterrand became first secretary of the party—both its electorate and the number of its participants have been increasing steadily, faster than any other European party in the past decade.

The case of the French PS is all the more interesting as its fast growth followed the adoption of a new strategy based on the European Social Democratic tradition: contemporary PS strategy is built on the idea of a breakdown of capitalist society.

On a tactical level, one of the main outcomes of this choice, already initiated with the electoral agreement concluded by the Left parties for the 1967 and 1968 parliamentary elections, was the adoption, in June 1972, of a common program of government by the PS, the Communist party (PC), and the Radicaux de Gauche (Movement of the Left Radicals —(MRG). This common program was, in 1972–78, the heart of the Propaganda Tactics of the French Left. The electoral alliance with the Communist party admitted of almost no exceptions after the parliamentary elections of 1973.

This evolution undeniably produced an effect upon the French working class: a large fraction of it has now ceased seeing the PC as the only defender of its interests. Furthermore, the numerous controversies the PS has engaged in with its Communist ally has improved its credibility in the opinion of liberal voters keen on rallying to a "democratic party," which defends "freedom" against the "Communist danger." Thus, even while hardening its orientation, the PS has been able to gain a more "open and liberal" image. The question however remains whether once at the head of a government—which it has not been since 1957—the PS would be able to adopt a program that accords with its new rhetoric and with the increasing support it has among the popular classes. Is there a new, more radical path for democratic socialism in Europe than that which has been followed in Great Britain, in West Germany, or in the Scandinavian countries? The distinctive symbol of the PS is a fist holding a rose. Will its policy, if it comes to power, be one of the fist or one of the rose? Will it be guided by its new political program and by the support of underprivileged classes, which have an interest in social change? Or, especially because of the social recruitment of many of the party leaders, will it encounter the same constraints as its European homologues and be compelled to take into account the contradictions existing within its own ranks?

A good way to approach these questions was to test precisely the degree of homogeneity existing between societal linkage, preferential linkage, and intraparty linkage. The existence of a gap—for example, a clear-cut predominance of societal linkage, at the expense of preferential linkage, with the working class, or a weak level of intraparty linkage— could be an important drawback when the time came to carry out in government policy the aspirations to *"changer la vie,"* as a PS slogan says. Will the quest for deep social change proclaimed by PS electoral propaganda be set aside once the party is in power because, in fact, significant numbers of its voters, militants, and leaders have a sociological interest in keeping the existing social system?

Societal Linkage and Preferential Linkage: The Structures of the New Socialist Electorate

The parliamentary elections on the twelfth and nineteenth of March 1978 resulted in an apparently contradictory situation for the Socialist party, which experienced both a major setback and a major victory. On the one hand, the Socialists did not manage to come to power within the framework of their alliance with the Communist party. Having obtained only 201 seats in Parliament, the Left was still far from the absolute majority (246 seats), whereas the Socialist party won, all in all, 102 seats, thus adding only 8 to its previous score. On the other hand, during the first ballot the Socialist party and its MRG allies obtained 24.9 percent of the valid votes cast in metropolitan France,[2] thus increasing their share by 4.2 percent, an increase that gave them the highest score ever in the history of French socialism. In post-Gaullist France, the Socialist party has been the principal beneficiary of the profound changes that have taken place in the electorate.

The newborn Socialist party is, at present, France's most important political party, despite its near disappearance from the electoral scene in 1969.[3] It has supplanted the Gaullists as France's foremost interclass

Parliamentary Elections (first ballot)	Valid Votes Cast	Votes for the Socialist Party	Percent Share
1967	22,389,473	4,224,110	18.9
1968	22,147,206	3,660,250	16.5
1973	23,750,731	4,945,922	20.7
1978	28,101,314	7,011,083	24.9

2. This analysis does not include the overseas *départements* and territories.

3. In the presidential elections of June 1969, which were provoked by de Gaulle's retirement, Gaston Defferre, candidate of the Socialist party, obtained only 5.1 percent of the valid votes cast.

party, in terms of both the geographical distribution of its suffrage and the sociological structure of its electorate.

A WELL-EQUILIBRATED GEOGRAPHICAL DISTRIBUTION

The geography of the Socialist vote in 1978 is still characterized by its traditional bastions—the North, the Aquitaine, and the Pyrenees in the southwest and the northwestern part of the Massif Central—and its traditional areas of weakness, Alsace and lower Normandy. However, the distribution of Socialist votes in France has become more evenly spread. In this respect the 1978 elections confirm and reinforce the general tendencies noticed in 1973: loss of votes in areas traditionally favorable to social democracy, counterbalanced by improvements achieved elsewhere.

Since 1967 the Socialists have been constantly losing ground in areas that were former strongholds. The mining district of the Nord-Pas de Calais, the western regions of the Massif Central, and the Mediterranean coast are particularly hard hit. Table 2.1 shows, for example, five *départe-*

TABLE 2.1. Socialist Party Losses in Some of the Départements Traditionally Held by the SFIO (in percent)

Département	1967	1968	1973	1978
Aude	41.9	33.3	35.8	33.7
Corrèze	31.3	28.3	17.0	18.6
Tarn-et-Garonne	39.7	36.0	30.4	28.1
Vaucluse	29.7	25.4	26.7	22.9
Haute-Vienne	31.6	24.6	28.6	26.7

TABLE 2.2. Some Examples of the Socialist Party's Gains (percent of valid votes cast)

Département	1967	1968	1973	1978
Mayenne	6.6	13.9	22.8	28.2
Meuse	12.9	17.7	26.7	29.9
Moselle	4.4	5.8	16.0	23.9
Savoie	10.0	10.8	23.3	32.2
Vienne	6.6	11.7	22.1	29.1

ments that were once Socialist strongholds in which the party has been losing ground ever since 1967.

Elsewhere, however, the Socialist party is progressing. The three main areas are: (1) the West, from the Haute-Normandie to the Poitou where none of the *départements* contradict this advance; (2) the East, from the Aisne to the Jura, including Alsace but bypassing Burgundy and Franche-Comté; and (3) the southern and western part of the Massif Central, extending from the Lot to the Haute-Savoie. In five traditionally weak départements the Socialist party has gained ground in each election since 1967 (table 2.2).

This uneven electoral balance sheet obeys the rule that Socialist party progress is inversely proportional to its past success. The percentage of constituencies[4] in which the Socialist party and its Radicaux de Gauche allies progressed in 1978 is calculated as follows in comparison with the Socialist levels attained in 1973:

Socialist Party Level in 1973 (*percent of valid votes cast*)	Number of Constituencies	Gains in 1978
More than 35	45	13
From 30 to 35	34	27
From 25 to 30	49	53
From 20 to 25	75	74
From 15 to 20	144	91
From 10 to 15	97	95
Less than 10	23	100

SOURCE: Adapted from G. Le Gall, "La gauche électorale, le 12 et 19 mars 1978," *Nouvelle revue socialiste*, n. 32, p. 44.

Progress is a rule in constituencies having low levels of Socialist voting in the past, whereas it is exceptional in traditional strongholds; as a consequence, the distribution of Socialist strength in France has become more uniform. The difference between the ten strongest and the ten weakest Socialist départements has been reduced to almost one-half of what it was in the past eleven years:

4. France is subdivided, administratively, into ninety-five départements. The legislative elections in the Fifth Republic are of the two-ballot majoritarian system. Each département is subdivided into constituencies (at least two per département).

| | *Percent of Valid Votes Cast* | | | |
	1967	*1968*	*1973*	*1978*
10 weakest Socialist départements	7.0	5.4	12.3	18.2
10 strongest Socialist départements	36.7	32.8	33.2	35.6
Difference	29.7	27.4	20.9	17.4

Thus it is obvious that a rapid change in voting patterns is taking place, resulting in the spread of Socialist influence on a national scale.

A DIVERSIFIED SOCIOLOGICAL STRUCTURE

A comparison of the 1978 Socialist electorate with the whole of the French adult population shows many similarities. Compared with the electoral body of all the other parties, the composition of the Socialist party's electorate is closest in structure to the average electorate in the first ballot of the 1978 elections. In fact, the sex and age of these two electorates are much the same. Some discrepancies do, however, appear in a comparison of the professions of heads of families, where the Socialist electorate shares the characteristics of the leftist electorate (table 2.3). Thus one finds that 26 percent of the Socialist electorate are white-collar workers and middle management (as compared with 22 percent in the entire electorate), and 6 percent are executives and professionals (as compared with 10 percent in the entire electorate).

An examination of the evolution of the Socialist electorate reveals a sociological dynamism that has permitted the party to rapidly eliminate its handicap in very different social categories: in the middle classes, plus 8 percent among the upper management and professional category between 1973 and 1978, and in the lower classes, plus 6 percent among the white-collar workers and middle-management category (table 2.4).

The Socialist party can be considered France's only interclass party when compared either with the Communist party, whose electorate is basically working class, or with the majority parties with their essentially middle-class electorate. The Socialist party is a composite party, well rooted in all the French regions and in all social milieus. On an electoral level it constitutes the *axis of the opposition* to Giscard d'Estaing's conservative coalition.

TABLE 2.3. The Electoral Makeup of the Socialist Party in 1978

	Electors = 100%	Socialist Electors = 100%
Sex		
Men	48	48
Women	52	52
Age Bracket		
18 to 24	11	12
25 to 34	21	21
35 to 49	27	26
50 to 64	22	22
65 and above	19	19
Profession of Heads of Family		
Farmer	8	6
Small shopkeeper, artisan	6	5
Upper management and professionals	10	6
Middle management and white collar	22	26
Blue-collar worker	29	31
Inactive or retired	25	26

SOURCE: SOFRES, postelectoral poll carried out 28 March–5 April 1978, based on a nationwide sample of two thousand electors.

TABLE 2.4. Electoral Penetration of the Socialist Party in the Various Socioprofessional Categories (in percent)

Profession of Heads of Family	*1973*	*1978*
Farmer	17	17
Small shopkeeper, artisan	23	23
Upper management and professional	7	15
Middle management and white collar	23	29
Blue-collar worker	27	27
Inactive or retired	20	26

Intrapartisan Linkage and Preferential Linkage: the Voters/Party and Rank-and-File/Leadership Contradictions

The study of intrapartisan linkage and the answer to the question asked in the introduction concerning the extent to which members of the working class are active at the different levels of the internal hierarchy of the PS will be derived from 1973–78 sociological data and, respectively, the French adult population, the Socialist electorate, the party's members and militants, its candidates in the legislative elections, its deputies in the National Assembly, and the members of its executive committee.[5] On the basis of this information the scope of the study can be defined more clearly at several levels: sex, age, socioprofessional category, degree of education, and type of union affiliation.

THE EXTENT OF MASCULINE PREDOMINANCE

The French Left has been known traditionally to be a predominantly masculine electorate. It is surprising, therefore, that the 1978 PS electorate resembles exactly that of the French adult population (table 2.5), which through the evolution of the last twenty years shows that differences in voting behavior based on sex are growing less marked, as women take a more and more active part in the social and economic life of the country.

5. The sources for the data used here are the following. Concerning the French adult population and the composition of the Socialist electorate in terms of sex, age and socioprofessional category: see Institut français d'opinion publique, 1973, and Société française d'enquête par sondages, 1978; for the composition of the Socialist electorate by degree of education and type of union affiliation: see Société française d'enquête par sondages, postelectoral surveys for *Le Nouvel Observateur*, 1973 and 1978; for the data on PS members: see P. Hardouin, "Les caractéristiques sociologiques du Parti Socialiste," *Revue française de science politique*, April 1978, pp. 220–56; for the data on militants: the survey carried out by Roland Cayrol among delegates to the PS Convention in Grenoble in June 1973, Roland Cayrol, "Les militants du parti socialiste, contribution à une sociologie" in *Projet*, no. 88 (September-October 1974), pp. 929–40; for the delegates to the convention held in Nantes in June 1977: see the IFOP report, *Parti Socialiste, Congrès de Nantes*, 1977; for the statistics concerning the candidates in the legislative elections: P. Laigre, *Les candidats de l'U.G.S.D. aux élections législatives des 4 et 11 mars 1973* (thesis presented at Institut d'études politiques in Paris, June 1975), and G. Fabre-Rosane and A. Guede, "Sociologie des candidats aux élections législatives de mars 1978," *Revue française de science politique*, October 1978, pp. 840–58; for the deputies: *Les élections législatives de 1973*, Ministry of Interior, 1973, pp. 11–26, and J. Edouard, "Le groupe parlementaire à l'Assemblée Nationale: renouvellement et continuité," *Nouvelle Revue Socialiste*, no. 1, pp. 34–42; for members of the executive committee, the organ that directs the party between national convention meetings: M. Benassayag, "Deux ou trois choses qu'on sait de lui: données anciennes et nouvelles sur le P.S." *Nouvelle Revue Socialiste*, no. 1, pp. 17–24.

35

TABLE 2.5. Socialist Strata and Sex (in percent)

Population	French Adult Population	Socialist Voters 1973 1978	PS Members 1973	PS Militants 1973 1977	PS Parliamentary Candidates 1973 1978	Members of PS Executive Committee 1973	Socialist Deputies 1973 1978
Sex							
Men	48	53 48	87	88 85	98 94	94	99 99
Women	52	47 52	13	12 15	2 6	6	1 1

Sexual differentiation, however, becomes more marked as soon as the party structures themselves are examined. Already among the rank-and-file militants the discrepancy is much greater: hardly more than one out of ten is a woman. And the higher the level in the internal party hierarchy, the more women are underrepresented.

This is true at the level of the executive committee and even more so at the level of candidates in parliamentary elections, a sphere that French political culture traditionally reserves for men—particularly when the voti: g system is a two-ballot election in single-member districts. And whatever the declarations of intention of the Socialist Left, it is obviously influenced by the traditional political environment.

A recent evolution in this respect is nevertheless worth mentioning. In the June 1973 Grenoble Congress, 62 percent of the women delegates had joined the PS since 1971, as against 43.4 percent of the men: Unless women stay in the party much more briefly than men, this means that the proportion of women in the party is now a little higher than formerly.

Moreover, since the March 1974 Suresnes Convention, the PS has reserved at least 10 percent of its positions of responsibility in the party for women. And the proportion of women on the executive committee has in fact passed from 6.2 percent in 1973 to 13 percent in 1975 (Pau Convention, February 1975).

In spite of this incipient change, however, it is obvious that the percentage of women in the party's militant population is not proportionate to their percentage in the Socialist electorate.

THE STRUCTURE OF THE ELECTORATE AS AN OBSTACLE TO
REJUVENATION

Distribution according to age groups is enlightening in several respects (table 2.6). First, a rather high degree of correspondence is evident between the distribution of the French population as a whole and that of the Socialist electorate: from this standpoint the PS is like a microcosm of French society.

But, in addition to that, the phenomenon already noticed in regard to sex is once again encountered: a sharp difference between the electorate and party members. In 1973 almost half of the party militants were under thirty-five years of age, much younger than the Socialist voters. The greater distance is not that separating the French population and the Socialist electorate but that which stretches between socialist voters and party militants.

37

TABLE 2.6. Socialist Strata and Age (in percent)

Population	French Adult Population	Socialist Voters 1973	Socialist Voters 1978	PS Members 1973	PS Militants 1973	PS Militants 1977	PS Parliamentary Candidates 1973	PS Parliamentary Candidates 1978	Members of PS Executive Committee 1973	Socialist Deputies 1973	Socialist Deputies 1978
Age											
Less than 35 years old	32	31	33	(16)[a]	46	35	22		(10)[a]	3	
35 to 49 years old	27	31	26	(44)[b]	36	44	41		(43)[f]	30	
50 to 64 years old	22	22	22	29	18	(12)[c]	32	(e)	(37)[g]	52	(h)
65 and over	19	16	19	11		(6)[d]	5		10	15	

a. Less than 30 years old.
b. 30 to 49 years old.
c. 50 to 59 years old.
d. 60 and above (and 3 percent without answer).
e. The data do not exist. Average age: 43 years 9 months.
f. 30 to 39 years old.
g. 40 to 49 years old.
h. The data do not exist. Average age: 48 years 3 months.

It would seem easier to transform a party of this type at the level of its executive bodies, such as the executive committee, than at the level of its parliamentary group. Table 2.6 shows this clearly: more than half of the members of the executive committee (elected directly by the PS Convention) were less than forty years old in 1973, whereas there is a noticeably lower proportion of young people among the party candidates in the parliamentary election designated by the organizations on the département level.

The deputies form the oldest group among the various strata of the party. This characteristic has a threefold explanation. First, candidates are often chosen because of their experience or because of the *cursus honorum* that they have already obtained on a local level (often they already hold local offices, as city councillors, mayors, general councillors). Second, it is usual for outgoing deputies to run for office again and again—has it not been said that in France deputies never withdraw from political life of their own accord and rarely die? These deputies therefore continue to play important roles in the Socialist party—even if less in 1978 than in 1973. Finally, although the party does present a certain number of young candidates for legislative office (22 percent of the candidates in 1973 were under thirty-five years of age), this is usually the case in constituencies considered to be "lost in advance," and these young candidates, consequently, are seldom actually elected to a seat in the National Assembly.

Therefore, in regard to age, the PS is confronted with a twofold problem of linkage: first, among the various levels of its activity (electors, members, executives, and elected representatives) and second, between the *militant* structures of the organization (militants and inner levels of management) and the *representative* structures of the party (candidates and those elected to Parliament).

THE "CLASS FRONT," THE VOTE, AND PARTY MEMBERSHIP

The PS organizes its strategy around what it calls the "class front," that is, "the regrouping of all those whose interests lie in the destruction of capitalist economic exploitation and political and ideological domination," a group that includes "the vast majority of salaried workers" but "rests mainly on the working class, which is the most directly and the most harshly exploited."[6] For a political organization that seeks to develop a strategy to achieve such goals there is obviously a crucial

6. Quotations from *Quinze thèses sur l'autogestion*, document adopted by the Socialist Party National Convention in Paris, 21–22, June 1975.

linkage problem: Is the party *for* the workers also a party *of* the workers? As table 2.7 points out, a marked difference is evident between the socioprofessional categories of the party's electorate, on the one hand, and its militants and officeholders, on the other.

As Table 2.7 makes clear, the electoral base of the PS appears in conformity with the party's political goals of having a predominantly working-class constituency, while at the same time standing as a microcosm of French society as a whole. In 1978 the most "bourgeois" professions were slightly underrepresented: the managers in trade and industry, professionals, and top-level executives represented no more than 11 percent of Socialist electors as opposed to 16 percent of the whole voting population. Middle-level executives and white-collar workers are found in equal proportions in the population as a whole and in the Socialist electorate in 1973 and are slightly overrepresented in the electorate in 1978 (22 percent of the general population, 26 percent of Socialist voters). Finally, a rather loose "lower-class" category of farmers, blue-collar workers, and the inactive groups includes 63 percent of the 1978 Socialist electorate and 62 percent of the population as a whole. Thus the party attracts a heterogeneous following, representative of the entire French population in general terms, but at the same time can honestly claim a "mainly working-class" constituency so far as voting support is concerned.

But once again there is a marked discrepancy between electoral support and the structures: table 2.7 shows the militants to be very different from both the population as a whole and the party leaders. The contrast between the population as a whole and that of the PS members and the party militants is particularly marked for two categories: the liberal professions and executives (7 percent of the adult population but 14 percent of the PS members and 47 percent of the militants) and the workers (29 percent of the adult population but only 16 percent of the PS party members and 5 percent of the militants).[7]

If the discrepancy between the electoral basis and the active members is the more striking, that between the militants and the elected representatives of the party is nonetheless very significant. It is noticeable not only in regard to the liberal professions and top-level executives (47 percent of the militants, 66 percent of the deputies) but also in the inverse

7. The figures cited are from different years, but are all within the six-year period of 1973–78.

TABLE 2.7. Socialist Strata and Socioprofessional Categories (in percent)

Population	French Adult Population 1978	Socialist Voters 1973	Socialist Voters 1978	PS Members 1973	PS Militants 1973	PS Militants 1977	PS Parliamentary Candidates 1973	PS Parliamentary Candidates 1978	Socialist Deputies 1973	Socialist Deputies 1978
Profession of Heads of Family										
Industry and commerce	9	5	5	9	4	2	4	4	5	7
Top-level executives and professionals	7	5	6	14	46	47	62	63	60	66
Middle-level executives and white-collar workers	22	22	26	29	35	37	23	28	15	26
Farmers	8	11	6	9	1	2	1	2	3	1
Bule-collar workers	29	36	31	16	3	5	3	1	—	—
Inactive or retired	25	21	26	23	11	7	7	2	17	—

relation as concerns the white-collar workers and middle-level executives (37 percent of the militants and 26 percent of the deputies). And not one Socialist deputy comes from the working class. It becomes clear that whereas the electoral support draws on relatively predominant lower classes, the party recruits its members and especially its activists mainly from the middle class and its deputies almost entirely from the wealthier categories.

In fact, the situation here is the old problem of European, and in particular of French, Socialist and Social-Democrat organizations. What is important—and also shows how precarious evolution can be in this field—is that whatever the recent evolution of the Socialist electorate may have been and however great the renewal of the Socialist politicians, the discrepancy between the voting populations and the elected representation is not growing smaller. Indeed, the professional structure of the Socialist parliamentary group has not become any more "popular" between 1968 and 1973 (table 2.8).

It should be noted that if the Socialist parties have up till now failed in their attempt to have the working class represented on the executive level and on the various elected committees, the Communist parties have been, from this point of view, more successful.

TABLE 2.8. Socioprofessional Structure of the Socialist Parliamentary Group (in percent)

Profession of Heads of Family	Socialist Parliamentary Group		
	In 1968	In 1973	In 1978
Industry and commerce	8.8	5	7
Top-level executives and professionals	54.3	60.4*	66
Middle-level executives	10.5	12.9	26
White-collar workers	—	2	
Farmers	5.3	3	1
Others workers	1.8	—	—
Others and inactive	19.3	16.8	—
	100	100	100

*The increase within this category is essentially due to the increase in the number of teachers (secondary and higher educaton), which rose from 14 percent in 1968 to 19.8 percent in 1973).

For example, 68 percent of the French Communist party electorate in 1973 came from lower-class categories (workers, white-collar workers, middle-level executives); at the Twentieth Congress of this party in December 1972, 67 percent of the delegates belonged to these categories; and in the 1973 parliamentary group 62 percent of the deputies came from these same categories. But it is clear that Communist organizations attach a great deal of importance to *intrapartisan linkage* and that they devote special attention to the social composition of party conventions and of the various bodies elected under the Communist label. It has become an organization principle for the Communist party in France to have minimum quotas for workers and also for women and young people. In this respect there is a great difference between the Communist and Socialist parties.

THE CULTURAL GAP

Because educational inequality in France is to a large extent bound up with social inequality, it is not surprising to find that distribution of the party hierarchy by educational level is in accordance with distribution by socioprofessional category.

Once more, as table 2.9 indicates, wide gaps separate the PS militants from both the electorate and the party leaders.

Table 2.9 shows to what extent the French PS recruits its members from culturally privileged spheres: more than half of the Socialist militants have studied at the university or at an institution of higher education (as opposed to one elector out of ten), and the higher in the party hierarchy, the greater the proportion of intellectuals (more than two-thirds of the members of the party executive committee are university educated).

Once again the basic discrepancy appears to be between Socialist

TABLE 2.9.   Socialist Strata and Level of Education (in percent)

Population	Socialist Voters 1973	1978	PS Militants 1973	1977	PS Executive Committee 1973
Level of Education					
Primary	58	59	5	12	6
Technical	19	19	10	8	—
Secondary	17	13	30	23	25
Higher	6	9	55	57	69

voters and the party structures, and once again there is also a significant difference between the rank and file and the leadership within the party itself.

THE DIFFERENT TYPES OF UNION AFFILIATION

Union membership is also a criterion that distinguishes sharply among the various strata of the PS (table 2.10).

Trade-union affiliation is much more widespread among the militants (and still more among the leaders) than among the electors. Only 50 percent of Socialist voters belong to a union, whereas 66 percent of the militants and 76 percent of the leaders do. This is easily explained by the higher level of social consciousness among socialist political militants than among mere sympathizers and by the fact that party rules require salaried workers who join the party to affiliate with a union.

Teachers form a large proportion of the party members (and in particular of the leaders) who belong to a union, because, obviously, the party draws heavily upon schools and universities.

If the party is compared with its electorate, it can be noted that the

TABLE 2.10. Socialist Strata and Union Affiliation (in percent)

Population	Socialist Voters 1973	PS Militants 1973	PS Executive Committee 1973
Union			
GGT[a]	24	7.4	11
CFDT[b]	7	19.4	11
FO[c]	8	10.2	20.5
Others	11	29[d]	33.4[e]
Non-unionized	50	34	24

a. The Confédération Générale du Travail is the largest French trade union. Its management is largely controlled by Communists. Its secretary is a member of the political bureau of the French Communist party.
b. The Confédération Francaise Démocratique du Travail, a union with Christian origins, became "areligious" in 1964. It stands for democratic socialism with the accent on workers' self-management. Several of its leaders are members of the Socialist party.
c. Force Ouvrière, which came into being as the result of a split within the CGT, is a reformist organization that claims to be apolitical, even though its secretary-general is a member of the PS.
d. 23.8 percent of whom belong to the FEN (Fédération de l'Education Nationale).
e. All belonging to the FEN.

CGT is underrepresented, that the CFDT and the FO are overrepresented, and that the FO holds an important place among the leaders, comparable to that of the CFDT among the members.

The PS members, as far as unionization is concerned, are thus out of step with their electorate; Socialist militants belong less often than Socialist electors to organizations under strong Communist influence; they tend to join "progressive" unions, whose ideology is assuredly closer to that of their party.

By contrast, party leaders often remain faithful to a yet more moderate union; they are obviously not attracted to the CFDT, which some probably consider to be too marked by its Christian origins or by its comparative "leftism." It is probably safe to assume that Socialist electors are guided, above all, by considerations of efficiency in choosing their union membership: The CGT is the most powerful union in France on a national level and is even more powerful in individual firms. Party militants seem more sensitive to ideology and party leaders to tradition.

The PS thus has many problems on the intrapartisan level. On the basis of all the variables examined, a considerable gap is observable between the electorate and the militant structures of the organization. A marked discrepancy also exists between the militant population and the party executives. In this respect the major problem seems to be to transform the parliamentary group, which is the structure most resistant to sociological transformation.

On the whole it can be concluded that the French Socialist party has undergone profound changes in recent years, and the modes of *linkage* that it has developed between the population and politics have been deeply modified. At the intrapartisan level, the PS has implicitly given up the idea of a *preferential linkage* and in this way appears very much like the other major European Socialist organizations. Like its British, Swedish, German, and Italian counterparts, the party finds its most active members and executives mainly from the upper levels of society, the middle and upper-middle classes who are politically active "in the name of the working class."

The French PS has also evolved on the social level, again coming closer to the position of its partners in the Socialist International. Like the British Labour Party, the Italian PSI, and the German and Swedish Social Democratic parties, the French PS has a wider following among the lower classes than among the affluent sections of society. But, also like the others, this party is progressively reducing the imbalance by acquiring followers from all segments of society and may soon constitute a microcosm of the society in which it functions.

The French PS, however, as mentioned earlier, continues to manifest a marked originality in comparison with the other European Socialist organizations: it is the only one to have opted for a strengthened anti-capitalist program. How has the party been able to move to a more radical ideological stance and at the same time come into closer sociological conformity with the population at large?

The explanation may lie in the fact that, in contrast with the other European Socialists, this party has not been in power for a long time. In light of the data collected here, one may wonder whether, once in power, the French PS would remain faithful to the strategic choice of breaking with capitalism or, having already drawn closer to the other European social democracies sociologically, would then move closer politically and ideologically as well. The importance assumed by societal linkage, at the expense of preferential linkage with the working class, makes the PS a more interclass party than ever. Simultaneously, the main characteristic of its intraparty linkage is the increasingly bourgeois composition of its strata as one moves up from voters to militants to leaders. Could not the configurations derived from these data provide, finally, serious obstacles to the radical social transformations implied in the party's ideological options?

3.

European Social Democratic Party Leaders and the Working Class: Some Linkage Implications of Trends in Recruitment

M. A. MARSH

Social Democratic parties[1] have played a considerable role in providing political leadership in most West European democracies over the last few decades. Most of these parties developed as citizenship was extended to the lower classes, seeing themselves, and being seen, as the channel through which the new participants could exercise their political rights. They organized participation, yet at the highest levels participation was often disproportionately middle class. The names of early Socialist leaders drawn from the upper reaches of

An earlier draft of this study, titled "Middle-Class Social Democratic Party Leaders: Some Trends and Implications," was presented to a Joint Sessions Workshop, "Theoretical and Empirical Analysis of Party Systems," European Consortium for Political Research, London, April 1975. I should like to thank members of the workshop for their criticisms. I am also grateful to Tom Mackie, Kjell Eliassen, Peter Gerlich, and Professor Per-Erik Back for assistance in collecting data and Keith Webb and Kay Lawson for comments on later drafts.

1. The term is used here to identify those self-described "Labour" and/or "Social Democratic" parties founded in Western Europe in the last third of the nineteenth century that today comprise most of the non-communist Left in Western Europe. The empirical examples discussed in this study all belonged to the Second International and today are affiliated with the Socialist International. The parties covered are detailed in the appendix.

society are widely known, and it is usually suggested that the middle-class element in higher party levels is even larger today.

The question this study asks is how does this aspect of the party's *recruitment* role affect the validity of its traditional claim to represent working-class interests and its ability to channel legitimacy, thus linking the working class and government in a number of different ways through the general representative process.

Linkage, of course, is the major theme here, and before proceeding further the concept should be clarified. In Otto Kirchheimer's terms, the concept signifies the party's function as a "transmission-belt"[2] conveying, for instance, political actors (recruitment function), political demands (interest-representation function), or political support from the mass public, or sections of it, to the political decision makers or governmental institutions. These are "input functions." The concept may describe "outputs" in so far as parties may influence public reaction to political events by their own reactions and interpretation.

Various labels can be given to linkage processes: integration, legitimation, social control, and so on. Used this way, the term "linkage" refers to particular "functions" when the latter term carries no implications for the stability of the political system. Linkage may also draw on the metaphor of communication, rather than biological systems, emphasizing signals as well as functions.[3] Here the term is used in both senses.

Recruitments, Interests, and Supports

The concern then is with three types of input linkage—recruitment, interest representation, and support—and their interrelations. Although various relationships could be explored, only those between recruitment

2. O. Kirchheimer, "The Transformation of Western European Party Systems," in J. LaPalombara and M. Weiner, eds., *Political Parties and Political Development* (Princeton: Princeton University Press, 1966), p. 177.

3. The above use of the term "function" has been described as "eclectic functionalism." For this and other implications of the term see W. Flanigan and W. Fogelman, "Functional Analysis," in J. C. Charlesworth, ed., *Contemporary Political Analysis* (London: Collier-Macmillan, 1967), pp. 72–85. An example of the communications metaphor is H. Heclo's interpretation of the concept "transmission line": "Parties have not served as the unfettered transmission lines between public demand and government social policy, partly because those responsible for the latter were not interested in or could not understand the messages, but mostly because the public were sending no clear signals." (*From Relief to Income Maintenance: Modern Social Politics in Britain and Sweden* [New Haven: Yale University Press, 1971], p. 293).

and interest representation and between recruitment and support will be examined. How does the recruitment of political actors socially representative of a party's sectional identity influence interest and support linkages?

Through recruitment, parties provide personnel for the governmental system. Electors legitimize these choices through their vote, and this recruitment and its legitimization are examples of both physical and psychological links between government and people for which parties provide a channel. When recruitment criteria include a strong emphasis on the social characteristics of the party's electoral clientele, the party is linking supporters and government through what is termed "social representation." For working-class parties this necessitates a strong bias in favor of working-class recruits. The declining importance of this aspect of linkage will be examined in this study.

The decline in social representation may have further implications; for example, in interest representation. Just as parties may provide for the selection and legitimation of political actors, so also they may permit the selection and legitimation of political policies. Thus representation can take on social or interest aspects. As emphasized above, these may be separated, at least analytically.[4]

The decline in social representation also has implications for the nature and pattern of political supports. Through support for prosystem parties[5] the electorate supports at least the ground rules of the political system. If social representation is salient for voting groups, they should react in some way to any decline in this form of recruitment. Thus a Social Democratic party that does not recruit workers for leadership

---

4. For a variety of interpretations of the concept of representation see H. F. Pitkin, *The Concept of Representation* (Berkeley and Los Angeles: University of California Press, 1967). Several recent studies have concluded that social background is a poor predictor of elite attitudes, which would indicate that the concepts are empirically separable. See L. J. Edinger and D. D. Searing, "Social Background in Elite Analysis: A Methodological Inquiry," *American Political Science Review* 61 (1967): 428–45; D. D. Searing, "The Comparative Study of Elite Socialisation," *Comparative Politics* 1 (1968): 471–500; D. Fairlie and I. Budge, "Elite Background and Issue Preferences: A Comparison of British and Foreign Data Using a New Technique," in I. Crewe, ed., *British Political Sociology Yearbook: Elites in Western Democracy* (London: Croom Helm, 1974), 1: 199–240. However, these studies did not treat party as an intervening variable, nor did they investigate the relationship between these factors at the party level as is done here.

5. It has been argued that support for antisystem parties can also have broadly "integrative" effects. See G. Roth, *The Social Democrats in Imperial Germany* (Totowa, N.J.: Bedminster Press, 1963).

roles would lose working-class support, and the party's linkage role as a channel of working-class support for the political system would be reduced.

A "class" party can link class and government through social representation, interest representation, and by generally mobilizing support and legitimacy. The implications of changes in the first linkage in relation to the nature of the other two will be examined.

The class background of Social Democratic party leaders, focusing on variations over time within and between parties, will be explored first. In general Social Democratic parties are now more middle class than in earlier years, although considerable differences exist in the weight of working-class leadership components and in the timing and rate of decline. A number of explanations for this decline are reviewed. As has been observed elsewhere (although no one has presented any systematic comparative evidence), some commentators believe that this trend has implications for policy as well as for the effectiveness with which parties will be able to maintain working-class support for the political system. The tentative conclusions here are that neither implication can be drawn.

Class Basis of Leadership

It is, perhaps, a reasonable expectation that party leaders will be drawn overwhelmingly from the social group that appears to constitute a party's main fund of voting support, the representation of which may be its raison d'être: Catholic or Christian party leaders should be church-goers, Agrarian party leaders farmers, and so on. Yet Social Democratic working-class parties have for the most part long been notable for containing within their leadership ranks relatively large contingents drawn from outside the working class.

The data presented here are the occupational backgrounds of the parliamentary groups of eight parties: the Austrian Social Democratic party, the French Socialist party, the German Social Democratic party, the Italian Socialist party, the Norwegian Labour party, the Swedish Social Democratic party, the Swiss Social Democratic party, and the British Labour party.[6] Occupation is taken to indicate class, and the parliamentary group is taken as representing the party leadership.

6. The names used here are the contemporary titles of parties listed and identified historically in T. T. Mackie and R. Rose, *The International Almanac of Electoral Behaviour* (London: Macmillan, 1974). The sample of parties here was partially restricted by both

Dealing comparatively with occupational classifications presents certain problems of equivalence. The problem of standardizing the categories has been met by electing to deal in simple, broad categories: nonmanual, manual, and those in agricultural employment. The terms "nonmanual" and "manual" workers are used synonymously with the terms "middle class" and "working class", respectively. Perhaps a more difficult problem is the temporal one—equating data on original occupation, occupation on entry to Parliament, and present occupation. Many parliamentarians change occupation through these separate time points. The aim here was to identify those who had at one time been engaged in manual work. Many manual workers experience social mobility through the labor movement, rising to white-collar status within it. Where there was no indication of other employment, it was assumed that trade-union employees had previously been manual workers but that party and other employees were nonmanual workers.[7] The data should be taken as an approximation rather than as a perfect indicator. The sources of the data (largely secondary) are given in the appendix.

TRENDS

Table 3.1 and figure 3.1 show the pattern of class changes, the former showing average class structure for prewar (pre-1918), interwar (1918–43), and postwar (1943–70) periods and the latter the trends in the postwar years. Averages were computed from as many data points as were available, but some cells are based on only one observation.

It is clear from table 3.1 that some leadership groups have become more middle class, although the Austrian and, to a lesser extent, the Norwegian, Swiss, and Italian cases all seem to indicate alternative

---

data availability and an intention to limit the context of the study to Western Europe to enable a "most similar systems" study design. (See A. Przeworski and H. Teune, *The Logic of Comparative Social Inquiry* [London: Wiley-Interscience, 1970], esp. chap. 3.) Heisler argues similarly in M. O. Heisler, ed., *European Politics: Structures and Processes in Some Post-Industrial Democracies* (New York: David McKay, 1974), pp. 19–22. The "Western" limitation is criticized by D. W. Urwin and K. Eliassen, "In Search of a Continent: The Quest of Comparative European Politics," *European Journal of Political Research* 3 (1975): 85–113. For "recruitment" comparisons across the Atlantic see L. D. Epstein, *Political Parties in Western Democracies* (London: Pall Mall Press, 1967), chap. 7.

7. Testing this assumption against more detailed Austrian information suggested that it has a reasonable empirical foundation. Generally, it would seem that the method underestimates the working-class component in earlier years and overestimates it in later years. The decline observed in the working-class component of leadership is thus probably greater than the data suggest.

51

TABLE 3.1. Class Breakdown of Social Democratic Parliamentary Groups: Selected Countries (in percent)

Country	Prewar Average				Interwar Average				Postwar Average			
	Non-manual	Manual	Farmers	(N)	Non-manual	Manual	Farmers	(N)	Non-manual	Manual	Farmers	(N)
Italy	94	6	0	(33)	—	—	—	*	88	12	0	(70)
Austria	72	26	2	(115)	64	36	0	(71)	49	50	1	(75)
Switzerland	69	31	0	(13)	60	40	0	(30)	60	40	0	(47)
Norway	66	18	16	(16)	61	19	20	(57)	55	25	20	(73)
France	50	41	9	(76)	—	8†	—	†	96	1	3	(64)
Sweden	48	44	8	(64)	56	27	17	(102)	66	20	14	(98)
Germany	25	75	0	(95)	29	71	0	(150)	78	21	1	(213)
Britain	12	88	0	(43)	26	74	0	(147)	66	34	0	(312)

SOURCE: See appendix.

NOTES: All Ns given except the Italian are the base from which the percentages have been calculated. The average size of the parliamentary group was therefore slightly higher because unclassifiable cases have been excluded. The postwar Italian N represents the average number of Socialist party deputies.

* Only two democratic elections took place in this period. No data is available.

† This single percentage (for 1936) is the only available data in the interwar period.

FIGURE 3.1.   Percentage of Workers in Postwar Social Democratic Parliamentary Groups: Selected Years and Countries

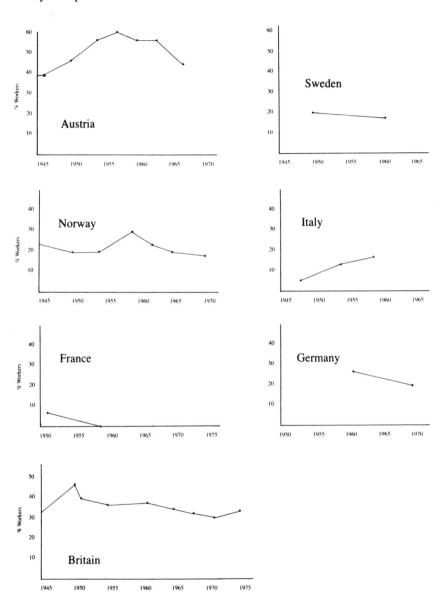

SOURCE: See appendix.

53

trends. The timing of change has not been regular: in Germany, for instance, it has been a recent phenomenon, whereas in Sweden the change has been a long-term one. Neither has the degree of change been standard, with Germany and Britain experiencing particularly large changes compared with small variations in Italy, Norway, and Switzerland. Generally, declines in working-class contingents have been large. Where increases have taken place, excepting Austria, they have been marginal.

Figure 3.1 suggests that the apparently "deviant" cases from table 3.1 may be following the same trend within the postwar period. In both Austria and Norway there have been steady declines in the working-class contingents since the mid-sixties. Only Italy (where data is for the 1950s only) clearly appears to resist the trend. Only one data point is available for postwar Switzerland. Elsewhere, postwar trends are in accord with the overall patterns of declining working-class and increasing middle-class representation.[8]

LEVELS

If the proportion of workers is declining almost everywhere, what is the meaning of difference in levels between parties? Is there a trend toward similarity despite the variety of origins and environments? Can any conclusions about the future be drawn from the overall picture?

Comparing the changing averages and ranges should provide partial answers, although missing data distorts the results. Nevertheless, whether ranges and averages are calculated simply for those countries with no missing data or for all countries, the results are quite similar, generally showing a fall in both maximum and minimum levels of working-class leadership (see table 3.2).

Before World War II the party leaders in Germany and Britain were about 75 percent working class; in other countries the composition was more scattered but well under the 50 percent mark. Now five parties— in Italy, Sweden, Germany, Norway, and Britain—are separated by only sixteen percentage points, with more working-class leaders in the Swiss and Austrian parties and fewer in the French. Apart from the

8. Farmers are treated as part of a separate "cleavage" in this study and there is little to say about them. They are numerous only in the Scandinavian parties and now seem to be a declining component, as indeed the primary sector of the economy itself declines. On socialists' attitudes toward "peasants" and agrarian problems generally see D. Mitrany, *Marx Against the Peasants: A Study in Social Dogmatism* (New York: Dover, 1961).

TABLE 3.2. Means and Range of Working-Class Percentage of Social Democratic Parliamentary Groups

	Range	Mean
Prewar	6–88	42
Interwar*	8–74	39
Postwar	1–50	26

SOURCE: See appendix.
*Does not include Italy.

dramatic fall in the level of French working-class leadership in the interwar period, the largest shifts have taken place in those parties that were originally the most working class: elsewhere any change has been relatively slight. Where prewar and interwar means suggest that the normal working-class component was around two-fifths of the group, the modern norm is only one-fourth. The normal prewar levels are exceeded only by the exceptional Austrian case. The data does not allow the positing of some "lower level" beyond which the working-class proportion will not fall, because it is not generally detailed enough to reflect any leveling out. However, the French case suggests that the result indicated by the logical extension of most trend lines is not impossible.[9]

The physical link maintained by Social Democratic parties between the working class and government is thus weakening. In Italy and in France, where the link is weakest in these parties, Communist parties have assumed the role of socially representing the working class;[10] in other nations there are no real political alternatives.[11]

9. R. W. Johnson suggests the possibility of no working-class leaders at all for the British Labour party by the next century, "The British Political Elite, 1955–1972," in *Archives européennes de sociologie* 14 (1973): 69. See also V. J. Hanby's comments on the National Executive Committee of that party, "A Changing Labour Elite: The National Executive Committee of the Labour Party 1900–72," in Crewe, op. cit., p. 152. An earlier author sees this as less likely, requiring certain structural changes: see Z. Bauman, *Between Class and Elite* (Manchester: Manchester University Press, 1973), p. 284.

10. Of twelve deputies in the French National Assembly of 1968 described as "*ouvriers*," ten were Communists. See R. Cayrol et al., *Le Deputé francais* (Paris: Armand Colin, 1973), p. 40. The comparable figure for the 1973 Assembly was sixteen out of sixteen: Ministère de l'Intérieur, *Les élections législatives de 1973* (Paris: Imprimerie Nationale/Direction de la documentation, 1973), pp. 119–20. For a more complete historical picture see M. Dogan, "Political Ascent in a Class Society: French Deputies 1870–1958," in D.

EXPLANATIONS

It is worthwhile to examine some of the reasons for the general decline. These are connected with political changes—within the parties themselves and in the political context—and with social developments. The wider political changes will be dealt with first.

The most significant change in the political context in which these parties operate is the increasing complexity of government. It can be— and is—argued that leaders must be men of proven intellectual ability, possibly having special expertise in some areas. Rather than the emphasis being on ascriptive criteria—notably class—it is on achievement, defined in educational and professional terms. This naturally makes things more difficult' for the manual worker. He can rarely display considerable formal educational achievement, and although trade unions provide opportunities to develop political and administrative skills, success in this area takes considerable time. Thus, well-educated non-manual aspirants are able to make their professional mark at an earlier age, gaining a considerable advantage when "youth" is a salient factor in candidate selection processes.[12]

The preceding factor is reinforced by the increasingly profession-alized status of parliamentarians.[13] To the extent that the profession becomes a secure one (and this is generally assisted by the proportional representation systems prevalent in Europe) and to the extent that material rewards are comparable with other professions, young professionals will be attracted to (or certainly not turned away from) politics.

Marvick, ed., *Political Decision Makers* (New York: The Free Press, 1961), pp. 57–90. In Italy, 25 percent of Communist party deputies 1946–58 were manual workers compared with 4 percent of Socialist party deputies and less than 1 percent of the dominant Christian Democratic party group (G. Sartori, "Parliament in Italy," *International Social Science Journal* 11 [1961]: 590).

11. Arguably, the trade unions still provide a vital link. Recent discussion of "neo-corporatism" or "neofeudalism," describing relations between interest groups (including trade unions) and government, suggests that parties may be bypassed. For a general view see M. O. Heisler with R. B. Kvavik, "Patterns of European Politics: The 'European Polity' Model," in Heisler, op. cit., esp. pp. 48–59.

12. This point is emphasized, for example, in two studies of British Labour party recruitment: see Johnson, op. cit., and J. W. Ellis and R. W. Johnson, *Members from the Unions* (Fabian Research Series, 316).

13. Observations by social scientists on this point have been common since Max Weber's time. Recent volumes by G. Sartori et al. and by E. Gruner et al. on Italian and Swiss parliamentarians respectively (see appendix, table 3.1) both emphasize the point. For a comparative review see the collection of articles in *International Social Science Journal*, vol. 11 (1961).

As Z. Bauman has pointed out, there is, therefore, both a *demand* for, and a supply of, nonproletarains as parliamentarians and, consequently, as party leaders.[14]

Certain aspects of Social Democratic party development have also served to increase the effect of the above process. As these parties have become governing parties, they have become both more attractive to middle-class aspirants and more eager to recruit such candidates for leadership positions.[15] Cabinet office is usually more demanding than a parliamentary position, and an emphasis on intellectual qualification in recruitment is even more understandable. The more "legitimate" status of the modern Social Democratic party compared with its late nineteenth century ancestors makes it more of a natural home for the middle-class radical-liberal. In addition, the more cynical have suggested that the prospective middle-class politician might see his chances of promotion as stronger in a working-class party where there is less competition.[16] Finally, to the extent that a middle-class group does come to dominate, it might be increasingly inclined to create a party in its own image.[17]

The important social changes concern social mobility. To the extent that more children of working-class parents can now obtain a good education than heretofore, middle-class leaders can be selected who have good working-class credentials to add to their proven intellectual abilities.[18] Available data from Italy, Norway, and France show a greater number of leaders whose parents were working class than of those who were themselves once engaged in manual labor.[19]

Social and economic change also seems to be reducing the relative

14. Bauman, op cit., p. 285.

15. In 1904 German Social Democrat leader August Bebel used this as an argument against Socialist "participation" in government. Such a policy would, he argued, attract to the party "a swarm of bourgeois of very dubious value." Quoted in R. Michels, *Political Parties* (New York: Dover, 1959), p. 213.

16. For example, ibid., pp. 266–67; Bauman, op. cit., pp. 285, 313–15.

17. This is argued by Johnson, op. cit., p. 73. For a general statement see M. Czudnowski, "Political Recruitment," in F. I. Greenstein and N. Polsby, eds., *Handbook of Political Science* (Reading, Mass.: Addison-Wesley, 1975) 2: 220–21.

18. The British Labour party's selection bias toward the teaching profession results from the search for this mixture according to M. Rush, *The Selection of Parliamentary Candidates* (London: Nelson, 1969), p. 210.

19. In Norway 29 percent of Labour parliamentarians in the postwar period had fathers who were manual workers, compared with 20 percent in the prewar period; the postwar figure for Italy is 20 percent. In the French party the level declined from 67 percent (prewar) through 45 percent (interwar) to 5 percent (Fourth Republic). For sources see appendix, table 3.1.

number of manual workers in many Western societies as a net shift from unskilled-manual to white-collar occupations takes place under the pressure of technological change. Cross-national evidence on the timing and magnitude of such changes is difficult to obtain and, if obtained, is equally awkward to evaluate. It would appear, however, that French development up to the late 1960s at least was contrary to this trend. Data for Norway, Austria, and Germany show no change in the 1950s, although other evidence points to a decline after that period. Even so, the magnitude of such change is small compared to the proportionate decline evident in figure 3.1.[20]

Thus, the professionalization of politics, the "governing party" status of Social Democratic parties, and the greater possibilities of social mobility through education all serve to increase both the demand for, and the supply of, middle-class leaders. Whether these explanations for the variations in timing and rates of change of working-class decline are adequate is dubious. Other factors would surely have to be taken into account to explain the originally very different levels of working-class leadership in Italy, Britain, and Germany, and why the Austrian trend seemed, at least in the fifties, to be toward an increasingly working-class leadership. A number of reasons why Social Democratic parties no longer link the working class strongly with government through a substantial degree of social representation have been reviewed. However, some parties never had this relationship (e.g., the Italian Socialists), and others (e.g., the Norwegian Labour Party) have always been predominantly nonproletarian (although the Scandinavian parties all recruited significant numbers of small farmers and peasants). These variations too are hardly explained by reference to the factors already discussed. Other possible explanations can be offered: for instance, it has been said that the social basis of early Socialist party leadership was dependent upon

20. For France, see the appropriate chapter in M. Archer and S. Giner, *Contemporary Europe: Class, Status and Power* (London: Weidenfeld & Nicolson, 1971). On Germany, Austria, and Norway up to 1960 see respectively L. Edinger, *Politics in Germany* (Boston: Little, Brown, 1968), table II.6; K. Steiner, *Politics in Austria* (Boston: Little, Brown, 1972), table II.3; S. Rokkan, "Norway: Numerical Democracy and Corporate Pluralism," in R. Dahl, ed., *Political Oppositions in Western Democracies* (New Haven: Yale University Press, 1965), p. 94n. For later information on Germany see Edinger, op. cit., 2nd ed. (1977). Data in the 1969 and 1973 volumes of *The Yearbook of Labour Statistics* (Geneva: I.L.O.): Table II B shows decline after 1960 everywhere except Italy, although only in Germany, Britain, and Sweden are 1960–70 differences more than one or two percentage points. Given the time required to establish a political career, the effects of such change will probably not make themselves felt at leadership level for some time.

previous national experiences of independent working-class organization. W. Galenson has offered this as an explanation of the low number of Norwegian working-class Socialist party leaders.[21] In Norway, unlike Britain or Denmark, labor mass movements had no traditions of skilled labor organization on which to draw for models and inspiration. This resulted in a leadership dominated by Socialists of middle-class origin. Institutional factors, such as the strength of union-party links, may also be important. These are traditionally weak in France and Italy, and the weakening of the links in postwar West Germany has been noted by several observers.[22] Of course, such factors in themselves require further explanation.

SIGNIFICANCE

However, before paying further attention to the *causes* of the decline in this aspect of linkage it is worthwhile to question the *significance* of the decline. Does it matter whether or not members of the working class are represented by their own class? As stated previously, the implications in the areas of policy and electoral support will be examined.

On the premise that political attitudes and values reflect the social structure, a change in the class composition of Socialist leaders will result in changes in policy; on the premise that communication is easiest between groups who share social background, the effectiveness of the party in maintaining electoral support is dependent on the class homogeneity of the party. These premises will be examined and three testable hypotheses derived.

Implications of Leaders' Social Class: Three Hypotheses

INTEREST REPRESENTATION

R. Michels argued the importance of social position.[23] At the time he was writing, the bourgeois element in Social Democratic parties was mainly comprised of "intellectuals," people cut off from their own class interests and the general social environment. In consequence, their

21. W. Galenson, "The Labour Movement in Scandinavia," in W. Galenson, ed., *Comparative Labour Movements* (New York: Prentice-Hall, 1952), p. 149: cf. Bauman, op. cit., p. 196.

22. See D. W. Rawson, "The Life-Span of Labour Parties," *Political Studies* 17 (1969): 313–33, for a review of general developments in this area.

23. Michels, op. cit., esp. part 4.

socialism was typified by a "more fervent idealism."[24] Not all were revolutionaries, as Michels admitted; in the great debate of his time, "bourgeois socialists" were to be found on both sides of the revolutionary-reformist conflict.[25] Nevertheless, Michels does seem to believe that "intellectuals" will usually be found on the Left of the socialist movement:

It is hardly possible to imagine the reasons which would induce refugees from the bourgeoisie to adhere to the extreme right wing of the working class party. It is rather the adverse thesis which might be sustained by psychological or historical arguments.[26]

The reasons for this are (a) the decisiveness of the bourgeois's break with his world, (b) his Marxist interpretation of the historical situation, and (c) his knowledge of bourgeois tactics to undermine and moderate the labor movement through reformist concessions. These three factors underlie Michels's thesis.[27]

In contrast, the Socialist party leader with a working-class background is inclined to become "bourgeois" and conservative. His newfound status in, and through, the labor movement and the consequent social mixing with predominantly middle-class (and non-Socialist) politicians tend to undermine his original principles. Furthermore, the common necessity for a manual worker to take paid employment within the labor movement means that his own livelihood becomes dependent upon the organizational success of the movement, rather than its ideological success, and thus inclines him, the paid functionary, to an essentially conservative position.[28] A working hypothesis at the party level could thus be: The stronger the middle-class element in the leadership, the more radical or leftist the party.[29]

However, F. Parkin points to the fact that an increasing middle-class element in European Social Democratic party leaderhip has not been accompanied by an increasing (or even constant) revolutionary socialism.[30] Why should this be so? Michels offered a clue. As has already been

24. Ibid., p. 248.
25. Ibid., p. 322.
26. Ibid., p. 317.
27. Ibid., pp. 317–19.
28. Ibid., pp. 297–315.
  29. Michels is followed here in using the terms "radical," "revolutionary," and "leftist" synonymously, although below two operational definitions are used.
  30. F. Parkin, *Class Inequality and Political Order* (St. Albans: Paladin, 1972), p. 131.

indicated, a factor causing middle-class radicalism was the necessity for the middle-class Socialist to cut himself off from his social origins; "his path," as Michels put it, "led through a thorny thicket" and necessitated violent struggle and much suffering.[31] Yet, "as the years have passed . . . the path of the bourgeois adherent to socialism has become so much easier,"[32] and thus the nature of the middle-class recruit changes; "the soil changes, and with it the quality of the fruit" was Michels's analogy.[33] Parkin takes up this argument, suggesting that the key factor in the change is the legitimation of the party through its acceptance of political parliamentary action as the road to socialism. This legitimation attracts the middle-class progressive, liberal, "moderate" socialist. Furthermore, the process is cumulatively self-reinforcing:

The greater the inflow of bourgeois recruits, the less militant the party becomes, so making it even more attractive to those who favour the interpretation of equality along meritocratic and welfare lines.[34]

Michels, it should be remembered, was also referring to intellectuals rather than to the bourgeoisie generally. In modern times there is probably far more differentiation between the middle-class recruits.[35] Thus, although middle-class recruits are a radical force in developing parties, operating in systems that have not accepted the Socialist representation of working-class interests as legitimate, once the party has accepted parliamentarianism (and been accepted), they are a moderating influence. The worker-recruit remains a potentially more radical force only in his tendency to pursue ends of material equality. Two simple hypotheses can be derived from this discussion:

1. In parties that have not accepted the parliamentary system, a higher level of middle-class leadership is associated with a greater radicalism.

31. Michels, op. cit., p. 322.
32. Ibid.
33. Ibid.
34. Parkin, op. cit., p. 132: cf. B. Hindess, *The Decline of Working Class Politics* (St. Albans: Paladin, 1971), p. 143.
35. As a proportion of the middle-class group, the "liberal professions" element is declining in many parties; for example, German, Swedish, and Austrian. If intellectuals are considered as "university educated" people (as Michels did), the overall proportions seem to be increasing in Germany, Britain, and France and declining in Norway and Italy. For sources see appendix, table 3.1.

2. In parties that have accepted the parliamentary system, a higher level of middle-class leadership is associated with a lesser radicalism.

Assuming that the objective interests of the European working class do not vary much between countries, these hypotheses, if proved true, would clearly carry implications for the nature of Social Democratic parties as representative links. The argument would be that the *social* representativeness of the party influenced its *interest* representativeness and that both linkages were interdependent. It will be observed, however, that neither hypothesis is supported by the available evidence.

SUPPORTS

The premise that shared social origins assist communication is related to the argument discussed above. The linkage concept here draws fruitfully on the notion that communications signals are more easily transmitted and interpreted between those of shared social background. Richard Rose has stated the general case:

Considerations of communication between electors and elected—by imaginative sympathy as well as face-to-face dialogue—argue for the importance of selecting some politicians because they are, in one or more senses, like the electorate.[36]

The result may be a more accurate transmission of demands. Beatrice Webb felt that working-class interests would not be neglected while working-class representatives were available to take care of them.[37] The result might equally well be that more trust is placed in working-class leaders by the working class; that is, whether or not interests are better represented, they may be perceived to be so.

Given that large proportions of electors seem to be "nonideologues," as the vast majority of voting studies suggest, and given relatively vague policy preferences, it can be argued that supporters who see in the party leadership some reflection of themselves would feel more closely linked with the party and, possibly indirectly, with the political system. In this way parties could manufacture and transmit system support through the

36. R. Rose, *Politics in England Today: An Interpretation* (London: Faber and Faber, 1974), p. 208. Earlier (p. 207) Rose noted: "The selective nature of political recruitment is undoubted. Its political significance is, however, controversial."

37. W. L. Guttsman, "Changes in British Labour Leadership," in Marvick, op. cit., pp. 131–32.

social-recruitment linkage: a case of a physical link creating a psychological one.

Several recent studies have emphasized the support-channeling (or creating) role of representative institutions in contrast to the traditional emphasis on demand transmission—interest articulation and aggregation—although most such studies have paid little attention to the importance of social recruitment.[38] A few have suggested that recruitment could be important; Kirchheimer, in his classic analysis of the "catch-all" phenomenon, implied that parties with a less sectional appeal could be dysfunctional for the maintenance of system support[39] as well as for the channeling of demands. Thus a more middle-class leadership could effectively reduce working-class attachment to parties. In the absence of alternatives, system support could decline. A third hypothesis therefore is:

3. The higher the level of middle-class leadership, the lower the level of working-class support for parties.

Implications of Leaders' Social Class: Some Evidence

Data collected and presented by J. C. Thomas will serve as a basis for consideration of the relationship between middle-class leadership, party

38. A good general statement is J. C. Wahlke, "Policy Demands and System Support: The Role of the Represented," *British Journal of Political Science* 1 (1970): 271–90. David Easton's particular approach has been influential; he has recently restated his ideas in "A Re-assessment of the Concept of Political Support," *British Journal of Political Science* 5 (1975): 435–48. A recent attempt to measure people's sense of being represented is E. N. Muller, "The Representation of Citizens by Political Authorities: Consequences for Regime Support," *American Political Science Review* 64 (1970): 1149–66, but Muller's response categories did not allow for the feeling of social representation suggested here.

39. Kirchheimer, op. cit., esp. pp. 198–200. The same general point is implied elsewhere: for example, L. S. Seligman, "Elite Recruitment and Political Development," *Journal of Politics* 26 (1964): 621; P. Medding, "A Framework for the Analysis of Power and Political Parties," *Political Studies* 28 (1970): 15. References to specific countries may be found in: J. Charlot, "Les élites politiques en France de la IIIe à la Ve Republique," *Archives européennes de sociologie* 14 (1973): 83 (France); H. Valen and D. Katz, *Political Parties in Norway* (Oslo: Universitetforslaget, 1967), pp. 321–23 (Norway); and Johnson, op. cit., p. 73 (Britain), although the last two are concerned with organizations (e.g., unions) as much as informal occupational groupings. Also W. L. Guttsman, "Elite Recruitment and Political Leadership in Britain and Germany since 1959: A Comparative Study of M.P.'s and Cabinets," in Crewe, op. cit., pp. 115–16, argues that the increasing size of the middle-class element in Socialist parties in both countries is due to the desire to attract the middle-class vote.

acceptance of parliamentarianism, and radicalism.[40] Thomas scored parties' issue-orientations on a wide range of subjects using a left-right dimension.[41] Two summary scores have been calculated here: (1) An average score for each party at each point (period) in time, giving a party's radicalism position relative to all other parties and (2) a score based on average deviation from national scores for the "status quo" position at each point in time, giving the party's position relative to the national situation. (This latter score Thomas defines as radicalism.)[42] Here the terms "socialist extremism" and "national radicalism" will be used. Both are considered to be aspects of radicalism. Data are available on only six of the countries previously discussed. Analysis is therefore confined to a smaller sample, but approximate positions of other parties can be indicated.

With respect to the next variable, parliamentarianism, two time periods are selected, prewar and postwar. It is argued that prewar Social Democratic parties generally were at best "ambiguous" in their parliamentary commitment, but that after 1943 all were explicitly and completely parliamentary parties. In most Social Democratic parties the transformation from "antisystem" to "system" party was made clear in the interwar years; refusals to join the Communist Third International, governmental cooperation with non-Socialist parties, programmatic commitments to "parliamentary democracy," all demonstrated this.[43] Some parties retained (or adopted) ambiguous, even hostile, positions, measured by one or more of the above indicators. Nevertheless, by the postwar period, the parliamentary system was accepted everywhere. Thus, hypothesis 1 will be tested on pre-1918 parties, and hypothesis 2 on post-1943 parties.

The term "middle class" is operationalized as the group of leaders from nonmanual occupations or rather those who were not previously manual workers or farmers.

Tables 3.3 and 3.4 show average levels of middle-class leadership and radicalism scores for parties in prewar and postwar periods. If

40. J. C. Thomas, "The Decline of Ideology in Western Political Parties: A Study of Policy Orientation," *Professional Papers in Contemporary Political Sociology*, vol. 1, series 06–012 (Beverly Hills, Calif: Sage Publications, 1974), appendix C.

41. Ibid., pp. 8–11 for a description of issues and coding rationale.

42. Ibid., p. 65.

43. This can be verified from any standard history: for example, H. W. Laidler, *History of Socialism* (London: Routledge and Kegan Paul, 1968).

TABLE 3.3. Average Middle-Class Proportion of Parliamentary Groups and Average Radicalism Scores for Social Democratic Party Before 1918: Selected Countries

Country	Average % Middle Class	Average National Radicalism Score*	Average Socialist Extremism Score
Italy	94	3.0 (1920s)	3.4
Austria	72	6.3 (1890s)	2.8
France	50	4.3 (1900, 1910s)	2.8
Sweden	48	5.0 (1890, 1910s)	2.3
Germany	25	5.4 (1870, 1890, 1910s)	3.1
Britain	12	4.3 (1900, 1910s)	2.5

SOURCE: See appendix.
*Decades for which scores were calculated in parentheses.

TABLE 3.4. Average Middle-Class Proportion of Parliamentary Group and Average Radicalism Scores for Social Democratic Party After 1943: Selected Countries

Country	Average % Middle Class	Average National Radicalism Score (1950s and 1960s)	Average Socialist Extremism Score (1950s and 1960s)
Austria	49	0.4	2.6
Sweden	66	0.1	2.5
Britain	66	0.6	2.9
Germany	77	0.7	2.2
Italy	88	1.6	3.0
France	96	1.0	2.3

SOURCE: See appendix.

hypothesis 1 is correct, table 3.3 should show most radicalism in the more middle class parties, and if hypothesis 2 is correct, radicalism should be more evident in the least middle class parties in table 3.4.

The evidence provides no strong support for hypothesis 1, that is, national radicalism does not correlate with class composition. A measure of support is provided by the socialist extremism scores; only the German cases are notably deviant, though the British and Swedish scores might be considered high. The potential effect of the two missing data cases on the pattern is not easy to judge. Norwegian and Swiss parties became more extreme in the second decade of this century after fairly moderate beginnings. Both parties sided with the "participationists" in the Communist International debates in 1900 and 1904, supporting the view that member parties could in some circumstances cooperate in government with non-Socialist parties. Yet in later years both parties revealed considerable support for the Communist Third International and adopted Marxist statements of principle. Overall, the evidence is inconclusive, offering little support and suggesting a number of deviant cases. Certainly the hypothesis offers neither a necessary nor a sufficient explanation of levels of radicalism in early Socialist parties.

Table 3.4 gives no support to hypothesis 2, as neither measure provides relationships in conformity with those expected. It is arguable that Thomas's data underestimates the socialist extremism of the French party, which has probably retained as much Marxist rhetoric as any in the sample.[44] Yet if that view was accepted, the data would even more clearly counter the expectations and support the earlier working hypothesis derived from Michels rather than hypothesis 2.

The absence of a clear pattern is reflected in the scattergrams, figures 3.2 and 3.3.

A tentative conclusion must therefore be that the social composition of leadership groups in Social Democratic parties bears little relationship to the goals and values of the party and its degree of opposition to the existing political, social, and economic systems. This would suggest that the trends observed earlier in the social origins of leaders have no clear implications for policy and the *interest* aspect of representation.

The second set of possible implications concerns the relationship between leadership class and the party's capacity to mobilize working-class support. Table 3.5 shows the proportion of working-class leaders, the party's share of the working-class vote, and the working-class element in the party's vote. A party with more working-class leaders would be expected, from hypothesis 3, to be more successful among the working class, and in addition the party's supporters might be expected to be more working class in composition.

Again, available data give the hypothesis no support; that is, the degree of success among working-class voters is not related to leadership

44. See F. L. Wilson, "The Persistence of Ideology in the French Democratic Left," in G. C. Byrne and K. S. Pederson, *Politics in Western European Democracies: Patterns and Problems* (London: John Wiley and Sons, 1971), pp. 217–32.

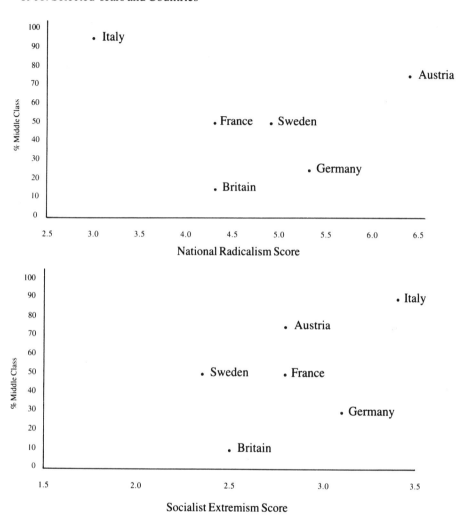

FIGURE 3.2.   Average Middle-Class Proportion of Parliamentary Groups and Average Radicalism/Extremism Scores for Social Democratic Parties Before 1918: Selected Years and Countries

SOURCE: See appendix.

67

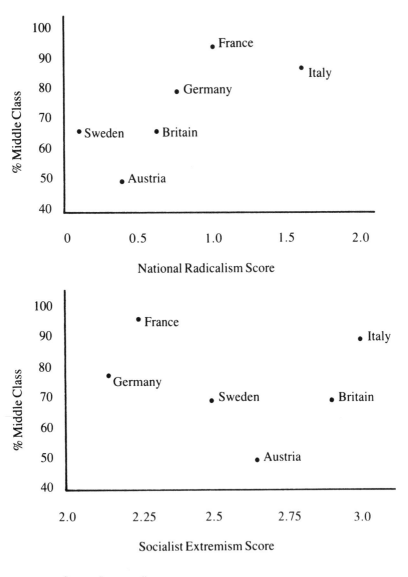

FIGURE 3.3.   Average Middle-Class Proportion of Parliamentary Group and Average Radicalism/Extremism Scores for Social Democratic Parties After 1943: Selected Years and Countries

SOURCE: See appendix.

TABLE 3.5. Class Composition of Parliamentary Group and Party Vote, Party Composition of Working-Class Vote: Selected Years and Countries

Country	Working-Class % of Social Democratic Parliamentary Group (Postwar)	Working-Class % of Social Democratic Vote (1960s)	Social Democratic % of Working-Class Vote (1960s)
France	1	38	17
Italy	12	76	20
Sweden	20	61	75
Germany	21	61	59
Norway	25	64	68
Britain	34	71	52
Switzerland	40	53	40
Austria	50	75	60

SOURCE: See appendix.

composition. Italian and French parties, with the least working-class support, are the least successful, but the two Scandinavian parties, which rank third and fourth in least working-class support, are the most successful; whereas the Swiss party, which ranks second highest in working-class support, is particularly unsuccessful. Overall variations with respect to the working-class component of the party vote are slight. French and Swiss parties are most notably heterogeneous in class terms but vary widely in their leadership composition, whereas leadership variations among the other parties are not related to even the slight variations in support characteristics. Leaders' social backgrounds would not seem to be a salient factor—conscious or unconscious—in voting choice and are probably, therefore, of little importance in the less manifest aspects of political support. Of course, voting habits change slowly, and a *continuing* decline in the working-class component of leadership may still have future consequences. Yet the Swedish party has remained successful and largely working class in electoral support despite a long-term decline in its proportion of working-class leaders; the Norwegian party, on the other hand, also successful and largely working class, has never had many working-class leaders. Thus, just as there are no obvious policy implications derived from the trend toward more middle-class leaderships, so there are no obvious implications for the party's efficacy as a support link between society and polity.

Conclusions

Several aspects of changing patterns in the recruitment of Social Democratic party leaders have been examined. Concentrating on social class, it has been observed that, in many cases, parties originally formed to represent the working-class interest were never particularly working class in leadership and have since become largely middle class with (even former) manual workers constituting no more than a significant minority. Most Social Democratic parties originally provided a link between working class and polity at least through their role as a recruitment agency for parliamentary and government office. Today this link is much weaker. It may be stronger intergenerationally. Upwardly mobile children of working-class parents may be attracted to Social Democratic parties in greater proportions than a middle-class status would predict. Even so, this would constitute only an indirect connection. The professionalization of politics may have weakened the link still further;

politicians may effectively be a separate class, having most in common with other politicians.

The changing composition of leadership has been examined, and the implications of some trends have been questioned. The further decline in the party's linkage role in the sense described above is one implication, but does this aspect of linkage itself matter? Some ideas from Michels and Parkin suggested that policy consequences would result from the different values and attitudes of leaders from different backgrounds. Two hypotheses were set out. Available data failed to support either hypothesis because extremism and radicalism are unrelated to class composition. *Interest* representation is unrelated to *social* representation. A third hypothesis, that social patterns of party support would generally reflect leadership composition, was outlined, based on work suggesting that socially representative leadership was important in maintaining electoral support. This was not validated: how electors feel when symbolically linked to party and government (as manifested by the vote) does not seem to depend upon shared social backgrounds. Thus social representation seems to be an unimportant factor in support linkage.[45]

It could be that voters' perceptions of leaders' class are determined less by objective criteria (leaders' past or present occupations or even their parents' occupations) than by the image those leaders deliberately seek to communicate. It would be interesting to ask Social Democratic voters: To what social class do you think the majority of your party's leaders belong? Answers could reveal remarkable differences between objective and perceived realities as well as more about the psychological dimensions of linkages. Alternatively, it could be that such voters favor middle-class leaders, that they feel they are more reliable or more expert. Rather than being ideological or sociological in nature, the linkage could be paternalistic, or simply, as indicated previously, analogous to the client-professional relationship existing in other areas of society.[46]

A word of caution is in order concerning the findings that underlie

45. For other factors, see Easton, op. cit., passim.
46. Personal analysis of the Butler-Stokes Survey Data on British Elections in the 1960s suggests less than 10 percent of Labour voters saw the Labour party leader, Wilson, in class-related terms. Most respondents emphasized more personal qualities, cf. D. Butler and D. Stokes, *Political Change in Britain* (London: Macmillan, 1969), chap. 17. In the Valen and Katz study (Valen and Katz, op. cit., p. 322) 24 percent of Norwegian voters felt they would consider withdrawing support if their occupational group was not represented on the party list.

these conclusions and speculations. Operationalization of all variables could be altered and consequently produce different findings. For instance, a "reputational" method of leadership definition might be used, rather than the "institutional" one used here. Those individuals perceived by the electorate to be leaders may not be those who are most important in decision making. These problems can be resolved only through further research. However, the comparative variations in the physical link between the working class and the parliamentary elite shown here through Social Democratic parties' recruitment patterns do strongly suggest that the implications of the declining strength of this link are far from obvious and are not necessarily in the direction usually assumed.

Appendix: Sources of Data in Tables and Figures

Table 3.1 and Figure 3.1

Austria (Social Democrats) 1897–1911: F. Freund, *Das Österreichische Abgeordnerenhaus 1907–13, XI Legislaturperiode* (Vienna and Leipzing: Weiner Verlag, 1911), pp. 22–23; 1918–66: O. Knauer, *Das Osterreichische Parlament 1846–66* (Vienna: Berglund Verlag, 1969).

France (Socialist Party) 1910: R. Michels, *Political Parties* (New York: Dover, 1959), p. 257n; 1936: J. Charlot, "Les élites politiques en France de la IIIe à la Ve Republique," *Archives européennes de sociologie* 14 (1973): 83; 1951, 1958, 1973: from the Ministry of the Interior's official publications on the elections of those years; 1968: R. Cayrol et al., *Le Deputé francais* (Paris: Armand Colin, 1973), p. 40.

Germany (Social Democrats) 1903, 1912, 1919, 1930: R. Hunt, *German Social Democracy* (New Haven: Yale University, Press, 1963), p. 92; 1961, 1969: W. L. Guttsman, "Elite Recruitment and Political Leadership in Britain and Germany since 1959: A Comparative Study of M. P.'s and Cabinets," in I. Crewe, ed., *British Political Sociology Yearbook: Elites in Western Democracy* (London: Croom Helm, 1974), 1: 108.

Italy (Socialist Party) 1903: R. Michels, *Il Proletariato é la Bourgesia nel Movimento Socialista Italiano* (Turin: Fratelli Boccia Editori, 1908), p. 98; 1948, 1953, 1958: S. Samogya, "Constituenti é Deputati 1946–58 Analisi Statistica" in G. Sartori et al., *Il Parlimento Italiano 1946–53* (Naples: Edizione Scientifiche Italiano, 1963), pp. 120–21.

Norway (Labour Party) 1906–73: Data kindly provided by K. A. Eliassen, University of Aarhus.

Sweden (Social Democrats) 1912, 1930, 1933, 1949, 1961: Tables kindly provided by Professor Per-Erik Back, University of Umeå, derived

73

from L. Sköld and A. Halvarson, "Den svenska viksdagens sociala sammansättning under hundra år," *Samhalle och riksdag I* (Uppsala: publisher unidentified, 1966), pp. 403–45.

Britain (Labour Party) 1906–74: R. Rose, *The Problem of Party Government* (London: Macmillan, 1974), p. 51.

Switzerland (Social Democrats) 1911, 1914, 1917, 1919: E. Gruner et al., *L'assemblé fédérale Suisse 1848–1920* (Berne: Éditions Franke, 1966), table 16; F. Masnata, *Le parti socialiste et la tradition démocratique en Suisse* (Paris: Armand Colin, 1963), p. 69.

Party names as listed in T. T. Mackie and R. Rose, *The International Almanac of Electoral Behaviour* (London: Macmillan, 1974).

Tables 3.2, 3.3, and 3.4, Figures 3.2 and 3.3
Leadership data as table 3.1. Policy data calculated from information found in J. C. Thomas, "The Decline of Ideology in Western Political Parties: A Study of Policy Orientation," *Professional Papers in Contemporary Political Sociology*, vol. 1, series 06–012 (Beverly Hills, Calif.: Sage Publications, 1974), appendix C.

Table 3.5
Leadership data as table 3.1. Working-Class Vote: German, Italian, Swedish, and British data derived from tables in respective chapters of R. Rose, ed., *Electoral Behavior: A Comparative Handbook* (New Haven: Yale University, Press, 1974), pp. 147, 190, 401, 502. Swiss percentage calculated from data in H. J. Kerr, Jr., "Social Cleavage and Partisan Conflict in Switzerland," mimeographed. French percentages from IFOP survey 1962 and Austrian percentages from 1969 survey, both by courtesy of the Social Statistics Laboratory, University of Strathclyde.

Social Democratic Vote: Swedish data as above. Other figures from R. Rose and D. W. Urwin, "Social Cohesion, Political Parties and Strains in Regimes," *Comparative Political Studies* 2 (1969): appendix.

4.

Linkage and Democratic Orientation of Party Elites in South Korea

YOUNG WHAN KIHL

Political parties in many developing countries are not serving as effective linkage mechanisms between the citizens and the government in power.[1] One reason for this situation is the ruling elite's use of party organization as an instrument for political mobilization and control of the citizens rather than as a forum of political participation and education. As a consequence, the rule of government in power is perpetuated and the voice of political opposition is suppressed.[2]

In many developing countries politics is a fierce and merciless competition between an elite that enjoys political authority and a counter elite that aspires to capture political power. Political-party competition, under these circumstances, becomes a serious matter of life and death

1. The meaning of "effective" linkage will become obvious as the study proceeds; see also footnote 14. Since this manuscript was completed, South Korea has gone through a radical political change as a result of the assassination of President Park Chung Hee on 26 October 1979. Some of the historical references are thus slightly outdated, but the basic theme and conclusion of the study remain intact.

2. The role of political parties in developing areas has not been given adequate coverage in political-science literature. Among the works that do investigate political parties in developing areas are: James S. Coleman and Carl G. Rosberg, Jr., eds., *Political Parties and National Integration in Tropical Africa* (Berkeley: University of California Press, 1964); Samuel P. Huntington, *Political Order in Changing Societies* (New Haven: Yale University Press, 1969); and Joseph LaPalombara and Myron Weiner, eds., *Political Parties and Political Development* (Princeton: Princeton University Press, 1966).

in which the winner takes all and the loser ends up with nothing. This means that (1) the linkage role of a political party in the developing world must be differentiated from that of a party in the developed world and suggests that (2) there may exist a significant difference between the cadres of the ruling party and those of the opposition party in their motivational basis for political participation.[3]

The purpose of this study is to ascertain the degree of difference between the elites of a ruling party and those of an opposition party in a developing country by examining the values and attitudes of each and to assess the meaning of such differences for the role of political parties.[4] The country selected for study is South Korea in the early 1970s and the data base is a survey of 354 party elites, which this author undertook in the summer months of 1972.[5] To achieve the objective, this study will delineate the linkage role of political parties in the political system, examine its applicability to the political process in developing nations, discuss briefly the nature of the Korean political system, formulate two hypotheses and test them in terms of empirical data, and conclude with a brief discussion and interpretation of the findings.

Linkage Role of Political Parties: Concept and Theory

The role of political parties in a political system, whether in developed or in developing countries, may be conceived as that of providing "a

3. For pleas urging a systematic comparative study of political parties and party organizations see William J. Crotty, "Political Parties Research," in Michael Haas and Henry Kariel, eds., *Approaches to the Study of Political Science* (Scranton, Pa.: Chandler, 1970), pp. 267–322; William E. Wright, ed., *A Comparative Study of Party Organization* (Columbus, Ohio: Charles E. Merrill, 1971). Also, for a similar plea as applied to Korea see Young Whan Kihl, "Research on Party Politics in Korea: An Analytical Scheme," *The Korean Political Science Review* (June 1972), pp. 279–96.

4. Research on party elites has been pioneered by Eldersveld in his study of party leaders in Detroit, Mich. See Samuel J. Eldersveld, *Political Parties: A Behavioral Analysis* (Chicago: Rand McNally, 1964). The ruling-party–opposition-party dichotomy, as conceptualized in the present study, may be objected to on the ground, as one distinguished student recently argued, that "bipolar social conflicts are rare, as opposed to multiple or segmented conflicts" (Robert Dahl, *Regimes and Oppositions* [New Haven: Yale University Press, 1973]). On the other hand, one cannot overlook the existence of polarized partisan conflict in certain areas of the world including South Korea.

5. Research site and design for the 1972 survey is further elaborated in an earlier study, Young Whan Kihl, "Leadership and Opposition Role Perception Among Party Elites in Korea," *Korea Journal* 13, No. 9 (September 1973): 3–22; also in *Asia Forum* 5, no. 3 (July–September 1973): 17–42.

comprehensive linkage" between the public and government decision makers.[6] The political party, according to prevailing theory, is a linkage mechanism, or an intermediary organization, that connects the *input* of citizen interest and demands and the policy *output* of government programs in the political system. By way of articulating and aggregating interests, political parties perform the input task of influencing public officials who are expected to reflect the public demand upon the process of policymaking and implementation.[7] Politics, according to systems-theory perspective, may be conceived as a system of communication and decision making whereby a message (influence in this case) is transmitted from the point of origin (i.e., input) to that of destination (i.e., output) in order to assure for the society collective decision making that is authoritative and binding.[8] The existence of intermediary structures, such as political parties, bureaucracies, and interest groups, will then facilitate the process of communication and the flow of influence in society by serving as "linkage" or "brokerage" agencies between citizens and public officials.

The concept of "linkage" or "political linkage" has become widely accepted in political-science literature in recent years. No standard definition of political linkage exists as yet, but the concept is rich and promises to be a useful tool for political analysis and especially for an understanding of the phenomenon of political parties and party activities. James Rosenau, who initiated the term "linkage politics," defines linkage as "any recurrent sequence of behavior that originates in one system and is reacted to in another."[9] The study of linkage politics is thus, in part, a reaction against the rigid disciplinary separation of domestic and international politics in political science.[10] Although the term "linkage" as used in this study also follows this new tradition, it is used in a some-

6. The term "comprehensive linkage" is borrowed from Crotty, op. cit., p. 294.

7. This view of the linkage role of the political party is reflected in the systems-functional theory of political development. See, for instance, Gabriel Almond and G. Bingham Powell, Jr., *Comparative Politics: A Development Approach* (Boston: Little, Brown, 1965).

8. This is a grossly simplified description of the communications model of politics. On systems theory and cybernetic conception of politics in general see David Easton, *A Systems Analysis of Political Life* (New York: John Wiley, 1965), and Karl Deutsch, *The Nerves of Government: Models of Political Communication and Control* (New York: The Free Press, 1963).

9. James Rosenau, ed., *Linkage Politics* (New York: The Free Press, 1969), p. 44.

10. Jonathan Wilkenfeld, ed., *Conflict Behavior and Linkage Politics* (New York: David McKay, 1973), p. 1.

what more general manner to describe the phenomenon of *relationship* between a set of objects in politics, whether domestic or international. More specifically, the term "linkage" will be used interchangeably with such terms as "connecting," "converting," "transmitting," and so on, applying it to the situation of domestic politics where the citizens and public officials are closely related through the instrument of political parties.

The linkage role of political parties, thus conceived, reflects a basically democratic value orientation toward parties as institutions in a society. The political party ideally is an approximation of a democratic institution, in the sense that it is a voluntary association of activists whose purpose is to capture political power through electoral means and to place its supporters in public offices. As a voluntary organization, the political party follows the principle of internal democracy: the membership is open to the public, and the leadership of the party is held accountable to the wishes of the rank-and-file membership. In actuality, however, a political party has come to acquire the dynamics of what is often referred to as "an iron law of oligarchy," which compels the party leadership to be oligarchic in the face of the reality of fierce intraparty as well as interparty competition vis-à-vis other parties.

The political party may also be conceived in ideal terms as an agency that provides an effective linkage between the government it aspires to control and the public it professes to represent. Party activists and followers, then, serve as "linkmen" between the electorate whose votes the party needs and the public officials whose stand the party hopes to influence. As linkmen, party elites would ideally be aware of the role of the party as a linkage agency and as a democratic institution and, in particular, of democratic ideals and a commitment to the values of democracy. The extent and degree of value commitment of party elites to democratic ideals therefore provide indices for the effectiveness of the party as a linkage agency.

However, "democracy" is an elusive concept, far from being uniformly applied and agreed upon. In this study democracy is defined as the principle of allowing the public an active role in the process of decision making for a society. Democracy, thus conceived, requires faith in the common man, as against the elite; faith in his rationality and in his capacity for self-rule.[11] The fact that the mass public in systems

11. For a comprehensive—now almost classic—treatise on the subject of democratic political theory see Giovanni Sartori, *Democratic Theory* (New York: Praeger, 1965).

loosely termed "democratic" does not always behave rationally and responsibly—which "fact," incidentally, reflects the normative judgment of the observer—does not eliminate faith in the possibility of that rationality and capacity for self-government as requirements of democracy in principle. Where political leaders do not possess that faith, the business of government may turn into a cynical and power-grabbing exercise among competing elites.

Related to the ideal of public self-rule is the additional requirement that elites be committed to the ideals of modernization, for a commitment to modernization facilitates the establishment of the socioeconomic base upon which participatory politics may be securely founded. A preference for the devolution and decentralization of power is also essential if the commitment to democratic ideals is to be effective, particularly given the tendency toward authoritarianism and the concentration of power in the central governments of many nations today. In short, the pursuit of democratic ideals includes a commitment to the principles of egalitarianism, modernization, and decentralization of power, as against those of elitism, traditionalism, and centralization of power. Each of these components of democratic ideals will be subjected to an empirical test later in this study.

Party Institutions and Developing Polities

In developing nations the role of the party as a linkage mechanism is made more difficult by the low overall level of political institutionalization and the imbalance in the relative potency and weight of influence of various agencies in the political system, with those involved in the process of input (e.g., demand and support) being considerably weaker than those involved in the process of output (e.g., policies and decisions).[12] The trends in many developing countries include fierce interelite conflict on values, increasing dominance by the executive branch, and the concentration of power in the hands of the central government.[13] These

12. Institutionalization, as Huntington defines it, may be conceived as "the process by which organizations and procedures acquire value and stability" and can be measured in terms of "adaptability, complexity, autonomy, and coherence" (Huntington, op. cit., p. 12).

13. These factors, of course, are also present in many developed countries. But the cumulative impact of these governmental trends, a result of the relative recency of independence, seems much greater in many of these developing countries.

facts, together with the "high-risk" nature of politics to be elaborated below, lead to a situation in which political parties fail to acquire institutional autonomy vis-à-vis government agencies. This lack of autonomy, coherence, and stability, in turn, prevents political parties from serving as effective linkage agencies between the public and the government decision makers.[14]

The failure of party institutionalization may be due primarily to the high-risk nature of politics that permeates the process of party competition in many developing countries. Politics in such a high-risk system may best be described as a zero-sum game in which the players are engaged in a deadly serious conflict and in which the difference between the winner and the loser is immense. Politics is often under-taken in a warlike, conflictual atmosphere in many of these countries.[15] An election resembles a contest on the battlefield where the fire of criticism and slander is exchanged between the contending parties, and the ballot box is jealously guarded against the possible danger of being rigged or even destroyed.[16] The political milieu of party activities in these countries is highly volatile, unpredictable, and full of risk.

The linkage role of political parties in developing countries differs, then, not only from that of parties in advanced and stable democracies but also in the relative importance of the ruling party and the opposition parties.[17] In the more established and developed systems, where politics is relatively less risky, the flow of message (i.e., influence) tends to travel from the input side to the output side of the political system in part through the conversion and linkage mechanism provided by all political parties, both in and out of power. In the less stable and developing countries, where politics is a high-risk business, the flow of influence rarely originates from the input side of the political system. Instead, the top

14. The choice of the word "effective" is deliberate. A distinction between "formal" and "effective" is useful in discussing various aspects of political structures and functions. For a convincing example of conceptualization along a similar line see Lester G. Seligman, "Political Parties and the Recruitment of Political Leadership," in Lewis J. Edinger, ed., *Political Leadership in Industrialized Societies: Studies in Comparative Analysis* (New York: John Wiley, 1967), pp. 294–315.

15. Ibid., p. 295.

16. An example of acute electoral contest and irregularity, which resulted in a student-led revolution and an overthrow of the regime, is the case of South Korea in April 1960.

17. A typical example in this regard is Norman R. Luttbeg, ed., *Public Opinion and Public Policy: Models of Political Linkage* (Homewood, Ill.: Dorsey Press, 1968), pp. 1–9.

leadership dispenses its authority unilaterally, allocating resources and determining policy, and the public is expected, or even coerced, to comply.[18] In high-risk politics, authority tends to flow from the leaders down to the citizens, and lines of influence traveling up from the citizens to the top leaders are difficult to find.[19]

The function of the ruling political party in such a system is to assist the process of resource allocation by the governing elite. The party is subservient to the government in power. The opposition parties are ineffective as linkage organizations because they are doubly handicapped: they not only are kept under close control by the ruling elite but also have not proven their efficacy to the public by capturing political power successfully in an electoral contest. In the high-risk system the ruling elite rarely—if ever—relinquishes political power voluntarily and the aspiring elites conspire to oust the incumbent by extraconstitutional methods. Under the circumstances, parties as political organizations are used by the ruling elites as instruments for the "ruler's imperative," which, following the Machiavellian dictum, is to capture political power by using whatever means are made available and, once in power, to maintain it and to stay in power.[20]

The high-risk nature of the political system may have a bearing also upon the composition of party elites in these countries. The recruitment basis of party activists and followers may be different between the ruling and the opposition parties.[21] The ruling party, as it continues to enjoy and monopolize political power, is likely to attract activists and

18. For a new conceptualization of politics as the process of allocating resources as values see David E. Apter, *Choice and the Politics of Allocation* (New Haven: Yale University Press, 1971), and Warren F. Ilchman and Norman Thomas Uphoff, *The Political Economy of Change* (Berkeley: University of California Press, 1969). Also see Young W. Kihl, "Urban Political Competition and the Allocation of National Resources: The Case of Korea," *Asian Survey* 13, no. 4 (April 1973): 366–79.

19. On the asymmetrical nature of authority structure in the political system see Harry Eckstein, "Authority Patterns: A Structural Basis for Political Inquiry," *American Political Science Review* 62, no. 4 (December 1973): 1142–61.

20. On the ruler's imperative see W. Howard Wriggins, *The Ruler's Imperative* (New York: Columbia University Press, 1969).

21. The extent of how recruitment policy varies from party to party is an empirical question that needs to be investigated. For an interesting approach to the study of party system based on a theoretical postulate of motivational analysis of party workers see James Payne, *Patterns of Conflict in Colombia* (New Haven: Yale University Press, 1968). Also, in this regard see Young W. Kihl and Chong Lim Kim, *Research on the Korean Political Party System: Some Conceptual and Methodological Considerations*, The Laboratory for Political Research, Report no. 39 (Iowa City: University of Iowa, 1971).

81

followers who are more supportive of government policies and who tend to reinforce the position of the executive leadership (i.e., incumbent power holder). The party elites of the ruling party may also be more elitist, submissive, and supportive of a centralized arrangement of power. The opposition party, on the other hand, is likely to attract those activists who are more criticial of government policies and leadership. It is possible that the opposition party elites are more egalitarian, self-assertive, and supportive of a decentralized arrangement of power. In terms of party characteristics, the ruling party is likely to be a party of organization and regimentation, a well-financed and tightly disciplined body, whereas the opposition party is likely to be an organization of factional grouping and strife, a less disciplined and loosely structured group of party followers. These observations, hypothetical postulates derived from a high-risk model of politics, require cross-validation in terms of empirical data and historical examples. For this discussion, the South Korean party system will be examined.[22]

The South Korean Party System (1945–79): An Overview

The development of political parties and a party system in South Korea closely approximates the logic of high-risk politics. The party system in South Korea may be characterized as semicompetitive, faction-ridden, authoritarian, and tending toward one-party domination.[23] Nominally, two major political parties are allowed to contest for power in electing members of the National Assembly. In substance, however, no opposition party has ever succeeded in ousting the party in power by electoral means since the Republic was proclaimed in 1948. Both the ruling and opposition parties in Korea tend to follow the line of personal leadership rather than to formulate a set of programs and policies for the party. The

22. For standard works on politics in Korea written in English see Gregory Henderson, *Korea: The Politics of the Vortex* (Cambridge: Harvard University Press, 1968); David Cole and Princeton Lyman, *Korean Development: The Interplay of Politics and Economics* (Cambridge: Harvard University Press, 1971); Hahn-been Lee, *Korea: Time, Change and the Administration* (Honolulu: East-West Center Press, 1968); and Edward Wright, ed., *Korean Politics in Transition* (Seattle: University of Washington Press, 1975).
23. The literature on the development of the Korean party system in English is notably sparse. For a useful survey see Han Ki-shik, "Development of Parties and Politics in Korea," *Korea Journal* 14, no. 9 (September 1974): 37–50, and 14, no. 10 (October 1974): 41–57. Also see C. I. Eugene Kim and Young Whan Kihl, eds., *Party Politics and Elections in Korea* (Silver Spring, Md.: Research Institute on Korean Affairs, 1976).

parties are often used as personal instruments of the leadership and they have also been paralyzed by intraparty factional strife in the leadership. Korean parties are generally nonideological cadre parties, rather than ideological, mass-membership parties.[24]

The ruling party in the Third Republic, the Democratic Republican party (DRP), was founded in February 1963 as an instrument to allow the leaders of the military government, following the coup of 17 May 1961, to continue in power.[25] General Park Chung Hee, then chairman of the Supreme Council for National Reconstruction, assumed the position of party leader of the newly formed DRP. He ran as a civilian candidate of the DRP in the presidential election in October 1963 against Yun Po-son of the Civil Rule party.[26] As the Third Republic was formally installed in 1963, the DRP emerged as the ruling party, a role it has maintained to the present. The effectiveness of the party as an instrument for policymaking has never been fully developed, however, owing to factional strife within the leadership and the skeptical view of the usefulness of parties that President Park, as party leader, had consistently held.

Initially, the DRP was founded as a "modern" party with an elaborate secretariat organization and policymaking bodies. The leaders of the military government in 1961 entertained the view that one of the ills of the First and Second Republics of Korea (1948–60; 1960–61) was the tendency toward party factionalism and the absence of an inspiring and modernizing ideology to guide the action and programs of the parties. They condemned the practice of party politics in the past as "old politics," being anxious to prove that they stood for "new" and "modern" politics. A so-called eight-point master plan, adopted on 18 January 1963 as a basis of forming the party, included these provisions: The DRP would be an open and mass party, with ideological cohesion,

24. For the distinction of the cadre and mass membership parties see Frank J. Sorauf, *Political Parties in the American System* (Boston: Little, Brown, 1964), p. 161.

25. The description of the DRP and the NDP in the following few pages is based on the author's previous work, "Leadership and Opposition Role Perception Among Party Elites in Korea," op. cit., pp. 8–9. For the circumstances leading to the founding of the DRP see Kwan-Bong Kim, *The Korea-Japan Treaty Crisis and the Instability of the Korean Political System* (New York: Praeger, 1971); and Se-Jin Kim, *The Politics of Military Revolution in Korea* (Chapel Hill: University of North Carolina Press, 1971).

26. The 1963 election is analyzed in C. I. Eugene Kim, "The Significance of the 1963 Korean Elections," *Asian Survey* 4, no. 3 (March 1964): 765–73, and John Kie-Chiang Oh, *Korea: Democracy on Trial* (Ithaca: Cornell University Press, 1968).

party discipline, centrally directed hierachical leadership, a major role in formulating and implementing policies and so on.[27] The blueprint of the DRP, then, reflects the concern of the founders to develop a "modern party" based on organizational direction and professional skill and dedication, as opposed to an "old party," which depended on factional bosses and money.[28]

The initial zeal and commitment of the workers of the DRP were not sustained for long, however, as the party was affected by ensuing strife over control of the party hegemony. In 1965 Kim Jong-pil, one of the original founders of the DRP, resigned under pressure from the post of secretary-general. Kim believed in strengthening the central control and power of the secretariat. He had to step down in favor of a moderate wing of the party, which advocated the loose structure of a decentralized party and a weaker party secretariat. The DRP has never succeeded in restoring the power initially envisioned by the founding fathers.

The opposition New Democratic party (NDP) was founded officially in 1967, with the merger of the former Sinhan (New Korea) party and the Minjung (Popular) party. The merger was designed to form a united opposition front against the ruling DRP in the presidential and parliamentary elections of 1967.[29] The party, however, was successful neither in unseating the incumbent president in 1967 nor in strengthening its control with more parliamentary seats.[30] In the 1971 elections the NDP fared better. It improved its position by increasing the margin of presidential votes received by its candidate and by winning 89 out of 204 seats in the National Assembly. By the end of 1972, however, the party, almost paralyzed by constant factional strife in the leadership, virtually split into two wings.[31] The annual party convention in 1972 was twice postponed. When it finally convened in the fall, the delegates split in two groups and ended by reinstating the former party chief, Yu Chin-san.

27. DRP Secretariat, *Minjugonghwadang Sa Nyon Sa* [Four-Year History of the DRP] (Seoul, 1967), p. 38, as quoted in Kwan-Bong Kim, op. cit., p. 182.

28. The founders of the DRP blamed factionalism as the root cause for the failure of the old parties in the First and Second republics.

29. Y. C. Han, "Political Parties and Political Development in South Korea," *Pacific Affairs* 43 (1969): 446–64.

30. C. I. Eugene Kim, "Patterns in the 1967 Korean Elections," *Pacific Affairs*, 42 (1968): 61.

31. The constant party splitting and merging is not an unusual aspect of South Korean party politics.

The outgoing party chief, Kim Hong-il, sued the former for allegedly mishandling party funds while he had been in office. In a desperate but unsuccessful attempt to save the party, Yu once again resigned from the post in February 1973, only to come back as party head a few months later. During the National Assembly election in February 1973 the opposition was divided into the NDP and the Democratic Unification Party, an offshoot of the minority wing of the NDP, but the latter failed to capture enough seats to become a viable political force in the Parliament.

The so-called Kim Dae-jung affair of 1973 gave the opposition force an opportunity to regroup and to improve its status by mobilizing public sympathy for Kim and by exploiting the public criticism of the government in mishandling the incident. Kim Dae-jung, the standard-bearer of the NDP ticket in the 1971 presidential election, running against incumbent President Park of the DRP, received 45 percent of the popular vote. While on a self-imposed exile abroad, Kim Dae-jung was actively engaged in the anti-Park movement and criticized the Seoul government as "dictatorial" and as denying the civil rights of individuals who opposed policies of the regime. On 8 August 1973, during one of his stopovers from the U.S., Kim was abducted from his Tokyo hotel room and returned to his house in Seoul. This kidnapping, allegedly by a South Korean agent of the CIA, was a diplomatic embarrassment; it was met by indignation at home and abroad and resulted in a series of antigovernment demonstrations organized by university students, Christian clergymen, and writers and newspaper reporters. The NDP, led by the youthful Kim Young-sam, attempted to capitalize on the situation by channeling the anti-Park forces into a mass-based movement.

In 1974 the Park government resorted to the strategy of repression, issuing emergency decrees and arresting those involved in the antigovernment demonstrations. Following the national referendum in March 1975, the government released many of those arrested but then returned to a hardline policy as the antigovernment demonstrations continued. The war in Vietnam created an atmosphere of national crisis in South Korea, temporarily putting an end to anti-Park activities. Intraparty factional strife resulting in the election of Yi Chul-seung as new party leader also weakened the role of the NDP as opposition party. With the return of Kim Young-sam as party leader in 1979, however, the antigovernment activities of the opposition party were resumed. The assassination of

85

President Park on 26 October 1979 gave the NDP a new opportunity to strengthen the basis of its popular support and thus to increase the possibility of its emerging as a government party in the future.[32]

In the history of the South Korean Republic since 1948 the fact remains that no political party has ever succeeded in replacing the party in power by peaceful means. Neither the ruling party of the First Republic (1948–60), the Liberal party of Syngman Rhee, nor that of the Second Republic (1960–61), the Democratic party of Chang Myon, relinquished power voluntarily as a result of electoral contest. In both cases extralegal means—the student uprising in 1960 and the military coup in 1961— overthrew the political order and led to the transition of power. The authoritarian tendency of President Park Chung Hee in the Third Republic was no exception. For this reason the party system in South Korea, for all practical purposes, has been a one-party-dominant system.[33]

A survey of the development of political parties in Korea indicates that political parties and the party system are far from being fully institutionalized and that party politics is closely associated with the characteristics of the high-risk system that provide the environment and setting for the activities of party politicians and activists. In such an environment the South Korean political parties are neither organizing the political participation of the citizens nor providing a meaningful linkage between the public and the government. Instead, the parties are often bypassed by the government on occasions of important decision making and are instead exploited by the ruling elite as an instrument for perpetuating its own dictatorial rule. In this connection one student makes the apt remark that "if the role of the legislature is handmaiden of the government, the role of the parties is a humble servant of the government administration."[34] Unless the master-servant relationship is reversed, by making representative institutions of the parties and the legislature co-equal with the executive branch of government, the prospect for the development of a democratic party system in Korea is dim indeed.

Also relevant to the role of parties in South Korea is the fact that the nation has been undergoing a period of rapid socioeconomic change,

---

32. The assassination ended eighteen years of authoritarian rule by Park Chung Hee.

33. The Korean Workers party of Kim Il Song of North Korea also exhibits an authoritarian and one-party-dominant tendency.

34. Han Ki-shik, op. cit., 14, no. 10: 54.

which affects the lives of many people. The change had been deliberately initiated by the government of President Park Chung Hee. In the form of a series of Five-Year Economic Development Plans the Park government pursured, with considerable success, a policy of modernization and socioeconomic development of the country. During the decade of the 1960s, for instance, South Korea achieved an annual rate of economic growth of almost 10 percent. It also centralized power and strengthened the executive branch by relying upon the efficiency and competence of the technocratic elite of the Economic Planning Board. In the process the Park government not only weakened the position of the representative institution, the National Assembly, but also did away with the constitutional provision for local autonomy and elections.[35]

In light of (1) the performance record of the Park regime in South Korea and (2) the existence of interparty variation in the pattern of value orientation of party elites, the following hypotheses regarding the value orientations of party elites in a high-risk system may be suggested:

Hypothesis 1.   In a high-risk political system, where authority is centralized and socioeconomic change is rapid, party elites tend to be more supportive of the values of modernization, elitism, and centralism than of the values of traditionalism, egalitarianism, and decentralization.

Hypothesis 2.   Party elites of the ruling party, as compared with those of the opposition party, are likely to be more supportive of modernization, more elitist and less egalitarian in their orientation, and more center- and less periphery-oriented in politics.

These hypotheses, when subjected to validation by attitudinal data of party elites, may provide further evidence and clues to the role of political parties as effective linkage agencies in the political system of South Korea.

The empirical data for the testing of these hypotheses are derived from a 1972 survey of party elites in Korea. The sample of party elites is not randomly selected, but members of the sample are fairly evenly distributed between the two parties and across various geographic

35. The so-called Revitalizing Reform of October 1972, following the coup in office, brought about the constitutional amendment that enhanced the position of President Park vis-à-vis the National Assembly and political parties. The subsequent demonstration and turmoils in South Korea, led by Christian clergymen, students, and the press, were a belated response to the condition created by Park in 1972 to strengthen his power.

TABLE 4.1.   Distribution of Party-Elite Sample by Party Status

	DRP	NDP	Total
Headquarters personnel (party cadres)	30	27	57
District party chairmen and their deputies	43	60	103
Local ward chiefs (*dong-ch'ek* and *kwalli-chang*)	98	87	185
Total	171	174	345

regions and levels of party hierarchy. Table 4.1 shows the distribution of the sample.[36]

The party elites in this study include three types of personnel related to party activities: party cadres of the central headquarters of political parties, party chairmen and their deputies in the electoral districts, and local party representatives or ward chiefs at the grass-roots level throughout South Korea. The ward chief of the ruling DRP is called *kwalli-chang*, whereas the opposition DRP calls its representative *dong-chek*. *Kwalli-chang*, in English, means "the person in charge of management" or simply "custodian," whereas dong-chek literally means "the person responsible for the dwelling unit" or "agent." Thus, different conceptions and philosophies of party cadres seem to be reflected even in the words chosen to designate the ward chiefs of the ruling DRP and the opposition NDP.

Party organization is set up on a constituency basis in South Korea. At the time of the 1972 survey the country was divided into 142 electoral districts for purposes of electing members of the National Assembly and of conducting the presidential election.[37] Each district, electing one representative to the National Assembly, had a district party chairman and several deputy district chairmen. When the party in the district succeeded in electing its candidate to the National Assembly, the assem-

36. Also see Kihl, "Leadership and Opposition Role Perception Among Party Elites in Korea," op. cit., p. 8.
37. Later, the election law was amended to abolish the presidential election and to increase the size of the National Assembly. In 1973 the electoral districts were reduced from 142 to 71, changing from a single-member small district to a plural-member medium-sized district, whereby each district now elected two members to the National Assembly. Together with the 71 appointed members of the National Assembly, under the revised constitution in 1972, the total of the National Assembly seats then stood at 213.

blyman became an ex-officio chairman of the party in the district. In that case the deputy chairman usually was the influential official of the party who managed the business of the party in the district and acted as a liaison between the constituency and the party in the central head-quarters. In the sample here no active National Assemblymen (i.e., incumbent members) were included.[38]

The central headquarters of both political parties are located in the capital city of Seoul. In addition to the formal structure of party organization, there were in 1972 many private offices near the National Assembly building or in representatives' homes or business concerns, which acted as centers for communication and contact between constituencies and National Assemblymen, as well as eleven branch party offices, which acted as intermediaries between the central party headquarters and the local district parties. These intermediary-level party offices varied in their efficiency and level of activities. However, they did not seem to exert great influence upon the process of party decision making. These inter-mediary offices of provincial party headquarters were further reduced in importance, at least in the case of the ruling DRP, when they were designated as simply "liaison offices" in 1973.

Value Orientation of Party Elites

It seems reasonable to assume that the action and behavior of party elites in South Korea are influenced largely by the specific pattern of their attitudinal makeup and psychological orientation toward a set of values in society. To discover their value-orientation pattern is therefore one of the basic tasks of behavioral research on party elites and leader-ship in Korea and is likely to yield important evidence regarding the structure of power and influence relationships in South Korean society.[39] With such a possibility of further inference in mind, the survey was

38. Research on the survey of the national assemblymen has been pioneered by Chong Lim Kim of the University of Iowa. See, for instance, Chong Lim Kim and Byung-kyu Woo, "Political Representation in the Korean National Assembly," *Midwest Journal of Political Science* 16, no. 4 (November 1972): 626–51. In this regard also see certain numbers of the Occasional Paper Series, Comparative Legislative Research Center, University of Iowa.

39. For a discussion of the structure of power and influence in Korea, and especially the role of local elites in the communities, see Young Whan Kihl, *Local Elites, Power Structure and the Legislative Process in Korea*, Comparative Legislative Research Center, Occasional Paper Series no. 8 (Iowa City: University of Iowa, 1975).

designed to include a number of questionnaire items to elicit the value orientation of party elites on such items as modernization, social change, the role of citizens in politics, local self-rule and so on.[40] The results of the survey are shown in tables 4.2, 4.3, and 4.4. Surprisingly, and contrary to the expectation of hypothesis 2, there is generally little variance between the ruling DRP and the opposition NDP elites in their value orientation toward many of the questionnaire items on democratic ideals. A discussion of the three ideals explored in the questionnaire follows.

Elitism-egalitarianism. The party elites in South Korea are generally more elitist than egalitarian in their orientation, irrespective of whether they are members of the ruling party or the opposition party. In both parties a majority considers that the public is badly informed, inactive in politics, and disrespectful of the leadership. Although in both parties a majority disagrees or strongly disagrees that only those who are fully informed should be allowed to vote or that most discussions should be left to the judgment of experts, large minorities (29.8 and 30.3 percent for the DRP, 45.8 and 35.5 percent for the NDP) take the opposite view (either agreeing or strongly agreeing with the questionnaire statements). Party elites in South Korea generally exhibit a low estimate of the role of the public in the political process. Thus hypothesis 1 is sustained in this respect.

Contrary to hypothesis 2, however, the DRP elites are not necessarily more elitist than NDP members. In fact, in most of the items that solicited their perception of the role of the public in South Korean politics, the NDP elites were more strongly elitist than their counterpart DRP elites. Thus, as table 4.2 shows, a higher percentage of NDP elites either agreed or strongly agreed that "the extent of political awareness of the public [in Korea] is low" (DRP: 62.4 percent versus NDP: 80.4 percent) and that "the degree of political participation of the public is [also] low" (DRP: 62.4 percent versus NDP: 81.5 percent). The elites of both parties also agreed or strongly agreed that "the public respect of political leaders is low" (DRP: 66.6 percent versus NDP: 73.5 percent),

40. For an example of recent research that relies on a similar research strategy see International Studies of Values in Politics, *Values and the Active Community: A Cross-National Study of the Influence of Local Leadership* (New York: The Free Press, 1971). Also see Gunnar Myrdal who advocates a research focus on the pattern of valuation of the ruling elite in pursuit of the ideals of modernization in many developing countries. Gunnar Myrdal, *Asian Drama: An Inquiry into the Poverty of Nations*, 3 vols. (New York: Pantheon, 1968), esp. vol. 1.

although interparty difference on the item is not so large as on the preceding two items. Interparty differences on these items are 18.0 percent, 19.3 percent, and 6.9 percent, respectively.

A considerable difference between the parties is noted, furthermore, for the items regarding qualifications for voting and the role of the expert in decision making. Thus, NDP elites either disagree or strongly disagree that "only those who are fully informed should be allowed to vote" and that "most discussions should be left to the judgment of experts" by margins substantially below those of the DRP elites. The interparty differences on these two items are, respectively, 17.2 and 9.8 percent. A chi-square test of significance, as table 4.2 shows, indicates that in all cases the distribution of party-elite attitudes on the values of elitism and egalitarianism is statistically significant.[41]

The responses of party elites to the elitism-egalitarianism items suggest that the NDP elites are more elitist than the DRP elites, thus rejecting this portion of hypothesis 2. One can speculate as to why the opposition NDP elites are more prone than the ruling DRP elites to the tendency of elitist rule in South Korea, contrary to initial expectations. Quite possibly the opposition party elites are victims of circumstance in that they suffer from what may be called "an opposition mentality" in a developing country where politics is a high-risk enterprise. The failure of the opposition to capture power may make its members less willing to endorse the free play of public opinion in the face of a formidable opposition that seems perpetually entrenched in power, that is, the ruling party.

Modernization. A majority of party elites of both the ruling DRP and the opposition NDP indicated that modernization is a desirable goal to pursue,[42] thus sustaining hypothesis 1 in this regard. Interparty differences, however, were not very large, contrary to hypothesis 2. As table 4.3 shows, an overwhelming majority of party elites said that they would either agree or strongly agree with these statements: "The poor and the rich should be given equal opportunity for bettering their life" (DRP: 89.4 percent versus NDP: 85.6 percent); "women should be encouraged to be self-reliant financially" (DRP: 84.2 percent versus

41. In this regard see the argument of the vortex of Korean politics by Henderson, op. cit.

42. In this connection see Alex Inkeles and David H. Smith, *Becoming Modern: Individual Change in Six Developing Countries* (Cambridge: Harvard University Press, 1974).

TABLE 4.2. Party-Elite Perception of the Role of Mass Public in Politics for Ruling and Opposition Parties (in percent)

Questions	Ruling Party (DRP) (N = 171)	Opposition Party (NDP) (N = 174)	X^2
The extent of political awareness of the public is low:			
Strongly agree	12.2	26.4	
Agree	50.2	54.0	
Disagree	33.9	12.0	
Strongly disagree	2.9	2.8	
NA	0.5	4.5	32.43*
The degree of political participation of the public is low:			
Strongly agree	12.2	22.4	
Agree	50.2	59.1	
Disagree	32.7	9.1	
Strongly disagree	1.7	2.8	
NA	2.9	6.3	32.36*
The public respect of political leaders is low:			
Strongly agree	15.2	25.8	
Agree	51.4	47.7	
Disagree	23.3	14.9	
Strongly disagree	5.2	2.2	
NA	4.6	9.1	12.77*
Only those who are fully informed should be allowed to vote:			
Strongly agree	7.6	20.1	
Agree	22.2	25.7	
Disagree	45.6	29.3	
Strongly disagree	19.2	18.3	
NA	5.2	6.3	16.52*
Most discussions should be left to the judgment of experts:			
Strongly agree	5.2	10.3	
Agree	25.1	25.2	
Disagree	58.4	41.9	
Strongly disagree	7.0	13.7	
NA	4.0	8.6	14.11*

*Significant at .05 level.

TABLE 4.3. Party-Elite Attitude Toward Modernization Items for Ruling and Opposition Parties (in percent)

Questions	Ruling Party (DRP) (N = 171)	Opposition Party (NDP) (N = 174)	X^2
Changes are desirable even if they do not seem to contribute as much as one might expect:			
Strongly agree	2.3	10.3	
Agree	53.2	56.3	
Disagree	32.7	16.6	
Strongly disagree	6.4	8.0	
NA	5.2	8.6	19.58*
The poor and the rich should be given equal opportunity for bettering their life:			
Strongly agree	43.8	44.8	
Agree	45.6	40.8	
Disagree	4.6	6.3	
Strongly disagree	0.5	1.7	
NA	5.2	6.3	2.04
If a certain area of the society is behind, it is the responsibility of those who made the mistake:			
Strongly agree	18.1	28.7	
Agree	59.6	48.2	
Disagree	19.2	14.3	
Strongly disagree	0	1.7	
NA	2.9	6.8	13.16*
Women should be encouraged to be self-reliant financially:			
Strongly agree	26.9	32.7	
Agree	57.3	55.1	
Disagree	12.2	4.5	
Strongly disagree	0.5	2.8	
NA	2.9	4.5	10.36*
Parents are expected to assist children in their social advancement:			
Strongly agree	7.0	16.6	
Agree	16.9	33.3	
Disagree	59.6	36.7	
Strongly disagree	12.8	6.8	
NA	3.5	6.3	29.80*

*Significant at .05 level.

93

NDP: 87.8 percent). A majority of them also endorsed the statements that "if a certain area of the society is behind, it is the responsibility of those who made the mistake" (DRP: 77.7 percent versus NDP: 76.9 percent) and that "changes are desirable even if they do not seem to contribute as much as one might expect." (DRP: 55.5 percent versus NDP: 66.6 percent). An interparty difference on these items is 3.8, 3.6, 0.8, and 11.1 percent, respectively.

The only exception in which a larger discrepancy between the two parties occurs is the item regarding the changing role of parents toward children. The sample either disagreed or strongly disagreed with the statement that "parents are expected to assist children in their social advancement" (DRP: 72.4 percent versus NDP: 43.5 percent). Here, agreement with the idea of parental assistance in their children's social advancement was taken as an index of resistance to modernization. Traditionally, South Korean youth were more dependent upon their parents for social advancement, a posture that is no longer widely accepted by many youth in today's Korea. Although the reason for the difference on this particular item is not immediately clear, it does suggest a relatively less modernized outlook on the part of the opposition NDP party members as compared with their counterpart DRP members. On the other hand, the greater commitment on the part of NDP elites to parental assistance may simply reflect the feeling of those in opposition (i.e., *not advanced*) that all possible means are to be used to secure advancement. A chi-square test of interparty difference proved to be statistically significant in four out of five survey items on modernization, thus lending strong evidence to support part of the hypotheses.

In interpreting these and other response items on party elites, utmost caution must be exercised not to accept the result at face value. It is possible that party elites were susceptible to a tendency to render lip service to the "right" and "desirable" answer in their responses to question concerning democratic ideals, and that this tendency has influenced the taking of one stance or another, if not the degree of difference between the parties. Much survey research is exposed to this kind of bias.

Center-periphery orientation. The party elites in South Korea are generally ambivalent on the question of whether the center or the periphery should be given priority in decision making. They seem to be torn between the idea of giving primacy to the local community and that of supporting the national government when conflict arises between the two.

TABLE 4.4. Party-Elite Orientation Toward Center-Periphery Focus in Decision Making for Ruling and Opposition Parties (in percent)

Questions	Ruling Party (DRP) (N = 171)	Opposition Party (NDP) (N = 174)	X^2
In case of conflict the needs of the local community should take precedence over national concern:			
Strongly agree	10.5	36.7	
Agree	40.3	29.3	
Disagree	42.1	22.4	
Strongly disagree	2.9	4.0	
NA	4.0	7.4	40.43*
Improving conditions of life in your own community is the best way to serve the nation:			
Strongly agree	45.6	50.5	
Agree	46.7	29.3	
Disagree	2.9	10.3	
Strongly disagree	0.5	1.1	
NA	4.0	8.5	18.24*
When in doubt, local leaders should decide in favor of the national government's objectives rather than the local:			
Strongly agree	15.7	12.0	
Agree	51.4	41.3	
Disagree	27.4	24.1	
Strongly disagree	1.1	8.0	
NA	4.0	14.3	21.73*

*Significant at .05 level.

The evidence suggests that the portion of hypothesis 1 that predicts a centralist orientation of party elites in a high-risk system is not sustained.

Thus, in evidence of a preference for decentralization, a majority of the party elites either agreed or strongly agreed that "in case of conflict the needs of the local community should take precedence over national concern" (DRP: 50.8 percent versus NDP: 66.0 percent), and that "improving conditions of life in your own community is the best way to serve the nation" (DRP: 92.3 percent versus NDP: 79.8 percent). On the other hand, two out of three sample elites either agreed or strongly agreed that "when in doubt, local leaders should decide in favor of the national government's objectives rather than the local" (DRP: 67.1 percent versus NDP: 53.3 percent). The interparty differences on all three items are, respectively, 15.2, 12.5, and 13.8 percent.

Hypothesis 2 predicts that the party elites of the ruling DRP will be more center- and less periphery-oriented in politics than those of the NDP. The findings show that this hypothesis cannot be entirely sustained. Although more DRP elites than NDP elites disagree that the needs of the local community should take precedence over national concern (item 1) and agree that local leaders should decide in favor of the national government's objectives (item 3), DRP elites appear more supportive of local initiative (item 2). Furthermore, a chi-square test reveals that the distribution of party elites on areal orientation is statistically significant in all three cases. Again, the reason for these rather unexpected results is not immediately clear, although one can argue that the South Korean ruling-party elites were rendering mere lip service to the textbook version of democratic principles including the efficacy of local initiative.[43] More will be said about this matter in the following summary.

Summary: Findings and Conclusion

The main findings of this survey of party elites' value orientations in South Korea and the implications the findings suggest for the linkage role of political parties may be summarized in the following propositions. First, party elites in South Korea are generally supportive of the values of modernization and elitism but are uncertain regarding the value of centralism. This means that party elites in South Korea, whether in the ruling or in the opposition party, are not clear-cut or unambiguous in their democratic orientation and that they may be giving merely pro forma answers to *some* ideals of democracy. Hypothesis 1 is only *partially* correct and should therefore be modified to exclude reference to central-

43. One possible explanation is the inauguration in 1971 of the New Community Movement, called the Saemaul Movement, which tended to cause the ruling DRP members to identify more with the local initiative and self-help program, the ideology of the Saemaul Movement. Elsewhere I have elaborated upon the politics of rural modernization policymaking in Korea, see Young W. Kihl, "Politics and Agrarian Change in South Korea: Rural Modernization by 'Induced' Mobilization," in Raymond Hopkins, Donald Puchala, and Ross Talbot, eds., Food, *Politics and Agricultural Development: Case Studies in the Public Policy of Rural Modernization* (Boulder, Colo.: Westview Press, 1979), pp. 133–69.

ism. Second, as far as an interparty variation on these value items is concerned, the findings are not at all supportive of hypothesis 2. In lieu of hypothesis 2 the new proposition is that "ruling party elites, as compared with those of the opposition party, are not *necessarily* more supportive of modernization ideas, more elitist and less egalitarian in their orientation, or more center- and less periphery-oriented in politics."

In short, no appreciable difference may be found between the ruling-party elites and the opposition-party elites in South Korea insofar as their attitudes toward modernization values are concerned. The difference is rather on other value items. The party elites of the opposition NDP are *slightly more elitist* than those of the ruling DRP in their perception of the role of mass public in politics and the latter's capacity for self-rule. Also, contrary to that part of hypothesis 1 regarding centralism, the party elites of both ruling and opposition parties are *not* centrally oriented, although the ruling-party elites tend to be more supportive than the opposition-party elites of a national focus in decision making when a conflict arises between the center and the periphery. Finally, hypothesis 2 generally does not stand valid in each of the three value items examined so far.

These rather anomalous findings do have some implications and significance, however. The ambivalent stand of party elites on democratic ideals, as revealed in the present study, may suggest two kinds of speculative observations on the possibility of assuring democratic viability in tomorrow's South Korea. The mixed result of the party elites' commitment to democratic ideals may suggest, in the first place, that party elites in South Korea are, in their heart, supportive of nondemocratic, authoritarian, elitist policies and that they are rendering mere lip service to democratic ideals, which are not indigenous to the political culture of South Korea.[44] This may also mean that the South Korean political system is in a state of flux and transition from the earlier days of a more democratic orientation at the beginning of the Republic in the 1950s to an increasingly authoritarian tendency in the later years of President Park's Yushin system. To measure the extent of the discrepancy between the aspiration and the action of party elites regarding democratic commitment is beyond the scope of the present

44. Young Whan Kihl, "Some Aspects of Political Participation and Culture of the Two Koreas" (Proceedings of the Thirtieth International Congress of Human Sciences in Asia and North Africa, Mexico City, 3–8 August 1976.

study. The above findings strongly suggest, however, that political parties in South Korea are not performing a "linkage" role in politics and that party elites are instead increasingly subservient to the supreme leader who wields absolute power and exploits the party as an instrument for perpetuating his personal rule.

One can also argue, on the other hand, that the mixed results in this survey suggest a brighter future for the democratic political tradition in South Korea. The fact that party elites are generally supportive of modernization and have some positive attitudes toward local control may mean that there still is hope for democracy in South Korea and for the restoration of the proper role of the political party as an effective linkage mechanism in the democratic process. For some time South Korea has suffered greatly from the ills of political centralization, which are associated with authoritarian systems. Prior to 1910 the Yi dynasty had been a model for the centralized bureaucratic polity based on the ideology of Confucianism. Under Japanese colonial rule, 1910–45, the Korean people were again subjected to a repressive and rigid form of centralized rule. Since the territorial division of the nation at the end of World War II and the Korean War in 1950, the political regimes in both parts of the divided land have become highly centralized once again. Measures for the decentralization of political power, strengthening the basis for local participation and autonomy, are clearly called for to legitimate claims of democratic political development in both Koreas.

Moreover, the political development of South Korea in the 1970s attests to the necessity of democratizing the political process by increasing local autonomy and opportunities for political participation by the citizens. President Park's economic development programs, although praiseworthy in their rapid rate of growth, were attained without giving a corresponding amount of attention to the need for political development.[45] The opposition NDP leaders, including Yi Chul-seung and Kim Young-sam, correctly asserted that what Korea needs is political development commensurate with economic development in the 1980s. As President Park's rule became increasingly authoritarian, the oppor-

45. Young Whan Kihl, "Policy Output and Electoral Support in a Centralized Developing Polity: The Case of South Korea," *Asian Forum* 2, nos. 3–4 (Fall–Winter 1977): 59–94.

tunity for democratic participation by the citizens correspondingly diminished.[46]

The assassination of President Park on 26 October 1979 abruptly changed the political landscape in South Korea; the possibility of restoring democratic political tradition was increased, as well as the danger of military intervention in politics. New President Choi Kyu-ha, elected as head of a caretaker, interim government until a new election is held, has pledged to carry out political reforms, including an amendment of the Yushin constitution. The calm with which citizens and leaders in South Korea reacted to the emergency situation following Park's assassination has been interpreted by some as expressing a determination that a new era of democracy will be ushered in, turning the tragedy into an opportunity for creative action. Whether such an expectation is warranted remains to be seen in the days ahead.

In view of the revived interest in democratic restoration in South Korea, it is rather encouraging to see that many of the party elites in our study exhibit support for, and commitment to, some of the values of democracy. From the value perspective of democratic development of South Korea one can argue that the right of democratic rule based on broader citizen participation in politics must be brought back by the many against the few at the top and that the repressive and self-serving tendency of the previous regime in South Korea must be brought to an end. Once this objective is achieved, there is reason to hope that the political parties will be able to play their rightful role in linking citizens and government decision making in South Korea.

46. Between 1961 and 1977 a total of three popular presidential elections (1963, 1967, and 1971), five National Assembly elections (1963, 1967, 1971, 1973, and 1978), two National Council for Unification elections (1973 and 1978), and four national referenda (1962, 1969, 1972, and 1975) were held. Under the Yushin constitution of 1972, President Park abolished the direct election of the president and created in its place the election of the members of the National Council for Unification, which acted, among other roles, as the electoral college to choose the president of the Republic.

5.

Political Linkage Functions of Rival Party Activists in the United States: Los Angeles, 1969–1974

DWAINE MARVICK

The aim of this paper is to report findings from three surveys of rival party activists in Los Angeles in 1969, 1972, and 1974. The findings concern their social credentials and campaign resources, their issue preferences and ideological distance from the voters, and the changing way their own policy views seem to be constrained by what they believe the voters want. In these years it emerges that the Democratic and Republican organizational rosters were closely matched in strength, that they provided quite different ideological rallying points, and that the brokerage implications of espousing the same issue positions in 1974 were quite different from what they had been in 1972 or 1969.

Each of these findings is significant for the clarification of political-linkage functions said to be largely the responsibility of rival party cadres in electoral democracies. They allow comment on certain features of linkage theory from an empirical reference point and not merely in terms of its conceptual utility and limitations. The analytical complexity involved in treating democratic elections as linkage processes has been emphasized by Eulau and Prewitt in their 1973 study of urban governance; and as long ago as 1961 V. O. Key stressed the systemic importance of the political substratum as an active force selectively linking public opinion to governmental action. In the mid-thirties, Lasswell repeatedly called attention to the ambiguous meaning of an ideological position in the absence of contextual knowledge about the stable and emerging political situation. These and related aspects of linkage theory will be briefly discussed. Thereafter a detailed presentation of the Los Angeles findings will be made. Finally, a tentative assessment will be put forward, asking whether the notions highlighted by linkage terminology, as well as the insensitivity it encourages to other aspects of the opinion-governance puzzle, make it, on balance, a worthwhile development in the professional study of politics.[1]

Political-Linkage Theory

"Linkage" is little more than a metaphor, but it directs attention to the persistent problem in democratic politics of connecting the few who manage the community's affairs with the many whose affairs are managed. All governance implies linkages ... but linkages take different forms depending on the nature of the regime. Democratic procedures seek to maximize communication between governors and governed both upward and downward.[2]

V. O. KEY

When V. O. Key gave sustained attention in 1961 to what he called political-linkage phenomena, he too recognized that popular government was only a special case. All governments, he argued, because they seek willing acceptance and conformity from the bulk of their citizens, find it worthwhile to pay heed to opinions of all kinds. "Lightly held views and transient anxieties, prejudices, preferences, demands and convictions all have their relevance for governmental action."[3]

By and large, the initiative rests with those in power. If they are prudent, they are likely to pay heed to private views of various kinds. All regimes are capable of placatory, as well as coercive, actions. Politics everywhere is an allocative process. In it, moreover, the crucial skills

1. Dwaine Marvick ed., *Harold D. Lasswell on Political Sociology* (Chicago: University of Chicago Press, 1977), esp. part 1, "Elite Analysis and the Contextual Approach."

2. Heinz Eulau and Kenneth Prewitt, *Labyrinths of Democracy: Adaptations, Linkages, Representation, and Policies in Urban Politics* (Indianapolis, New York: Bobbs-Merrill, 1973).

3. V. O. Key, *Public Opinion and American Democracy* (New York: Knopf, 1961).

are those cultivated by the practicing politician, namely, the ability to trace influence relationships and to anticipate changes in what people with influence want.[4]

Key defined public opinion as anything that a "prudent politician" would pay heed to. With this definition he moved away from others' excessive concern with propaganda analysis, on the one hand, and over-preoccupation with underlying social and psychological factors causing opinion phenomena, on the other. Key wanted to take opinion configurations as political facts of life. Whether stable or changing, opinions had consequences if they were *linked* to the thinking of those in high places. Then, too, Key was convinced that opinions were shaped by governmental actions as well as by underlying factors, and not only by the consciously propagandistic efforts of those in politics either.

Out of prudence, all regimes pay some attention to the state of opinion among their peoples. But those in political life in democracies are expected to give deference to public opinion and to incorporate public wishes into government policy wherever possible because it is right to do so and not simply because it may be expedient. To be sure, the availability of alternative leaders capable of governing sharpens the sense of vulnerability felt by those in power:

Governments may pay heed to public wishes and preferences in part because of the norms of value and behavior internalized by the impact of the political culture on the political activists. They may also pay heed because of the fear that if they do not do so, another crowd of politicians will.[5]

In any event, responsiveness to public opinion can never be complete and unmediated. Key repeatedly stressed the active contribution

---

4. In 1950 H. D. Lasswell and A. Kaplan, writing *Power and Society* (New Haven: Yale University Press), tried—vainly, as it turned out—to adumbrate the notion of influence into a general-purpose descriptor for any and all political relationships. Power, they said, is actual participation in decisions; influence is being taken account of by those who participate. Thus policymakers might react negatively to union demands, find themselves using the ideas of Keynes but not of Marx, remember the results of last year's elections, and realize the financial cost of a proposal before them: all of these manifestations of the content of their deliberations are—by definition—matters of influence. Nor surprisingly, their conceptual scheme called for considerable taxonomic effort in order to classify different kinds of influence at different stages of decision making. Presumably, "linkage" schematics will proliferate in similar fashion, apart from their other potentialities.

5. Key, op. cit., p. 456.

made by what he called the political substratum in effectuating much of the linkage between public opinion and government action. In democratic systems each party's upper echelon leadership "bundles up the preferences and aspirations of individuals—in the process contributing to the formation of those preferences and aspirations—and seeks over the long run to move public policies in the appropriate direction."[6] Faced with the puzzle of how democratic regimes manage to function, Key found much of the explanation in the "elite"—

in the motives that actuate the leadership echelon, the values that it holds, in the rules of the political game to which it adheres, in the expectations which it entertains about its own status in society, and perhaps in some of the objective circumstances, both material and institutional, in which it functions.[7]

It is possible, Key argued, that mass opinion may be greedy and unconcerned with individual rights. It may also be that democratic governments are inclined often to take the easy and popular route and thus lose their decisiveness and credibility. But it is not inevitably so, both because the masses are not demonstrably and persistently corrupt and because "politicians enjoy a considerable range of discretion within which to exercise prudence and good sense."[8] Key's articulation of a "democratic elitism" is nowhere put more persuasively than in his closing paragraph:

The masses do not corrupt themselves; if they are corrupt, they have been corrupted. . . . The critical element for the health of a democratic order consists in the beliefs, standards and competence of those who constitute the influentials, the opinion-leaders, the political activists in the order.[9]

How do the key linkage mechanisms—popular elections and other machinery for securing representative government—appear to work? Political brokers must always assess public opinion, not simply yield to it. Key posed several illustrative cases. Given a fitfully aroused public and a placatory governmental leadership, has opinion influenced policy

6. Ibid., p. 455.
7. Ibid., p. 537.
8. Ibid., p. 557.
9. Ibid., p. 558.

or vice versa? Or, to take a different case, given a cumulative buildup of public sentiment for a certain kind of government action, fed by ex parte versions of relevant news developments and further distorted by sensationalizing practices used to sustain audience attention, what kind of public demand for action may confront those in leadership positions? Key is concerned about the fact that sometimes the public expresses unrealistic and dangerous preferences of the kind that prudent leaders are expected by that same public not to accept uncritically. Instead, responsible governments are expected to treat an aroused public as a political fact of life with many facets. What is posed is an intricate task, that of "estimating what kinds of people have what opinions and of a search for a decision that will give appropriate weights to conflicting equities and interests."[10] As an immediate problem, caution and placatory moves may be called for; over the long haul, policies that give different weights to conflicting equities may be required. Not in either short run or long should there be a surrender of leadership to public mood.

It is clear, then, that mass opinion must always be interpreted and evaluated critically by policymakers, both for its content and its political implications.

Opinion cannot be treated in isolation from its institutional setting. In considerable measure it must be a product of mass interaction with points of leadership—both formal political leadership and the many nonofficial centers for the dissemination of intelligence and the advocacy of points of view.[11]

In addition, Key placed special emphasis on the work of "out" parties in democracies. Governments almost inevitably tend toward a monopolization of the flow of information and of the function of molding opinion:

10. Ibid., p. 412.
11. Ibid., p. 455. Key was a throughgoing pluralist, of course, but not in a simplistic sense, not if it meant a "society divided into great groups whose interactions produced a precipitate of public policy" (p. 529). In a noteworthy footnote, Key suggested that a pluralistic order might well have as one of its prerequisite conditions a relatively weak attachment to group causes by ordinary people: "The pluralistic interactions among leadership echelons may occur, and may be tolerable, precisely because leadership clusters can command only a relatively small following among the mass. That circumstance both predisposes leadership sectors toward a practice of give-and-take, and avoids the paralyzing conflict that might come with intense mass attachment to group causes" (p. 530).

They try to conceal their errors and derelictions ... to present their actions in the most favorable light possible ... to bring public opinion to the service of their allies and supporters in the political system.[12]

Hence the "out" parties have a special role to play—to break the government's information monopoly, to expose misdeeds and errors, to inform the public, and to stand ready to take over.

Furthermore, "out" parties help shift the grounds for political debate. By their acceptance of a changed set of policy options after years of insisting on an earlier formulation, the spokesmen for "out" parties contribute to what is taken for granted by all—to issue consensus on certain policy fronts:

Party leaders focus their attention on the attainment of office and are not much disposed to fight for lost causes. They tend to abandon positions that have clearly been rejected by majority opinion. As they do so, they also tend to bring their followers around to acceptance of that which has prevailed. In this manner the minority leadership plays a part in the reconciliation of its followers to the new order of things.[13]

EULAU AND PREWITT

In their fascinating journey through the *Labyrinths of Democracy* that characterized city life in the San Francisco Bay Area during the 1960s Eulau and Prewitt make their analysis at a transindividual level, in terms of action units like city councils, electorates, and communities. In their view, the small governing unit of a municipality takes collective steps that, whether unanimously adopted or passed by a bare majority, commit the resources and the citizens of the larger community to joint actions and complex programs. Linkage for them means bridging the political distance between council and community as collectivities rather than between individual councilmen and citizens. Elections, both as periodic opportunities for affirming "the consent of the governed" in a democratic tradition and as culminating stages in leadership selection, are prime linkage mechanisms. Electorates are characterized in light of their history—or sometimes in terms of what political leaders expect them to do—as assertive, passive, hostile, supportive, and so forth. Much of their inquiry is concerned with whether council structures, processes, and activities vary in tune with the prevailing type of electorate.

12. Ibid.
13. Ibid., p. 457.

For Eulau and Prewitt, the prime question is not whether linkages exist but which forms and practices are relied upon and whether they are adequate to the changing tasks of governance:

The linkages established between governors and governed through institutional arrangements and political processes are critical components of governance. Because linkages vary in kind and extent, any government will be partly explained by investigating how the distance between governors and governed is bridged. The form and extent of the linkages will differ depending on the constitutional rules under which a polity is organized.[14]

Wherever a particular linkage practice is operative, it necessarily has a substantive form; it is, so to speak, clothed in cultural garments. In small residential communities councilmen tend to grow irritated with too much organized group petitioning; in larger cities councilmen tend to express disapproval of the group process when there is too little such associational activity.[15] In the more complex urban environment an intermediate organizational level of activity is sustained and accepted; in the simple small-town environment councilmen more often deal with citizens informally and individually. Group spokesmen seem unnecessary, annoying.

Cities vary in their record of evolving a uniform and appropriate response to the stresses and strains of urbanization. In some large Bay Area cities public policy was still cast in terms of small-town governance problems and the goal of maintaining a residential community. Only when councilmen came to a fuller appreciation of the magnitude of urban growth were they likely to change their conception of the future kind of city they wanted and adopt policies that contemplated land-use development as well as the provision of residential services. "What is and what ought to be are dimensions of political behavior which constitute an interlocking series of events through time."[16] Eulau and Prewitt report that sometimes "the linkages between the council and its constituencies are impaired or ineffectual."[17] On the one hand, when the council's internal structures and processes are characterized by obstruction, lag, or deviancy, it is not likely to be a forceful or consistent policymaking

14. Eulau and Prewitt, op. cit., p. 218.
15. Ibid., p. 326.
16. Ibid., p. 588.
17. Ibid., p. 593.

body. On the other hand, in the disjointed circumstances of a transition state, although the linkages may not be disrupted across the full range of activities connecting governors and governed, the linkages that are deviant tend to form a consistent pattern—one of crowded contests, close races but relatively few incumbency defeats, one of well-established and generally cooperative associational life but with unusual reliance on informal contacts by council members.[18] The linkage practices of the past may continue to be used, but the "environmental challenge" may create problems of governance for which those linkage practices are simply inadequate.

Eulau and Prewitt devote much attention to the implications of electoral accountability for a theory of representation. If leaders are to be held accountable, it must be for something they do; it must be for their conduct in office. Moreover, when electoral arrangements permit the public to hold representatives accountable for what they are doing, it is argued that a responsive relationship between governors and governed is most likely to occur.

The existence of linkage machinery—in this case, the holding of periodic elections—does not guarantee the achievement of responsiveness on the part of leaders, that is, genuinely representative government. Eulau and Prewitt propose a model that predicts responsive leadership when certain conditions are present. The institutional conditions are high turnout, vigorous opposition, and frequent eviction of incumbents; the psychological conditions are desire to pursue a political career and sensitivity to the possibility of electoral defeat. With data from their eighty-two cities, they can measure each of these conditions appropriately.

In large cities, the model applies quite well. Responsive conduct is substantially more likely to occur when the two psychological conditions supplement the three institutional ones. That the initiative still rests with the political aspirants is underlined by the fact that the institutional conditions alone do not produce more responsive conduct by incumbents. Only when the leaders want to hold office and worry about losing office at the hands of the voters is the serious use of electoral machinery to enforce accountability shown to correlate with more responsive conduct by incumbents.

However, the model does not work in small cities. The explanation

18. Ibid., pp. 596–609.

offered by Eulau and Prewitt is that small communities do not need to rely upon such occasional, formal, and artificial methods as political elections in order to apprise their leaders of discontent; instead, social pressures of a more continuous, diffuse, and subtle kind operate to explain responsiveness:

The councils in small communities will often know directly or indirectly most of the active and concerned citizens. . . . Councils will be sensitive to discontent and to implied criticism. . . . This sensitivity will not depend on their own ambitions or concern about the termination of their political careers. Rather it will depend on patterns of social relationships and involvements, often of a face-to-face nature.[19]

THE USEFULNESS OF LINKAGE THEORY

When Key used the term "linkage" in 1961, it was little more than plain speech; he asked how governmental action and public opinion are linked. As a synonym for "interrelated," or as an alternative way of noting "interdependence," or even as a proxy term for referring obliquely to reciprocal "influences," to say that things were "linked" must have seemed a straightforward, unpretentious, and innocuous way to make his points to readers put off by social-science jargon.

It was useful to have a term that equated all the different ways in which "opinion" and "governance" were related. It was a term that treated institutionalized arrangements like elections or representative assemblies as linkage mechanisms along with ad hoc developments like labor strikes, mob actions, or citizen protest movements. It helped readers to look for the common features and to discount the distinctive details when they were asked to analyze political events.

Its danger lay no doubt in overlooking important features of the event by abstracting too quickly away from the substantive context and mistaking the form for the substance. Distortion was to some extent inevitable when using so lifeless and mechanical an image as "links in a chain." Applied to difficult questions of shared subjectivity, it might be hard to retain an adequate appreciation of how fluctuating and dynamic "opinions" could be.

Still, "linkage" was a term that suggested a sensible starting point for inquiry—a search for empirically verifiable practices and arrange-

19. Ibid., p. 459.

ments by which "opinion" and "governance" were put into a give-and-take relationship—before turning to yet more elusive considerations such as democracy, responsiveness, leadership, or policymaking.

Linkage referred to something more than a channel of communication or a route of access to power centers. It was the communication itself—the flow of information about events or developments—that made a linkage mechanism interesting. It was the people on the receiving end, moreover, who judged the meaning of linkage phenomena. The appraisals made by prudent politicians were necessarily intuitive and might often be wrong. In America they were keyed both to calculations about electoral potency and to respect for democratic norms. Often they engaged the substantive preferences of the political activists themselves.

Nevertheless, for Key—and also for Eulau and Prewitt—the political substrata are not passive or neutral figures in the linkage process. Typically, they are seen as actively trying to shape opinion as well as to assess it. The opinion configurations of relevant publics are sometimes persistent and sometimes undergo quite rapid change. In some contexts formal mechanisms are invoked; in other contexts the channels for expression of citizen viewpoints are diffuse and casual. But, as Eulau and Prewitt insist, "the linkage process should not itself be taken as representation."[20] What the political leadership of a community *does*, individually or collectively, comes after the linkage process has alerted its members to the opinion topography ahead. Some political moves are realistic, others are folly, some look safe, others risky.

In sum, both versions of linkage theory considered here have tended to treat a "link" as providing a prerequisite condition rather than as necessarily producing a certain political result. Both leave the assessment task largely up to the political elite. Both use linkage notions to refer to systemic implications, to man-made arrangements, to observable forms and processes about which comment is worthwhile and at the same time inconclusive. There is evidence, too, that both are aware that linkage is a mechanical, static, and lifeless term, that it distracts attention away from contextual and substantive details, and that it sometimes diminishes the thrust of inquiry by providing a language for reaching academically respectable conclusions about a process while remaining noncommittal on the substantively controversial features of the political events in question.

20. Ibid., p. 405.

Empirical Inquiries in Los Angeles

One way to give greater life and meaning to the concept of linkage is to postulate the conditions that would enhance the capacity of a particular agency to transmit information about political choices accurately from citizens to policymakers. The political party is an agency that lends itself to this form of inquiry. In a two-party system it is possible to suggest three conditions that will improve the capacity of the parties to function effectively as linkage agencies:

1. Party activists in the two parties are closely matched in strength. Where rival camps of party activists are well matched, the probability of closely contested elections is greater. Closely contested elections stimulate interest and participation, and thereby increase the parties' capacity to convey *numerous concerned* voters' choices.
2. Activists in the two parties have sharply contrasting policy preferences and maintain a wide ideological distance between each other. The probability of meaningful policy choices for the voters is heightened, thereby increasing the parties' capacity to convey the voters' *more important* choices upward.
3. The political meaning of policy stands on particular issues changes for the rival party cadres in response to shifting voter preference patterns. Parties capable of accommodating shifting issue stances are better able to convey voters' *current* choices upward.

The determination of whether or not the three above conditions obtain depends on an analysis of the attitude structures of partisanship. The activities undertaken by party units depend upon the composition of the local personnel roster and upon the interaction patterns that ensue among those who must work together within the same "effective structural extent" of their party's apparatus.

The research for this study into the lives of party activists in Los Angeles was designed to explore the attitudinal structure of party cadres in such a way as to determine whether or not the three conditions postulated above were present. To permit cumulative longitudinal analysis, a series of inquiries, using virtually the same interview forms, was conducted in 1969, 1972, and 1974. Informants were asked to express their policy preferences on the same set of public issues. They were also asked to say what they thought most voters in their district wanted the federal government to do on those same public issues—most Democratic voters and, separately, most Republican voters. Other batteries asked them to

110

classify themselves ideologically—as liberals, moderates, or conservatives—and to characterize their social backgrounds, rearing experiences, and political histories in various ways. For each time period surveyed, equivalent information on these and other points was gathered.[21]

An effort too has been made in these Los Angeles party-cadre studies to be systematically comparative, seeking each year to relate the campaign experiences and political perspectives found among a sample of active Democrats with the equivalent phenomena among a counterpart sample of active Republicans. In 1969, 1972, and 1974, the samples of rival party cadres were matched by using the legal grid imposed by California law on major parties and defining the makeup of their county central committees. For Los Angeles County, the apportionment formula required equal representation for each of the thirty-one district party organizations into which the county was divided. This legal grid ensured geographic diversity. Moreover, the resulting samples gave equivalent weight in each party to the currently prevailing range of interparty competition and intraparty factionalism. Even without technical weighting to reflect minor differences in response rates, the completed interviews each time provided well-matched twin samples of "the middlemen of politics" in Los Angeles—those who were significantly active in the Democratic and Republican party organizational structures at district and countywide levels in recent years.[22]

21. The Los Angeles party-cadre studies began in 1956 with a study of voluntary-club participants. In 1963 and 1968 interviews were also carried out with county central committee members of each major party, so that for many purposes the longitudinal analysis can cover more than a decade. Here, however, attention centers on the constraining effects on one's own issue preferences of thinking that local voters have supportive (or hostile) preferences on the same questions. See Dwaine Marvick and Charles Nixon, "Recruitment Contrasts in Rival Campaign Groups," in D. Marvick, ed., *Political Decision Makers: Recruitment and Performance* (Glencoe, Ill.: Free Press, 1961), and D. Marvick, "The Middlemen of Politics," in W. Crotty, ed., *Approaches to the Study of Party Organization* (Boston: Allyn & Bacon, 1968), for reports on those earlier investigations.

22. In California the county committee is the lowest level of official party organization, as prescribed by statutes promulgated around 1910 during the Progressive era. There are no statutory provisions for precinct, ward, or city party units, perhaps because of the nonpartisan character of city and school-board elections. Rank-and-file party voters, at primary election time, elect county central committee members for two-year terms, either by assembly or supervisorial districts. Each of the thirty-one state assembly districts located within Los Angeles County is entitled to seven seats on each party's county committee. These district delegations are chosen in even-numbered years at the June primary. Rival slates are often sponsored by intraparty factions. In both parties it is not uncommon for ten to fifteen people to compete for these party leadership posts. On the other hand, the

111

Finding: Year after year, in social credentials and campaign re-sources, the rival party organizational rosters were closely matched in strength.

In each party, most of the committee members were men and women whose commitment to party work, during and between campaigns, was unflagging, clearly engrossing to them, and extraordinarily time con-suming. About half in each party reported having been active in party work for at least fifteen years. In each case, too, clear majorities reported themselves to be currently "very active" at the voluntary club level as well as on the county committee.

Many were politically ambitious, although by no means all. Of those on each Los Angeles county committee, one in every four or five reported having held public office ,at some time, usually at the local level. Asked also whether they would consider taking a "responsible party post if the opportunity arose," in each year approximately half of the Democratic and Republican informants said "definitely yes."

Party organizations in Los Angeles are loosely knit structures. At the neighborhood or locality level, voluntary political clubs flourish in both parties. There is a persistent nucleus of organizational activity at the state assembly and congressional-district levels. But there is virtually no direction or control exercised by the countywide structures of either party, except with respect to campaign finances in some degree.[23]

Grass-roots personnel are indispensable to partisan campaign efforts under such conditions. Local activists possess certain residual controls over how the campaign is waged in their locality. It is, after all, up to the active partisans and enthusiasts to carry the party messages into lukewarm or even hostile quarters. They personalize the standardized campaign appeals that are broadcast to mass-media audiences. Whether

---

ordinary primary voter *does not* pay much attention to this set of questions. Incumbency practically guarantees retention. Openings arise chiefly because substantial numbers of incumbents fail to file for reelection. The resulting party conclave is not an authoritative control unit but it provides a convenient and comprehensive sample frame to use in selecting the matched samples of rival party cadres year after year.

23. See the analysis of Los Angeles activities at club level in James Q. Wilson's *The Amateur Democrat* (Chicago: University of Chicago Press, 1956). Standard sources include W. W. Crouch, D. E. McHenry, J. C. Bollens, and S. Scott, *California Government and Politics* (Englewood Cliffs, N. J.: Prentice-Hall, 1978), and Bernard L. Hyink et al., *Politics and Government in California*, 9th ed. (New York: Crowell, 1975).

they make speeches, contact voters systematically and door to door, or engage in informal politicking with their daily associates, party activists convey more than the basic campaign themes. Inevitably they also add their own ethical and ideological commentary through words and gestures; their social and political credentials, in most of the face-to-face contacts with voters that occur, are credentials fused and intertwined with their personal style and status.

Despite differences, both parties were basically staffed by upper-middle-class volunteers. Neither party could really boast a roster that was a representative cross section of ethnic groupings, social classes, or occupational categories.

From table 5.1, a few trends can be discerned. The ranks of both parties are somewhat older in the seventies; the proportion of professional men is declining. The typical activist in 1974 is a little more likely than in 1969 to have a full college education. Another constant is sex and family status; both parties are heavily staffed by men. Most activists have stable marriages with children, though this is down somewhat in 1974.

There are also some persistent differences that give special social "access" to one party and place its rival at a handicap. The Republican party is the party of Protestants; Jews make up a substantial segment of the Democratic roster. In the Democratic party also, the proportion who claim no religious affiliation has doubled since 1969 and now accounts for one in every four. Businessmen and executives are more likely to be found in the Republican camp, although the proportion in both parties is notably higher than in 1969. Lawyers and other professional people are more frequent among Democrats, although in both parties the figures are substantially lower in the seventies. Only the Democrats have a full complement of blacks, and neither party is well represented by Chicano activists.

In the context of electoral democracies, several parties typically perform the parallel functions of sponsoring candidates for key governmental positions and formulating basic programs calling for government action. The crucial point of the functional redundancy is, of course, to vest the power to "hire and fire" in the electorate—and indirectly, therefore, to choose between the policy alternatives for which the rival candidates and contending parties stand. As Joseph Schumpeter incisively pointed out many years ago, the electorate possesses this power *whenever*

113

TABLE 5.1. Selected Social Credentials and Political Resources of Rival Party Organizational Personnel in Los Angeles: 1969, 1972, 1974 (in percent)

(Cases)	Democratic Cadres			Republican Cadres		
	1974 (215)	1972 (173)	1969 (223)	1974 (189)	1972 (185)	1969 (214)
Age:						
Up to 30	34	30	33	23	38	40
31 to 49	28	28	35	38	31	36
50 plus	38	42	32	39	31	24
Sex: Female	24	22	21	27	32	20
Married with children	75	83	83	73	88	89
Occupation						
Professional	44	43	69	29	32	54
Business & executive	29	29	14	41	35	25
Other	27	28	17	30	33	21
Education						
No college	5	6	10	4	12	9
Some college	25	29	29	29	30	30
Full college or more	70	65	61	67	58	61
Religion						
Protestant	30	34	34	70	75	70
Catholic	18	18	20	18	16	12
Jewish	21	26	25	3	3	3
Other	6	4	8	2	3	9
None	25	18	13	7	3	6
Ethnicity						
Anglo	89	86	79	96	94	90
Chicano	1	3	10	2	0	2
Black	9	10	9	2	6	7
Other	1	1	2	0	0	1
Very active in voluntary party clubs	38	64	53	46	53	57
Would take responsible party post if asked	36	56	50	37	49	51

the rivals compete seriously from roughly equivalent resource positions.[24]

To compete seriously, the rival organizations must be well matched, though to be sure one party may compensate for a lack of money by an abundance of voluntary help or may seek to offset the opposition's attractive program for governmental action by choosing a candidate whose personal magnetism and community stature are effective counter-weights. Given these and other strategies, something that can be called "performance symmetry" serves to make the election-day outcome *doubtful* as people go to the polls. Then and only then does the electorate actually wield the power to "hire and fire."

On the other hand, where the "social credentials" of cadres in clientele-oriented party structures like those in Los Angeles are "well matched," it can be argued that the core support base for each party will be less certain to be loyal because it is also catered to by the rival party. Traditional affinities are likely to be weakened; it is less plausible for one party to feel itself to be the only spokesman for such groups. Voters who think in terms of group interests and subcultural priorities can hope to implement their goals on election day in some measure whichever party wins when both have openly catered to the social group in question.

Thus it is necessary to establish in what sense the rival parties are *asymmetrical*. When attention turns to the substance of policy alternatives embodied in election-day choices, dimensions of asymmetry may emerge. It is quite possible for rival parties to be well matched in campaign resources and in social credentials and to be nevertheless heavily weighted in opposite directions when it comes to philosophies of public policy. In a political system where parties draw from substantially the same overlapping segments of the social structure, a rudimentary linkage function is achieved. But it is significantly complicated and, ultimately, enhanced by ideological considerations that provoke political activists of roughly the same social background and status to become advocates of quite different philosophies for government: on the one hand, defenders of the dominant interests of the political community; on the other hand, champions of subordinate status groups.

Finding: Year after year, in policy preferences and ideological distance, the rival party cadres in Los Angeles were sharply contrasting groups.

24. Joseph A. Schumpeter, *Capitalism, Socialism, and Democracy* (New York: Harpers, 1943), esp. chaps. 19 through 22.

In the Los Angeles surveys, informants were asked to express policy preferences on a set of public issues. In form, they were asked whether they preferred more, less, or the current level of federal action on each policy front. Seven issues were common to the 1969, 1972, and 1974 sets. As table 5.2 shows, each year and on each issue the Democratic cadre scored distinctly to the political Left, whereas the Republican cadre took Center or Right positions.

In an influential article on "Issue Conflict and Consensus among Party Leaders and Followers," Herbert McClosky and his associates compared the issue preferences of equivalent sets of Republican and Democratic party leaders—delegates at the 1956 nominating conventions who answered their questionnaire. At the same time, a nationwide professional polling organization administered the same questionnaire to those in a representative cross-section sample of the American electorate who indicated themselves to be party followers. The findings in this study established in some detail (*a*) that there were consistent, substantial, and predictable ideological differences between the rival party elites thus identified, (*b*) that ordinary Democratic voters held views on many issues that were quite similar to the views of ordinary Republican voters, and (*c*) that the views of the Democratic leaders were quite similar to those held by Republican voters as well as by Democratic voters, whereas the views of Republican leaders were quite distant from both kinds of party followers in the electorate. In short, the Republican leaders were "off in right field"—out of touch with their own electoral following and even more distant ideologically from the "floating vote" needed to carry closely contested elections. By implication, their political-linkage potential was low. It was, of course, a period of Republican ascendancy under Eisenhower, and the Republican convention of 1956 had little serious work to do.[25]

McClosky and his associates noted that two quite different conceptions of American parties were possible and that they tended to be seen as opposites. One viewed the parties as *brokerage organizations* with leaders whose policy views were flexible and opportunistically held, views that tended to become rather similar to those of their counterparts in

25. H. McClosky et al., "Issue Conflict and Consensus among Party Leaders and Followers," *American Political Science Review* 54 (June 1960): 406–27. For evidence of the atypical character of the 1956 Republican convention, see D. Marvick and Samuel J. Eldersveld, "National Convention Leadership: 1952 and 1956," *Western Political Quarterly*, March 1961.

TABLE 5.2. Issue Preferences of Party Cadres, Their Appraisals of Voter Preferences, and the Ideological Distance Between Cadres and Voters in 1969, 1972, 1974 (ratio of support scores from 0.0 to 1.0)*

| | Issue Preferences of | | What Most Democ. Voters Want according to | | What Most Repub. Voters Want according to | | Ideological Distance Between | | | |
	Democ. Cadre	Repub. Cadre	Democ. Cadre	Repub. Cadre	Democ. Cadre	Repub. Cadre	Democ. Voters and Democ. Cadre	Democ. Voters and Repub. Cadre	Repub. Voters and Democ. Cadre	Repub. Voters and Repub. Cadre
Seven Issue Average										
1974	.80	.39	.68	.73	.30	.37	+ .12	− .34	+ .50	+ .02
1972	.84	.45	.67	.69	.35	.43	+ .17	− .24	+ .49	+ .02
1969	.83	.51	.63	.70	.39	.49	+ .20	− .19	+ .44	+ .02
Help Poor People										
1974	.91	.37	.75	.86	.18	.34	+ .16	− .49	+ .73	+ .03
1972	.94	.53	.72	.85	.20	.50	+ .22	− .32	+ .74	+ .03
1969	.96	.53	.68	.80	.22	.44	+ .28	− .27	+ .74	+ .09
Cut Defense Spending										
1974	.89	.34	.74	.74	.20	.27	+ .15	− .40	+ .69	+ .07
1972	.87	.33	.67	.65	.24	.30	+ .20	− .32	+ .63	+ .03
1969	.86	.54	.60	.71	.36	.47	+ .26	− .17	+ .50	+ .07
Speed Desegregation										
1974	.78	.24	.52	.68	.12	.21	+ .26	− .44	+ .66	+ .03
1972	.86	.29	.50	.59	.18	.28	+ .36	− .30	+ .68	+ .01
1969	.87	.41	.49	.67	.21	.35	+ .38	− .26	+ .66	+ .06

TABLE 5.2.—Continued

Get Nuclear Disarmament										
1974	.89	.53	.78	.79	.40	.47	+ .11	− .26	+ .49	+ .06
1972	.90	.49	.79	.77	.42	.46	+ .11	− .28	+ .48	+ .03
1969	.87	.46	.64	.73	.36	.43	+ .23	− .27	+ .51	+ .03
Control Cost of Living										
1974	.93	.54	.96	.91	.56	.62	− .03	− .37	+ .37	− .08
1972	.89	.60	.90	.79	.54	.60	− .01	− .19	+ .35	0.0
1969	.86	.59	.84	.79	.70	.71	+ .02	− .20	+ .16	− .12
Curb Air/Water Pollution										
1974	.92	.59	.85	.84	.55	.59	+ .07	− .25	+ .37	0.0
1972	.98	.73	.93	.88	.82	.74	+ .05	− .15	+ .16	− .01
1969	.99	.86	.92	.89	.81	.84	+ .07	− .03	+ .18	+ .02
(Don't) Get Tough with Urban Violence‡										
1974	.25	.15	.13	.31	.09	.10	+ .12	− .16	+ .16	+ .05
1972	.41	.18	.19	.27	.07	.13	+ .22	− .09	+ .34	+ .05
1969	.39	.19	.23	.30	.08	.22	+ .16	− .11	+ .31	− .03

*To simplify presentation, use is made of McClosky's ratio-of-support scores. This is a simple weighting procedure, which assigns a weight of 1.0 to a preference for a "leftist" policy stand, a weight of 0.0 for a "rightist" stand, and a weight of 0.5 for satisfaction with the current level of federal action. On six of seven policy issues posed, the leftist position as conventionally understood was clearly one that favored "more" federal action. In one case, calling for more federal action to "get tough with urban violence," such a position was considered a rightist policy preference. For any group of respondents, the sum of their weighted scores on an issue is divided by their number, producing an average score for that group on that issue. Scores above .67 manifestly are strongly supportive of leftist government action; scores below .33 are clearly negative. In his use of these scores, McClosky suggested that the .46 to .55 range might reasonably be interpreted as favorable to the status quo.

‡ Whether to "get tough with urban violence" has been reverse scored.

rival party organizations. The 1956 data did little to support a brokerage conception, especially in the Republican case.

The alternative view held that rival parties in America, because their leaders strive for clearly distinguishable and logically defensible issue positions, have become rallying points for electoral adherents concerned about issues of public policy. McClosky's evidence supported such a picture in 1956, with a further discovery that the Democratic leaders were successful in rallying nominally Republican voters as well as Democrats.

The party cadres in Los Angeles, as already noted, were similarly contrasting groups. Democratic and Republican county committee members—in 1969, 1972, and 1974 alike—were persistently, pronouncedly, and predictably different in the "left-to-right" policy preferences they held on all issues—though not with equal force on all seven.

Direct data from samples of party followers in the Los Angeles electorate with which to carry out an inquiry paralleling McClosky's, point for point, is not available. From the standpoint of linkage theory— especially that of Key, which stresses the importance of leadership *discretion* and the need to *assess* public opinion in the process of taking it into account—a somewhat more closely joined question can, however, be explored: What did the party cadres think the voters wanted by way of federal action on different public issues?

Table 5.2 provides this data for the Los Angeles voters, Democrats and Republicans separately, as rated on seven policy issues by the two rival party cadre groups, first in 1969, then in 1972, again in 1974. In form, the question was posed as follows:

In this Assembly District, would you say that *most* DEMOCRATIC VOTERS want the federal government to do more, the same, or less?

A comparable question was posed concerning "most Republican voters."

As the table shows, there is an impressive degree of cognitive agreement about where the two voting blocs stand on issue after issue. The ratio-of-support index is calibrated from zero to one; on the average, the ratings given by both party cadre groups for the Democratic position hovered around .7, whereas the Republican voters were judged to stand near .4 by both groups. The Republican cadre located each set of voters slightly farther to the political Left than did the Democratic cadre.

119

With few exceptions, both groups of party cadres judged the Republican voters to be *moving* toward the political Right during these years. As for the Democratic voters, there is little agreement about a trend, from issue to issue, but both sets of judges agree that they stand markedly to the Left on six of the seven issues.

As figure 5.1 illustrates, it is possible to use these data to measure the ideological distance that separates each group of party activists or cadres from what they believe to be the typical stand taken by their own party followers and the rival party followers among the electorate in their districts. This can be done, as the details of table 5.2 show, by subtracting the support score attributed to the voting bloc from the support score of the cadre group in question. The patterns thus revealed show remarkably little variation from question to question and rather clear longitudinal patterns that hold across many of the issues. Figure 5.1 permits a graphic appreciation of how differently the two sets of rival cadres locate themselves in ideological space relative to the two voting blocs. Year after year, the Democratic cadres as a group stand conspicuously to the Left of Republican voters and substantially to the Left of Democratic voters as well. Whereas there is evidence that overall Democratic voters are visualized as moving leftward and hence moving closer to where the Democratic cadres stand, the opposite applies to the rival party's voting bloc. Year after year, the Republican voters are viewed by Democratic cadres not only as being far to their political Right but as *moving* in that direction even more so from 1969 to 1972 to 1974.

Quite a different picture characterizes the world of Republican cadres. Year after year, they themselves are moving toward the political Right; year after year, they feel themselves to occupy almost the same ideological position on these seven issues as they attribute to Republican voters in their area; year after year, they locate the Democratic voters in approximately the same leftist posture on these issues (agreeing with their Democratic counterparts in this judgment). Because they and their party supporters in the local electorate are steadily moving rightward, the net effect is for the distance separating them from Democratic voters to increase noticeably.

The Los Angeles data suggests conclusions different from those reached by McClosky in 1956. Clearly, the Democratic cadres have created an ideological rallying point on the Left; they themselves seem

FIGURE 5.1.   Ideological Distances between Party Cadres and Partisan Voting Blocs on a Composite Measure of Seven Policy Issues

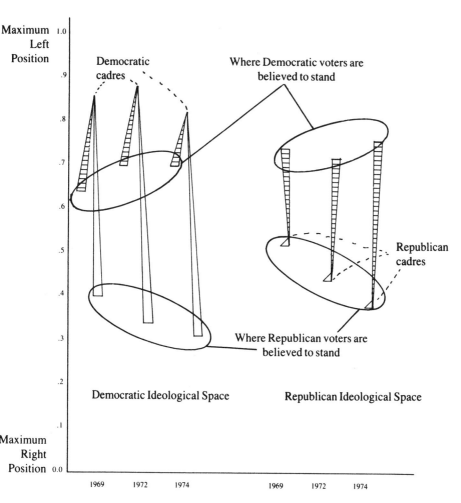

to feel it is increasingly attractive to Democratic voters *and* increasingly unattractive to Republican voters. Conversely, the Republican cadres stand close, year by year, to their own partisans in the electorate and, because they themselves are shifting to the Right, a growing ideological gulf is acknowledged to separate them from Democratic voters. One cannot say whether they and their electoral followers are shifting simultaneously in that direction. One conclusion is amply warranted, however. The ideological positions taken up by the rival party cadres are *not felt by them* to be attractive politically to the rival party's following in the local electorate.

The analysis is suggestive but inconclusive. Whereas McClosky's data base permitted him to examine the *coincidence* of issue positions taken by party leaders and party followers, the Los Angeles data allowed the examination of the ideological terrain in the electorate as viewed from the issue position taken by each party cadre group. The linkage is closer, but it is still not individualized. What is needed, one can suggest, is to characterize the perspective of each individual party activist on each issue. Following Lasswell and Kaplan, a perspective is defined as "a pattern of identifications, preferences and their supporting expectations."[26] To a Democratic activist, conscious of his identity as such, his personal preference on an issue of public policy *remains academic until* it is linked in his mind to "supporting expectations" about what the voters want. A Republican woman, thinking of her party activist "self" and of the policy goals she wants to see implemented through effective campaigning and electoral success, necessarily considers whether she feels consensus in the electorate on certain issues and whether she senses cleavage along party lines on others. These are the intricacies that must be grappled with if something of the individual activist's way of thinking about issues and their utility for the impending electoral campaign is to be captured.

Finding: Year after year, the political meaning of policy stands on particular issues changed for the rival party cadres in Los Angeles. As they observed the electorate's views shift from consensus to cleavage, they sometimes felt isolated or in conflict because they were "in the wrong party" on a given issue.

Before studying table 5.3, which summarizes the data on cadre preferences characterized in light of where they think most voters stand, attention must be given to the issue-alignment perspectives distinguished by the operational steps. Eight optional perspectives can be logically distinguished. In practice, on issue after issue, each party cadre group tended to prefer one or two perspectives, but there were always some colleagues who took other, atypical stands. Half the options can apply to those who, on a given issue, take a "leftist" stand personally; the other

26. Lasswell and Kaplane, op. cit., chap. 2.

TABLE 5.3. Issue Alignment Perspectives of Rival Party Cadres in Los Angeles, 1974, 1972, 1969—Cadre Preferences Characterized in Light of Where They Think Most Voters Stand

Issue Position of	Democrats								Republicans							
Cadres	R	R	R	R	L	L	L	L	L	L	L	L	R	R	R	R
R. Voters	L	R	R	L	L	R	R	L	R	L	R	L	R	L	R	L
D. Voters	L	R	L	R	L	R	L	R	L	R	R	L	L	R	R	L

Type

Isolated Rightists							
Mainstream Rightists							
Conflicted Rightists							
Party-backed Rightists							
Mainstream Leftists							
Isolated Leftists							
Party-backed Leftists							
Conflicted Leftists							

(in percent)																
Seven-Issue Average																
1974	1	8	6	2	13	16	52	2	7	4	4	11	45	6	16	7
1972	2	8	3	1	16	17	50	3	8	4	4	18	33	4	24	5
1969	3	6	3	2	24	25	33	4	8	8	8	24	9	17	14	12
Help Poor People																
1974	1	1	3	0	5	12	76	2	6	2	3	4	63	10	7	5
1972	0	1	3	0	8	19	66	3	12	1	2	22	39	7	11	6
1969	1	0	1	1	11	24	56	6	15	13	3	23	11	20	5	10
Cut Defense Spending																
1974	2	3	4	1	2	14	71	3	11	6	4	2	50	7	11	9
1972	3	3	2	1	4	17	66	4	11	4	3	4	41	6	29	4
1969	3	5	4	3	12	27	41	6	12	11	8	16	9	15	15	14
Speed Desegregation																
1974	2	6	7	1	2	28	51	3	7	2	6	2	55	9	16	3
1972	3	7	2	1	3	32	46	6	5	2	4	5	39	5	33	7
1969	1	3	2	2	10	38	37	7	8	7	8	9	10	27	19	12
Get Nuclear Disarmament																
1974	1	5	5	2	16	16	52	3	13	5	4	17	37	4	15	5
1972	4	4	3	0	17	11	58	3	8	4	4	17	38	6	19	4
1969	3	7	2	0	17	27	39	5	7	8	10	15	13	22	10	15
Control Cost of Living																
1974	1	2	5	0	38	1	52	1	4	6	2	34	39	4	2	9
1972	3	2	2	3	33	4	50	3	7	10	3	31	25	5	12	7
1969	10	4	3	2	47	9	21	4	4	5	3	34	10	14	8	22
Curb Air/Water Pollution																
1974	1	4	5	1	27	12	47	3	6	4	5	20	35	5	13	12
1972	2	1	1	0	48	7	39	2	6	1	2	49	20	1	11	10
1969	1	1	1	1	70	7	17	2	2	6	5	70	3	5	4	5
(Don't) Get Tough with Urban Violence																
1974	0	41	10	7	0	26	14	2	5	5	6	1	33	3	44	3
1972	1	40	3	2	0	28	23	3	5	6	8	1	25	1	53	1
1969	2	17	5	2	2	46	22	4	8	7	16	4	8	15	36	6

NOTE: One issue, whether to "get tough with urban violence," has been reverse scored.

123

half are for those who prefer "rightist" policy. Two of the four possible leftist perspectives involve expecting the electorate to hold a consensus preference on the issue; the other two entail viewing the electorate as split along party lines.

Thus, some informants on a given issue place both voting blocs on the Left; others put both sets of voters on the Right. Moreover, when a party-line cleavage is seen by an informant, it sometimes is an alignment with the Democratic voters farther Left than the Republican voters, and sometimes it is the other way around.

If both party voting blocs are seen to prefer a leftist-issue posture, a "leftist consensus" is defined. Similarly, a "rightist consensus" is defined when both blocs are seen to favor a rightist position. If a cleavage situation exists, it is either a "leftmost Democratic cleavage" or a "leftmost Republican cleavage."

Taken together, these characterizations of where the two voting blocs stand constrain the personal issue preference of the party activist in meaningfully different ways. Consider what it means to be an "isolated rightist" in Los Angeles during these years, as were 1 to 3 percent of the Democrats and 5 to 12 percent of the Republican cadres. It means that on issue after issue they personally prefer a rightist policy but think the electorate overwhelmingly wants a leftist line to prevail. As table 5.3 shows, this lonely posture was especially common in 1969 among Republicans, on such issues as "controlling the cost of living" and "getting nuclear disarmament" and "cutting defense spending." Having captured the White House in 1968, the Nixon administration had moved actively on all these policy fronts, taking the popular and conventionally "leftist" line. Understandably, there were many disgruntled Republican activists who felt themselves to be "isolated rightists." In a corresponding way, there were sizable numbers in the Democratic camp and a modest fraction of Republicans who felt themselves to be "isolated leftists," especially in 1969 when, confronted by Nixon's successful use of the "law and order" theme and the seeming popularity of the rightist demand to "get tough with urban violence," fully 47 percent of the Democratic cadres characterized themselves on that issue as "isolated leftists." Almost as impressive that same year is the fact that 38 percent of the Democratic cadre roster felt that a rightist consensus prevailed against taking action to speed desegregation of schools and housing. As table 5.3 shows, the proportion of Democrats in later years who consider themselves isolated leftists on these two issues runs from one in three to one in four.

Consider the other consensus cases, those in which the voters of both parties are seen as in agreement with the party activist's own stand. Defined as "mainstream rightist" viewpoints, they are more commonly found in Republican than in Democratic circles. By 1972 nearly a third of the Republicans had come to feel that their opposition to defense cuts and their reluctance to speed desegregation with federal machinery were views widely shared among Democratic and Republican voters alike. Likewise, more than half were convinced that "mainstream rightist" sentiment existed for a "get tough with urban violence" policy. On this last count, moreover, between 1969 and 1972 there seems to have been a dramatic revision of personal policy preferences among Democratic cadres. Whereas in 1969 there were 46 percent who felt like "isolated leftists," by 1972 there were far fewer. And the number of "mainstream rightists" on this issue has jumped from 17 percent to 40 percent. The electorate is sized up the same way; what is different is whether the activist opposes or favors a "get tough" policy.

In 1969 roughly a quarter of those in both party cadre groups tended to make "mainstream leftist" appraisals of the issues. The most dramatic instance was "curbing air and water pollution"; 70 percent in each party wanted such action and believed the voters of both parties also wanted it. Similar sentiments at somewhat lower levels held in 1972. In 1974, however, only 25 percent of the Democratic cadres and 20 percent of the Republican cadres took a mainstream-leftist view of this issue. What has taken place? Evidently that issue, like a number of others, has been transformed into a Left-Right partisan question at the voter level. Appropriately, among Democrats the "party-backed leftist" view has risen from 17 to 39 to 47 percent. Among Republicans at the same time the "party-backed rightist" view has grown from 3 to 20 to 35 percent. For the Democrats, this chiefly involved reassessing where Republican voters stood. But for many Republican activists it must have meant both reassessing where Republican voters stood *and* changing one's own personal stand from Left to Right.

A similar transformation from a mainstream-leftist assessment common in both parties to a party-backed assessment, leftist for Democrats and rightist for Republicans, seems to have taken place on the "control cost of living" issue during these same years.

What of those who feel "conflicted" after thinking about how the voters line up, because the lines of party cleavage are such that their party followers want the wrong policy and the rival party followers want the correct one? Surprisingly, on the seven-issue average, there were almost as many "conflicted rightists" as "conflicted leftists" in both parties. From 6 to 8 percent of the Democrats had to wrestle with such considerations. In 1972 and 1974 from 12 to 14 percent of the Republicans faced such problems, but in 1969, after the Republican party had been in power nationally for about one year, fully one-fourth of the Los Angeles Republican cadres on one issue or another character- ized themselves as holding views that put them "in the wrong party," so to speak. On "helping to create opportunities for poor people," "speeding desegregation," and "getting nuclear disarmament" at least 20 percent felt that the Democratic voters shared rightist views with them, whereas Republican voters favored a leftist posture! On the first of these issues, ironically enough, another 15 percent of the Republicans sized up the electorate in just the opposite way, but also found themselves out of step with their own party following, as "conflicted leftists."

Analysis has scarcely begun, using a typology of issue-alignment perspectives, to explore the transformation of issues in the thinking of party activists. Surely the realities of political linkage must entail dy- namics of the kind illustrated here. A few general conclusions are worth noting. In these years, changes in the way the voters lined up on these issues were being monitored by the party cadres of both camps. The remarkably high cognitive agreement about where each voting bloc stood on each issue strongly suggests that political realities were being skillfully appraised. It is difficult to imagine two sets of political fantasies, one for Democratic activists and the other for Republicans, that for quite different reasons could have led these men and women in rival camps—themselves with sharply contrasting policy preferences—to reach the same conclusions about the preferences of Democratic and Republican voters.

By and large, the years have seen a decline in "consensus" align- ments and a rise in what cadres believe to be partisan cleavages on issue after issue. In 1969 Democratic voters were seen as *not* routinely taking a leftist stand, nor where most Republican voters seen as favoring rightist alternatives. Rather, many activists in both parties were convinced that a near-consensus situation prevailed on many issues, with most voters in both parties preferring a leftist (or rightist) policy. In addition, there were those in each party who, realistically or not, believed Republican voters to be mostly on the Left, Democratic voters mostly on the Right. If such unconventional appraisals are treated as probably confusing to

TABLE 5.4. Over-all Shifts in Issue-Alignment Perspectives of Cadre Groups, 1969, 1972, 1974 (in percent)

	Lonely	Confused	Conventional	Consensual		Total
Republicans						
1974	11	17	45	27	:	100
1972	9	20	33	42	:	100
1969	20	33	9	38	:	100
Democrats						
1974	17	10	52	21	:	100
1972	19	7	50	24	:	100
1969	28	9	33	30	:	100

those who hold them and are combined with the two kinds of conflicted outlook that are possible, the summary in table 5.4 is instructive. Both kinds of "isolated" perspectives are here merged as "lonely"; both kinds of "mainstream" perspectives are added together under the heading "consensual."

The contrasting ideological environments in which Republican and Democratic cadres lived during these years can readily be seen. Democrats were substantially more prone to feel isolated and "lonely" as here defined; Republicans were more likely to be "confused"—because of either a conflicted situation or an unconventional partisan one. Both sets of activists show a decline in consensus perspectives; both show a rise in the "conventional" partisan alignment that puts Democrats on the Left, Republicans on the Right.

A TENTATIVE ASSESSMENT

The version of political-linkage theory set forth in works by Key and by Eulau and Prewitt has a special pertinence for interpreting the findings about rival party activists in contemporary Los Angeles that have been reported here. It is a version of linkage theory that gives special attention to how the electoral mechanism works; following Schumpeter, democratic choice rests with the voters when (a) the campaign has been closely fought by well-matched contenders, (b) the election-day choice is meaningful in terms of issue positions and ideological alternatives made available by those who offer rallying points for issue-conscious voters, and (c) the election-day choice is shaped by realistic appreciation on the part of the rival party activists that the voters have changed their stance on different issues, perhaps shifting from Left to Right or from general agreement to partisan disagreement. It is a version of linkage theory that uses the core notions heuristically. Opinions are complex and changing things; catering to them in order to increase the electoral chances for one's party calls for skill and realism and much hard work. The Los Angeles data suggest that many activists on both sides were political brokers who at the same time held consistent and informed views about a range of public policy issues.

6.

The Australian Labor Party and the Trade Unions: Linkage as Penetration and Reaction

TOM TRUMAN

Linkage Theory

Linkage theory is across-systems theory. James N. Rosenau says that its initial formulation arose out of a conviction that specialists in comparative politics and specialists in international politics needed a method of analysis that facilitated the convergence of the two fields and the crossing of the boundaries. Rosenau defines "linkage" as "any recurrent sequence of behavior that originates in one system and is reacted to in another."[1] "The original formulation," he states, "posited the initial and terminal stages of a linkage as, respectively, outputs and inputs for the national or international system in which the sequence of behavior either originated or culminated."[2] It is possible to have "fused" linkage in which an output fosters an input, which in turn fosters an output, in such a way that they cannot meaningfully be analyzed separately. Apart from this there are three basic processes by means of which the outputs and inputs get linked together. A *penetrative process* occurs when members of one system serve as participants in the political processes of another. A *reactive process* is the contrary of a penetrative one: it is brought into

---

1. James N. Rosenau, "Theorizing Across Systems: Linkage Politics Revisited," in Jonathan Wilkenfeld, *Conflict Behavior and Linkage Politics* (New York: David McKay, 1973), pp. 42–43.
2. Ibid., p. 43.

being by recurrent and similar boundary-crossing reactions rather than the sharing of authority. The third process is a special form of the reactive one. Referred to as an *emulative process*, it is established when the input not only is a response to the output but essentially takes the same form as the output.[3]

Although Rosenau's theory was developed to deal with cross-national relations, it can also be applied to systems within nations. The events described in this study took place in Australia and the systems explored include trade unions, Catholic organizations, the Australian Communist party, and the Australian Labor party. The study will show that trade-union personnel penetrate the ALP by consent or design of the ALP and that the trade unions themselves are penetrated by members of both the Communist party and Catholic organizations. This second level of penetration, which results in the influence of those groups in the ALP by reason of the linkage between the unions and the party, may be actively resisted by the ALP, as it has been in the case of the Communists, or at best viewed ambivalently, as in the case of the Catholic Social Movement.

This study focuses on Australian domestic political events that have been connected with certain international happenings. It would be going much too far to say that a causal or deterministic relationship existed between the international and the domestic events. But it is clear that the domestic events would have been different if the international events had been different. Both the Australian Communist party (before 1956 and the shattering of the unity of the international Communist movement) and Catholic Action in Australia had organizational links to their respective world centers and looked to those centers for ideological leadership and for cues in setting policy. In addition, Australian politics was affected by the American decision to withdraw troops from Vietnam and to acknowledge implicitly the failure of its Vietnam policy. Australia was more affected by this event than other Western countries because it had sent troops to Vietnam to aid the United States: the American defeat was also an Australian defeat. In terms of linkage theory, the Australian responses to these international events constitute linkage by way of a reactive process. To illustrate this process four cases will be described.

3. Ibid.

Case 1
International Events:
  a. Nazi-Soviet Pact of 1939.
  b. Nazi attack on Russia June 1941 and subsequent alliance of USSR with the West (1941–45).
Linkage Pattern Affected:
  Australian Communist party → trade unions → Australian Labor party.
Nature of Changes:
  a. Reduced influence of Communist party over the Australian Labor party (1939–41).
  b. Increased influence of the Communist party over the unions and the Australian Labor party (1941–45).

Case 2
International Event:
  Vatican launches offensive against international communism.
Linkage Pattern Affected:
  Catholic Action → Catholic Social Movement → ALP Industrial Groups → trade unions → Australian Labor party.
Nature of Changes:
  Organized Catholic influence in the ALP increases (1945–54), disrupting normal power relations in unions and party and thus precipitating conflict.

Case 3
International Event:
  Fall of Beria in the USSR.
Linkage Pattern Affected:
  ALP Industrial Groups → Australian Labor party → Democratic Labor party.
Nature of Changes:
  The Royal Commission on Soviet Espionage increases the conflict in the Australian Labor party between the ALP Industrial Groups and their enemies. In the ensuing split, the "groupers" leave the Australian Labor Party to form the Democratic Labor party, bringing about left-wing dominance in the ALP (1954–68).

Case 4
International Event:
  American (and Australian) failure in Vietnam War, decision to withdraw troops, LBJ retires, Nixon visits China, détente.
Linkage Pattern Affected:
  Middle-class suburban voters → Australian Labor party (1968–75) → trade unions.

Nature of Changes:

The effects of international events on Australian middle-class suburban voters inclined them to vote for the ALP in 1969 and this tendency increased in 1972, resulting in a Labor government that lasted until December 1975.

Before proceeding to develop the four cases outlined above it is necessary to provide the reader with some background to the Australian Labor party and its place in the Australian political party system and to demonstrate the linkage by penetration that exists between the trade unions and the ALP.

Background

The Australian party system is mainly a class-based system. There are lesser cleavages of some importance, namely, the differences between Protestants and Catholics and the regionalism typical of a country of continental proportions,[4] but the Australian Labor party regularly wins between 65 and 80 percent of the votes of manual workers in every one of the six states in federal elections (and in state elections), and the Liberal-Country party coalition obtains a similar proportion of the votes of nonmanual workers[5] in what is virtually a two-party system. Robert R. Alford in his comparative treatment of the Anglo-American democracies gives Australia an index of class voting of 33 compared with Great Britain 40, United States 16, and Canada 8.[6]

The rise of the Australian Labor party to major party status in the years 1891 to 1909 converted a party system based on regionalism and a contest between two liberal capitalist parties over the tariff into a competition between the social-democratic Australian Labor party and the merged liberal-capitalist forces (the Liberal party and the small Country party are always in alliance). The ALP, built on the rapid expansion of trade unionism, was made militantly class conscious by both the sudden ending in the 1890s of thirty years of remarkable prosperity and the influx of many British workers whose class consciousness

4. See Robert R. Alford, *Party and Society* (Chicago: Rand McNally, 1963), pp. 172–218.
   5. Ibid., pp. 184–87.
   6. Ibid., p. 102.

was intensified by similar conditions in the United Kingdom.[7] After their disastrous defeats in the great strikes of the nineties, the trade unions created the Australian Labor party to try to achieve by political means the goals they had failed to accomplish by industrial action. The ALP is even more strongly based on trade unions than is the British Labour party. The middle-class intellectual element, so influential in the British party, is relatively weak in the ALP and has less prestige in general in more egalitarian Australia.

One consequence of egalitarian values has been the party's stress on the sovereignty of the rank-and-file members of the trade unions and the ALP branches (constituency associations). The extraparliamentary organization of the party has on some occasions successfully directed the parliamentary party to change its position on parliamentary matters or has expelled parliamentarians from the party for refusing to do so. Constitutionally, between conferences, the party delegate conference and the party central executive are the masters of the parliamentary party. In practice, power is wielded by trade-union leaders representing their largely passive rank-and-file members. In the principal state branches of the ALP union delegates on the governing bodies outnumber the constituency branch members six to four, and the number of parliamentarians is deliberately restricted to a mere one or two besides the state parliamentary leader and his deputy.

However, there is very rarely any confrontation between parliamentarians and trade unionists as such. Much more frequent and meaningful are divisions along ideological lines defined by distance from, or closeness to, the various Communist parties, which constitute the extreme Left of the labor movement and into which the ALP imperceptibly merges and shades off on the Left in the spectrum of Australian politics (see figure 6.1). (The larger trade unions in industry, mining, and transport have a tradition of radicalism and militancy going back fifty years or more, and their leaders are usually in the left wing of the ALP; many of them are actually Communists of one of the three varieties: national line, Moscow line, or Peking line.) In these internal power struggles the

7. The earlier success of the Australian and New Zealand Labor parties and their closer similarity to the British Labour party compared with the Canadian New Democratic party owe much to the purer "Britishness" of Australia and New Zealand and their more recent settlement by Europeans as compared with Canada, partly American in origin, where the influence of the United States continues to be a factor in the culture of the country.

133

FIGURE 6.1.   Approximate Spectrum of Australian Party Politics 1972–75

Australian Country
Party-National Party
(minor party)*

Australia Party
(very small breakaway from Liberal Party)

Liberal Party of Australia
(major party)

Australian   Labor   Party
(major party)

Liberal Movement
(very small breakaway from Liberal Party)

Democratic Labor Party
Communists   (very small breakaway from ALP)
(three very small parties)

L _____ C _____ R

* The Australian Country Party in some states changed its name to National Party in seeking a
foothold in the cities in the face of a declining rural population.

more pragmatic Center usually prevails, reflecting the party's quest for
votes among groups outside the labor movement, such as middle-class
suburbanites and dwellers in country towns.

The ALP is the largest party in terms of popular vote, but the anti-
Labor parties (the Liberal party and the Country party in coalition
under one of the several changes of name) have enjoyed by far the greater
share of years in office in the national capital (see table 6.1). In the seventy-
five years since the founding of the Australian Commonwealth, the
capitalist parties have ruled fifty-five years to the ALP's twenty years
in office. But at the state level, where ideological and policy differences
between the rival party teams are not so salient, Labor has done much

TABLE 6.1. House of Representatives—Percentage of Total Votes and
Seats Won by Parties, 1969 and 1972

Party	1969		1972	
	Percent of vote	Seats	Percent of vote	Seats
Liberal	37.79	46	32.04	38
Country	8.56	20	9.44	20
Coalition	43.35	66	41.48	58
Australian Labor	46.95	59	49.59	67
Democratic Labor	6.02	0	5.25	0
Australia	0.88	0	2.42	0
Others	2.74	0	1.26	0
Total	100	125	100	125

better; in the state of Queensland, for example, a Labor government ruled from 1915 to 1929 and from 1932 to 1957, and there have been long periods of Labor rule in Tasmania and New South Wales, although not quite so long as the Queensland stretch.

Penetration: The Trade Unions and the Australian Labor Party

Australia has a very high percentage of its work force in trade unions. In the peak year of 1954, 62 percent of *all* employees, including agricultural employees, were in unions. This fell to 50 percent by 1970 but rose slightly to 52 percent by 1971. Over the same period, however, the total number of trade-union members rose by about 30 percent to 2,427,000 (the Australian population was then approximately 12.5 million).[8] In contrast, only 26.2 percent of United States employees were in unions in 1955 and only 22.6 percent in 1970.

The Australian Council of Trade Unions, established in 1927, represents Australian unions at the national level. In 1969 the ACTU unions represented 77 percent of all unionists in Australia, and by 1971 the figure was 79 percent. (The British Trade Union Congress, which the ACTU resembles in its powers and functions, represented 92 percent

8. D. W. Rawson, *A Handbook of Australian Trade Unions and Employee Associations*, Occasional Paper no. 8, (Canberra: Department of Political Science, Research School of Social Sciences, Australian National University, 1973), p. 81.

of British trade unions in 1970; the AFL-CIO unions comprised 77 per-cent of all American unionists in 1968.)[9] The ACTU was founded as the executive committee of the Inter-State Congresses of Australian Trade Unions.[10] Each state had then a central labor organization to deal with matters of common interest to the trade unions, including at times the direction of a strike involving a number of unions.[11] After the ACTU was formed these councils became, in addition, the state branches of the ACTU. Today unions affiliate separately with the state councils and the ACTU. Affiliation with the ACTU, or with one of its branches, implies support for the idea of "the labor movement" and for the Australian Labor party as the movement's political wing (as the unions are the industrial wing). Such affiliation suggests the sentiment of class solidarity, a relatively militant industrial stance, and a relatively radical political stance. The ACTU has as its objective "the socialization of industry, i.e., production, distribution and exchange." Union leaders often take it as their duty to lecture erring Labor politicians who depart from the true faith or dissemble to please middle-class and rural voters.

Even when under Communist influence, Trades and Labor councils and the ACTU support the Labor party and regard it as their instrument in politics. Robert Hawke, president of the ACTU, doubles as president of the Australian Labor party (i.e., the federation organization). John Ducker, assistant secretary of the Sydney Trades and Labor Council, is the New South Wales president of the ALP. Jack Egerton served as president of the Queensland TLC and president of the Queensland branch of the ALP. F. E. (Joe) Chamberlain, state secretary of the Tramways Employees, was in 1949 elected to the combined office of secretary of the Perth Trades and Labor Council and secretary of the Western Australian branch of the ALP and held both offices up to 1970. Thus it is a common pattern for leading trade unionists to become presidents of state branchs of the ALP and fairly common for them to become federal president or hold some other high office.

Like the Australian government, the Australian Labor party is organized on a federal basis. Each state branch of the party is ruled by a conference, annual in most states, with delegates coming from the trade unions and the state electorate councils (which combine a number of

9. Ibid., p. 16.
10. J. T. Sutcliffe, *A History of Trade Unionism in Australia* (Melbourne: Macmillan, 1921), pp. 46–48.
11. Ibid., p. 45.

membership branches for each state parliamentary seat). The conference is constitutionally the supreme power in the state branch. It develops the party platform and the rules of the branch, which are binding on all members of the state branch, and it hears appeals from the decisions of the state executive. But the state executives, which rule the state branches between conferences, are in fact the most powerful state organs because they exercise power on a day-to-day basis. Among these powers are the right to determine membership, to expel members, and to suspend or expel constituency associations (membership "branches"); they also, on occasion, issue instructions to the state parliamentary parties regarding their stances on bills and parliamentary strategy. Since 1970 the Victorian State Branch and the New South Wales State Branch have been given new constitutions, which created a new institution, the state council. These councils are much more broadly representative than the old state executives in that they resemble small conferences, meeting monthly.

The ALP Federal Conference is the supreme policymaking and rule-making organ of the party. It meets regularly every two years but is often called into special session by the ALP Federal Executive. The federal executive tends in practice to be more powerful than the federal conference because it meets more frequently (about once a month), is smaller, and its dominant members are in constant touch by telephone. The state conferences (and the new state councils in Victoria and New South Wales) are delegate bodies that directly represent the rank-and-file members of trade unions and party branches. But the federal conference and the federal executive are truly federal organizations, representing the state branches, which means, actually, the state executives.

The trade unions created the Labor party to be their instrument in politics. Since the split over conscription in World War I, when the Labor prime minister held a referendum on conscription against their wishes and was expelled, the unions have been at pains to exert control over the party in each state. The way they exercise this control varies from state to state, but in general they follow the principle that the number of delegates from each affiliated body should be based on the capitation fees paid to the state executive. Because the unions have memberships running into tens of thousands and hundreds of thousands and a party branch is very large if it has five hundred members, the union delegates easily outnumber the party branch delegates, even though the latter are much more active as party members—big unions sometimes have trouble finding enough ALP union members in their groups to fill their delegations. In the New South Wales State Conferences the union delegates usually outnumber the party branch delegates three to one. In Victoria between 1955 and 1970 the trade-union delegates outnumbered the delegates from the state electorate councils by seven to one. In Tasmania the proportion of union delegates to those from the party branches was ten to one. In Queensland where the Labor-in-Politics Convention is triennial, the party branch delegates have something like parity in numbers with the union delegates, but on the state executive, where the numbers matter more, only about one-fourth of the places are filled by election from the convention, and all the other positions on the executive go to the unions on the basis of the number of members in their unions for whom they have paid capitation fees. In Western Australia the unions in the conference have a card vote.

Thus, by one device or another the unions dominate the state executives.[12] Under the reforms of 1970, which set up state councils in Victoria and New South Wales as more representative ruling bodies, the unions are guaranteed 60 percent of the places to 40 percent for the state electorate councils.[13]

The federal executive forced these reforms on reluctant state branches in which there had been a power shift brought about by the realization (after Labor's good showing in the federal election of 1969) that the ALP could win in 1972 if left-wing influence ceased to antagonize middle-class suburban voters. From 1955 to 1970, however, the federal executive and the federal conference had been dominated by left-wing trade-union officials.[14]

---

12. There are estimated to be some 1.6 million unionists, or 65 percent of the total unionized, affiliated with ALP. Most of the larger unions are affiliated in every state in which they operate. For example, the Amalgamated Metal Workers' Union (167,445 members), which is the largest union and is Communist led, is affiliated in all states. The next largest union, the Australian Workers' Union (147,000 members), has been controlled by extremely anti-Communist officials for more than forty years. It is a union with a broad constitution covering most of the rural industries. It is affiliated with the ALP in every state except Queensland, where its leaders had a violent quarrel with the Communist-influenced group of TLC unions that got control of the Queensland branch of the ALP.

13. Laurie Oakes, *Whitlam, P. M.* (Sydney: Angus and Robertson, 1973), p. 205.

14. The federal conference was increased from thirty-six to forty-seven by the addition of the federal parliamentary leaders, the six state parliamentary leaders, and a representative of the Northern Territory. The federal executive was increased from twelve to seventeen by the addition of the federal parliamentary leaders and a representative from the Northern Territory. See ibid., p. 159.

The federal conference decisions are binding on all members of the ALP, including the federal leader, the parliamentary party, and all the state branches. The federal executive, which rules the party between conferences, has the power to declare state executives "bogus" and to remove them from office for contravening federal conference decisions or acting against the general welfare of the labor movement in the opinion of a bare majority of its members (until 1967 just seven of twelve). The federal executive has on four separate occasions exercised those powers (1931, 1940, 1954–56, and 1970), but on the first occasion it had to back down and sue for peace because the New South Wales State Branch remained united in support of the state executive. However, if the federal executive has powerful allies within the state branch, as was the case especially in Victoria from 1954 to 1956 and in 1970, the state executive cannot resist successfully.

The federal conference and the federal executive have the power to make decisions binding on the federal parliamentary Labor party. The 1916 special conference expelled Labor Prime Minister Hughes, some of his ministers, and his supporters for contravening the federal platform on the conscription issue.[15] In 1950 the federal executive instructed the federal parliamentary party to reverse the stand it had taken in opposition to the Communist-party dissolution bill introduced by the Liberal-Country party government.[16] The present leader of the federal parliamentary Labor party, Gough Whitlam, barely escaped expulsion at the hands of the federal executive in 1966 for referring to them, in a fit of pique, as "the twelve witless men."[17]

Labor party members of state and federal parliaments are under discipline not only from the party outside Parliament but also from their own ranks inside Parliament. Members of the parliamentary party decide all parliamentary issues by majority vote in party caucus and bind all members to act in unison in Parliament. All caucuses, state and federal, instruct their leaders and give orders to all state and federal Labor cabinets. By exhaustive ballot, caucuses select the members of Labor party ministries and leave to the Labor prime minister or state premier the right only to allocate the portfolios to the elected ministers. In the case of the federal Labor government of 1972–75 the party caucus

15. However, they had already been expelled by their own state branches.
16. L. F. Crisp, *Ben Chifley* (Croydon, Victoria: Longmans, 1960), p. 395.
17. Oakes, op. cit., pp. 128–52.

insisted that legislation, as well as the principles of the budget, receive its approval before being introduced into Parliament.

Trade-union officials have traditionally made up about one-half of the members of state and federal parliamentary Labor parties. From their positions of strength on the state executives of the ALP, trade-union leaders control the official endorsement of candidates for parliamentary honors even when the selection is done in the electorate by the state and federal electorate councils representing the branches.[18] So trade-union officials of the faction dominant on the state executive are well placed to get the party's endorsement of their candidacies and appear to have a lien on safe seats in the industrial areas where the workers live.[19] All members of the ALP are expected to join a union if there is one for their calling. Parliamentarians who come from a nonunion background, like the present leader, Gough Whitlam, can only hope that officials of a friendly union will confer membership on them as a special favor, as the Australian Workers' Union did in Whitlam's case. Of the 111 men who have been ministers in state and federal Labor governments, 48 were trade-union officials before entering Parliament.[20]

The affiliation fees of trade unions constitute the main source of funds for the operating expenses of the state branches of the Labor party, but the federal executive and the federal secretariat depend almost entirely on the fees paid to them by the state branches.[21] Large donations by unions, including Communist-led unions, just before an election constitute the principal source of campaign funds for the ALP.[22] Sometimes unions try to use their financial power to manipulate ALP policy; when the ALP was temporarily under right-wing control in 1953–54 some left-wing unions reduced the number of members for whom they paid capitation fees.

18. Selection and endorsement of candidates in Victoria and New South Wales is now done by special selection councils.

19. See S. Encel, *Equality and Authority: A Study of Class, Status and Power in Australia*, (Melbourne: Cheshire, 1972), p. 229.

20. Ibid., pp. 236–37.

21. In 1960 the income of the New South Wales branch was £30,000 (about $67,500), but the federal executive's income, before the federal secretariat was established, was only £3,500.

22. The ALP does pick up some large donations from businessmen who either have been antagonized by a Liberal-Country party government or, more commonly, have to live with a Labor government or expect to. Jewish businessmen also contribute to ALP campaign funds as the Labor party is the antiestablishment party.

In short, in the tight-knit relationship between the Australian trade unions and the Australian Labor party the members of the first system serve as participants in the political processes of the second. Unions and party are closely linked. Changes in the unions are likely to be reflected by changes in the party. The following four case studies illustrate how specific changes in the composition of the trade-union movement in Australia have effected important changes in the party's policies, factions, and/or electoral support.

Case 1
International Events:
  a. Nazi-Soviet Pact of 1939.
  b. Nazi attack on Russia June 1941 and subsequent alliance of USSR with the West (1941–45).
Linkage Pattern Affected:
  Australian Communist party → trade unions → Australian Labor party.
Nature of Changes:
  a. Reduced influence of Communist party over the Australian Labor party (1939–41).
  b. Increased influence of the Communist party over the unions and the Australian Labor party (1941–45).

Although the Labor party has repeatedly declared that members of the Communist party will not be admitted to the ALP and has also repeatedly refused the Communist party the right of affiliation, not all members of the Labor party have believed in this policy of keeping the Communists at arm's length. In fact, there has been a more or less open alliance of left-wing ALP men and Communists in the trade unions in the coal-mining, engineering, metalworking, and transport industries, especially in New South Wales, the most populous and most industrialized state. Left-wing ALP men and Communists think alike, frequent the same pubs, and are natural allies. They often share positions on the same union executive Committee with the frequent result that Communist policies are introduced in Labor party conferences and executives by ALP men who belong to Communist-led unions.

The Communist party's membership at the height of its popularity in 1945 stood at 23,000. It is now estimated to be only 2,465.[23] The CP has negligible support from the voters, but it has been, since the 1930s,

23. *National Times* (Sydney), 8 February 1974.

a formidable force in the trade unions. From 1930 to 1965 the Australian Communist party was very subservient to Moscow. Democratic centralism helped to enforce a rigid adherence to the Moscow line among the CPA membership. Thus the policies of the USSR in the international system had an impact on Communist policies in the trade unions and were, in turn, felt in the ALP.

In the late thirties the Soviet Union was desperately trying to build alliances with the West to prepare for the expected attack from Nazi Germany. The right wing and the center of the ALP were isolationist and pacifist like their counterparts in the British Labour party. But the left wing, especially the socialist industrial union leaders, was convinced that the "united front" policy of the Communists was absolutely necessary to stop Hitler.

In 1935 the ACTU, like the ALP, adopted an isolationist position in international affairs. But in 1937 under pressure from the Communists and their allies, the ACTU changed direction and came out in support of world wide trade-union unity and for collective security. At the 1939 Congress the radicals were stronger still, and the ACTU adopted the Communist party's policy on the role of Australia in the international political system in preference to that of the Australian Labor party.

The Nazi-Soviet Pact of 1939 came with the impact of an earthquake, confusing the Communists and their allies in the trade unions and the ALP. The Communist party suffered some defections and even lost some of its longtime leadership group. However, the remaining leaders faithfully responded to the Comintern line requiring them to oppose the Allied war effort (J. D. Blake, for example, urged party members to struggle for revolution "even it means aiding the military defeat of our own and Britain's soldiers").[24] The Communists mounted a campaign to oppose the recruitment and dispatch of men to fight overseas. They infiltrated the armed services to spread disaffection but had very little effect in reality. More serious were the go-slow movements and the sabotage in the factories and on the docks, which their cadres in the unions encouraged. The Australian federal government, then a conservative United Australia party (Liberals under another label) and Country party coalition, responded by declaring the Communist party illegal. So strong was public disgust with the Soviet Union's pact with the Nazis and with the local Communists' behavior that the Labor

24. Ibid., p. 79.

party made no move to save the Communists. The ALP Federal Executive intervened in the affairs of the New South Wales branch of the party when the branch at its 1940 state conference carried resolutions of support for the Soviet Union and replaced the state executive with another group of men whose loyalty to Australia and the Allied cause could be relied on. The Communists and their allies thereupon set up in August 1940 the rival State Labor party, so-called to distinguish it from the official Australian Labor party. The State Labor party became, in effect, a front for the banned Communist party in New South Wales.

During this time the ALP virtually lost its radical and militant element of trade-union leaders. Although some of them were strongly critical of the Communist party line, they could not support the Labor party action, which they regarded as an attack on the Left, splitting the working class and playing into the hands of a reactionary government that threatened the freedom of the trade-union movement. The result was that the membership of the Communist party increased from 4,000 to 7,200 while it was banned.

The attack by Nazi Germany on the Soviet Union in June 1941 and the declaration by the British government of support for Russia changed the situation again. The Australian Communists were now enthusiastic supporters of the Australian effort in the "people's anti-Fascist war." The result for the ALP was to bring about the reconciliation of the Left with the Center and the Right and so to promote party morale and confidence. Simultaneously, the weaknesses of the coalition government's conduct of the war effort and the dissatisfaction of some of its members with the leadership of R. G. Menzies came to the fore in the national Parliament and induced two of them to "cross the floor" of the chamber to vote with Labor, bringing that party to office in 1941.

In late 1942 the Labor government lifted the ban on the Communist party. By that time the distinction between the politics of the Communists and that of the Labor party had disappeared. Many ALP members joined Communist-front organizations and many undercover Communists were in Labor party branches in the constitutencies. The line dividing the parties became blurred. Communist party membership grew from 7,200 in May 1942 to 23,000 in 1944, and more than half the new members were middle class.

Communist influence in the trade unions was considerable in 1939. That year they and their allies wrote many of the resolutions adopted by the ACTU, including the foreign-policy resolution. Communist union leaders and radical ALP union leaders were generally much superior in ability, education, industry, and effectiveness to those union officials espousing more moderate political views. Their natural ability, together with their unprecedented popularity during the war years, resulted in their taking power in most of the important industrial unions. By 1945 the Communist party had at least 300 members in top-level union positions, which gave them direct control of 275,000 unionists out of a total of 1.2 million. In addition, the Communists were very well represented in lower level union positions (shop stewards, job representatives, and delegates) and had the support of their union allies, the left-wing ALP men. In sum, the Communists controlled about 40 percent of all trade unionists.[25] Communist union leaders showed up with ALP trade-union officials as members of various federal government boards and production agencies during the war and performed very creditably in those positions. This position of respectability was to contrast strongly with their role in the cold-war period, which is described in Case 2.

The linkage between the trade unions and the ALP in the case described permitted the transmission of Communist influence to the Labor party. The next case shows how trade-union linkage with the party made it possible for an anti-Communist organization to reduce Communist influence in the trade unions.

Case 2
International Event:
  Vatican launches offensive against international communism.
Linkage Pattern Affected:
  Catholic Action → Catholic Social Movement → ALP Industrial Groups → trade unions → Australian Labor party.
Nature of Changes:
  Organized Catholic influence in the ALP increases (1945–54), disrupting normal power relations in unions and party and thus precipitating conflict.

Catholic Action, an organization of the laity to convert the social life of a country, including its trade unions and political parties, to Catholic principles and policies, developed out of the church's position in Italy. In 1929 Pope Pius XI issued a call to the laity throughout the world to enlist in Catholic Action for an "advance" on all fronts. Soon

25. Ibid., p. 92.

many countries with sizable Catholic populations had Catholic Action movements. Members of Catholic Action penetrated host organizations after the fashion of the Communists and set up cells to influence the host toward Catholic policies. Catholic Action in Australia was established by decision of the Australian Catholic bishops at their synod in 1937. The Catholic Social Movement came into existence in 1943 as a secret organization for the express purpose of organizing Catholics in the trade unions to stem the Communist advance and to try to place anti-Communists in union positions.[26] The assistance of the CSM was welcomed by a number of influential union officials, both Catholic and non-Catholic, who were also powerful in the ALP, because their jobs were threatened by the advancing Communists. With their help, CSM members established a front organization, the ALP Industrial Groups, which recruited anti-Communists to attend union meetings, contest union ballots, and go door to door in the evenings to solicit votes from union members. Previously, Catholic candidates acting without the cover of the ALP Industrial Groups had been confronted with the hostility of Protestants and other non-Catholics, such as the Freemasons, and these animosities were sedulously fostered by the Communists and their allies. This disability did not affect the ALP Industrial Groups, especially as they were careful to choose non-Catholics for candidates as often as possible. This latter tactic was also meant to disguise the fact that CSM people controlled the ALP Industrial Groups' organization and planning of operations and were the most zealous and the best disciplined and organized of all the "groupers."[27] (Many joined the party with the express purpose of manning the ALP Industrial Groups.[28])

The ALP Industrial Groups were set up in New South Wales in 1945, in Victoria in 1946, and in Queensland in 1947. (These were the states where Communist control of the trade unions had advanced the farthest.) They were set up by the ALP State Conferences and thus represented a considerable innovation in relations between the ALP and the trade unions. Trade-union officials had always insisted that they

26. See Paul Ormonde, *The Movement* (Melbourne: Thomas Nelson, n.d.); Thomas Truman, *Catholic Action and Politics* (Melbourne: Georgian House, 1960), chaps. 3 and 4, pp. 52–97; B. A. Santamaria, "The Movement: 1941–60, An Outline," in Henry Mayer, ed., *Catholics and the Free Society* (Melbourne: Cheshire, 1961), pp. 54–103.

27. Ormonde, op. cit., pp. 37–39; Robert Murray, *The Split: Australian Labor in the Fifties* (Melbourne: Cheshire, 1970), p. 15.

28. Murray, ibid.

145

ought to control the Labor party. Now an organization created in part by the political party was reaching back into the unions and deciding who should hold office in them—an interesting case of reverse linkage.

The ALP Industrial Groups were very successful. They were helped by the aggressive foreign policy of Stalin, which ushered in the cold war, and the Russian use of Communist parties to take over Eastern and Central Europe, policies that made the Australian Communist party unpopular. The Communists assisted the strategy of the Industrial Groups by their indiscriminate attacks on all ALP men in the unions and in the federal Labor government who were not actually fellow travelers. Their desire to sabotage the Australian economy in the interests of weakening the Western powers led them into the disastrous coal miners' strike of 1949, which was supported by other Communist-led unions. This strike united the Labor government, the ACTU (which combination was in itself enough to be fatal to the Communist cause), the opposition parties, the employers, the press, and nearly all Australian public opinion against the Communists. The hardship and inconvenience caused by the coal strike were bitterly resented by the public, and the Liberal-Country party team exploited this feeling in the federal elections of 1949 by charging the Labor government with being "soft" with the Communists. The Liberal-Country party coalition won the elections and subsequently introduced legislation to ban the Communist party.

The ALP Industrial Groups were helped in their struggle with the Communists by compulsory, secret union-ballot legislation introduced by the federal Labor government and strengthened by the Liberal-Country party government that followed. This legislation enabled a minority in a union to petition the Industrial Arbitration Court for a court-conducted ballot that was in practice run by the Commonwealth Electoral Office, which conducts federal elections. By 1950 the Communists were on the defensive. They were defeated in the Clerks' Union, the Ironworkers, the Amalgamated Engineering Union, in branches of the Boilermakers, Builders, Laborers, Waterside Workers, Painters, Postal Workers, and Electricians unions. In 1951 and 1952 the defeats continued. The Communists lost control of all the labor councils except the Queensland TLC. The ACTU was now dominated by the Industrial Groups. It withdrew its affiliation from the Communist-led World Federation of Trade Unions and affiliated instead with the International Confederation of Free Trade Unions. The ACTU threatened the remaining Communist-led unions with expulsion if they did not sever their ties with the WFTU, and they complied. The ACTU, led by the groupers, prevented the success of several Communist strikes, which were aimed at destroying the compulsory industrial arbitration system.

Through their control of the main part of the trade-union movement, the Industrial Groups put considerable power into the hands of the Catholic Social Movement and its leader, Bartholomew Santamaria. Because of the penetration of the trade-union system into the Labor party system, Santamaria, not himself a member of the ALP, came to exercise formidable influence in the Labor party. The groupers controlled the Victorian State Executive, were the main force on the New South Wales State Executive, shared power with the right-wing Australian Workers' Union on the Queensland State Executive, and had considerable influence in Tasmania and some in Western Australia. They constituted the right wing of the ALP Federal Executive and were believed to have a majority; at least they were able to see to it that the federal executive instruct the parliamentary Labor party to cease resisting the passage of the Liberal-Country party's Communist-party dissolution bill in 1950. In the federal parliamentary caucus they constituted a cohesive right wing and in the state parliamentary Labor parties they were also powerful.

In addition to directing the Catholic Social Movement, which in turn guided the Industrial Groups, Santamaria was also the lay director of Catholic Action. Because of the Catholic Social Movement's power in the labor movement, he developed grandiose plans for a Catholic ascendancy in Australia that was to lead to an eventual "conquest of Asia for Christ," thus converting the ALP into an instrument for achieving the aims of the church. However unlikely of success, the plan makes clear the strength of Catholic-union-party links during this period in Australian politics.

Case 3
International Event:
    Fall of Beria in the USSR.
Linkage Pattern Affected:
    ALP Industrial Groups → Australian Labor party → Democratic Labor party.
Nature of Changes:
    The Royal Commission on Soviet Espionage increases the conflict in the Australian Labor Party between the ALP Industrial Groups and their enemies. In the ensuing split, the "groupers" leave the Australian

147

Labor party to form the Democratic Labor party, bringing about left-wing dominance in the ALP (1954–68).

On 5 March 1953 Stalin died. In the second half of December Lavrenti Beria, minister of the interior of the USSR and head of the secret police, and all his principal assistants in the state security service were put on trial, found guilty of various crimes against the state and the party, sentenced to death, and shot. There followed a purge of Beria's supporters.[29] In Australia on 13 April 1954 the Liberal prime minister, R. G. Menzies, announced the defection of Vladimir Petrov, the third secretary of the Soviet Embassy and a secret MVD agent who was engaged in espionage. Petrov, ordered to return to Russia, believed that as a follower of Beria he would be in danger. He therefore made contact with the Australian Security Intelligence Organization, and the Australian government promised him asylum in return for documents purporting to reveal the names of disloyal Australians who were passing confidential information to the Russians.[30]

Prime Minister Menzies set up the Royal Commission on Soviet Espionage, presided over by three eminent judges, to make a public inquiry into Petrov's allegations. Among these charges was the sensational revelation that members of the personal staff of the leader of the federal parliamentary Labour party, Dr. H. V. Evatt, had passed confidential information to Petrov. The scandal was compounded by the fact that Evatt had been assiduously cultivating leaders of the anti-Communist ALP Industrial Groups, because he believed that an anti-Communist stance would find favor with the Australian voters.

The groupers had supported Evatt without being aware that his professed anti-Communist view was not so pure as he claimed. They continued to support him until Evatt began to use his considerable legal talents to make a shambles of the Royal Commission. He charged that Petrov's documents were forgeries and that the prime minister and the Australian Security Intelligence Organization had entered into a conspiracy to "frame" him and the Labor party. The Communists were

29. See Frederic C. Barghoorn, *Politics in the U.S.S.R.* (Boston: Little, Brown, 1966), p. 233. Barghoorn relies on Wolfgang Leonhard as the authority on these events. See his book, *The Kremlin Since Stalin*, Elizabeth Wiskemann and Marian Jackson, trans. (New York: Praeger, 1962), pp. 68–75. Leonhard says: "It was not Beria's person which was at stake but the omnipotence of the secret police represented by him."
30. Murray, op. cit., pp. 149–51.

delighted with the confusion Evatt created, but the groupers were beside themselves with anger. In the federal Labor party caucus they attacked Evatt as an ally of the Communists and called for his resignation. Seeing that his alliance with the ALP Industrial Groups was finished, Evatt decided on a bold counterstroke, which at one blow was to throw the groupers into confusion and put himself at the head of the gathering revolt against them.[31]

Evatt's master stroke was a press statement that made front-page headlines in every daily morning newspaper throughout Australia on 6 October 1954. The statement alleged that a disloyal group controlled from outside the labor movement, whose organ was *News-Weekly* (the CSM paper), was "adopting methods which strikingly resemble both Communist and Fascist infiltration of larger groups.... Some of these groups have created an intolerable situation—calculated to deflect the Labor Movement from established Labor objectives and ideals." Evatt concluded by saying: "I am bringing this matter before the Federal Executive with a view to appropriate action being taken by the Federal Conference in January."[32]

Evatt's attack on the groupers was well planned. He was well informed and expertly advised.[33] The innuendos concerning the secrecy of the CSM and its Catholic connections were explosive in a country where religious antagonism between the Protestant and Catholic churches was not far below the surface. As the story in the newspapers developed, it began to appear that the Catholic Social Movement was using the ALP Industrial Groups to take over the Labor party. Protestant clergymen rushed into print to voice their indignation at the imperialism of the Catholic church, the Catholic bishops were embarrassed, and many Catholics were dismayed at the revelations that Santamaria was plunging the church into politics.

ALP and union members who had been opposed to the groupers but reluctant to expose themselves were now emboldened to rally to Evatt's standard and declare their support of his charges. Evatt found anti-grouper allies in twenty-seven rebel unions in Victoria and in twenty-four unions in New South Wales, as well as in the ALP Federal Executive, where anti-groupers outnumbered pro-groupers seven to five.

31. Truman, op. cit., pp. 1–17; Murray op. cit., pp. 158–74.
32. Truman, op. cit., pp. 1, 2.
33. Ormonde, op. cit., pp. 58, 59.

149

Evatt's contribution to the anti-groupers was to lend a leader's prestige to their cause, thereby influencing the loyal but uninformed rank-and-file members in their favor. Boldly using their narrow majority on the federal executive and that body's formidable constitutional powers, the anti-groupers found the grouper Victorian State Executive guilty of disloyalty to the party and called a special conference of the Victorian branch. This conference chose a new anti-grouper state executive made up, for the most part, of officials from the rebel unions.

The groupers took their case to the federal conference in March 1955, but again the federal executive's powers were used ruthlessly. An expected grouper majority of twenty-three to thirteen in the conference was turned into an anti-grouper majority of nineteen to seventeen by the dubious expedient of having the federal executive assume the power to credential the delegates to the conference. The groupers tried to render the conference abortive by boycotting it, but the nineteen-delegate rump conference forged ahead relentlessly, withdrawing the official ALP endorsement of the Industrial Groups. The conference swung the ALP away from its previous anti-Communist positions on foreign policy by endorsing the seating of Communist China in the United Nations and seeking the withdrawal of Australian troops from the jungles of Malaya where they were fighting Communist guerrillas.

The CSM and grouper command in Victoria, faced with the certain purge of their leaders and overestimating the support they would get, chose to split from the ALP to form the separate anti-communist Democratic Labor party. In 1956 the split spread to New South Wales and in 1972 to Queensland. Branches of the DLP were also set up in South Australia, Western Australia, and Tasmania. Table 6.2 shows what effect the split had on the Labor vote. Catholic bishops throughout Australia divided over the issue, and the DLP vote was larger in those states where the Catholic bishops supported it and smaller where the bishops opposed it.

The DLP split off about one-third of the Catholic vote from the ALP. Furthermore, it took advantage of Australia's preferential voting system (sometimes called the alternative vote) to direct its voters' second preferences toward Liberal candidates and so get them elected in close-fought seats that would otherwise have gone to the ALP.[34]

The split unbalanced the Australian Labor party; by weakening

34. Alford, op. cit., pp. 197–98.

TABLE 6.2. House of Representatives—Comparison of Percentage of Votes for DLP and ALP, 22 November 1958

State	Democratic Labor Party		Australian Labor Party	
	Votes	% Total	Votes	% Total
New South Wales	106,805	5.59	900,843	47.14
Victoria	207,247	14.75	555,470	39.52
Queensland	80,035	11.08	270,676	37.47
South Australia	27,703	6.05	217,727	47.52
Western Australia	34,944	10.51	116,302	34.98
Tasmania	12,989	7.88	77,323	46.83
Total	469,723	9.41	2,137,890	42.81

the Right, it gave to the Left an influence in the party that it could not otherwise have gained. In Victoria this was especially marked; the left-wing state executive was virulently anti-Catholic, anti-American, and pro-Communist. It opposed state aid to Catholic schools, urged Australian troops in Vietnam to lay down their arms, and gave its whole-hearted support to street marches and demonstrations protesting Australia's involvement in the Vietnam War. The left-wing unions, organized as the Trade Union Defence Committee, exercised complete control over the Victorian branch. They permitted ALP members to join the Communists in "unity tickets" in union ballot against the policy laid down by the federal conference. This successful defiance of party policy by the Victorian State Executive was made possible because its left-wing allies on the federal executive protected it. But the net effect was that the Victorian State Executive and its left-wing allies provided the DLP and the Liberal party with some of their most effective propaganda against the Labor party, thus helping to keep Labor out of power.

In sum, Case 3 is a good example of the surprising influence external events may have on a nation's internal linkage patterns. Beria's removal and the Petrov case first weakened left-wing influence in the ALP (as the accusations against Evatt were made), then weakened the right wing of the party (as Evatt turned the tables on the groupers), then weakened the entire party's role in government by bringing about the departure of most of its right-wing membership and the consequent loss of electoral support.

Case 4

International Event:
   American (and Australian) failure in Vietnam War, decision to with-
   draw troops, LBJ retires, Nixon visits China, détente.
Linkage Pattern Affected:
   Middle-class suburban voters → Australian Labor party (1968–75)
   → trade unions.
Nature of Changes:
   The effects of international events on Australian middle-class suburban
   voters inclined them to vote for the ALP in 1969 and this tendency
   increased in 1972, resulting in a Labor government that lasted until
   December 1975.

In the federal election of November 1966 the Liberal-Country party
coalition won its greatest electoral triumph since Labor had gone down
to defeat in 1949 on the nationalization-of-the-banks issue. The Liberal
prime minister, Harold Holt, won this election on support for the policy
of fighting alongside the United States in Vietnam, support for the
American alliance ("All the Way with LBJ"), and a strong defense
policy.[35] However, by the time of the October 1969 federal elections
the war had turned sour for the majority of Australian voters. Australian
society, like American society, had been deeply divided over the war.
But as long as the Americans were prepared to fight, the majority of
Australian voters returned Liberal-Country party governments committed to keeping Australian troops fighting alongside them. During this
time Labor failed to attract the middle-class voters it needed because
it was pledged to withdraw the conscripted soldiers and to end the conscription, because it was lukewarm on the defense issue, and because the
party's left wing (especially the Victorian State Executive) was anti-
American and pro-Communist. When the Americans decided to pull out
of Vietnam and to enter into peace negotiations, the Labor party was
able to claim to have been right all along.

A second important factor in bringing middle-class voters—and
especially middle-class Catholic voters—into Labor was that the party
succeeded at last in toning down the pro-Communist image given to it
by the Victorian State Executive. The federal executive moved into
Victoria in late 1970, suspended the existing state executive, and called
a special conference of the Victorian branch on federal executive rules.

35. "Australian Political Chronicle," *Australian Journal of Politics and History*
13, no. 1 (April 1967): 101.

The result was a "balanced" state executive, made up of elements of Left, Center, and Right, which was committed to carrying out federal conference policy to assist nongovernment schools on the basis of financial need, which meant, in practice, state aid to the great majority of Catholic schools.[36]

The third important factor in Labor's ability to attract new voters was connected with the first. The swing voters who turned away from the ruling coalition's emphasis on defense and foreign policy found Labor's reform program attractive. Labor promised vast sums for the problems of the cities, education, preschool child centers, free universities, a national superannuation plan and higher pensions with the abolition of the means test in three years, cheaper houses, adequate fuel and energy at low prices, conservation, protection of the environment, and assistance to the arts.[37] The results of the three federal elections, 1966, 1969, and 1972, given in table 6.3 show the steady increase of Labor voting.

After its success at the polls the new Labor government initiated the promised reforms. However, the expense of the new programs in turn initiated a period of rapidly increasing inflation: from 3 percent in December 1972 to 13.2 percent by July 1973 and on up to 16.9 percent in September 1974. Unemployment rose to 5 percent by August 1975, from a base of 1.8 percent when the party first came to power. The result for Labor was the loss of many of its new supporters and defeat in the elections of December 1975. Thus the new linkage pattern in Australian politics provoked by American defeat in Vietnam and Australian middle-class malaise proved short-lived.

The events described above demonstrate how linkage by penetration facilitates the movement of policy ideas from one subsystem to the next in a political system, how linkage patterns change over time, and in particular how such changes may be triggered by changes in the policies of other nations—even when those policies are in no wise directed at the nation in question. The links described between Communists and

36. Robert Murray, "Fifteen Years of the Victorian Problem," *Australian Financial Review*, 18 September 1970; Brian Johns, "The State Aid Affair," *Sydney Morning Herald*, 22 June 1970; Eric Walsh, "Broken Hill and After: An Exercise in Self-Destruction," *Australian Quarterly* 42, no. 4 (December 1970).
37. *The Courier-Mail* (Brisbane), 14 November 1972; Malcolm Mackerras, "The Swing: Variability and Uniformity" in Henry Mayer, ed., *Labor to Power* (Sydney: Angus and Robertson, 1973), pp. 234–41.

TABLE 6.3. Federal Elections 1966, 1969, 1972—House of Representatives

Party	Percent of Votes			Seats		
	1966	1969	1972	1966	1969	1972
Liberal	40.2	34.79	32.1	61	46	38
Country	9.7	8.56	9.4	21	20	20
Australian Labor	40.0	46.95	49.6	41	59	67
Democratic Labor	7.3	6.02	5.2	0	0	0
Liberal Reform	1.03	—	—	0	0	0
Australia	—	0.88	2.4	0	0	0
Other	1.23	2.74	1.3	0	0	0

trade unions (Case 1), Catholics and trade unions (Cases 2 and 3), trade
unions and the Australian Labor party (introduction), and the Australian
middle class and the ALP (Case 4) form part of a larger network of
interconnecting linkage patterns in contemporary Australia. As these
patterns shift, in response to domestic as well as foreign developments,
the personnel and the ideas reaching the arena of authoritative decision
making will also shift. Examining how specific linkage patterns change
in response to international events is one way to achieve a better understanding of the *dynamics* of political change in Australia.

PART III

Policy-Responsive Linkage

7.

Political Elite Linkages in the Dutch Consociational System

SAMUEL J. ELDERSVELD

The phenomenon of "linkage" in political systems has become the focus of theoretical interest and empirical analysis recently. This is significant, for it is only through an understanding of the interactions, associations, and congruences of system actors that an understanding can be obtained of how and why the system functions as it does and in what respects it is not functioning well. In pursuit of this intellectual interest the concentration has been on "mass-elite" linkages to the neglect, unfortunately, of "inter-elite" linkages, which may be as, if not more, important. The discussion here is primarily concerned with the linkages of certain elite actors in the Dutch system, and an attempt will be made to assess what should be and what is the pattern of such relationships for the historic model of Dutch pluralist democracy, which has been going through a transitional period since 1967. In particular, the "linkage function" of Dutch parliamentary party leaders in their associations with the Dutch bureaucracy will be explored. The observations presented here are based on interviews conducted and taped in 1973 with samples of Dutch higher civil servants and members of Parliament.

The Netherlands was one of nine countries in which a University of Michigan group completed very similar studies of "elite political culture" between 1970 and 1974. Other countries in which the study was completed, using the same basic theory and design were: Sweden, Britain, Italy, Germany, France, United States, Jamaica, Morocco. For a description of the theory and methodology of these studies, see the following articles or papers: Thomas J. Anton et al., "Bureaucrats in Politics: A Profile of the Swedish Administrative

SAMUEL J. ELDERSVELD

General Theoretical Concerns

In attempting to develop a theoretical perspective for the analysis of elite orientations and behavior it is not enough to proceed with general systemic formulations. What is needed also is a set of theoretical propositions that are "country specific," that is, relevant to the political culture and environment of a specific political order. In this regard, we have for a long time noted the importance of *bureaucracies*, calling them as Carl Friedrich does "the core of modern government"[1] and claiming as Gabriel Almond does that they "tend to monopolize outputs."[2] And we have also asserted since 1900 the functional centrality of *political parties*, contending as Avery Leiserson, among others, does that they are "strategically central" to the system.[3] Further, we have recently begun to develop an interesting theory about the interrelationships of these two elite structures in *general systemic terms*. Thus, Fred Riggs, particularly concerned about developing societies, advances some general insights concerning the difficulty in maintaining a proper balance between the bureaucracy and the party leadership, particularly the difficulty of sustaining a "rational-efficient" bureaucracy in a highly power-expansionist and patronage-conscious party-leadership context. He speaks of the "inner tensions and contradictions" of the development

Elite," *Canadian Public Administration*, 1974, pp. 627–51; Robert D. Putnam, "The Political Attitudes of Senior Civil Servants in Western Europe: A Preliminary Report" (1972 Annual Meeting of the American Political Science Association); Joel D. Aberbach et al., "Exploring Elite Political Attitudes: Some Methodological Lessons" (1974 Annual Meeting of the Midwest Political Science Association); S. J. Eldersveld et al., "Elite Perceptions of the Political Process in the Netherlands—Looked at in Comparative Perspective" (ninth World Congress, 1973, International Political Science Association). The Putnam and Eldersveld papers are published in Mattei Dogan, ed., *The Mandarins of Western Europe —the Political Role of Top Civil Servants* (New York: Wiley, Sage Publications, 1975).

For the Dutch project I am particularly indebted to my two coinvestigators, Jan Kooiman, formerly of the University of Leiden and now holding a new chair at the Graduate School of Management at Delft, and Sonja Hubee-Boonzaaijer, formerly of the University of Leiden.

The Dutch study was based on interviews with seventy-five civil servants at the second and third levels below the minister; we also included a one-third sample (fifty) of the lower house of the Dutch Parliament.

1. *Man and His Government* (New York: McGraw-Hill, 1963), p. 464.
2. Gabriel Almond and G. Bingham Powell, Jr., *Comparative Politics—A Developmental Approach* (Boston: Little, Brown, 1966), p. 153.
3. *Parties and Politics* (New York: Knopf, 1958), p. 35.

process in such societies.[4] It might be argued, given the recent revelations of presumably "advanced" societies (note especially Watergate), that such "tensions and contradictions" are found in "modern" societies also.

These general theoretical perspectives are valuable. But the functional roles of elites and the linkage patterns of the different elite actors (as well as mass-elite relationships) must be operationalized and visualized in the context of the specific system, with its own traditions and political practices, its own needs for governance, and its own apparatus and procedures for elite interaction and decision. The key questions for each society are: What types of orientations and behavior by what actors (in this case, elite actors) and what interaction patterns by these actors are important if the system is to maintain or achieve stability or if it is to change (incrementally or radically)? This requires an assessment of what actors are relevant to system performance and what cognitions, beliefs, values, and actions are central to comprehending that system.

The Classical Model of the Dutch Political System

The Netherlands is of great interest in this context. It illustrates well the need for such "country-specific" theory and also the problems resulting from an attempt to specify theory and to test it. The Netherlands system is presumably one where certain sets of beliefs and actions by different elites have been crucial for system maintenance. The Dutch system has been classified as a "consociational democracy," in the typology developed by Arend Lijphart and applied by other scholars also to the Belgian and Swiss systems as well as to other countries.[5] Val Lorwin characterizes these societies as "segmental pluralism," defined as "the organization of social movements . . . along the lines of

4. *Administration in Developing Countries* (Boston: Houghton Mifflin, 1964), p. 237.

5. Arend Lijphart, "Typologies of Democratic Systems," *Comparative Political Studies*, no. 1 (1968), pp. 3–44. Hans Daalder has also written at length on the Dutch system. See particularly his disagreement with Lijphart on grounds of historical interpretation, in his "On Building Consociational Nations: The Cases of the Netherlands and Switzerland," *International Social Science Journal* 23, no. 3 (1971): 355–70. The author is indebted to both Arend Lijphart and Hans Daalder, as well as Jan Kooiman, for their insights into developments in the Dutch system, which led to the present formulation for this paper. These gentlemen are not responsible, however, for the ideas expressed here.

159

religious and ideological cleavages."[6] The characteristics of the consociational system are well known. It is a system in which there are clearly defined and separate subcultures across whose boundaries social and political intercourse is negligible and within which subcultures there is high internal cohesion and deference of rank and file to subcultural leadership. No subculture has a majority, and the system, in fact, rests on the assumption of a multiple balance of power among several subgroups that are relatively equal in size. Within each subculture there is a political party, encapsulated by the subculture as well as a manifestation of it, just as there is also found within each subculture other groups— religious, labor union, educational, social, welfare, and other societies —contained by the subculture and supported almost exclusively by individuals born into, and ideologically committed to, the social system and belief system of the subculture. In ideal-typical terms one finds a highly compartmentalized and pluralized social and political system at the infrastructure level.

What should such a consociational system look like at the elite level? Theorists of the Dutch system, such as Lijphart and Daalder, have been fairly precise in their specifications of the requirements of the system. Elite behavior must be "joint," "coalescent," "accommodationist." In the Netherlands, according to a system theorist like Lijphart, this means specifically that elites at the apex of the system must accept the following principles[7] for governing the system:

1. The governing elite structure must include representatives of the major subcultures; for example, cabinets should be inclusive, if not "grand," coalitions.
2. Mutual veto rights for the representatives of subcultures—something similar to Calhoun's doctrine of concurrent majority—are recognized.
3. Proportionality is necessary in the elections to legislatures, in civil service appointments, in cabinets, and in the allocation of public resources.
4. A coalition formation bargaining process takes place *after* the election

---

6. Val Lorwin, "Segmental Pluralism: Ideological Cleavages and Political Cohesion in the Smaller European Democracies," *Comparative Politics* 3, no. 2 (January 1971): 141–75.

7. See particularly Arend Lijphart, *The Politics of Accommodation: Pluralism and Democracy in the Netherlands* (Berkeley: University of California Press, 1968); also his "Consociational Democracy," *World Politics* 21 (1968–69): 207–25.

and is not influenced by actions (promises, threats, maneuvers) *before* the election.

5. "Accommodationist" attitudes and behavior are expected for elites, attitudes "transcending cleavages," emphasizing "joining in a common effort," recognizing divergent subcultural interests, and strong commitments to making the system work.

Thus at the elite level the consociational model deals directly with the problem of linkage between elites representative of the different subcultures. Furthermore, different linkage tasks are implied for different elite roles: The member of Parliament and the higher civil servant each has his own way of facilitating the accommodationism of the consociational system.

Theoretical Expectations About the Dutch Member of Parliament

The role of the Dutch member of Parliament in this system has never been as precisely specified as the role of the cabinet member, but to fit the model of the consociational system the M.P. should not be primarily engaged in challenging the right of the cabinet to govern. Theoretically, M.P.'s would be partly representatives of subcultures in legislative matters, but because of the deference to leaders, they would be more "Burkean" than "delegates" in role expectations. They would be legislators in the sense of reviewing government proposals, initiating legislation, scrutinizing the budget and approving it, debating policy at length if they want to, and in the last analysis approving or disapproving cabinet proposals. But they would not be involved in the final stages of problem solving, in the critical bargaining decisions among subcultural leaders. That critical problem-solving process is eventually the prerogative of the grand coalition in the cabinet (none of whose members can sit in the Parliament). Yet most of the preliminary groundwork and preparatory or anticipatory discussions must take place in the interactions of party leaders in Parliament. M.P.'s have important links to the public, interest groups, and the bureaucracy, but in the Dutch system they are not "the government." Nevertheless, their perspectives toward the system and the decision-making rules of the system and the roles of other actors in that system are crucial. For one must not forget that defections by parliamentary party leaders in support of the cabinet can bring down the government. This indeed has happened. It underlines the

161

important intermediary role of M.P.'s as critical for the accommodationist model.

Theoretical Expectations About the Dutch Higher Civil Servant

What image should one have of the bureaucracy in a consociational system? Not much has been written on this subject. One could hypothesize either a very politicized bureaucracy or one that is depoliticized. The latter construct, that of a "depoliticized bureaucracy" but yet one that reflects certain characteristics of the consociational system, is preferable and logically most defensible in such a society.[8] One major expectation would be that the bureaucracy would not perceive itself as central to the resolution of political conflict. Its function should not be that of political bargaining. It would be aware that certain problems are clearly "political" and others "administrative," that politics is conflict, and that conflicts are resolved by political elites at the apex of the system. As Daalder has pointed out, the Dutch bureaucracy historically was "of modest size" and was not a "central bureaucracy" playing a leading role in the system.[9] In addition to perceiving its role as not one of potential conflict resolution, the bureaucracy should also reflect the irrelevance of partisanship in its actions and performance. One can well expect that civil servants will come from the cultural and political subcultures, in roughly equal proportions to the strength of these subcultures in the population. There may be some imbalance if particular subcultural groups (the socialists, for example) cannot meet the educational qualifications for entrance into the civil service. But since there is no discrimination and rough proportionality is the rule, one should not find the career civil service monopolized, "colonized," or dominated by one or two subcultures. Bureaucrats should not act as partisan advocates. Nor should there be any evidence that the political parties exploit the bureaucracy for their own advantage. Yet the bureaucracy, as Daalder puts it, can function as "points of brokerage between highly differentiated subgroups of society."[10]

Further, civil servants should support system goals as defined by politicians and work equally well with whatever government (and in their immediate administrative life with whatever minister) is in office. It

8. Conversations the author has had with both Arend Lijphart and Hans Daalder reinforce this preference.
9. "On Building Consociational Nations," op. cit., pp. 358–60.
10. Ibid., p. 360.

is essential that civil servants perceive their roles and that of M.P.'s and other party leaders correctly, for the development of incongruence in system perspectives or what Shils in another context calls "the oppositional mentality" would be hazardous to the system. If hostility to politicians as conflict resolvers emerged or if the bureaucracy reflected an ideological polarization in the system—a locus of conservatism, for example, in contrast to political elite liberalism elsewhere in the system—the consequences for the consociational system could be serious.

These are then the theoretical prescriptions, admittedly tentative and speculative, for elite orientations and behavior in the classical Dutch consociational system. The following characteristics can be expected:

1. Party leaders in the Parliaments who reveal "accommodationist" perspectives but do not challenge the "coalescent" behavior of the cabinet too frequently.
2. A "depoliticized" cadre of top civil servants who reflect the subgroup structure of the system but engage in administrative decision making immune from subcultural and partisan conflict, clearly aware of the nature and function of conflict in the consociational system and their own neutral role, as well as the government's critical role, in conflict resolution.
3. Patterns of linkage between civil servants and M.P.'s as well as between these elites and other elites (as, for example, interest-group representatives), which are functional to the success of the consociational system.

Revision of the Classic Consociational Model in the Netherlands

The classic Dutch model leading to the above derivations is, in the opinion of recent observers, undergoing significant modifications. Lijphart is now arguing the "breakdown of the politics of accommodation."[11] Lorwin speaks of the "decline of segmented pluralism."[12] The explanations for these developments and the evidence that they are occurring (and to Lijphart the breaking point was 1967) are complex. Suffice it to say here that the evidence is impressive that social and political cleavages between the blocs are much less sharp and that leaders seem to be modifying certain rules of the game (particularly with reference to

11. In the second edition of *The Politics of Accommodation*, 1975, chap. 10.
12. Ibid., pp. 163–72.

163

the practice of proportionality and postelection bargaining in cabinet formations). The public seems much less deferential and also more supportive of system change.[13] If this is so and the Dutch system is in a period of transitional pluralism, the expectations about elite behavior in such a system undergoing transition become difficult. In a state of operational uncertainty, however, the following findings about elite behavior become perhaps of greater relevance and may lead to the discovery of the directions in which the Dutch system is moving.

Purposes of Analysis

This analysis of the Dutch M.P. and civil servant was undertaken to determine whether they do indeed reveal the perspectives that the classic Dutch model implies. Is there convergence and mutual acceptance of the "accommodationist" perspectives as the model predicts? And, above all, do elites, as they interact with each other, seem to communicate these perspectives? What is particularly important is the extent to which party elites and civil servants, as they associate together, tend to influence the orientations of each other to the system. The model *assumes* linkage that is functional to system stability. But it may be asked, as elites are linked to each other, whether a common elite political culture *does* emerge, or does such contact become dysfunctional and lead to dissensus and thus to system instability? This, in a sense, is the major query to be answered here: Are party elites (M.P.'s in Parliament) in contact with other elites (such as bureaucrats), and what is the relevance of this contact for system perspectives, for themselves as well as for civil servants? Related to this is the question of what *other* elites M.P.'s and civil servants are in contact with, and what the consequences of such inter-elite contacts are for system orientation. These questions cannot be answered conclusively, but perhaps the data can begin to shed some light on these problems.

Comparison of Social Backgrounds

The first way to approach "linkage" (and thus, "consociation") is to discover whether different elite sets share common backgrounds. In the Dutch case it is also important to note the proportionate representation

13. For a review of some of this evidence see Lorwin, op. cit., pp. 163–72.

TABLE 7.1.   Social Backgrounds of M.P.'s and Civil Servants (in percent)

	M.P.'s	CS
Age		
36 and under	18	0
37–46	36	13
47–56	36	41
57–66	9	44
67 and older	0	1
Education		
University	57	85
Law	23	38
Economics	14	23
Natural science	7	16
Theology	5	0
Other	9	8
No university education	43	15
Occupational Class Status (based on father's occupation)		
1–Highest	27	35
2	18	24
3	14	26
4	32	11
5–6	9	4
Percent who were "laborers"	20	11

of social groups among the elites. As table 7.1 shows, there are considerable differences in certain social characteristics of these two elite groups. The civil servants are much older than the M.P.'s—54 percent of the M.P.'s are forty-six and under, but only 13 percent of the civil servants are. Far fewer of the M.P.'s have had a university education, whereas almost all (85 percent) of the civil servants have gone to the university (a finding that holds for all the other European communities in which this study was undertaken).

There are certain parallels in social background also, however. Both elite groups come predominantly from the higher prestige occupational groups (60 percent of M.P.'s and 85 percent of the civil servants), few of them had fathers with manual-labor backgrounds, and those who did go to universities were inclined to specialize in a variety of fields but concentrated in three disciplines particularly: law, economics, and natural science. One gets the clear impression from these data that there is a diversity of intellectual interests in each elite group. Nevertheless, the M.P. is clearly younger, less well educated, and probably comes from more humble class origins. In "linkage" terms this is highly suggestive not only of certain overlaps in social experience but also of possibly serious incongruence and imbalance: two socially unrepresentative elite groups in relation to the public, but also two elite groups by no means congruent in social backgrounds. Although interesting, this by itself reveals little about "linkage." It describes, however, the parameters within which elite consensus (or conflict) can develop.

Subcultural Group Representation Among Elites

The principle of "proportionality" has in the past been central to the Dutch consociational system. The proportional-representation election system permits all groups access to the Parliament and comes as close as possible to a perfect arithmetical translation of votes into seats. In addition, as Lijphart has argued, there is the expectation of rough proportionality in the bureaucracy and the basic assumption that there will be no discrimination against the subcultures in the recruitment of career personnel. The question is to what extent is this principle adhered to and how much congruence is there, therefore, in the subcultural and partisan complexion of the Parliament and the civil service? Even though Dutch civil servants are presumably nonpartisan, when queried as to their religion and party, three-fourths of them had a partisan affiliation and willingly identified their preference. And 70 percent revealed their religious preference.

According to the 1971 census, 22.5 percent of the population did not indicate a church affiliation (compared with 18.4 percent in 1960). Civil servants tend to be more religious than M.P.'s and are about as affiliative with churches as the public. But Catholics are still less represented among civil servants than one might expect if one looks at their proportion among M.P.'s and the population.

A considerable coincidence in partisan backgrounds existed for M.P.'s and civil servants (table 7.2). Nine parties had supporters among the civil-servant sample (compared with fourteen in the Parliament). True, some of the smaller parties (Communists, Farmers, Political Reformed, Reformed Political League, and a new, small Catholic splinter party) were not represented in the civil-servant sample. But

TABLE 7.2. "Proportionality": The Representation of Subcultures Among Dutch Elites (in percent)

	M.P.'s[a]	Civil Servants[b]	Population (1970)
Religious Affiliation[c]			
Catholic	30	20	35
Hervormd	18	31	28
Gereformeerd	7	8	14
Other	2	12	4
None (or N.A.)	43	29	19
			1972 Vote for the Lower House
Party Affiliation			
Left			
PSP (Pacifist Socialist)	1.3	1.8	1.5
PPR (Left Radicals)	4.7	1.8	4.8
PVDA (Left Labor)	28.7	23.6	27.3
D '66 (Democrats 1966)	4.0	3.6	4.2
Center-Right			
DS '70 (Democratic Socialists 1970)	4.0	7.3	4.1
KVP (Catholic Peoples)	18.0	18.2	17.7
CHU (Christian Historical Union)	4.7	7.3	4.8
ARP (Anti-Revolutionary Party)	9.3	1.8	8.8
VVD (People's Party for Freedom and Democracy)	14.7	34.5	14.4
Other parties	10.6	—	12.4

a. The M.P. data are the actual proportion of seats held by each party in the lower house.

b. The CS party affiliation data are based on those who expressed a party preference. In our sample 25.7 percent had no party preference.

c. Religious percentages come from S. B. Wolenitz, Canadian Political Science Association Paper, 1973. Hervormd is a "liberal" Protestant sect; Gereformeered is a "fundamentalist" Protestant sect.

these parties were minor in percentage of popular support. And given the presumably nonpurposive recruitment of administrators, the presence of identifiers from nine parties is impressive. Further, although there are instances where party strength in the Civil Service is at some variance if compared with that in the Parliament, the representation of parties is reasonably satisfactory. The greatest "overrepresentation" is of those from the Hervormd religious persuasion and supporters of the Liberal (VVD) party. The latter reveals the most overrepresentation in the Civil Service. The Catholic party supporters seem to be evenly represented, the Socialists only slightly underrepresented, and the Protestants some-what underrepresented. One can perhaps summarize the incongruence in social representation of elites in the following way:

	M.P.'s	*Civil Servants*
The Big Five (the five major parties)	75%	63%
Conservative parties	51	51
Coalition parties	65	36

Keeping in mind the fact that 25 percent of the civil servants revealed no party affiliation, the above comparisons are highly suggestive. Almost one-fourth of the higher civil servants are of liberal partisan persuasion and about 50 percent are of conservative persuasion (see table 7.2). This means that the current coalition, heavily Left in its ideology and led by a Socialist prime minister, is considerably more "liberal" in its parliamentary representation than in its civil-servant complexion. Whether this is a significant disjunction depends on the perspectives and attitudes of these elites.

System Orientations of Parliamentary and Civil-Servant Elites

The important questions here are to what extent do these elites demon-strate "accommodationist" attitudes, and are their attitudes highly consensual or conflictual? Table 7.3 presents the relevant evidence from this first analysis of the data based on the responses to short-answer items.

What stands out in these data is that Dutch elites are very worried about conflict and polarization and are very supportive of political compromise. Thus 76 percent of the M.P.'s and 93 percent of the civil servants are in favor of compromise. On the other hand, these elites are quite aware of the "political" character of the decision-making

TABLE 7.3. Differential Perceptions of System Roles and Processes by Dutch Elites (in percent)

	Civil Servants	M.P.'s
Attitudes		
Social conflicts not necessarily functional to progress	69	48
Extremism should be avoided in political controversy	82	52
Clash of interest groups is harmful	57	38
Parties often exacerbate conflict	74	50
Compromise with political adversaries is not dangerous	93	76
Citizens have a perfect right to exert pressure for legislation	79	88
Recognition that "political factors" are as important or more important than "technical factors" in policymaking	68	87
Resent interference of politicians in affairs of civil servants	17	—
Resent interference of civil servants in affairs of politicians	—	22
Feels M.P.'s should have "some" or "great" influence in policy decisions	96	100
Role Perceptions (perceived role—feel the actor should have "considerable influence" in system)		
Cabinet ministers	83	41
High civil servants	65	52
M.P. policy specialists	87	91
Party organization leaders	27	48
Churches	28	16
Employer organizations	31	26
Trade unions	34	52

process. They do not feel that technocrats should take over the political process. Only 32 percent of the civil servants see "technical factors" as more important than "political factors." Further, there is very little evidence of hostility and resentment between civil servants and politicians. For example, only 17 percent of the civil servants resent the interference of politicians (in Italy it is 79 percent, in Germany 47 percent, and in Sweden 37 percent). Thus, there is strong evidence here that both elite groups take "accommodationist" orientations. One must understand, however, that although Dutch civil servants are anxious about conflict and do not feel it is necessary or functional, they nevertheless recognize the right of citizens to exert pressure on governmental leaders. In a sense one can interpret these data as quite in accord with the model of a system of accommodation. Civil servants accept the goals of the system (68 percent favor state intervention in social and economic affairs, compared with 81 percent of the M.P.'s in the sample), recognize the need for political compromise, see the need for conflict to be resolved and for citizen pressure to be heard, and are highly cognizant of the role of the politician, such as the M.P., in the system.

There is some disagreement on the role of certain actors in the system. Thus cabinet ministers should have a major decisional role in the view of 83 percent of the civil servants, but only 41 percent of the M.P.'s agree. And national party organization leaders should have a major role in the opinion of 48 percent of the M.P.'s, but only 27 percent of the civil servants agree. But these differences pale into relative insignificance when one notes the congruences in "desired role" perceptions of a variety of actors (table 7.3). Above all, civil servants and M.P.'s both agree—at the 90 percent plus level—that M.P.'s should have a major role in governmental decision making. This is a remarkable convergence of role expectations and suggests great political elite consensus in the Netherlands in system orientations, although M.P.'s demean the system role of ministers.

What emerges here then is that Dutch elites, administrative as well as political, are high in support of system goals, are conflict conscious (and in the case of a majority of civil servants are opposed to too much conflict and extremist manifestations of conflict), see problem solving as highly "political," are clientelistic in their views of the system, and accept the right of citizens to press for legislation. The differences between civil servants and M.P.'s indicate a much more consistent picture of conflict anxiety among civil servants and a small minority of civil servants who oppose politicians. But basically there is strong congruence suggestive of socialization into, and support for, the consociational model.

Although in aggregate terms this is the picture of elite congruence that emerges, more evidence of dissensus appears when differences by party preference are examined (table 7.4). This occurs in two patterns: (1) when partitioned by party, sharp differences among civil servants occur and also, of course, for M.P.'s; (2) sizable differences also occur between civil servants and M.P.'s who have the same partisan orientations. The illustrations of this in table 7.4 are suggestive and by no means

170

TABLE 7.4. Elite Dissensus by Party Within Dutch Elite Structures (in percent)

		All Left Parties	Center and Right Parties	PVDA (Labor Party)	VVD (Right of Center Liberal Party)
Dissensus Within Civil Servant					
or Parliamentary Elites					
Fears state intervention					
in economic and social	CS	6	46	8	72
spheres	MP	5	33	6	(75)
Clash of interest groups					
endangers the welfare	CS	38	66	33	72
of the country	MP	26	50	19	(75)
Politics should deal with					
short-run, rather than	CS	7	31	8	46
long-range, plans	MP	5	33	6	25
Dissensus Between Elite					
Structures (Civil Servants vs.					
M.P.'s)					
The civil service, rather					
than parties or Parlia-					
ment, guarantees satis-	CS	38	51	25	50
factory public policy	MP	9	0	13	0
Political parties	CS	63	71	50	83
exacerbate conflict	MP	30	78	25	100
Governmental efficiency					
is more important than	CS	56	69	58	67
program	MP	14	39	19	50

constitute all the evidence of dissensus. They indicate that elites who identify with, or are representative of, more conservative parties are, when contrasted to those affiliated with the parties on the Left, more opposed to state interventionist policies, much more concerned about group conflict, and less interested in long-range policy planning. There is then a conceivable polarization by party among elites on certain attitudes toward the system.

There are also attitude conflicts between civil servants an M.P.'s within the same party, however. The persistently more conservative orientations of civil servants are manifest concerning the role of parties, the harmfulness of political conflict, the importance of efficiency versus program, and so on. Labor (PVDA) civil servants disagree just as fundamentally with their M.P.'s as do the Liberal (VVD) civil servants with their VVD M.P.'s over the role of the Civil Service in the Dutch system. On certain matters it appears that bureaucrats are bureaucrats irrespective of party affiliation; on other matters they follow party convictions.

One should be cautious about these data. To conclude that significant dissensus by partisan commitment has invaded the top bureaucracy in the Netherlands is tempting but premature. It is true the evidence here indicates that on certain critical attitudes about the system Dutch civil servants differ, and by party. How central these attitudes are to them and whether they act upon them, or whether their behavior is influenced by them, is another matter. If they continue to function as a politically neutral and depoliticized elite sector despite these differences of opinion there is no threat of divisive polarization. Further, one should not forget that on certain key dimensions civil servants are very like-minded, if not completely united, despite political-party preference. Examples are the following:

	Percent of Civil Servants Identifying With	
	PVDA (Labor Party)	VVD (Right of Center Liberal Party)
Feel political compromise is dangerous	0	11
Feel citizens have the right to exert pressure	58	72
Worry about the interference of politicians in Civil Service affairs	33	17
Approve clientele relationships between a ministry and affected groups	83	83

Congruence of civil servants is high on certain major orientations, therefore, and these may be of overriding importance. On these attitudes the M.P.'s also reveal remarkably high congruence. Although ideological matters and concerns about the role of conflict in the system do divide elites, the respect of M.P.'s for civil servants, and vice versa, the absence of a pervading "oppositional mentality," a commitment to the role of citizens, and an overwhelming belief in compromise as necessary and beneficial for the system are perceptions and beliefs that are widely shared and may still be major factors in the stability of the system.

The Relevance of Political Communication for Elite Attitudes

One of the most important types of linkage in a system is that of contacts among the elite actors in the system. What the extent and pattern of that interaction is, in formal as well as in informal contexts, may be critical for understanding system performance. The first question is, do M.P.'s and high civil servants maintain contact with each other and with other actors in the Dutch system?

The data on elite contacts reveal for M.P.'s the importance of party organization leaders in their communication network—64 percent see them at least weekly. And the Dutch M.P. is also citizen oriented. On the other hand, the M.P. does not apparently neglect his associations with interest-group representatives, ministers and high civil servants—from 60 to 80 percent see these elites regularly (table 7.5).

There is an interesting difference in M.P. contacts by party "ideology," with M.P.'s from Left parties having less frequent contacts with civil servants than do M.P.'s from Center and Right parties—a sizable difference of almost 30 percent (table 7.5). Perhaps this is not surprising given the finding that no more than 23 percent of the total sample of civil servants supported parties of the Left, whereas 51 percent supported Center and Right parties (and 26 percent had no affiliation). One might argue that it also fits with the finding in table 7.6 that only 6 percent of the civil servants of Left party affiliation had contact with the M.P.'s.

A curious disjunction in the data appears at this point. M.P.'s report a higher frequency of regular contact with civil servants than civil servants do with M.P.'s (31 percent compared with 1 percent, or 66 percent for M.P.'s if all "regular" contacts are included, compared with 16 percent for civil servants). This is explicable, of course, if one realizes that the level of the bureaucracy that the M.P.'s may be referencing (either the higher, ministerial, or lower, civil servant, level) may be different from the level of the sample. Higher civil servants in the sample, nevertheless, report limited contact with M.P.'s and national party leaders, although they are much more in contact with interest-group

173

TABLE 7.5.   The Frequency of Elite Contacts in the Netherlands (in percent)

	Weekly or More Frequently	Regularly but Less Than Weekly	Irregularly or Seldom
Contacts by M.P.'s with			
Ministers	49	29	22
High civil servants	31	35	35
National interest groups	31	50	19
National party leaders	64	26	10
Citizens	71	17	12
Contacts of High Civil Servants with			
Ministers (own department)	45	28	26
Other high civil servants	55	36	9
Representatives of organizations active in the department's work or area	24	40	35
National party leaders	1	3	96
Citizens	13	16	71
Individual M.P.'s	1	15	84

NOTE: Each percent is the proportion of each elite group that is in contact with other actors.

TABLE 7.6.   The Role of Party Affiliation in Elite Contacts (in percent)

	Often	Less Often	Seldom or Never	N
Contact of Members of Parliament with Civil Servants				
M.P.'s of Left parties	39	39	22	23
M.P.'s of Center and Right parties	67	22	11	18
Contact of High Civil Servants with Members of Parliament				
Those who affiliate with Left parties	0	6	94	16
Those who affiliate with Center or Right parties	0	20	80	35
Those who have no party affiliation	6	18	76	17

representatives. In one sense this accords with the expectations for the Dutch model of a "depoliticized bureaucracy." Civil servants interact primarily with other civil servants and with clientele group leaders, with whom they are performing a brokerage function. Yet, one wonders at the consequences of such limited contact of higher civil servants with party leaders. Does this lead, in those who are isolated, to less acceptance of accommodationist perspectives or is there a type of congruence by elites despite minimal communication, a type of "autonomous congruence"? This key question leads to the analysis of the consequences of inter-elite contacts as well as of inter-elite nonassociation.

The Effects of Elite Linkages on Elite Perspectives

Having looked at the pattern of contacts, the possible consequences of exposure of elites to each other can now be examined. The two main questions here are:

1. Does inter-elite contact lead to a convergence in perspectives, that is, do bureaucrats in contact with M.P.'s reveal a tendency to adopt M.P. views of the system (or vice versa)?
2. Is the change in perspectives that occurs as a result of communication "functional" to system performance, that is, in this case, supportive of the Dutch consociational model?

The data presented here can only be suggestive because the analysis of the Dutch data from this theoretical vantage point is still in the early stages.

It is clear from the data, first, that a consistent pattern of differences is found for those bureaucrats who are in contact with M.P.'s and for those who are isolated from parliamentary leaders (table 7.7). Those relatively few civil servants who are in weekly contact with M.P.'s are clearly more "politicized" or, to put it differently, are more inclined to accept the position of the M.P. in their images of the political process. Thus, civil servants with little or no contact with M.P.'s are more likely to emphasize "technical" over "political" considerations (34 to 17 percent), see parties as exacerbating conflict needlessly (40 to 25 percent), are more opposed to conflict, are more worried about interest-group clashes, and so on. This is a fascinating finding in its own right—that bureaucratic elites may be influenced by the orientations of political elites. "May" is used because no causal relationship has been established,

TABLE 7.7. Orientations of Bureaucrats by Frequency of Contact with M.P.'s (in percent)

Civil Servant Orientation (or Attitude)	Civil Servant Contact Patterns with M.P.'s	
	Interactors (N = 12)	Isolates (N = 60)
Technical considerations more important than political factors ($\%$ who agree)	17	34
See life in zero-sum terms ($\%$ who agree)	17	40
Parties uselessly exacerbate conflicts ($\%$ who agree without reservations)	25	40
Social conflicts are functional to the achievement of progress ($\%$ who agree)	42	29
To compromise with political adversaries is dangerous ($\%$ who agree)	0	8
In political controversies, extreme positions should be avoided ($\%$ who agree)	92	80
Welfare of the country is endangered by the clash of special-interest groups ($\%$ who agree without reservations)	8	24
The interference of politicians with the work of civil servants is worrisome ($\%$ who agree)	8	19
Politics is "the art of the possible" and should focus on short-run plans ($\%$ who agree)	33	21
Clientele relations between a ministry and the group most affected by it are improper ($\%$ who agree)	0	17
Basically, it is not the parties and Parliament but the civil service that guarantees satisfactory public policy ($\%$ who agree without reservation)	8	5

only a linkage, or association. It is particularly to be noted, in terms of the Dutch accommodationist model, that civil servants in frequent contact with M.P.'s are less worried about compromise, are less interested in advocating extremist positions, and are much less likely to see the political process in zero-sum terms. They are also much less likely to be critical of, or hostile to, politicians. To test this, an Index of Tolerance of Politics, based on six agree-disagree items, was developed. Significant difference by frequency of contact was observed:

	Civil Servants	
	Interact with M.P.'s	Isolated from M.P.'s
Percent intolerant	25	46
Mean score (range was from 0 to 8, zero for most intolerant)	5.8	4.8

Thus the level of hostility seems to be "reduced" by contact or "associated with" inter-elite contact.

A final point should be noted here. Civil servants not in touch with M.P.'s (and the great majority say they are not) are nevertheless very inclined to give responses indicative of support for the consociational model. Thus, 66 percent of the "isolates" are willing to concede that political factors are more important than technical considerations in policymaking, 29 percent see social conflict as functional, 80 percent want to avoid extreme positions, and so on. Obviously, other types of socialization experiences, or other factors, are basic to explaining these functional perspectives.

When the analysis is turned around to ask to what extent it appears that M.P. views are altered as the result of contact with bureaucrats, the obverse set of findings is, to some extent, seen (table 7.8). Those M.P.'s who interact frequently with bureaucrats are somewhat more inclined to emphasize "technical" over "political" considerations (19 to 0 percent) and to oppose party conflict (19 to 10 percent). But on certain crucial orientations for the Dutch accommodationist model, the relevance for the system of M.P. contact with bureaucrats is more ambiguous. Thus, M.P.'s in frequent contact with bureaucrats are more likely to avoid extremes (57 percent) and less likely to find compromise dangerous

TABLE 7.8. Orientations of M.P.'s by Frequency of Contact with Bureaucrats (in percent)

M.P. Orientation (or Attitude) (Refer to table 7.7 for more complete description of item)	M.P. Contact Patterns with Civil Servants	
	Constant Interactors (N=21)	Less Frequent Interactors (N=20)
Technical over political	19	0
Zero-sum	43	20
Party conflict exacerbation	19	10
Social conflict functional	48	55
Compromise dangerous	10	35
Avoid extreme positions	57	40
Vs. clash of interest groups	14	10
Worried about interference of bureaucrats	24	15
Politics "art of the possible"	24	10
Clientele relations of ministry improper	10	5
Civil service preferred to parties/Parliament	0	0

(10 percent), whereas those less frequently exposed to bureaucrats are less likely to desire avoidance of extremes (40 percent) and more likely to find compromise dangerous (35 percent). The evidence does not, therefore, suggest that bureaucratic "influence" over M.P.'s as a result of communication contacts is very strong or runs counter to the requisites of the consociational system.

One way to evaluate these findings in systemic terms is by use of a set of fourfold tables, using the above data but computing percentages for the total bureaucratic or M.P. group. If we examine tables 7.9 and 7.10 the comprehensive picture of bureaucratic orientations in relation to inter-elite linkages emerges. And the paradox in the Dutch elite context begins to unfold. Although more than half (55 percent) of Dutch higher civil servants are isolated from elite contacts *and* take a "modern" view on the importance of technical over political consideration in policy-making, more than half (59 percent) are isolated *and* take a "classical view" on the role of conflict in the system. True, earlier findings indicated that isolates are more concerned about conflict than are interactors. Nevertheless, the Dutch higher bureaucracy is obviously an elite set that

TABLE 7.9. Total Distribution of Dutch Civil Servants in "Classical" and "Modern" Orientations: The Relevance of Technical or Political Factors in Decision Making

	Dutch Civil Servants (in percent)	
	Interactors with M.P.'s	Isolates from M.P.'s
"Classical view":		
Technical factors take precedence over political	3	28
"Modern view":		
Political factors take precedence over technical	14	55
	Total = 100%	

TABLE 7.10. Total Distribution of Dutch Civil Servants on "Classical" and "Modern" Orientations: The Question of the Function of Social and Political Conflict in the System

	Dutch Civil Servants (in percent)	
	Interactors with M.P.'s	Isolates from M.P.'s
"Classical view":		
Feel conflict is not functional	10	59
"Modern view":		
Feel conflict is functional	7	24
	Total = 100%	

is by and large isolated from parliamentary leadership contact *and* also reflects divergent views concerning the "proper" functioning of the Dutch system. The saving grace of the bureaucracy in one sense is that despite the absence of political elite contact it has not developed deep-seated hostility to politicians, has not overexpanded its own conception of the role of the bureaucrat, and is willing to argue for moderation and compromise in the system. But on the other hand, the isolates

179

particularly see conflict as dysfunctional and parties as conflict-arousing (61 percent of the civil-servant sample are isolates who are worried about parties' "uselessly exacerbating conflict"). If more contact between civil servants and M.P.'s could occur, the data suggest that these orientations might be considerably changed.

Concluding Observations

To summarize the relevance of these data at this stage of investigation is difficult. It appears that for civil servants the following observations may be tenable:

1. The general patterns of civil-servant and M.P. orientations are supportive of key elements of the consociational democratic system.
2. A minority of civil servants take positions that appear oppositionist to the proper functioning of the Dutch system.
3. Although overall the Dutch elites exhibit high consensus on system orientations, when distinguished by party affiliation significant dissensus appears. There is no evidence, however, that these differences in attitudes are central, polarizing, or as yet disruptive of elite accommodationism.
4. Contact of civil servants with M.P.'s is functional to the development of what might be called a more "politicized" and "conflict-acceptance" orientation toward the system.
5. But for sizable proportions of civil servants not exposed to M.P.'s, there is also the acceptance of consociational norms, suggesting "autonomous convergence" and the presence of other learning influences.
6. M.P.'s who report much contact with bureaucrats are generally inclined to be slightly more sympathetic to what might be called "classical" bureaucratic orientations, but the evidence is not consistent on this point. There is also a slight tendency for M.P.'s in contact with civil servants to be more worried about the role of bureaucrats in the system. But on balance among all M.P.'s, irrespective of frequency of civil-servant contact, there is strong support for the accommodationist orientations presumably integral to the Dutch system: necessity and functionality of conflict, role of compromise, the dangers of extremism, the importance of "politicized" approaches to the policy process, and support for parties and interest groups.

In short, there is no clear evidence of a polarization of perspectives or of dysfunctional orientations within elites or between elites. This can be illustrated finally with two other types of data. When asked whether they were worried about "the growing intervention of the state in eco-

nomic and social spheres," 81 percent of the M.P.'s and 68 percent of
the civil servants favored such intervention and did not fear it. The
relevance of elite contact is demonstrated as follows:

	Percent Opposing Intervention	
	Civil Servants	M.P.'s
Frequent interactors with other elites	17	19
Less frequent interactors with, or isolates from, other elites	36	15

Obviously, association of civil servants with M.P.'s "reduced" opposition
to state interventionism (although the reverse was not true). More
important probably is the fact that for M.P.'s the overwhelming majority
did not oppose state policy. The Dutch elite (bureaucratic and political)
is a highly consensual set of leaders on the aims of governmental policy.

A second final measure concerns the extent to which Dutch elites are
"elitist" in their attitudes toward the role of citizens in decision making,
in their right to vote, in the right of groups and individual citizens to
exert pressure and make demands, and so on. A variety of questions
probed inclinations in these respects and combined them into an Index
of Elitism. Dutch leaders revealed a remarkably high level of support
for citizen involvement, and a very high congruence between bureaucrats
and M.P.'s occurred on this index. Thus, for example, 61 percent of the
M.P.'s and 66 percent of the civil servants were not opposed to increasing
the citizen's role in governmental affairs. The relevance of inter-elite
contact for this is suggested by:

	Percent Scoring High on Elitism Index	
	Civil Servants	M.P.'s
Frequent interactors with other elites	17	10
Infrequent interactors with, or isolates from, other elites	25	5
Total	24	7

Although "elitist" tendencies are minimal in these data for Dutch leaders, there appears to be consistent evidence that contact with M.P.'s may indeed be marginally functional to reduction in "elitism" among bureaucrats.

The attempt here has been to present some suggestive evidence from an ongoing analysis of parliamentary and bureaucratic elite data in the Netherlands as to the relevance of elite linkages for the system. Obviously civil servants and M.P.'s are not the only actors in the system, and the relevance of other elite contacts will be assessed subsequently, particularly the relevance of linkage relationships with interest groups, party organizational leaders, and subcultural sector leaders. It is also obvious that causal connections have not been demonstrated here but merely the patterns of orientations that emerge from the association of elites. This is basically a configurationist approach to data. It is important to ask what the meaning of the data is in the context of a theory of how a particular system does function or is supposed to function. The Dutch consociational democracy provided that opportunity. The data suggest that elite linkages constitute one factor among others that may be important in explaining both the viability of Dutch democracy and the possible threats to the system in the orientations of bureaucrats. Further analysis is necessary to discover the processes and patterns of socialization, transmission, and reinforcement of elite orientations supportive of, or antagonistic to, the "politics of accommodation."

8.

Cleavage Crystallization and Party Linkages in Finland, 1900–1918

WILLIAM C. MARTIN AND KAREN HOPKINS

The Meaning and Significance of Cleavage Crystallization

Political scientists tend to assert that the maintenance of democratic processes is hindered by the presence of a strong threat of external domination to a state. Also accepted is the premise that the co-alignment of structural cleavages tends to produce intense internal conflict that makes difficult the sustenance of democratic processes. Thus, when one finds a country where language, ethnic, and socioeconomic groupings are historically coterminous and when one further finds a persistent threat of external domination, one expects *not* to find a stable democratic government. However, the existence of a stable democratic government in Finland for the past half century challenges these generalizations.

Historically, Finland moved from Swedish domination to Russian domination. In the beginning of this century Finland was an autonomous part of the Russian Empire. Its political system was one of representation in the Diet of Estates with the bulk of the population remaining unrepresented and nonparticipant. During the 1905–18 period Finland developed highly effective and inclusive political party organizations, the population became highly mobilized, and a constitutional democracy was established that remains effective to the present day. The theoretically significant fact is that this democracy remained viable despite the continuing threat of Russian domination and despite the co-alignment of internal cleavages based on language, ethnic background, and socioeconomic divisions.

Political development is viewed here as the process by which a social system develops political structures and institutions that allow the system to adapt successfully to the problems generated by heterogeneity, structural conflict, complex organization, and high levels of mobilization. Political development can be seen as resolving certain structural problems: national integration, political participation, legitimacy, and the management of conflict.[1]

Political parties occur everywhere as a part of the political systems of the modern nation-state. Whatever the character of the political system, the political party performs similar functions: the organization of public opinion and its communication to the governmental center, the articulation and aggregation of interests and the legitimation of the political system, and recruitment of political leadership. La Palombara and Weiner suggest that the emergence of political parties is a product of the level of complexity of political systems and/or the idea that political power should involve mass public participation. In modern societies the political party may take on a further function as a symbol of "modernity."[2]

Whatever the function of political parties, however, a fundamental element is that of linking the political public with its interests and goals to the political state with its formulation of policy and maintenance of social order. The political party thus tends to be the prime political agency for linkage in the modern state. This study examines the intricate pattern of linkages of the party system to the Finnish cleavage structure during the period of organization, mobilization, and institutionalization of the Finnish political system, examining in particular the process of cleavage crystallization. "Cleavage crystallization" is defined as the process by which interest and identity cleavages within a society become articulated and organized into political bodies capable of influencing public policy and recruitment of political leadership. Cleavage crystallization thus involves the organization of citizens around social issues, the effective linking of citizens to the political system in which they live, and the estab-

1. Joseph La Palombara and Myron Weiner, eds., *Political Parties and Political Development* (Princeton: Princeton University Press, 1966), and J. P. Nettl, *Political Mobilization* (New York: Basic Books, 1967).

2. Joseph La Palombara and Myron Weiner, "The Origin and Development of Political Parties," ibid., pp. 3–7.

lishment of legitimate mechanisms for citizen participation in political decision making.

Political mobilization and organization reflect the changing alignment among cleavage structures in a society. Stratificational cleavages develop within the context of broad institutional systems or orders. Cleavages are also a function of the more general character of society, for example, rural or urban, agrarian or industrial, relatively stable or transitional. But the cleavage structure of a society does not determine its political or social life. Rather, it establishes the constraints, the limitations and potential, for political development. Cleavages must crystallize into interests and organizations (parties or interest groups) in order to effect political action.[3] Value controversies must become political issues and these issues must be articulated and aggregated by organizations.[4] These structural cleavages in the process of crystallization may develop their distinctive organizations or may co-align to develop organizations based on a number of cleavages.

Pluralistic theory has generally assumed that the crystallization of cross-cutting cleavages tends to promote stable democratic systems, whereas crystallization of fundamental and co-aligned cleavages tends to polarize the political system.[5] The political party system in Finland has been characterized by a high degree of co-alignment of critical cleavages since its very beginning. Furthermore, during the critical period of political development, Finland has been threatened (and in part subjected to) external domination, a situation that traditionally is considered inimical to the establishment and maintenance of democratic government. This study shows how in this instance the *interaction* of these two variables permitted the development of a strong party system, effectively crystallizing existing cleavages and helping to maintain a viable democracy. In order to understand how this pattern of development proved possible, it is necessary to begin with a brief summary of the history of the development of the Finnish party system, a development that began toward the end of the nineteenth century.

3. Seymour M. Lipset and Stein Rokkan, *Party Systems and Voter Alignments: Cross-National Perspectives* (New York: The Free Press, 1967), and Douglas W. Rae and Michael Taylor, *The Analysis of Political Cleavages* (New Haven and London: Yale University Press, 1970).

4. Nettl, op. cit.

5. Rae and Taylor, op. cit., pp. 1–17.

Origins and History of the Finnish Party System

The development of Finland's political parties, and the concomitant crystallization of cleavages in that nation's pattern of political linkages, must be understood within two sets of political conditions: the character of Finland's internal social system and the peculiar pattern of domination of Finland by Russia.

Finland's social structure. At the end of the nineteenth century the Finnish Diet of Estates was probably the only Parliament in Europe in which the medieval division into separately voting Estates or Orders still existed, and it was certainly the only Parliament where division was into four Estates, or Houses: the Nobility, the Clergy, the Burghers, and the Peasantry.[6] Representation in the Diet of Estates was narrow and limited to privileged sectors of the population, but the status dimensions established there were reinforced by distinctions of language and education in the broader society.[7] Major cleavages formed along these status dimensions and tended to co-align and reinforce each other.

By the end of the nineteenth century, the nobility and other gentry formed an almost unified whole—an upper class distinguished from the common people.[8] The former group included independent peasants, and tenant farmers (*torpparit*) and agricultural laborers belonged to the lower group.

Language was a key variable in distinguishing these two status groups. During the nineteenth century, the language of the upper class, with the exception of the clergy, had increasingly become Swedish. Most high status positions were held by those who spoke Swedish; those who spoke Finnish were generally relegated to low status. The Swedish-speaking population was on the whole more affluent, held significant government positions, and composed an educational elite (higher education was usually conducted in Swedish). Furthermore, the estate system was

6. Joseph R. Fisher, *Finland and the Tsars, 1809–1899* (London: Edward Arnold, 1899), p. 134.

7. Martti Noponen notes statistical records that show in 1890 more than 70 percent of the country's population remained outside the body of electors of the Estates Diet with the consequence that political power was concentrated in the hands of a small fraction of the population. *Kansanedustajien sosiaalinen tausta Suomessa* [The social background of Parliament representatives in Finland] (Helsinki: Werner Söderström, 1964), p. 25.

8. Hannu Soikkanen, *Sosialismin tulo Suomeen. Ensimmäisiin yksikamarisen eduskunnan vaaleihin asti* [Socialism's advent to Finland: up to the first elections to the unicameral Parliament] (Helsinki: Werner Söderström, 1961), pp. 1–4.

structured so as to limit effective participation to a minority segment of the population, and the Estates of the Nobility and of the Burghers were generally drawn from the Swedish-speaking population.

At the beginning of this century, Finland began the transition from an agrarian and rural society to a relatively urbanized society with a sizable industrial base. By 1900, some 70 to 80 percent of the population still gained its livelihood from agriculture and forestry, but industry was becoming a more important factor in both the internal and external trade of Finland (primarily the wood industry).[9] The number of industrial workers grew rapidly, tending to concentrate in the cities, and the new economic cleavages that developed tended toward congruence with status (language, estate, education) cleavages.[10] Political organization and mobilization could be expected to reflect the changing alignments among these cleavage structures. The stage was being set for a drama of classes that would last for two generations.

Domination by Russia. In assuming control of Finland from Sweden in 1809, the Russians declared Finland an autonomous grand duchy with its own fundamental law or constitution.[11] In 1886 the right to make legislative motions was restored to the Diet, and in 1906 Finland obtained universal suffrage. Nevertheless, Parliament's authority remained within a very narrow constitutional framework.[12] The governor-general of Finland, directly representing the czar, was chairman of the Senate. Although the Senate conducted the government and was usually composed of Finnish citizens, it remained totally dependent upon the czar. It was neither responsible to the Diet nor did it have any authority based on any constitution.[13] Finland was not a sovereign state.

Controversy over the power of Parliament meant more than the

9. K. O. Alho, *Suomen uudenaikaisen teollisuuden synty ja kehitys 1860–1914* [The rise and development of modern Finnish industry 1860–1914] (Helsinki: Suomen Pankin Taloustieteellinen Tutkimuslaitos, 1949).

10. Carl Erik Knoellinger, *Labor in Finland* (Cambridge: Harvard University Press, 1960).

11. Päiviö Tommila, *La Finlande dans la Politique Européenne en 1809–1815* (Helsinki: La Société Historique de Finlande, 1962), and K. R. Brotherus, *Översikt av statsskickets historiska utveckling i Finland* [Overview of the historical development of the constitution in Finland] (Helsinki: Söderström, 1947).

12. O. Seitkari, "Valtiosääntömme perinteet autonomian ajalta" [Our constitution's heritage from the period of autonomy], *Valtio ja Yhteiskunta* 14 (1954): 25–34.

13. M. G. Schybergson, *Finlands Politiska Historia, 1809–1919* [The political history of Finland, 1809–1919] (Helsinki: Söderström, 1923), pp. 46–47; Brotherus, op. cit., pp. 55–58.

mere limitation of the power of the executive; it meant also the weakening of the power of Russia over Finland. This created a systematic source of dissatisfaction, conflict, and strain, which could only be resolved by total Russification or by separation of Finland from Russia.

The first political parties. Finland's earliest parties evolved in response to the historical development and interplay between these two sets of political conditions. When parties first appeared on the scene, the dominant issues were those arising from the social structure. Attempts to expand and equalize suffrage were frustrated by the language problem and the resultant entrenchment of the Swedish-speaking minority in positions of privilege. The first major political cleavage in Finland was thus between the Finnish Nationalists and the Swedish Nationalists, with the latter in control of the Noble and Burgher estates, the former dominating the Clerical and Peasant estates. The first political parties were organized to demand universal and equal suffrage (which would have meant control of the Diet by the Finnish-speaking group) and were immediately countered by the formation of the Swedish party to defend the privileges and power of the minority. A short-lived Liberal party formed in the early 1880s in an unsuccessful attempt to bridge the language cleavage. These early parties were for the most part groupings in the Diet, but gradually they became important in elections for the Peasant and Burgher estates.

In the 1890s, as Finnish industry began to develop and trade unions and business associations were being organized, political parties began to articulate new interests and issues. The Finnish Nationalists split into the conservative Old Finn and the more liberal and progressive Young Finn parties. The Workers' party was formed in Helsinki in 1899 and became the Social Democratic party in 1903.[14]

But by the end of the century, the issue of relations with Russia was assuming renewed importance in Finland and became the new focus of political organization. At that time efforts to make Finland an integral part of Russia were intensified.[15] Not content with control of the government via the Senate and with an earlier demand for increased use of the Russian language in secondary schools and in the university, the czar

14. Yrjö Sirola, "Sosialidemokratinen puolue" [The Social Democratic party], *Yhteiskunnallinen Käsikirja* (Helsinki: Kansanvalistusseura, 1910), pp. 431–35.
15. Schybergson, op. cit., pp. 260–76, and John H. Wuorinen, *Nationalism in Modern Finland* (New York: Columbia University Press, 1931), pp. 190–203.

issued the Imperial Manifesto of 15 February 1899.[16] The import of the February Manifesto is simply stated: all Finnish matters of imperial interest were hereafter to be dealt with by Russian institutions, and the czar would determine which matters were imperial and which were local and Finnish.

The effect on Finland was profound. Language conflict ceased. A national protest was organized in complete secrecy from the Russians. Within a week a petition was drafted, read from every pulpit in the country, and obtained 522,931 signatures of adult men and women from every parish in the country. On 13 March 1899 a Committee of Five Hundred —one representative for every parish—assembled in Helsinki to take the petition to St. Petersburg. The delegation was refused audience by the czar as were also European delegations protesting the coup d'état. The Russian response was immediate and repressive: sharp restrictions on rights of assembly and freedom of the press, dissolution of the Finnish army, political arrests, the importation of Russian police, reduction of the Senate to an instrument of Russian control, and efforts to exploit internal differences.

As a consequence the whole Finnish population mobilized politically against the Russians. Finnish politics, which had been inward directed and centered on the language split, now became externally directed against the Russian oppression. Resistance generally took two forms: the strategies of the Constitutionalists and of the Compromisers.[17] In the majority, the Constitutionalists, primarily members of the Young Finn party and the Swedish Nationalist party, argued that constitutional rights should not be surrendered and pursued a strategy of passive resistance to all Russian initiatives. The far less militant Compromisers consisted primarily of the Old Finn party. A third strategy proposed by various secret revolutionary organizations urged the dissemination of propaganda and direct action against the Russians and cooperation with revolutionary groups in Russia.[18] Their readiness for action became apparent in 1904 when the governor-general was assassinated

16. Wuorinen, op. cit., pp. 190–92, and Schybergson, op. cit., pp. 263ff.

17. Olavi Borg, *Suomen puolueet ja puolueohjelmat 1880–1964* (Finland's parties and party programs 1880–1964) (Porvoo-Helsinki: Werner Söderström, 1965), p. 21.

18. Wuorinen, op. cit., p. 198, and Konni Zilliacus, *Revolution och kontra-revolution i Ryssland och Finland* [Revolution and counterrevolution in Russia and Finland] (Stockholm: Albert Bonnier, 1912).

—and his assassin became a national hero.[19] In sum, the overall effect of the period of attempted Russification was to raise Finnish national consciousness and to give that consciousness new political form.

The General Strike of 1905. Following the devaluation of czarist authority, a result of the Russian defeat in the Russo-Japanese War and the acts of revolution taking place inside Russia, a General Strike was proclaimed in Helsinki on 30 October 1905.[20] In the Finnish labor movement, the strike was seen as a means of regaining the political rights lost during Russification, as well as an expression of sympathy for Russian comrades. However, because all social classes in Finland favored the restoration of autonomy and political rights, the strike soon spread across the nation. In many parts of the country officials were forced to resign, and the police either joined the strike or were disarmed.

But the newfound unity proved short-lived. Attempts to form a national front composed of Constitutionalists and the workers' movement were unsuccessful.[21] This failure sharpened the cleavage between the two classes: radicalism gained ground among the workers as their belief in the idea of class struggle grew and traditional attitudes of submission to authority no longer prevailed.[22] At the same time, the bourgeois parties became persuaded that the goal of Finnish nationalism, to which they remained committed, could be obtained through peaceful means. As a result of negotiations between the governor-general and the Constitutionalists, the czar issued an Imperial Manifesto on 4 November 1905 repealing the February Manifesto of 1899 and most of the Russification measures related to it.[23]

Political mobilization, 1905–17. After the General Strike of 1905 the stage was set for a radical reform of the electoral system and the Diet.

19. Eino Jutikkala, *A History of Finland*, trans. Paul Sjöblom (New York: Praeger, 1962), p. 239.

20. R. H. Oittinen, *Työväenkysymys ja työväenliike Suomessa* [The labor question and labor movement in Finland] (Helsinki: Tammi, 1954); Jarl von Schoultz, *Bidrag till belysande av Finlands Socialdemokratiska partis historia. Del I: Tiden före representations-reformen år 1906* [Contributions to the illumination of the history of the Finnish Social Democratic party. Part I: the period before the Representation Reform of 1906] (Helsinki: Söderström, 1924), pp. 292–329; Soikkanen, op. cit.

21. Hannes Ryöm, "Vuoden 1905 suurlakko" [The General Strike of 1905], *Sosia-alidemokraattinen Puolue 25 Vuotta* (Helsinki: Sosialidemokraattinen Puoluetoimikunta, 1924), pp. 156–59; Soikkanen, op. cit., pp. 225–28; von Schoultz, op. cit., pp. 293–97.

22. *Kansan Lehti*, 11 November 1905.

23. Klaus Törnudd, *The Electoral System of Finland* (London: Hugh Evelyn, 1968), p. 28.

A new Senate, dominated by Constitutionalists, appointed a committee to prepare a reform of the system of representation, and the first election under the new system took place on 15–16 March 1907. Finland had moved from perhaps the most reactionary representative system in Europe to the most democratic parliamentary system in the world. With only slight modification, the electoral and parliamentary system achieved in 1906 remains in effect in Finland today. The reforms as provided for in the Parliament Law and the Election Law of 1906[24] may be summarized as follows:

1. The Parliament Law abolished the Estates Diet and established a unicameral Parliament of two hundred representatives.
2. Representation in the Parliament would be on the basis of proportional representation.
3. The country would be divided into a minimum of twelve and a maximum of eighteen electoral constituencies.
4. Suffrage was to be universal and equal for all adults over the age of twenty-four with minimal restrictions.
5. The Election Law divided the country into sixteen constituencies.
6. The Election Law also specified that nomination to Parliament would be by a voters' association of not less than fifty enfranchised citizens whose signatures on the nomination document were to be submitted to the central electoral board of the constituency.
7. Election was determined for each constituency rather than for either election districts or the country at large.

Neither the Parliament Law nor the Election Law provided for political parties, but the specifications for electoral alliance operating under the same name and the eligibility of candidates in several election lists and alliances meant that political parties would have an advantage in elections over individual candidates or separate election associations. At the same time the division of the country into sixteen election constituencies had the effect of limiting the number of political parties. A political party would be represented in Parliament according to its capacity to get its candidates elected in each constituency; it could not expect representation in Parliament on the basis of its proportion of votes in the country as a whole. Regional parties and parties representing ethnic or economic

24. Jussi Teljo, *Suomen valtioelämän murros 1905–1908: Perustuslaillinen senaatti—viimeiset säätyvaltiopäivät—ensimmäinen eduskunta* [Crisis of Finnish political life 1905–1908: constitutional Senate—last Diet of Estates—first Parliament] (Helsinki: Werner Söderström, 1949), pp. 49–128, and Törnudd, op. cit., pp. 33–70.

minorities were thus destined to be systematically underrepresented in Parliament.

Party organization. The fundamental structure of participation established in 1906 remains in effect today. Changes in the constitutional and statutory context in which the parties evolved led inevitably to changes in the structures of the parties themselves. Prior to 1905 the cadre party with a caucus structure was the typical form of political organization in Finland. The great mass of the Finnish people were politically unmobilized and without voting rights. Political activity was for the elite and was mainly confined to the capital, the Estates Diet, and relations between the Senate and the governor-general. No relations existed to allow the establishment of nation-wide electoral organizations. The Old Finn party in 1900 had no expressly elected party management except for a delegation appointed separately for each session of the Estates Diet to draft the outlines of a common policy to be supported by the party.[25]

The Workers' party (after 1903 the Social Democratic party) was the first party in Finland to develop the structure of a mass party.[26] Established in 1899 by the express resolution of a representative meeting of Finland's worker associations, this party from the start had a detailed ideological program and an organizational network of party center and branches that was soon supplemented by women's and youth leagues. Representatives elected by the party's branch associations met regularly at party conventions. It adopted a precise and detailed party program, which was reviewed and supplemented by the decisions of regular party conventions. Because most members of the party had no vote in the Estates Diet, during the early years the party functioned as a mobilizing organization for political education and political pressure for working-class interests.[27] The party was financed from the proceeds of its membership fees. The elaborate party machinery was characterized by strict adherence to the principles of democratic control provided for in its rules. For many years it was the only political party in Finland that

25. Jaakko Nousiainen, "The Structure of the Finnish Political Parties," *Democracy in Finland: Studies in Politics and Government* (Helsinki: Finnish Political Science Association, 1960), pp. 28–43.

26. Teljo, op. cit., pp. 31–32; Nousiainen, op. cit., pp. 29–30.

27. Yrjö Sirola, "Sosialidemokratinen puolue" [The Social Democratic party], *Yhteiskunnallinen Käsikirja* (Helsinki: Kansanvalistusseura, 1910), pp. 431–35, and Y. K. Laine, *Suomen poliittisen työväenliikkeen historia* [History of Finland's political labor movement], 3 vols. (Helsinki: Tammi, 1946), vol. 1.

published annual data on its membership. When general suffrage was achieved, the party also attempted to control the activities of its parliamentary delegation.

After 1905, parliamentary reform and the achievement of general suffrage led to further changes in party organization.[28] General elections increased the electorate and prompted parties to organize to compete for votes. The prior establishment of the Social Democratic party also required the bourgeois political groups to respond. Development of these small cadre parties into political electoral organizations with party programs was very rapid during the years 1905–08.[29] The small, loosely structured language parties strengthened their party organizations and developed broad party programs under central party leadership. However, the bourgeois parties continued to rely on influential persons and experts for the management and funding of their election campaigns. Hence, even after reorganization, recruitment of members had less significance for the bourgeois parties than for the Social Democrats.[30]

Certain party organizational forms imposed by the electoral reforms of 1906 remain in effect today.[31] The basic organization consists of local divisions in each commune where the party has numerical support. These local divisions are united into electoral district associations. Above the district organizations is a central administration called a party council, central administration, or party administration. An extended form of this central executive organ, consisting of additional representatives from the district organizations in the countryside, decides more important matters between party conventions. The highest level in the party is the party convention, which usually meets every one to three years to ratify programs and rules for the party. Representatives of the local and district organizations (in proportion to membership numbers), the party press, the parliamentary group, and the party's central administration

28. Borg, op. cit., pp. 8ff., divides the development of the Finnish party system into three major developmental periods: a "prehistory" of language parties, the actual birth of electoral parties following parliamentary reform, and the period following Finnish independence in 1918.

29. Nousiainen, op. cit., pp. 28–36, and Göran von Bonsdorff, *De politiska partierna i Finland* [The political parties in Finland] (Stockholm: Fahlcrantz and Gumaelius, 1951), pp. 9–54.

30. Nousiainen notes that even a generation after suffrage and parliamentary reform the majority of local party organizations were not active except at the time of elections and internal party contacts remained weak (op. cit., p. 30).

31. Von Bonsdorff, op. cit., pp. 52–54; Nousiainen, op. cit., pp. 32–36.

make up the party convention. The Social Democrats set up the machinery for party referenda and a nominating system comparable to a party primary in which the membership selects the party candidates. They also introduced membership dues and parallel organizations for trade unions, women, and youth, two innovations subsequently adopted by the other parties.

As the parties developed stronger organizations, they came to exercise greater control over their members in Parliament, a key stage in the evolution of parties as agencies of political linkage between citizens and policymakers.[32] In Finland the member of Parliament represents his party rather than the electorate, because he is dependent on the party administration for nomination and election. Campaigns are fought by parties; only candidates of the major parties have a significant chance of election. The elector in a proportional-representation system tends to give his vote first to the party and only second to the candidate. Furthermore, members of Parliament have seldom held important positions in the administrative organs of any party. However, the independence of parliamentary representatives of the bourgeois parties has been historically greater than that of the Social Democratic party, dating back to the days at the beginning of the century when power in the bourgeois parties resided in members of the Estates Diet.

The parties in contemporary Finland reflect the general organization, ideology, and voting constituencies developed in the 1907–17 period. Today's major parties include the Social Democratic party (from which the Communist party broke off in 1919), the bourgeois parties (the two Finnish parties under various names and the Swedish party), the Agrarian party (now the Center party), and certain small parties, which have appeared for varying periods on the Finnish political scene (e.g., the Christian Workers' party).

Cleavage Crystallization and the Growth of Democracy

Having explored the origins and history of the Finnish party system, this study will now examine whether these parties do in fact each serve distinct social-ideological unities within the electorate, a phenomenon referred to as cleavage crystallization. Parties that represent distinct units are at both an advantage and a disadvantage in serving as linkage agencies.

32. Nousiainen, op. cit., pp. 37–38.

194

Their advantage is their greater representativeness: each party serves only one body of political thought. Their disadvantage is—or can be— the difficulty of achieving either dominance (given their inability to appeal to more than a limited sector of the electorate) or compromise (given the unambiguous nature of their programs), and consequently, the difficulty of making public policy on the basis of party principles. The following discussion will examine how the parties do crystallize Finnish cleavages, and why this characteristic has not severely limited their capacity to make government policy on the basis of compromise and negotiation among the parties.

Cleavage crystallization: the electoral record, 1907–17. The process of cleavage crystallization in Finland can be studied in the record of political mobilization for elections to the Parliament. Between 1907 and 1917 there were eight parliamentary elections in Finland, because of the repeated dissolutions of Parliament by the Russian ruler. This may be contrasted with the fourteen elections of the Estates Diet between 1863 and 1905 and the nine elections of the Parliament between 1919 and 1939. Between 1907 and 1917 only the 1913 Parliament survived a full term without dissolution. Finnish political parties can be grouped according to their relations to the more fundamental social cleavages as follows:

1. *The Social Democrats.* This party's appeal and support came primarily from working-class components of the population, for example, industrial workers, landless farm workers and *torpparit*, and other nonpropertied elements of the urban population.
2. *The Finnish bourgeois parties (Finnish party and Young Finn party).* These parties made their fundamental appeals to landowning, business, religious, and other propertied or educated segments of the Finnish-speaking population.
3. *The Swedish People's party.* This party primarily represented the more educated and wealthy Swedish-speaking population but attempted to mobilize all segments of the Swedish-speaking population for electoral support.
4. *The Agrarian Union.* In its formative stage for the greater part of the 1907–17 period, this bourgeois Center party appealed to the small, independent, Finnish-speaking farmer and tended to cut into the electoral support of both the Social Democrats and the Finnish bourgeois language parties.

The small Christian Workers' party has little relevance for this analysis except to demonstrate the difficulty individual electoral associa-

195

TABLE 8.1. Distribution of Votes by Political Party in Parliamentary Elections, 1907–17 (in percent)

Parliamentary Election	Social Democrats	Finnish Party (Old Finns)	Young Finns	Agrarian Union	Swedish People's Party	Christian Workers' Party	Proportion of Electorate Voting
1907	37.0	27.3	13.6	5.8	12.6	1.6	70.7
1908	38.4	25.4	14.2	6.4	12.8	2.3	64.4
1909	39.9	23.6	14.5	6.7	12.3	2.8	65.3
1910	40.0	22.1	14.4	7.6	13.5	2.2	60.1
1911	40.0	21.7	14.9	7.8	13.3	2.2	59.8
1913	43.1	19.9	14.1	7.8	13.3	1.8	51.1
1916	47.3	17.6	12.4	9.0	11.8	1.8	55.5
1917	44.8	30.1*	—	12.4	10.9	1.6	69.2

SOURCE: *Soumen Virallinen Tilasto*: 29. Vaalitilasto, 1–8 (1907–17).

*United Finnish Party Front consisting of Finnish party, Young Finns, and newly created People's party. Actual distribution of seats was a matter of negotiation among the parties involved.

196

TABLE 8.2. Distribution of Parliamentary Seats by Political Party, 1907–1917

Parliament Election	Social Democrats	Finnish Party	Young Finns	Agrarian Union	Swedish People's Party	Christian Workers' Party
1907	80	59	26	9	24	2
1908	83	54	27	9	25	2
1909	84	48	29	13	25	1
1910	86	42	28	17	26	1
1911	86	43	28	16	26	1
1913	90	38	29	18	25	0
1916	103	33	23	19	21	1
1917	92	61*	—	26	21	0

SOURCE: *Suomen Virallinen Tilasto*, 29. Vaalitilasto, 1–8 (1907–17).
*United Finnish Party Front consisting of Finnish party, Young Finns, and newly created People's party. Actual distribution of seats gave Finnish party 32 seats, Young Finns 24 seats, and People's party 5 seats.

tions or small parties have in gaining effective representation in Parliament. The effect of the rules for representation, allowance for electoral associations, and proportional representation in sixteen electoral constituencies rather than for the country as a whole was to promote the parliamentary strength of the major national parties organized around fundamental social cleavages. The effect in representation can be measured by comparing the proportion of the votes cast for a party (table 8.1) with the number of seats the party received in the Parliament (table 8.2). The single most significant political effect of the weighting of the electoral system in favor of the national parties took place after the 1916 election when the Social Democrats with 47.3 percent of the votes received an absolute majority of 103 seats in Parliament. Thus the Social Democrats in Finland, having already in 1907 become the first socialist party in any country to achieve an electoral plurality, became the first socialist party to achieve a parliamentary majority.

As tables 8.1 and 8.2 show, the Social Democratic party steadily increased its electoral support and its parliamentary representation until 1917. To a great extent the Social Democratic electoral achievement must be attributed to its more efficient party organization and to its socially militant appeals as a class-struggle party. The Agrarian Union also gained steadily in popular support among the rural population.

197

This support for the Agrarian Union came largely at the loss of the two Finnish-language parties, particularly the Finnish party, which was characterized by a steady electoral decline between 1907 and 1917. The Young Finn party and the Swedish People's party generally maintained their political position during these years; both lost sharply, however, in the 1916 and 1917 elections. The association of the language issue with the higher economic position of the Swedish minority may account for part of its loss of effectiveness in the generally more class-conscious elections of 1916 and 1917.

In sum, during this era the parties were organized around the dominant social cleavages in Finland. Furthermore, the Social Democratic party, which was best organized and whose program was most focused on the dominant cleavage of the times, social class, was the most successful among the parties. The potential for a deeply divided polity, incapable of forward movement, was clearly present, particularly as the Social Democrats alienated their bourgeois support by moving more openly toward identification with the Finnish working class, Russian freedom movements, and Marxist socialism.

The growth of democracy: nationalism as a spur to compromise. How was Finland able to maintain the advantages of crystallized politics (greater representativeness) and at the same time avoid its common disadvantages (inability to achieve the level of compromise necessary in democratic systems)? The answer is twofold, and both parts of the answer have to do with Russian domination during the formative period of Finnish party politics.

1. *An ineffective Parliament.* Reexamination of table 8.1 will demonstrate that a significant characteristic of Finnish electoral politics during this period was the decline in voter turnout, from 70.7 percent in 1907 to only 51.1 percent in 1913. A major reason for the drop in proportion of electorate voting was the public loss of confidence in the capacity of Parliament to pass social legislation. Although demonstrating a high degree of cleavage crystallization and political mobilization, Parliament still had little effective power as a political institution so long as ultimate decision-making power was in foreign hands. Furthermore, with its broad electoral representation, Parliament was strongly opposed in more conservative bourgeois circles in Finland. This weakness of Parliament clearly weakened the capacity of the parties to attract voter support and thereby serve as effective agencies of linkage. On the other hand, Parliament was the one arena where organized political interests faced each

198

other. The inactivity of the Parliament, therefore, took on importance for party formation rather than policy; it had the effect of creating a period when parties could organize, propagandize, stabilize their support, and learn techniques of parliamentary debate and compromise without having to assume responsibility for government policy.

2. *Russification II, revolution, civil war.* The period of liberal treatment of Finland by Russia was relatively short-lived.[33] A new policy of Russification began in 1908, and in 1910 the Duma, over the opposition of the Finnish Senate and Parliament, passed the Imperial Legislation Act for Finland, which, in effect, abolished the constitution of autonomous Finland. All parties in Parliament moved to the defense of autonomy.

The cleavage between Finland and Russia became the central fact of political life in Finland during the period 1908–17. Russification seemed aimed at the annihilation of Finland's autonomy and nationality. Even as the Parliament became a center of popular resistance, the Senate became the instrument of integration of Finland into the Russian state. In November 1914 the Finnish press published a program proposed by the czar for the complete Russification of Finland.[34] With the 1914 declaration that Finland was in a state of war, repressive measures increased. But Finland had no army and did not wage war.[35] Student leaders and other Finnish activists began to explore possibilities of foreign support for Finnish independence.

Within Finland other major cleavages were also intensifying. Social reforms by Parliament were either vetoed by the czar or were minimal in order to avoid a czarist veto. Political emotion and frustration became general to the Finnish polity. The lack of effective legislative power in Parliament under Russian domination served to frustrate solution of major social problems inherent in the industrialization and urbanization of Finland. The 1917–18 period was thus a time of intense political activity as Finland moved from Russian control to national independence, underwent revolution and a bitter civil war, and moved to formalize a new political arrangement. When the Russian Revolution of March 1917

33. Schybergson, op. cit., pp. 310–44; and Uuno Tuominen, "Autonomian ajan yksikamarinen eduskunta 1907–1916" [Unicameral Parliament of the autonomy period 1907–1916], *Suomen Kansanedustuslaitoksen Historia* (Helsinki: Eduskunnan Historiakomitea, 1958), vol. 5, pt. 2: 165–170.
34. Schybergson, op. cit., p. 291.
35. Jutikkala, op. cit., pp. 248–49.

took place, the Finnish parties divided as to how to exploit the new political situation.[36] The Social Democratic party, with some support in the bourgeois parties, attempted to achieve internal independence for Finland during July 1917. However, the conservative bourgeois leadership feared such independence while a workers' party held a majority in Parliament. They joined with Russian opposition to support the governor-general in dissolving Parliament and calling new elections. These 1917 elections resulted in a parliamentary majority for the bourgeois parties. The bourgeois leadership now began to form a new Senate made up of conservative politicians and to seek independence under a strong executive form of government. The new Senate also opposed the reform program of the Social Democratic party. Political polarization continued through the summer and fall of 1917 as the Social Democratic party and the bourgeois parties mobilized increasingly as political fronts.

While this was happening on the level of political organization, the country faced a crisis of social control.[37] Finland under Russia had no police force or military force of its own. Now economic and political cleavages began to be manifest in the formation of rival order guards, with the workers organizing Red Guards while the bourgeois parties supported Protective Guards (White Guards). These armed guards now formed national organizations and mobilized for class warfare. Neither Parliament nor the Senate was able or willing to control these extragovernmental armies.[38] In November 1917 the Social Democratic party proclaimed a General Strike in support of its "We Demand" program of reforms.[39]

36. Gunnar Landtman, *Finlands väg till oavhängighet* [Finland's road to independence] (Helsingfors: Söderström, 1919); Väinö Tanner, *Kuinka se oikein tapahtui: Vuosi 1918 esivaiheineen ja jälkiselvittelyineen* [How it really happened: the year 1918 with its prephases and postsettlements] (Helsinki: Tammi, 1948); Oskari Tokoi, *Sisu: Even Through a Stone Wall; Autobiography* (New York: Robert Speller & Sons, 1957); and Juhani Paasivirta, *Suomen itsenäisyyskysymys 1917. II. Eduskunnan hajoituksesta itsenäisyysjulistukseen* [The Finnish independence question 1917. II. From the dissolution of Parliament to the declaration of independence] (Porvoo: Werner Söderström, 1949).

37. E. Huttunen, *Sosialidemokraattinen puoluejohto ja kansalaissota* [The Social Democratic party leadership and the civil war] (Helsinki: Kansanvalta, 1918), and Hannes Ryömä, *Vallankumousvuoden tapahtumista* [On the events of the revolution year] (Helsinki: Helsingin Uusi Kirjapaino, 1918).

38. Hannu Soikkanen, *Kansalaissota dokumentteina: Valkoista ja punaistassänankäyttöä v. 1917–1918*. Vol. 1: *Mielipiteiden muovautuminen kohti kansalaissotaa* [The civil war in documents. White and Red phraseology in 1917–1918. Vol. 1: opinion formation toward civil war] (Helsinki: Tammi, 1967).

39. Finnish Social Democratic Party Council, Minutes of Meetings, October 1917; Tanner, op. cit., pp. 179–80.

When the Senate finally moved to form a military and police force, it was interpreted by the leadership of the Social Democratic party as a declaration of war on the working class.[40] On 27 January 1918 the party leadership, expanded to include militant representatives, moved to seize the government.[41] The coup d'état succeeded in Helsinki and southern Finland, but public support failed to develop for the new government, the People's Commission. In addition, the legal government escaped arrest and formed a military and political headquarters from which they mobilized internal and foreign military support. In the meantime, almost simultaneously with the Red coup in Helsinki, the White Guards had begun military action in the north. There followed a civil war from January to May 1918 with the White Army winning.[42] The military failure of the Red Guard cannot be attributed to lack of war matériels.[43] Rather, the cause of failure lies in the extreme democratic character of its organization—in the election of officers on charismatic bases rather than military expertise and in the making of military plans according to democratic political considerations. The White Army under Mannerheim had professionally trained officers and much tighter discipline. In addition, the German Army intervened, substantially shortening the war and eliminating any chance of victory by the Red Guard.

The major issue now became the form of government of independent Finland. A bitter debate followed the civil war, resulting in the adoption of a strong presidential form of government rather than a monarchy.[44] Factors contributing to this determination were the loss of World War I by the Germans and the reentry of the Social Democratic party into

40. Finnish Social Democratic Party, Minutes of Tenth Convention (description), 1917; Tanner, op. cit., pp. 240–43; Juhani Paasivirta, *Suomi vuonna 1918* [Finland in 1918] (Porvoo: Werner Söderström, 1957), pp. 64–67.

41. Finnish Social Democratic Party Council, Minutes of Meeting, January 1918; *Suomen Työväen Vallankumous 1918: Arviota ja itsekritiikkiä* [The Finnish workers' revolution 1918: evaluations and self-criticism] (Leningrad: Kirja, 1928), pp. 180–81.

42. Kai Donner et al., eds., *Suomen Vapaussota* [Finland's freedom war], 6 vols. (Jyväskylä: Gummerus, 1921–22), and H. Ignatius et al., eds., *Suomen Vapaussota vuonna 1918* [Finland's freedom war in 1918], 6 vols. (Helsinki: Otava, 1921–25).

43. Y. W. Sourander, "Vapaussodan punainen armeija sodankäyntivälineenä [The freedom war Red Army as a war tool], *Tiede ja Ase* 1 (1933): 31–54; and Arvid Luhtakanta, *Suomen Punakaarti* [The Finnish Red Guard] (Kulju: E. A. Täckman, 1938).

44. *Form of Government Act and Diet Act of Finland* (Helsinki: Ministry of Foreign Affairs, 1947); Georg Schauman, *Kampen om statsskicket i Finland 1918: Fakta, betraktelser och hågkomster* [The fight about the constitution in Finland in 1918: facts, reflections, and reminiscences] (Helsinki: Holger Schildts Förlag, 1924).

political activity. The new constitution retained essentially the same parliamentary law and electoral law that existed before independence.

By 1919 the party system was reestablished and functioning in the first parliamentary elections after the revolution. The Old Finn party was renamed the National Coalition party and received 15.7 percent of the vote (twenty-eight elected members). The Young Finn party became the National Progressive party and received 12 percent of the vote (twenty-six members). The Swedish People's party received 12.1 percent of the vote (twenty-two members), the Agrarian Union 19.7 percent (forty-two members), and the Christian Workers' party 1.5 percent of the vote (two members). The Social Democratic party retained its position as the largest party in the country with 38 percent of the votes and eighty members elected to Parliament. The only significant shift in voting patterns was the growth of the Agrarian Union to second-largest party in the nation. The one notable change in this political balance during the next fifty years was the splitting of the workers' movement into the Social Democratic party and a left-wing party (the Communist party under various names). The political party system in Finland maintained its structure with little significant change for two-thirds of a century. The major effect of the revolution was to consolidate the structural cleavage between the proletariat and the bourgeoisie.

Thus the revolution and associated events of 1917–18 gave formation to the political system that endures to the present day. During this revolutionary period Finland achieved its national independence, something that was barely conceivable only a few decades earlier. The trauma of revolution and civil war, together with the earlier experience of Russification, established a national identity and a determination to maintain that identity, which has remained the foremost political concern of all Finns, including party politicians. The Finnish Constitution achieved a symbolic position in the ongoing political culture, which is probably equaled in only the United States. The legitimacy of the Finnish Constitution and the mandated governmental structure have been maintained for the past sixty years. Indeed, Finland was the only country established after World War I that escaped either Fascist or Communist dictatorship. In spite of social revolution, depression, and war, Finland has maintained its democratic character and fundamental constitutional structure to the present day.

The sharpness of internal cleavages in Finland might have precluded democratic processes had the Russification issue not occurred. However, in both 1899 and 1908 attempts to extend Russian control inspired widespread resistance among nearly all segments of the Finnish population. Thus the persistent threat of external domination served to promote cooperative action among disparate population groupings. The 1905–17 period of parliamentary ineffectiveness also contributed to the establishment of democratic processes by providing a period when political parties could organize and mobilize support without assuming direct responsibility for legislative or political programs. The 1918 civil war revealed the seriousness of the cleavage split in Finnish society; nevertheless, after this period the various population groupings were able to reestablish relations of compromise and negotiation. Central to this process were the Allied victory in World War I and the resultant external pressure for a republican and liberal democratic government in Finland. Thus, having organized around existent cleavages, Finnish parties today represent distinctive interests in their nation's politics. And having originated in an era of intense nationalism under the persistent threat of external domination, Finnish parties are committed first to the identity and interests of Finland and only second to more narrow party objectives. The two qualities in combination make Finnish parties strong exemplars of the role political parties can play as agencies linking a divided society to a democratic political process.

9.

Party Linkages and Strife Accommodation in Democratic India

A. H. SOMJEE

In his presidential address to the International Political Science Association in 1970 at Munich, Professor Carl Friedrich maintained that political scientists have so far given most of their attention to understanding the positive aspects of the democratic process. In so doing they have left out those negative characteristics that have sometimes proved deleterious to the very existence of democratic systems, such as the circumvention of accountability, undue influence on public officials, corruption, nondecision, violence, and so on. Similarly, one could argue that party-linkage theorists have so far paid much of their attention to the interest-aggregation function of party organization to the exclusion of other less positive forms of linkages. Such theorists also tend to overlook those pursuits of party organizers that do not help either to sustain the existing linkages or to forge new ones. Like all other organizations, the political party has its own inner dynamics, geared to a variety of pursuits. The linkage functions that one reads about in standard works on the subject seem to be drawn from what the party does during elections. What takes the place of such functions between elections? Does the party organization continue to work toward maintaining the already created linkages at all levels or does it neglect them or even enter into pursuits that erode them?

I am grateful to the Macmillan Company, London, for permission to use certain passages relating to my formulation of the strife-accommodation model from my *Democratic Process in a Developing Society* (1979), pp. 107–13.

This study argues that a functional distinction must be made between three different kinds of linkages: interest linkages, normative linkages, and operational linkages. Of the three, the focus will be on operational linkages, and the argument will contend that the activity of men who run the party organization during and between elections is materially different and that their activity can be explained with the help of what is called a strife-accommodation model. This argument will be substantiated by empirical data collected during a study of party organizations in a middle-sized town in western India called Anand, where fieldwork was spread over eleven years (1966 to 1977), a period that also included four elections.

The Three Different Kinds of Linkages

The following examination of the characteristics of the three different kinds of linkages, namely, interest, normative, and operational, will provide the background for a subsequent detailed analysis of the way in which operational linkages work.

Interest-linkage theorists have supplied a number of useful studies.[1] They point out that various structures in society articulate their respective interests and that the party organization, in order to have their support, formulates programs balancing the demands of such structures. In so doing the party organization undertakes a twofold linkage function: on the one hand, it links the competitive demands of different structures to a common program and, on the other, it relates citizens to the political system by asking them to support the party program electorally.

Around such a core activity, the party organization also becomes the supplier of information and brings together "unacquainted individuals who share political beliefs, interests, and aspirations."[2]

Few studies, however, have taken note of what Morton Grodzins calls "the internal dynamics" of party organization. In his view party activity is more likely to exacerbate than to aggregate the claims of com-

1. See in this connection G. A. Almond and G. B. Powell, *Comparative Politics: A Development Approach* (Boston: Little, Brown, 1966), pp. 98–128.
2. Kay Lawson, *The Comparative Study of Political Parties* (New York: St. Martin's Press, 1976).

205

peting social groups.[3] In fact, as this study will indicate, between elections party organizations may pursue activities that have very little to do with interest aggregation, and at times such activity may even undo whatever interest aggregation the party has achieved for election purposes.

Normative linkage has received hardly any attention from linkage theorists. Yet for any political system and for the various subsystems within it, such as party organizations, the existence of shared normative perspectives is crucial. Shared normative perspectives provide necessary links within, as well as between, different systems. At the level of the political system itself, the ideals of the commonweal are provided by the ruling elite, by the media, and by the exponents of party programs. These leaders of public opinion evaluate the quality of public life, identify critical issues facing the society as a whole, and indicate new directions to take. They also engage in mutual criticism and evaluate competing policy proposals in terms of what would lead to an improved common welfare. This form of linkage activity occurs at a normative level within the community as a whole, and the party organization is but one of many groups involved.

There are occasions in the history of every democratic society when the contribution of the party organization to normative linkage is minimal. A party organization can become obsessed with the game of power and the denunciation of adversaries. On such occasions the voter may show more concern for national interest than does the party and may even endeavor to link himself to the system unaided if not obstructed by the party.

A number of illustrations can be cited in support of this argument. The thinking men and women in the United States during the summer of 1974, for instance, seemed much more concerned with the quick resolution of the Watergate problem than did the two national political parties. While the parties were engaged in viewing the Watergate episode from the point of view of its effects on their respective electoral fortunes, others were demanding the rule of law and public accountability in the highest office in the nation.

A further illustration is found in India. During the first regime

3. See in this connection Morton Grodzins, "Political Parties and the Crisis of Succession in the United States: The Case of 1800," in *Political Parties and Political Development*, Joseph La Palombara and Myron Weiner, eds. (Princeton: Princeton University Press, 1966), pp. 317–23.

of Indira Gandhi, the demand grew for a leadership that would protect the civil liberties of the citizens. But when Morarji Desai came into office in 1977 and restored civil liberties at the expense of administrative firmness, the resultant changes were not well received. The political alternatives represented by Indira Gandhi and Morarji Desai, of administrative firmness *or* civil liberties, one excluding the other, had become unacceptable. A new political norm began to be articulated, not by the parties but by the population: a demand for civil liberties *within* a framework of firmness in routine administration. This new political norm gave the Indian people a common perspective on the problems of their society and thereby served to link a diverse community.

Operational linkage,[4] the activity of men and women who direct their energies to the task of building and sustaining a structure of support for their party organizations, is what sustains, in the last analysis, a system of party linkages. Most of these hardworking activists are motivated by the hope of personal benefits. They seek their reward in the form of power, status, or material benefit, and without such a payoff, most would not be interested in the linkage work of the party.

The linkmen involved in operational-linkage activity are the officeholders, the party activists, and the marginals. The marginals consist of the fringe people who periodically get involved in partisan politics. They are not fully assimilated into party organizations. Party organizations, nevertheless, need their support to put across the vote-catching items in the party programs. Apart from a few public-spirited individuals, the marginals make their services available to party organizations for a potential political advantage to themselves.[5] The greatest single problem for any party organization is to sustain the interest of its activists and marginals *as* linkmen. Because the party activists and the marginals get involved in extraparty and nonparty political activity, especially between elections, the consequences of such involvements for party linkages become unpredictable. During the period preceding elections the linkmen build a patchwork of support structure for the party organization, but between elections they are likely, as shall be

4. For the want of a better expression, I have used the term "operational linkage" in order to indicate the diversity of motivations and pursuits among men *actually* involved in linkage activity.
5. In the Indian situation, the marginals are often drawn from the ranks of lawyers, businessmen, industrialists, ethnic and religious leaders, and men of means and influence generally.

seen, to join competing support structures that do not necessarily run parallel to the existing party cleavages. The activists and the marginals often cut across such cleavage structures. Neither the activists nor the marginals, with few exceptions, don the party uniform all the time. Many enter into a dialogue across the party fence as soon as the electoral rhetoric dies down, and erstwhile enemies may form peculiar and sometimes unpredictable political combinations.

Consequently, it is important to examine closely the operational conduct of the activists and the marginals between elections and more specifically their off-election "demembering." No analysis of linkage activity will be complete unless we also take into account the extra-linkage activity of its linkmen. In many political systems, the activity of linkmen alternates between building up a patchwork of support for electoral strife and then dismantling it for a variety of accommodations at the party and individual levels. In the case study explored later the emphasis will be on examining this third form of linkage and examples of the kinds of situations that lead to its dismantlement in the post-electoral period.

A Model of Political Party Strife Accommodation

In the various writings on party organization, linkage activity is rarely considered against the background of interparty behavior. The activists and the marginals are often considered to be pursuing linkage activity and nothing else. Horse-trading activity between elections, especially across the party fence, is often lost sight of. This is partly due to the fact that party conflict, which figures prominently during electoral contests, is taken far too seriously. Because their mutually exclusive linkages are built out of the gross mass of common potential supporters by stressing points of conflict, the rivalry between the linkmen of contesting political parties is considered to be an ever-present phenomenon. It is not surprising, therefore, that the phenomenon of interparty activity has received little or no attention.

INTERPARTY ACCOMMODATIONS: PARTY TO PARTY
However, two studies of Indian political parties provide an exception. The views of Myron Weiner on the linkage activity of Congress party organizers and those of W. H. Morris-Jones on Congress interparty behavior are both significant for the purpose here.

Weiner has formulated a sophisticated model, employing Avery Leiserson's[6] notion of the "manipulative" function of party organization and Samuel Eldersveld's[7] concept of party as "a conflict system," to explain the success of the Congress party in India. According to Weiner, the secret of success of the Congress party was twofold: it manipulated a close "fit" between its own interests and those of its members, and it developed an effective mechanism for manipulating and resolving internal conflicts. In his words:

Congress adapts itself to the local power structure. It recruits from among those who have local power and influence. It trains its cadres to perform political roles similar to those performed in the traditional society before there was party politics. It manipulates factional, caste, and linguistic disputes and uses its influence within the administration to win and maintain electoral and financial support. It utilizes traditional methods of dispute settlement to maintain cohesion within the party.[8]

Morris-Jones proposed a conversation-bargain model for explaining the interparty behavior of the Congress party. According to him the Congress, despite its "dominance," stood in a peculiar relationship with those other parties that "dissented" from it. He likened the Congress to a flabby shopkeeper in an Indian bazaar where "bargaining and dissent are the languages of discourse." Such a relationship was made possible by what he called the "openness" of the Congress. In his words:

There is a most important "openness" in the relation between the Congress and the other political parties; not merely is there an absence of barriers, there is a positive communication and interaction among them. The opposition parties neither alternate with the Congress in the exercise of power, nor do they share power in any coalition form. Rather they operate by *conversing* with sections of Congress itself.[9]

6. Avery Leiserson has accorded to the party organization the function of "manipulation" of the structural relationship between the social system, on the one hand, and the political party, on the other. See in this connection his *Parties and Politics* (New York: Knopf, 1958), p. 65.

7. Samuel J. Eldersveld, *Political Parties: A Behavioral Analysis* (Chicago: Rand McNally, 1964).

8. Myron Weiner, *Party Building in a New Nation* (Chicago: Chicago University Press, 1967), p. 15.

9. See W. H. Morris-Jones, "Dominance and Dissent: Their Inter-relations in the Indian Party System," *Government and Opposition* 1 (July–September 1966): 455.

A similar conclusion, especially on the behavior of opposition parties in India vis-à-vis the Congress, was reached by R. Kothari.[10] Morris-Jones's conversation-bargain model, underlining the "positive communication and interaction" between the Congress and other parties, comes quite close to identifying the endless sequence of political linkages built for electoral strife and interparty accommodations between elections.

INTERPARTY ACCOMMODATIONS: INDIVIDUAL TO INDIVIDUAL

The interparty accommodations at the individual level across the party fence—particularly between individuals of common religious, ethnic, regional, or class origins—have received much less attention. No party organization in a democratic society can impose a formal cast of hostility on the entire range of sociopolitical relationships that exist between the members of contesting political parties. Despite hostile partisanship, the undercurrent of primary social ties quite often opens up avenues for political accommodations at an individual level. Postelection periods are conducive to the resumption of normal sociability and political accommodation across the party line.

EXTRAPARTY ACCOMMODATIONS

Then there are occasions that give rise to extraparty accommodations. In such situations, political parties are not directly involved in the political fray, and local party officials may connive at various liaisons and accommodations arranged between supposedly competitive party activists and marginals, on the governing boards of nonpartisan institutions, for example.

NONPARTY ACCOMMODATIONS

Finally, there are nonparty accommodations. Between elections, several new issues of common concern are likely to develop. Until a partisan approach to such issues crystallizes, individuals belonging to different political parties will often enter into situations of mutual accommodation.

In short, it is important to identify the nature and extent of involvement of party officeholders, activists, and marginals in situations of interparty, extraparty, and nonparty accommodations, together with the significance of such an involvement to the linkage structure itself.

10. Ibid.

In a sense the politics of accommodation alternates and undercuts the politics of linkage. Because most political parties are essentially electioneering parties, their accent on linkages is revived only during periods preceding elections.

Party-to-party accommodations, between the erstwhile competitors, are entered into with a view either to maximize political advantage or to ensure political survival. The individual-to-individual accommodations and liaisons across the party fence, on the other hand, are brought about with indifference to their long-term effect on parties' following. Within the support structures themselves the party-to-party accommodations may cause confusion in the minds of people who had swung behind the competitive parties, whereas the pacts made at the individual level by former hostiles are often cynically written off as "politics." Nevertheless, all accommodations—whether entered into by parties themselves or by their irrepressible activists and marginals—hasten the process of dissolution of the patchwork of electoral linkages.

In democratic political systems, which are based on *periodic* mandates from the people rather than continuous accountability, political parties have neither the incentive nor the urgency to guard against the disintegration of their support structures between elections.

During the period between elections, the activists and marginals have time to spare. There is more time and energy for political pursuits in the local unit of a party. The local unit's time, energy, and organizational power are available to the people who control, influence, or manipulate them. All are used to enter into a variety of political accommodations with uncertain effects on party linkages.

A summary of the involvement of party workers in different types of accommodations and the significance of such involvements to linkage structure is provided in table 9.1.

The Background of Party Politics in Anand

Anand is a rapidly industrializing middle-sized (population approximately one hundred thousand) town in western India. Before describing the variety of accommodation patterns in Anand, a word on the background of Anand party politics is in order.

The Congress party in India has always been challenged by different political parties in different states. In the western state of Gujarat, where Anand is located, the principal contender for power in the sixties was a

TABLE 9.1. Party Accommodation and Linkage

Type of Accommodation	Party Personnel Involved	Significance to Linkage Structure
Interparty accommodation (formal party-to-party accommodation)	Office holders in charge of accommodation. Activists play a supporting role. Marginals involved only if the accommodation takes place soon after election.	Linkage structure likely to be sustained if accommodation takes place soon after election.
Interparty accommodation (accommodation among individuals of different political parties)	No specific party direction. Office-holders and activists individually involved in accommodation. Marginals follow independent course of action.	Linkage structure bypassed.
Extra party accommodation (party not involved in political fray)	Office holders become spectators. Activists get involved. Marginals follow independent course of action.	Linkage structure bypassed.
Non party accommodation (party's approach to new issues not crystallized)	Office holders and activists involved so as not to be left out of the main current of events. Marginals follow independent course of action.	Explorations for picking up support for a new linkage structure.

right-wing political party called the Swatantra party. In the seventies the main opposition to the Congress came from a combination of political parties including Swatantra. For the purposes of this study analysis will be confined to the accommodation patterns forged by the two chief contending parties, Congress and Swatantra.

In 1921 a branch of the Congress party was established in Anand with the twin purposes of recruiting new members and launching political agitation. Political agitation influenced a generation of young men who were still in school. In 1921 Mahatma Gandhi exhorted the students to boycott the British-run schools. In response to his call, twenty-five students from Anand dropped out of school and went to an institution called Vidyapeeth, an indigenous educational institution in the nearby metropolis of Ahmedabad that was devoted to the regeneration of Indian cultural values and emphasis on the upliftment of rural India by means of social work and political awakening. That generation dominated the politics of Anand and the district itself for the next half century. One of the towering individuals who emerged was T. K. Patel, popularly known as TK.

Political agitation between 1933 and 1942 brought TK and his associates into close contact with the political workers in the district. TK found the district political elite much more responsive to his way of thinking than the urban political elite of Anand. After Indian independence, therefore, he concentrated not only on building up various district infrastructural bodies but also on refashioning the Congress organization to ensure control, under his leadership, from the district.

Anand is often described as one of the most prosperous towns of India. It has Asia's largest milk cooperative dairy, a large number of medium-size industrial units, and a flourishing grain and vegetable trade. The locus of economic power in the district, therefore, is Anand. But so far as the Congress organization under TK was concerned, the organizational political power had shifted to the district.

Such a dichotomy forced TK to make some concessions to his comrades who preferred to organize a base of political power in Anand itself. TK allowed them a great deal of latitude in civic politics and also in running various other institutions of Anand as long as they did not involve the district-based Congress too deeply in their own politics.

As a result of TK's strategy, the Congress did not have a separate party unit for Anand. The Anand Congress party merely functioned as one of the many units of the Congress district organization.

Within the Congress district organization, the political workers based in rural areas were invariably accorded higher positions within the party hierarchy than those who were located in Anand. Even the Congress members of the Legislative Assembly (M.L.A.'s) and the member of Parliament (M.P.) were not given any extraordinary position

213

within the party hierarchy. They were merely treated as vote-catching individuals. In a sense, there were two forms of status and power: that acquired through the elective machinery by the M.L.A.'s and M.P. and the effective political influence wielded by TK and the district leaders. Such a division was possible because the M.L.A.'s and the M.P. preferred to have influence in Ahmedabad (the state capital) and in New Delhi, respectively, rather than in the district. The district body periodically looked after the economic interests of the elected deputies and their relatives so as to keep them in good humor.

The founding father of the Swatantra party in the state of Gujarat was Bhailalbhai Patel, popularly known as Bhaikaka. The headquarters of the Swatantra party was in Vidyanagar, which is on the outskirts of Anand. Bhaikaka was closely associated with Sardar Patel, one of the principal architects of Indian independence and of the integration of the princely states into the Republic of India. Bhaikaka wanted to build and dedicate a university to the memory of Sardar. But Morarji Desai, a person who held a great many top positions in free India including that as deputy prime minister, created many obstacles for him to overcome. In the end Sardar Patel University was established, but Bhaikaka bore a lasting grudge against Desai. One way for Bhaikaka to express his anger was to try his hand at organizing a political party opposed to the Congress. Thus in 1952, during India's first general election, Bhaikaka formed his own party, the Lok Paksha, contested the election against the Congress nominee for the Legislative Assembly, and lost. Although the Congress party won the election, it began to experience more and more opposition in various institutions of Anand. In the following general election, in 1957, the opposition forces appealed to regional sentiment for the bifurcation of a composite Bombay state and against the Land Tenancy Act. But again they failed to dislodge the Congress candidate.

The forces of opposition lacked a sound organizational base from which to launch their drive against the Congress. This was finally provided, on the eve of 1962 election, by the establishment of the Swatantra party. Apart from becoming a rallying point for all those forces that were frustrated in their drive for power inside the Congress, the new party prospered when an ethnic organization of the warrior caste, the Kshatriya Sabha, decided to support it during the election of 1962.

Bhaikaka subscribed to the view that India should avoid the concentration of its economic resources in a few urban centers. Instead, the national government should provide development facilities in rural areas, attract talent there by giving it modern amenities, and thereby bring about a more balanced development of urban as well as rural areas. He expressed these views in his various writings. Nevertheless, in his political strategy, unlike TK, he did not believe in bypassing the urban base of political power. On the contrary, the Swatantra party unit of Anand not only was encouraged to enter into civic politics *as* a party but was given additional weight and extra facilities within the party organization.

The party's formal organization provided a place for the town unit along with district and state units. Moreover, all the top officeholders, such as president, secretary, and treasurer, were expected to be from Anand. Thus, as opposed to TK's strategy of keeping the Anand Congress members organizationally controlled by the district, the Swatantra party honored the standing of its political workers in Anand by allotting them important positions in the party.

The Swatantra party's decision to fight for the control of the Anand municipality in 1967 opened up the field to a relatively younger group of men from commerce and the professions, with their own electoral strategies and achievement-oriented style. Disgruntled ex-Congress members were soon surpassed by younger men in their late thirties with superior political skills and intelligence but without any experience of office. Whereas the Swatantra high command worried over the younger group's sudden rise to power in civic politics and its potential demand for a greater share of power in the district, the party bosses preferred the younger group to the ex-Congressmembers. The group was given a free hand in planning its strategy and, after electoral victory, in formulating its policy. Out of a total of twenty-five seats in the Anand municipality, the Swatantra party captured sixteen. The Congress party could capture only five, and the remaining four went to Independents. Between 1967 and 1971, the Anand municipality achieved tremendous progress under Swatantra leadership. Great strides were made in town planning and widening roads, a new vegetable market was constructed, and the municipal administration of schools and hospitals was greatly improved.

Strife Accommodation in Anand

A variety of accommodations took place between the two contending parties in Anand.

215

INTERPARTY ACCOMMODATIONS: PARTY TO PARTY

Despite the struggle for power between the local units of the Congress and the Swatantra during and between elections, there were a number of occasions when the spirit of give-and-take between the two hostile parties also prevailed. As could be expected, each party tried very hard to reduce and eliminate the other's influence and advance its own in the various institutions of Anand. Nevertheless, such a game of power was played within the framework of certain tacitly acknowledged rules, normative as well as practical. Both sides studiously avoided zero-sum-game situations where the winner took all.[11] The political leadership on both sides of the party fence, largely drawn from the commercial and agricultural classes, was deeply aware of the vicissitudes of public life. Any defeat of their adversaries led them to ponder their own situation a few years hence. In treating their adversaries with some degree of respect and compassion, they worked to ensure for themselves a similar treatment, should the future bring a change in mutual positions. There was greater glory in achieving desired objectives than in going it alone, and traditional ethics, which had a remarkably clear practical application, taught them that in asking for a helping hand for a common cause they never demeaned themselves. Induced by these considerations, the party and individuals in relatively stronger positions frequently worked to accommodate the opposition's point of view and thereby widen the scope of concerted action. A few examples will illustrate how the process worked.

1. The Anand Milk Consumers Union bought bulk milk from the Amul Dairy and distributed it in Anand. The union was a cooperative body and every year its managing committee was elected. In the past the union and its managing committee had been controlled by the Congress. In 1967, however, the Swatantra party captured the union with a large majority. After their victory, the Swatantra members suggested that they and the Congress should have five members each on the managing committee, in addition to two nonpartisans. The Congress refused to cooperate. Eventually the Congress and Swatantra distribution was four and eight, respectively. The rationable behind the Swatantra offer

11. See in this connection Arend Lijphart, *The Politics of Accommodation: Pluralism and Democracy in the Netherlands* (Berkeley: University of California Press, 1968), particularly his model for explaining the politics of accommodation within a society with "an extraordinary degree of social cleavage" (p. 2), building minimal political consensus around "programmatic solutions" (p. 103).

was practical. Because the committee was required to deal with Amul Dairy, a body dominated by the Congress, the suggested Swatantra composition would have been more effective in dealings with the dairy. Despite the lack of agreement between the two parties as to the composition of the managing committee, their relationship remained extremely cordial. Finally, when the committee was asked to nominate a representative to an outside body, the Swatantra majority deliberately elected a well-known Congress party member.

2. In 1968–69 the Swatantra-dominated municipality decided to construct a new building for the town library. A library committee was composed to supervise the construction of the building. Once again the Swatantra majority elected a leading Congress party member.

3. Similarly, in 1969, when the local tuberculosis hospital committee, entirely composed of Congress members, approached the Swatantra-dominated municipality for funds, party considerations were kept in the background and the request was immediately met.

4. When the question of housing the prestigious National Dairy Development Board (NDDB) arose, the most suitable place for it was on land belonging to the Institute of Agriculture. The institute promised to give the land, provided the municipality changed the classification of the land. The credit for the coming of the NDDB to Anand was likely to go entirely to the Amul Dairy and therefore to the Congress. This was because the Congress, together with the highly efficient administrative staff of Amul Dairy, had succeeded in developing a scheme for the expansion of cooperative dairying in the rest of the country. The Swatantra-dominated municipality could have been awkward about it but preferred not to, placing community interests before partisan advantage.

5. The local Congress, too, proved equally accommodating in certain cases. In 1962 K. M. Munshi, a national leader of the Swatantra party, asked for a donation of land near Anand for the establishment of a branch of Bhavan's College. Knowing full well that the Swatantra party would claim credit for it, the Congress gave a helping hand in the acquisition of land for the college.

6. Finally, the case of the transport bus service may be mentioned. Run by an organization called Charotar Vidya Mandal, which was controlled by members of the Swatantra party, the bus traveled between Anand railway station and Vidyanagar. Orginally it was meant for the students of Anand to go to Sardar Patel University in Vidyanagar, but the Mandal used it as a commercial bus service, carrying nonstudents

as passengers. Within the state, the State Transport Service had the sole right to run such a service. The Congress-dominated state government could have created problems for the Mandal had the local unit of the Congress brought the matter to its attention, but the latter deliberately turned a blind eye to this infraction.

These, then, are some of the instances of strife accommodation by the parties between elections. One could cite equally numerous illustrations of obstructionism and willful attempts to frustrate each other's maintenance and enhancement of power, but the purpose here has been to give evidence of those accommodative interparty relationships so seldom documented in the literature on party linkage.

INTERPARTY ACCOMMODATIONS: INDIVIDUAL TO INDIVIDUAL

One peculiar fact about the Anand Swatantra party was its strong Anand sentiment. This was true of the young as well as the not so young in the party. The regional leadership of the Swatantra party was located in Vidyanagar. Vidyanagar, the seat of Sardar Patel University, was classed by the census authority as a new town with a sizable residential population of its own, an identity that the Swatantra leadership located in Vidyanagar were eager to maintain. However, for the Swatantra members in Anand, Vidyanagar would never be more than a suburb of Anand.

Moreover, the top leadership of the Swatantra party came from the six *mota gam* ("prestigious villages") of the Patidar caste. Within the social stratification of the Patidars themselves, the people of the mota gam looked down upon the Patidars of Anand. The status differentiation within the Patidar community had created a curious problem across the party line. In the decision-making processes of various institutions, the Patidars of Anand, regardless of their diverse party affiliations, felt a strong affinity toward each other vis-à-vis the Patidars of the mota gam. This facilitated what Morris-Jones aptly described as "conversation" across the party fence. The Patidars of Anand, on either side of the party divide, did not act as pressure groups on each other but rather as a transmission belt for conveying the proposals of compromise and accommodation. Particularly within the top decision-making body of Sardar Patel University, the party divide often melted away when the interests of Anand were at stake, creating a pronounced cleavage between Anand Patidars and the rest.

Limitations of space prevent the mention of parallel examples of compromise and accommodation, brought about as a result of Anand sentiment and the peculiarities of Patidar social stratification, across the party line in other institutions of Anand. Such accommodations often came on the heels of intensely contested elections.

EXTRAPARTY ACCOMMODATIONS
As stated earlier, the Congress party boss allowed the party activists to involve themselves in local politics as long as their involvement was not deleterious to the party's influence in Anand as well as in the district generally. Consequently, the Congress activists and marginals often entered into peculiar deals with the personnel of the Swatantra party in various public institutions of Anand.

Despite partisan conflict of varying degrees of intensity within the major institutions of Anand, contests for certain elective positions were made a mere formality in accordance with certain prearranged deals between individuals and groups of the two officially warring sides. Sometimes a favorable decision for an individual Congress member in the minority in a Swatantra-dominated institution was immediately rewarded by another favorable decision for a Swatantra member within a Congress-dominated institution. Such deals, essentially made at individual level, often facilitated the decision-making process within the civic (municipality), educational (Charutar Education Society, which administered a number of schools and colleges), economic (Amul Dairy, one of the largest economic units in the state), and agricultural (Agricultural College, which revolutionized agriculture in the area) institutions. All these are public institutions with mechanisms for electing many members of their governing bodies. The activists and marginals from both parties played a leading role in the decision making of these bodies. The officeholders of the two political parties kept an eye on their respective personnel and their extraparty accommodations. The farther the parties were from the elections, the greater was the leeway given to party personnel for accommodations in these ostensibly entirely nonpartisan institutions.

NONPARTY ACCOMMODATIONS
Anand has a long tradition of public-spiritedness and voluntary social work. This is largely due to the emphasis on social concern and involvement on the part of its various schools. Consequently, its commercial, professional, managerial, and technocratic classes were invariably involved in the public causes that developed between elections. So were

the party personnel of the Congress and the Swatantra party. So far as the new projects and issues were concerned, the party personnel worked side by side with the public-spirited citizens. There was often a feeling of comradeship and give-and-take across the party line as long as the political parties themselves did not take partisan positions on these new projects and issues.

Two of the most active and socially concerned organizations of Anand were the Lions Club and the Rotary Club. They provided ideal meeting places for Anand's burgeoning commercial and professional class, technocrats, and industrialists. The bulk of the activists and marginals of the Congress as well as the Swatantra party were recruited from these classes. They regularly attended meetings of the clubs and actively participated in various social-work activities undertaken by them. The clubs launched fund-raising activities for famine and flood relief and expanded the General Hospital in Anand; they collected used clothing and blankets to be sent to different parts of India; they organized year-round cultural activities. As nonpartisan bodies, the clubs did not have difficulty in obtaining the active support of members of all political parties. Similarly, whenever groups of concerned citizens undertook any relief or social-work activity, party activists and marginals gave a helping hand, and when elected to steering committees, they worked in the spirit of give-and-take.

The variety of accommodations discussed here take their own toll of party linkages. Every incidence of accommodation potentially weakens the ties between party personnel, party organization, and party supporters. Party accommodations between elections encourage the movement of some activists and a large number of marginals from one side of the party divide to the other, encourage movement out of party politics altogether, and seriously undermine the linkage structure so laboriously built during the preelection periods.

Conclusion

The foregoing discussion stresses the need to look at linkage activity and what takes its place between elections for the activists and marginals within the party organization. During the election period the activists and the marginals are engaged in building a support structure for their party. Between elections they cut across such structures and enter into fresh political alliances and accommodations. This is not to say that political parties do not continue to retain their hold on specific bases of support over a prolonged period of time. What is maintained here is that the complex linkages brought about for the purposes of specific elections do not remain intact in the postelection periods.

Some insights for wider application are gained in the study of linkage processes in the developing countries, where the formation of political parties is a relatively new phenomenon. Political parties in those parts of the world represent what David Apter calls "a set of sub-group variables."[12] Their sociopolitical compositions make them the target of diverse pressures, and it is understandable that their solidarities may not outlast periodic elections. However, political parties in the developed countries are subject to similar pressures, and if similar studies were to be replicated in developed countries, chances are that the linkage/nonlinkage activities of party organizations would register some striking parallels.

Political scientists are accustomed to identifying the linkage function of party organizations and turning a blind eye to what is contrary to it. Carl Friedrich's reminder to look to the other side of the political reality is well taken, as these examples from the local politics of Anand may serve to illustrate.

12. See in this connection David E. Apter, *The Politics of Modernization* (Chicago: Chicago University Press, 1965), p. 222.

10.

People, Parties, Polities:
A Linkage Perspective on
African Party-States

FRANCES HILL

African politics have been, to a remarkable degree, party politics. Political parties are linkage-seeking, linkage-building organizations. Yet the study of African politics has not produced a theory of interactive political linkages. The emphasis has been on only selected aspects of linkage, seldom, if ever, explicitly designated as such. The effort here is to develop a theory of interactive political linkages for the study of party politics in Africa.

Linkage is an ongoing interaction that is sufficiently sustained and significant to modify the linked actors.[1] The concept of linkage involves direction and salience. The differential direction of the linkage and the differential salience of the linkage to the linked actors become the basis for distinguishing among linkage systems.

A fully specified political system in interactive linkage terms almost always involves the following actors and linkages: citizens ↔ party ↔ state.[2] Political parties become the focus of a linkage approach to poli-

1. Peter Blau, *Exchange and Power in Social Life* (New York: Labus Wiley & Sons, 1964). Marcel Mauss, *The Gift: Forms and Functions of Exchange in Archaic Societies* (Glencoe: The Free Press, 1954). George Simmel, *Conflict* and *The Web of Group Affiliations* (Glencoe: The Free Press, 1955). The implications of interaction for constituting the individual are discussed in George Herbert Mead, *Mind, Self and Society* (Chicago: University of Chicago Press, 1934).

2. Unified entities (the state, the party) are discussed as actors in sketching the initial contours of a linkage approach. These general characterizations will be modified in specific case studies as well as in the formulation of more detailed hypotheses.

tical inquiry because of their intermediate position between citizens and the state. A party's intermediate position does not imply or guarantee primacy. A party is not necessarily a primary actor capable of defining the nature, direction, and salience of its own linkages. The paradoxes of interaction—that interaction defines the actors as well as the rules and conditions of interaction—apply with special force to parties. A party's centralness can become the base for political influence only to the extent that the party facilitates interaction between citizens and the state, between two demand-forming and demand-granting actors. The party's capacity to gratify citizen or state demands is limited: states want support, citizens want access to a body that can meet their ongoing demands for services. A party can provide access; it can provide a linkage; but it cannot provide a substitute for either citizen support or state responsiveness. Thus, both citizens and the state will treat parties instrumentally as second-order actors that each seeks to define. Citizens will speek to impose a citizen → party linkage as a prelude to a citizen → party → state linkage system. The state will seek a state → party linkage as a prelude to a state → party → citizen linkage system. A party will seek to approximate a state ← party → citizen linkage system.

A linkage approach requires that the nature of the linked actors be carefully specified in interaction terms and that the direction and salience of the linkages among these actors be carefully delineated. Finally, the policy implications of particular linkages can be examined. A linkage approach should be able to suggest fresh perspectives on each of these themes. It should suggest new questions for future research as well as facilitate a reanalysis of existing studies.

African parties offer interesting potential for such reanalysis. African parties have been studied in virtual isolation from the other components of a political system and the idea of linkages has been either neglected or rejected. Nevertheless, there are several landmark studies of parties that can serve as a basis for a linkage approach. The differing perspectives suggested by a linkage approach thus become particularly clear in comparison with previous conceptualizations.

Prelude to a Linkage Approach: Two Generations of African Party Analysis

The potential analytical contributions of a linkage approach to the study of African political parties can be best understood in light of a brief examination of the existing literature on African party politics. This research can be divided into two generations, distinguished by their research foci and their leading concepts.[3] Although neither generation articulated an explicit linkage perspective, each operated with an implicit linkage concept. The first generation examined party → citizen linkages in which the party was primary and directive. The second generation operated with a de facto interest in citizen → party linkages with the party studied as a component of local society. Neither generation considered a fully specified linkage system of state ↔ party ↔ citizen interactions.

The first-generation scholars of contemporary African politics focused on the central leadership of the nationalist movements. This preoccupation is readily understandable. New leaders were attempting to form new organizations that would, in turn, found new polities. Emphasis on the creative power of the nationalist parties made the past seem less relevant then the posited future for understanding the political moment of nationalist creation. Discounting the forms of social cohesion among citizens as traditional or ahistoric and dismissing the colonial state as an alien intrusion, scholars remained content to focus on the nationalist party. When Kwame Nkrumah urged his followers to "seek ye first the political kingdom,"[4] political researchers responded, confident that their preoccupation with the national organization of the dominant party presented the elements central to both the present and the future. Some Africanists even suggested that there were no African political systems, only the embryo of the future embodied in the party.[5] The party was thus not the component of a system, linked with other political actors, but Gramsci's Prince, the party that created a system.[6]

3. Although these generations are not perfectly chronological, the first generation derived from the African nationalist era and the second generation developed in the later 1960s as the problems of the nationalist parties in power became apparent.

4. Nkrumah's Convention People's party, the first popular nationalist movement to form an independent African government, provided a model to many other African nationalist movements and to many scholars, to whom it seemed the prototype of the African political party. Nkrumah's ideas of the political party are found in his own writings, especially *Ghana: The Autobiography of Kwame Nkrumah* (New York: Nelson, 1957); *I Speak of Freedom: A Statement of African Ideology* (New York: Praeger, 1961); *Africa Must Unite* (London: Heineman, 1963).

5. James S. Coleman, "The Politics of Sub-Saharan Africa," in Gabriel A. Almond and James S. Coleman, eds., *The Politics of the Developing Areas* (Princeton: Princeton University Press, 1960), p. 294.

6. Antonio Gramsci, the Italian nationalist Communist, shared with a later genera-

No African nationalist leader or first-generation analyst of African politics would have disagreed with Gramsci's description of the party as "the first cell containing the germs of collective will which are striving to become universal and total."[7]

This tendency to analyze the party in terms of its unfettered directive capacity, or in terms of an implicit party → citizen linkage, facilitated the blend of social mobilization and political development assumptions fundamental to the analysis of first-generation Africanists. The party was seen as the only "modern" universal in the midst of diverse and dangerous "traditional" particularisms.[8] The people were not so much members as they were targets of the party. In such a situation, the party's primary duty, other than removing the alien colonial presence, was to modernize the citizens, "to make them available for new forms of association."[9] Such "social mobilization" is much more profound than mere political mobilization. Social mobilization aims at a redefinition of the person as an individual and as a member of a social group. Thus, the party becomes the embryonic representation as well as the creator of new forms of social relations. Gramsci, in detailing the duties of the Modern Prince, says:

The Modern Prince, in developing itself, changes the system of intellectual and moral relations, since its development means precisely that every act is conceived as useful or harmful, as virtuous or wicked, only in so far as it has the Modern Prince itself as a point of reference and helps to increase its power or oppose it. The Prince takes the place, in the conscience, of the divinity or of the categorical imperative, and becomes the basis of a modern laicism, of a complete laicisation of the whole of life and of all customary relations.[10]

First-generation Africanists endorsed this view of the historic role

---

tion of African nationalists the desire to vindicate the honor of his country by uniting its areas and peoples under a strong central national government, the lack of which he saw as the basis for Italy's weakness.

7. Antonio Gramsci, *The Modern Prince and Other Writings* (London: Lawrence and Wishart, 1967), p. 137.

8. For a critique of the modern-traditional dichotomy see J. R. Gusfield, "Tradition and Modernity: Misplaced Polarities in the Study of Social Change," *American Journal of Sociology* 72, no. 4 (January 1967): 351–62.

9. Karl W. Deutsch, "Social Mobilization and Political Development," *American Political Science Review* 55 (September 1961): 494.

10. Gramsci, op. cit., p. 140.

of the nationalist parties without reservation. Yet they did not elaborate a view of this basic role and the implications for the other components of a political system of the unfettered activity of such a party. Rather, these scholars presented a typology of political parties based on the degree of the party's unfettered control over the society. Such typologies derived from Maurice Duverger's distinction between mass and cadre parties but with important departures from Duverger's approach.[11] Africanists' typologies, notably those by Hodgkin, Schachter Morgenthau, Coleman and Rosberg, and Apter, all gave ideology, as an articulated prospective purpose, much greater emphasis than organization,[12] while Duverger did the obverse.[13] Moreover, Duverger analyzed political parties as components of larger political systems and analyzed particular parties as components of party systems, whereas Africanists posited the absence of system, denied the legitimacy of nonparty actors, and tended to focus on that one nationalist party that had succeeded in taking control of the colonial apparatus and becoming the governing party even before independence. Africanists asked primarily whether the party reflected, or planned to re-create, the societies in which it operated.[14] All first-generation Africanists assumed that African society and ordinary Africans were "traditional" and that nationalist parties and some few Africans associated with the party were "modern." African parties were commonly divided into mass or elite parties with the mass parties held to be "modern" and more "radical" than the elite parties that depended more on notables within the existing society for support than did the "mass" parties.[15] To this generation of scholars a citizen → party linkage posed a danger to the party's modernizing mission.

Ruth Schachter described African mass parties as "national

11. Maurice Duverger, *Political Parties* (London: Methuen, 1954), appeared in French in 1951, coinciding with the emerging academic interest in African nationalist parties.

12. Thomas Hodgkin, *Nationalism in Colonial Africa* (London: Mueller, 1956) and *African Political Parties* (Harmondsworth: Penguin Books, 1961); Ruth Schachter Morgenthau, *Political Parties in French-Speaking West Africa* (London: Oxford University Press, 1964); James S. Coleman and Carl G. Rosberg, eds., *Political Parties and National Integration in Tropical Africa* (Berkeley: University of California Press, 1965); David Apter, *The Politics of Modernization* (Chicago: University of Chicago Press, 1965). Each of these works presents a wealth of data that remains basic to contemporary work in the study of African politics.

13. Duverger, op. cit., pp. xiv–xv.

14. Hodgkin, *African Political Parties*, op. cit., p. 69.

15. Ibid., pp. 73, 161–65.

'melting pots,' educating people as Africans."[16] Thomas Hodgkin used even more forceful language in describing the party as an agent of social mobilization, suggesting that, "like Jehovah, the mass party is a jealous God. It permits the worship of no gods but itself."[17] In language remarkably similar to that of Gramsci, Hodgkin goes on to describe the historic responsibilities of the African mass party:

A mass party, while it may on occasion make use of traditional ties, is normally faced with the problem of buiding up an entirely new set of loyalties to a new form of organization under a new type of leader. A new sense of solidarity, based upon the party, has to be substituted for the solidarity based upon older, more restrictive groupings, associated with kinship, locality, language, religion. At the same time the mass party has to dispel the inertia and irresponsibility which colonial systems, by their nature, tend to produce among the governed; to put in its place a belief in the "historic role" of Africans in general and of a given African community in particular; and to refer to past periods of greatness and the achievements of folk heroes in order to stimulate a confidence in the possibilities of the present. Hence the importance which mass parties attach to propaganda and re-education, and the remarkable variety of techniques which they employ.[18]

By analyzing the African mass party, political observers were confident that they would also understand the African sociopolitical future. They predicted that mass parties would replace elite parties throughout Africa and that these triumphant mass parties would then be able to forgo even those instrumental ties with "traditional" notables that seemed analytically deviant and politically retrogressive.[19]

The second generation of African political inquiry was a logical and predictable reaction to this first generation. Second-generation observers questioned the primacy of the party, the validity of the elite-mass distinction, and the desirability of the mass party's unfettered directional role. This second generation took two distinct forms that have yet to coalesce. One thrust questioned the macrosystemic assumptions

16. Ruth Schachter, "Single-Party Systems in West Africa," *American Political Science Review* 55 (June 1961): 299.

17. Hodgkin, *African Political Parties*, p. 104.

18. Ibid., pp. 133–34.

19. Schachter, op. cit., p. 302, noting that the high traditional status of such mass-party leaders as Sekou Touré and Modibo Keita challenges her model, nevertheless asserts that, "on the whole, they used their nobility to preach equality."

and assertions of the first generation. Aristide Zolberg's seminal work, *Creating Political Order*, argued that the nationalist parties were organizationally weak, that there was little practical difference between mass and elite parties, and that parties were rapidly becoming less important than the administrative arm of the new independent states.[20] Zolberg retained the first generation's uncertainty about the possible constructive political role of ordinary Africans. He restricted his study to what he regarded as the "modern" sector and eliminated what he regarded as the "residual" or "traditional" sector.[21] By his own definitions his work still excluded the vast majority of the African population and most citizen-initiated organizations. He disputed the existence of parties capable of imposing a party → citizen linkage or a party → state linkage, but he neither examined empirical evidence of citizen → party linkages nor presented an analytical framework in which such a linkage could be either important or desirable. Zolberg remained content to negate the first-generation Africanists on their own macrosystemic grounds.

The other thrust of second-generation reaction to the initial concept of the African political party produced a variety of micropolitical studies that introduced a great variety of new data to the study of African politics.[22] Hodgkin had noted during the first generation that there was little evidence about local politics.[23] The second-generation Africanists rectified this omission. These observers questioned the first-generation assumption that a citizen → party linkage was atavistic, subversive, or regressive. Viewed as a local political actor, enmeshed in a web of local socioeconomic ties, the party did not seem as uniquely determinate as the nationalist party had seemed, viewed from the center. The party came to seem, and in fact was, less important than it had been during the nationalist era. Second-generation researchers were more interested in and tended to identify with local influentials and ordinary citizens more than with central party-state leaders who had often been the personal friends of the first-generation Africanists. This change had a normative

20. Aristide Zolberg, *Creating Political Order: The Party-States of West Africa* (Chicago: Rand McNally, 1966).

21. Ibid.

22. Lucy Behrman, *Muslim Brotherhoods and Politics in Senegal* (Cambridge: Harvard University Press, 1970); Audrey Smock, *Ibo Politics: The Role of Ethnic Unions in Eastern Nigeria* (Cambridge: Harvard University Press, 1971); C. S. Whitaker, *The Politics of Tradition and Continuity in Northern Nigeria, 1946–1966* (Princeton: Princeton University Press, 1970) are some of the outstanding second-generation monographs.

23. Hodgkin, *African Political Parties*, op. cit., p. 13.

base as well as an empirical one. Second-generation theorists generally endorsed Fanon's condemnation of the new African elites who had organized the parties and then forgotten the party members and ordinary citizens in the interest of institution-building and self-aggrandizement.[24]

The strength of second-generation studies lies in demonstration of the political relevance of a great variety of citizen organizations and their questioning of the premise that Africans must be socially mobilized before they can be constructive citizens. The shortcoming of this research is the relative neglect of citizen interaction with the central level of the party-state and the underemphasis on the increasing importance of the new African states. There is as yet no theory of a citizen ↔ party ↔ state linkage system.

Political Actors in Linkage Perspective

The basic actors of any political system are the state, the party or parties, and the citizens. A linkage approach directs attention to all three actors and notes the implications of the absolute or relative neglect of any actor in presenting an interpretation of either the entire political system or of any other single actor. A linkage approach not only includes all three but also raises particular questions about their nature specified in interaction terms. A linkage approach rejects a priori or essentialist characterizations as well as hypotheses that flow from such characterizations. Specification of these broad actors in interactive linkage terms offers the basis for a linkage-focused typology of actors. Such a typology is a prelude to typologies of linkage systems and to hypotheses about the operations and policy implications of such systems.

Such characterizations of the actors of a linkage system will point to some general features of all political systems. This study makes no attempt to operate at such an all-inclusive level of generalization. Rather, the study focuses on the political actors of the African party-state and its nationalist-party predecessor during the past twenty-five years. After the nationalist parties became official partners in party-states, the major failure of all students of African politics was the failure to develop a heuristic theory of the state in interactive linkage terms. The first-generation idea that the party would create and control the state quickly gave way to the idea that the state would create the new nation. The

24. Frantz Fanon, *The Wretched of the Earth* (New York: Grove Press, 1963).

centrality of party → state and party → citizen linkages gave way to a focus on state → citizen linkage.

At independence, African nationalist leaders virtually abandoned the task of party maintenance and party adaptation for the new tasks of building the institutions of rule. Nationalist heroes like Nyerere, Nkrumah, Senghor, Touré, whatever their ideological position, whatever their rhetoric about the primacy of the nationalist party, became heads of state. Although they invariably kept their previous positions as chairman of the nationalist party, their daily attention turned to state rather than to party issues. Likewise, their closest lieutenants in the party-central apparatus became cabinet ministers with new responsibilities for their respective departments. At the regional and local levels, a similar process occurred.

This tendency of African political leaders to devote themselves to building the institutions of the state as energetically as they had set about the task of winning control of the state is simply the practical politicians' recognition of the state's primacy in any political system.

Only the state commands a "monopoly of the legitimate use of physical force."[25] Although every state depends on citizen consent to some degree, the state's monopoly on legalized violence gives the state primacy in defining the form that consent will take, the organizations through which consent can be expressed, and the range of issues that consent organizations will be allowed to address. The state alone defines the "structure of political opportunities,"[26] and, in so doing, the state establishes its primacy in the ongoing process of engineering consent. The state thus defines the rules of interaction and influences profoundly the nature of the political actors. In so doing, the state seeks procedural-structural congruence as a prelude to substantive agreement on policies. A state can tolerate substantive disagreements more easily than it can endure the strain of disagreement or incongruence in the method of policy formulation and implementation, the process of political interaction. Any state is both a self-interested actor and the agent of other self-interested actors. In directing this process, the state imposes structural-

25. Max Weber, "Politics as a Vocation," in H. H. Gerth and C. W. Mills, eds., *From Max Weber* (New York: Oxford University Press, 1946), p. 78.

26. Alfred de Grazia, "Representation: Theory," in David L. Sills, ed., *International Encyclopedia of the Social Sciences* (New York: Macmillan and The Free Press, 1968), 13:463.

procedural congruence directly through laws and regulations that apply to other political actors and indirectly by organizing itself in particular ways.

A state is a multifaceted actor. The almost limitless number and variations of agencies and departments within a state that would be crucial for understanding a particular linkage in detail can be subsumed for present purposes under two broad categories of state structures—the administrative and the legislative. An administration by its very nature fragments all issues into their smallest and most disconnected technical dimensions. Each agency and department will seek maximum jurisdiction over its particular part of any issue or problem. Decision making is to be done according to rules and procedures rather than through the marshaling of external pressure. It is clear, of course, that bureaucracies operate "politically," through the application of power and influence and not the mere application of rules.[27] However, a bureaucracy is open to a particular type of influence from particular types of linked actors. The specialized components of an administration will deal most readily and most comfortably with special-interest associations restricted in interest and membership to the particular area of expertise of that one component of the bureaucracy. The bureaucratic department will enter an ongoing linkage with the type of organization that can give the department support in its wars with other sectors of the bureaucracy. The capacity of the interest group to provide broad citizen support will be counterproductive from an intraadministration perspective if the group cannot give undivided support to its allied administrative department. An administrative state thus fragments issues and constituencies and the constituencies' organizations.

A legislature cumulates precisely where an administration fragments. Legislatures can be dominated only by a party or a coalition of parties that establishes commonalities among the concerns of diverse constituencies. The legislature requires not unidimensional commitment but the capacity for forming policy packages that can unite discrete problems and issues and generalize these disparate concerns to the level of basic legal principles.

The nature of the state—administrative or legislative—has a direct impact on the nature of parties, the type of linkages they can enter, and

27. V. O. Key, *Politics, Parties, and Pressure Groups* (New York: Crowell, 1952).

the likely effectiveness of these linkages in pursuing particular policies. There is little room for parties in an administrative state, whereas they are fundamental in a legislative system.

Some states allow markedly incongruent actors and linkages to function within the political system. African states have not been this tolerant of incongruence. Instead, African states shortly after independence began to equate state-building with administration-building. In important ways this was a continuation of the colonial legacy of administrative states. It was also a serious departure from the rationale of nationalist-party politics.[28] Nationalist parties found their forums in the colonial legislatures, newly opened to elected representatives with actual decision-making authority. At independence, African nationalist leaders did not simply carry on an unambiguously administrative colonial legacy. They consciously chose to establish administrative states. In so doing they sacrificed the nationalist parties.

African citizens and the question of citizenship in African polities have not engaged the interest or attention of most political scientists. An interactive linkage approach to African politics reveals this omission and its implications and suggests descriptive-analytical concepts that can mitigate the deficiencies of the language now used in reference to African citizens and party members. Studies of political development commonly assess citizens' "fitness" for participation, or even for inclusion, according to socioeconomic criteria. It is far less common to examine actual linkage in terms of their effect on facilitating, precluding, or regulating participation.

African citizens are generally regarded as tribals, a concept taken from the kinship-focused literature of early twentieth-century anthropology. Political scientists have not really investigated local socioeconomic political organizations; they have merely derived certain hypotheses from this anthropological literature. To many political scientists, the concept of a tribe implies self-imposed isolation, intergroup hostility, a parochialness amounting to primitiveness that precludes citizenship in the "modern" state.[29] Coleman and Rosberg summarized the view of first-

---

28. For a more detailed discussion of colonial-administrative and nationalist-conciliar regimes as precedents for the postindependence party-states, see Frances Hill, *Ujamaa: Mobilization and Participation in Tanzania* (London: Frank Cass, 1980).

29. Clifford Geertz, "The Integrative Revolution," in Clifford Geertz, ed., *Old Societies and New States* (New York: The Free Press, 1963).

generation Africanists when they concluded that "traditional Africa" had "in most cases . . . played an obstructive role."[30]

Predictions about the destructive effects of tribalism seem, when examined superficially, to be corroborated by the experiences of contemporary Africa—the Nigerian civil war, the chaos in the Congo, Ashanti hostility to Nkrumah, Kikuyu-Luo confrontations in Kenya, the Eritrean disinclination to accept Ethiopian rule, the continuing tensions between the northern and southern Sudanese, the civil war between the Arabs and the Bantu in Chad, to mention only a few. The fact of these confrontations and the human suffering they entailed is indisputable. What is open to question is the simplistic assertion that these complex events were the direct result of primitive tribalism and did not grow out of very complex configurations of interests among which a tribal loyalty was present but was not necessarily primary.

The concept of a local power system is designed to free such terms as "tribes" of their "non-modern" connotations. A century or more of incorporation into colonial administrations, nationalist movements, and independent polities has changed what anthropologists call "tribes" into local power systems operating within larger political-economic systems.[31] A local power system is studied through the matrix of its external interactions.[32]

Citizens develop their own politically relevant forms of cohesion. The party need not start de novo aggregating the disparate elements of a fragmented mass. Indeed, the citizens may seem too organized for either the party or the state, either of which will then demand that citizens abandon their own forms of association and relate to the party or the state only as fragments of a mass. Much of the first-generation discussion of mass parties operates with a fundamental conceptual ambiguity: Is the mass party an all-embracing party or does "mass" refer to the lack of organization in its membership? A linkage approach offers the possibility of understanding the party's and the state's orientation to autonomous citizen organization as well as the political implications of particular forms of cohesion.

30. Coleman and Rosberg, op. cit., p. 658.
31. Peter C. Lloyd, "Traditional Rulers," in Coleman and Rosberg, op. cit., pp. 382–412.
32. For an analogous approach to the study of caste, see McKim Marriott, "Interactional and Attributional Theories of Caste-Ranking," *Man in India*, vol. 30 (April–June 1959).

A linkage approach directs attention to the position of politicals parties between citizens and the state. This does not automatically mean that parties define their own linkages nor that they determine their own organization with a view to imposing a particular kind of linkage on other political actors. The question of whether a party can or should impose its own organizational structures and procedures on other political actors is not easily solved at either the empirical or normative levels. Michels's classic study of *Political Parties* warns against the inevitability that party leaderships will overdetermine their relations with the party's members.[33] This possibility, and evidence that some parties were capable of imposing this degree of high salience directionality on party → citizen linkages, drove Rosa Luxemburg to distrust party organization as almost inevitably inimical to the pursuit of progressive social-economic policies of vital concern to citizens.[34] Lenin had the same confidence in the party's determinative role but accepted the normative implications as the only road to progressive policies.[35] Political development theorists have tended toward a statist Leninism free of the empirical or normative doubts of the socialist practitioner-theorists.[36] If anything, political-development theorists are disquieted only by the party's potential failure to impose a party → citizen linkage, not by the party's willingness to accept a state → party linkage.[37]

The African parties that have survived into the independence era did so as official partners of the state in the party-state. This would seem to suggest that statist-Leninist models of theorists like Huntington are heuristically appropriate. However, much of the data collected by second-generation Africanists suggest that this is not the case. Indeed, the idea of a unified party, with operative intraparty links between members and

33. Robert Michels, *Political Parties: A Sociological Study of the Oligarchical Tendencies of Modern Democracy* (New York: The Free Press, 1962).

34.. Rosa Luxemburg, *The Mass Strike: The Political Party and the Trade Unions* (New York: Harper & Row, 1971); "Organizational Questions of Social Democracy," in Mary Alice Water, ed., *Rosa Luxemburg Speaks* (New York: Pathfinder Press, 1970), pp. 112–30.

35. V. I. Lenin, *What Is to Be Done?* (New York: International Publishers, 1932) and *Organizational Principles of a Proletarian Party* (Moscow: Novasti, 1972).

36. Samuel P. Huntington, *Political Order in Changing Societies* (New Haven: Yale University Press, 1968).

37. A notable exception is Robert Dahl, *Polyarchy: Participation and Opposition* (New Haven: Yale University Press, 1971). Dahl sees participation, defined as contestation and opposition expressed through both political parties and interest groups, as a fundamental and positive process in any political system.

leaders, is seen as a misleading reification of the much more complex reality.

African parties are components both of local power systems and of the central governing apparatus. The local ties of parties are so important that national parties are better understood as multilocal parties.[38] Multilocalism implies the primacy of citizen → party linkages. It further suggests that the nature of these linkages varies in different areas. Most parties are more active in some areas of their countries than in others, and even in those areas where they are active, they owe more to their local linkages than to autonomous party organization.

The multilocal component of the party is not necessarily well integrated with the party that is the partner in the central government. The official party is a much more formalistic entity, determined more by a state → party linkage than by its own organization or by a citizen → party linkage. Most commonly these strains are resolved by maintaining a low intensity of interaction between the party's multilocal and its official components.

As an official party, a partner in a party-state, the party may be either a governing or a symbolic party. The governing party will have an important impact on government decision making; it will approximate a state ↔ party linkage. In so doing, it will be able to draw upon its membership of ordinary citizens to strengthen its claim to an important role in government circles. A symbolic party is determined by the state in a state → party linkage. The party's primary function is to symbolize, and thus to legitimate, actions taken by the state, often in the party's name. The party may occasionally exert considerable influence as a "significant symbol,"[39] but this influence has little relation to any party → citizen linkage. The symbolic party presides over, rather than participates in, the political process.

Party Linkages and Party-State Dynamics

First-generation theorists posited a close and determinate relationship between the party's linkages and the party's ideology. With little or no opportunity to observe the translation of parties' nationalist rhetoric

38. See Frances Hill, "TANU: Single-Party Multi-Localism," in Dunstan Wai, ed., *Political Parties and Political Participation in Africa* (London: Frank Cass, forthcoming).
39. Mead, op. cit., pp. 61–75, 122–25, 146–47.

into governmental policies, these first-generation theorists assumed that party → citizen linkages produced socialist, Pan-Africanist, nonaligned policies, whereas citizen → party linkages produced capitalist and neo-colonialist policies.[40] Second-generation theorists documented numerous deviations from these assumptions, without presenting any systematic explanation of them.

A linkage approach suggests several hypotheses that help to systematize deviations from first-generation assumptions noted by second-generation researchers. These hypotheses do not individually or severally produce a complete linkage theory of the African party-states. They do suggest a direction for future research and for the reinterpretation of existing materials.

Hypothesis I: Parties' policies cannot be distinguished or predicted by the presence or absence, direction, or salience of a party's ascriptive linkages.

> *Postulate A:* The lack of correlation relates partly to the lack of variation in the posited dependent variable, the nature of parties' policies. Policies pursued by the nationalist parties once in power have differed less than their various preindependence rhetorics. All have pursued not socialism or capitalism but a statist Africanization. Houphouet-Boigny describes his economic policy as "state capitalism" but has built the state-controlled sector faster than did his neighboring socialist, Kwame Nkrumah.[41] Houphouet's policy of nationalization has not differed appreciably from that of Africa's most determined African socialist, Julius Nyerere. One of Africa's most purposive and successful "modernizing" regimes has been the ascriptively determined northern Nigerian regime of emirs and technocrats.[42]

> *Postulate B:* Any differences that may be found cannot be causally related to the official party's historic linkages. All parties relied for electoral support on local power-system influentials during the critical elections that gave them control of the state apparatus. Once in control, the party—and its linkages—became largely irrelevant to the formulation and implementation of regime policy. Those few regimes that continue to permit elections that are not

---

40. Such hypotheses are summarized in the "pragmatic-pluralistic" and "revolutionary-centralizing" regimes outlined in Coleman and Rosberg, op. cit., p. 5.

41. Frances Hill, "Ghana and the Ivory Coast: Single-Party Systems and Their Policies" (M.A. thesis, University of Birmingham, Centre for West African Studies, 1967).

42. Whitaker, op. cit.

simple endorsements of the single party's single list do not allow elections to become issue oriented. In the midst of a major effort to foster rural socialist transformation, the Tanzanian party-state did virtually nothing to make Ujamaa the focal issue of the election.[43]

Postulate C: Factions within a ruling party do not generally represent different policies and any differences that do exist cannot be causally related to ascriptive linkages.

Senegal is the most French of the former French colonies.[44] Its "citizens" in the four coastal communes began sending deputies to the French Assembly in the 1880s. Once political parties began to form, they were linked closely with metropolitan parties, defined to a marked degree by French metropolitan ideological positions, and joined in parliamentary coalitions in Paris. Senegalese leaders have themselves, both personally and politically, been far more French cosmopolitan than their brother nationalists. Yet, Senegalese politics and Senegalese parties have all become enmeshed in a web of linkages with well-organized Muslim brotherhoods that control the area of the country producing Senegal's chief export, groundnuts. Once the election law changed to permit a broadened and ultimately universal adult suffrage, the key to a party's electoral success, the precondition for acceptance established by the colonial regime, lay in these alliances.[45] Leopold Senghor, a teacher of the French language and the French-language poet of negritude, was the first and most successful Senegalese nationalist to make such alliances with the most powerful of the brotherhood leaders.

For those socialists who tend to dismiss Senghor's negritude as romantic mysticism, a folklore and not an ideology, these linkages seem to define Senghor's political party and prescribe his policies. Senghor's confrontation with his lieutenant, Mamadou Dia, is most commonly

43. Frances Hill, "Electoral Participation and Ujamaa Mobilization in Tanzania" (Paper delivered at the African Studies Association Conference, Syracuse, N.Y., 1973) and "Elections in the Local Context," in the Election Study Committee, University of Dar es Salaam, *Socialism and Participation: Tanzania's 1970 National Elections* (Dar es Salaam: Tanzania Publishing House, 1974).

44. Michael Crowder, *Senegal: A Study in French Assimilation Policy* (London: Oxford University Press, 1962).

45. Kenneth Robinson, "Senegal: The Elections to the Territorial Assembly, March 1957," in Kenneth Robinson and J. M. Mackenzie, eds., *Five Elections in Africa* (London: Oxford University Press), pp. 281–390.

seen as a confrontation between a socialist modernizer (Dia) and the ascriptive romantic (Senghor).[46] Yet, a study of linkage politics in independent Senegal suggests that both sides in the dispute had the same kinds of linkages and that their differences of ideology cannot be accounted for in linkage terms.[47] One possible explanation is that the Dia-Senghor confrontation was not primarily about ideology but about the control of state apparatus, irrespective of its subsequent instrumental utility in facilitating particular policies. Another explanation is that there was a meaningful difference between the two but that their linkages with ascriptive groups were so similar that ideological differences cannot be related to these linkages.

Hypothesis II: As administrative regimes, African party-states are vulnerable to pressure from interest groups that can establish effective long-term linkages with the relevant section of the bureaucracy.

> *Postulate A:* The African party-state seeks to preclude such citizen → state linkages by putting the interest groups under formal party control and such party → state linkage by rendering Parliament peripheral.

> *Postulate B:* These new responsibilities do not allow the party to develop operative party → citizen linkages or a citizen → party linkage. The party's branch organization and its subsequent functional organization are used to neutralize each other. Nkrumah pioneered this tactic of political control in the 1959 reforms of the Convention People's party.[48] The resulting tensions between party wings and party branches effectively destroyed the CPP and any hope of citizen participation through it without advancing the cause of socialism in Ghana. Nyerere used the same tactic to control the Tanzanian trade unions and cooperatives *before* he had formulated his ideology of Ujamaa socialism.[49]

46. William J. Foltz, "Senegal," in Coleman and Rosberg, op. cit., pp. 63–64.

47. Behrman, op. cit., and Donald B. Cruise O'Brien *The Mourides of Senegal: The Political and Economic Organization of an Islamic Brotherhood* (Oxford: Clarendon Press, 1971), pp. 262–84.

48. David Apter, *Ghana in Transition* (New York: Atheneum, 1963) and "Ghana," in Coleman and Rosberg, op. cit. Hodgkin, *African Political Parties*, op. cit., pp. 118, 124. Maxwell Owusu, *Uses and Abuses of Political Power* (Chicago: University of Chicago Press, 1970).

49. William Friedland, "Cooperation, Conflict, and Conscription: TANU-TFL Relations, 1955–1964," in Jeffrey Butler and A. A. Castagno, eds., *Boston University Papers on Africa: Transition in African Politics* (New York: Praeger, 1967), pp. 67–114.

Hypothesis III: Only in rare cases does a state's policy of economic development or national integration require an active citizen commitment that, in turn, requires a high salience party → citizen linkage.

Postulate A: Mobilizational parties pose a risk of developing citizen → party links or party ↔ citizen links, both of which are challenges to the state's power to impose structural-procedural congruence on the political system. This risk is often not worth the level of mobilizational effectiveness the relatively weak African parties are able to contribute to the implementation of state policies.

Postulate B: The government will sacrifice the implementation of any particular policy to preclude the establishment of these citizen → party linkages, even a party ↔ citizen linkage.

Postulate C: The state will weaken the party in the interest of maintaining a state → party linkage, even if this means losing the party's services as a mobilizational ally in implementing a particular policy.

Corollary 1: These regime tactics are based on the regimes' recognition of the difference between the multilocal and the central-symbolic aspects of the party.

Tanzania is one of the very few African states to pursue a policy that requires active citizen involvement, not merely passive citizen acquiescence. The Nyerere regime's attempts to foster rural socialist transformation through rural resettlement has involved TANU, the official party, as a mobilizing partner of the state bureaucracy. When the multilocal party finally endorsed peasant resistance to this nationwide resettlement program, the regime was constrained to modify its policy temporarily.[50] However, the major result of this ability of the multilocal party to oppose, within party-state decision-making circles, the policy legitimated by the central symbolic party was to force Nyerere to choose between components of the party as well as between the party and his policy. The outcome is by no means clear, although it seems that Nyerere is attempting to purge the TANU membership. The possible advantages of a party → citizen linkage did not seem worth the risk of a

50. This attempt to purge TANU was announced by Nyerere at a November 1974 meeting of the TANU National Executive Committee, which was convened in Nyerere's home area. See news reports and editorials in the government newspaper, *The Daily News*, of 28 November, 2 December, and 9 December 1974.

possible citizen → party linkage that promised to become a citizen → party → state linkage. Any linkage that involves the party in a high salience, high intensity interaction with citizens will thus be avoided, even by the mobilizing party-state.

In seeking political linkages with the state through political parties, citizens of the African party-states face a formidable array of obstacles. Nevertheless, such citizen-initiated linkages are the citizens' chief hope of influencing the course pursued by the states that control their destinies to such a significant extent. Linkages, even those controlled by citizens in their own interest, do not promise a political millennium. Political systems will continue to reflect the self-interested offensives of all political actors—citizens, parties, and states. The assumption common to African leaders and students of African politics of a previous decade—that the self-interest of states was progressive, whereas the self-interest of citizens was regressive and subversive—is untenable. This does not suggest that the obverse is correct. The maximum good a political system can offer is that "this cruel game will continue without end"[51] and the parties and citizens will become allies in monitoring and restraining the state. The present status of the African parties and the African party-states does not justify even this minimal hope by African citizens.

51. Michels, op. cit., p. 371.

240

PART IV

Linkage by Reward

11.

Political Power Linkages in Italy: The Nature of the Christian Democratic Party Organization

ROBERT LEONARDI

In recent years there has been a considerable amount of debate over how the Italian Christian Democratic party has been able to maintain a position of hegemony over the political system for more than thirty years despite what seems to be a never-ending series of internal conflicts that have produced periodic upheavals in the party organization and governmental coalitions at both national and local levels.[1] Its success is even more surprising when it is remembered that the largest, best financed, and intellectually most dynamic Communist party in the Western world is among its national opponents. What has been the basis for the continuing success of the Christian Democrats in Italy? This question can only be adequately answered by looking at the set of linkages that the party has been able to forge in connecting its administration of political power to a highly complex and fragmented societal structure.[2]

1. See Giorgio Galli and Paolo Facchi, *La sinistra democristiana* (Milan: Feltrinelli Editore, 1962), and Ruggero Orfei, *L'occupazione del potere: I democristiani '45/'75* (Milan: Longanesi, 1976).
2. For a discussion of the fragmented nature of the Italian political and social structure see Joseph LaPalombara, "Italy: Fragmentation, Isolation, and Alienation," in Lucian Pye and Sidney Verba, eds., *Political Culture and Political Development* (Princeton: Princeton University Press, 1965), pp. 282–329.

The linkages to be discussed in this study are those institutions and groups that serve to transmit the demands and wishes of the populace to the political leaders who occupy positions of decision making in the political system and implement governmental decisions in the society. Thus, the linkage system transmits demands up to the centers of power and conveys decisions down to the citizenry. In Italy, as in most other countries, any consideration of the primary linkages between the exercise of political power and the citizenry leads to an initial consideration of the role played by political party organizations. As Kay Lawson has written, only political parties "openly claim to link the general public to political power by placing representatives of their organizations in positions where they may exercise that power on behalf of that public."[3] The main emphasis here is on the upward, rather than downward, linkage function. However, in certain societal settings political parties have performed *both* functions or have shared with other societal subgroups or public institutions responsibilities in the two areas.

Figure 11.1 presents a classification of groups and institutions that have, under various conditions, provided political systems with vital linkage units. These linkages can be distinguished along two dimensions: (1) the "public" versus "private" nature of the link between centers of decision making and the society and (2) the "constitutional" versus "organizational" status of these linkages in the political system. The first dimension is important in establishing exactly *who* is being linked and what is the relationship of the linked group to the rest of society. A public linkage is by definition potentially open to all of the members of the society, and the institutions acting in this area do so in the name of the public good. Heads of public institutions are ultimately responsible to all enfranchised citizens or to their representatives. Private groups, on the other hand, draw support from defined subgroups of the society. These groups represent primarily the interests of their membership and only secondarily (based on some form of extrapolation of the interests of their members to the rest of society) a more general, societal good.

The second dimension of the constitutional versus organizational nature of the linkage attempts to distinguish the *source of authority* for the linkage system. The constitutional cell assumes the existence

3. Kay Lawson, *The Comparative Study of Political Parties* (New York: St. Martin's Press, 1976), p. 3.

FIGURE 11.1.   Classification of Linkage Units

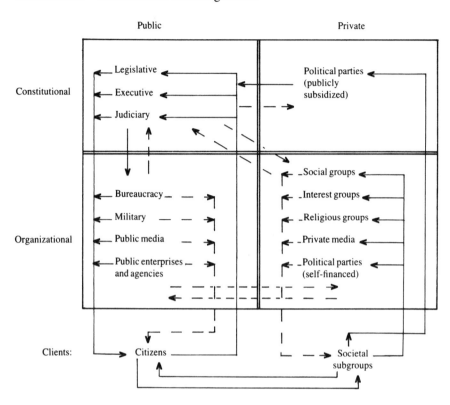

Solid arrows represent the normal linkage patterns.

Broken arrows represent the ad hoc, informal linkage patterns.

of two distinct types of linkage patterns: (1) an upward linkage usually represented by the electoral process or some other kind of annointment procedure that grants legitimacy to the decisions taken by the leadership and (2) a downward linkage that is necessary for the implementation of decisions. The nature of the downward linkage is a vital element in any political system because it effectively measures the "space" between the citizen and the decision-making apparatus of the society. In small and simple societies the decision makers can also be the decision implementators. However, in more complex societies the usual pattern is to create a decision-implementation apparatus to rationalize the process. The daily contact of the citizen with the decision makers is coordinated through an organizational network over which the citizen has only an indirect control by means of the constitutional electoral process. In this manner, the direct contact between citizens and decision makers is diminished and the necessary organizational space is created for the growth of alternative linkage patterns.

In figure 11.1 the solid lines represent the normal linkage patterns that are supposed to articulate the contacts between the citizenry, societal subgroups, and various components of the political system. However, in practice this linkage pattern can be (and often is) short-circuited at various points and other ad hoc, informal linkages are substituted. The broken lines are an attempt to illustrate the possibilities for alternative linkage patterns. The importance assumed by the informal linkages is dependent upon the strength of the separation of the public from private centers of decision making and the maintenance of the distinction between the decision-making and administrative functions in a political system. If these distinctions are not maintained, there will be a process of cross-fertilization and interpenetration taking place among the units in the four cells contained in figure 11.1. There are numerous examples of interpenetration of functions and linkages in the everyday workings of government. For example, when the bureaucracy assumes the function of making basic policy decisions it is undertaking decision making that would otherwise be the role of the political organs of the society, and in cases where societal subgroups are given "governmental" functions—for example, interest groups in the Fascist corporate state and religious organizations in theocratic regimes—the distinction between public and private spheres breaks down. Accordingly, in the case of countries in which political parties have been granted state subsidies in recognition of their vital linkage function it would be accurate to think of these parties as occupying a constitutional linkage role even though they still maintain their private membership nature.

In practice, maintaining the separation of the decision-making and administrative functions depends on the socioeconomic development of the society, the degree of institutionalization of the various political organs and processes of government, and the absence of unexpected upheavals (e.g., coups d'état, revolutions, decolonialization, etc.), which can upset the normal distribution of roles. These factors can influence the amount of importance assumed in the political system of the informal linkage patterns. It is conceivable that a pattern of ad hoc linkages that effectively nullifies the role of constitutional linkages can be created, but in most cases ad hoc linkages become complementary to, rather than a complete alternative for, constitutional linkages. However, when informal linkages begin to assume a predominant role over the formal ones, it is usually done in accordance with a set of principles that are not normally tied to the functioning of that organization in society. Samuel P. Huntington has argued that societies with highly developed traditional political institutions (bureaucracies, military organizations, religious groups, etc.) may be able to adapt these institutions to higher levels of political participation without parties, but at some point "political parties become necessary to organize and to structure the expanded participation."[4] Theoretically, the opposite can also hold. Once parties become institutionalized, the state system can be used to consolidate or perpetuate their control of political power by the creation of a system of ad hoc linkages that bypasses the formal constitutional linkage pattern.

It is the contention of this study that the Italian Christian Democratic party has pursued a strategy of establishing a far-reaching system of ad hoc linkages to preserve its control of political power. The process has been characterized by the growing interpenetration of the political party organization and the public administrative and economic structure. This system of ad hoc linkages seems to have effectively reduced the ability of the constitutional linkage system in maintaining a normal flow in the relationship between the public sphere and the citizens. To evaluate objectively the possible importance of the ad hoc linkage system created in the post–World War II period by the DC to manage to its advantage the flow of decision making and implementation in the Italian political system, an investigation must: (1) look at the historical context within which these developments took place and (2) find an empirical verification of the existence of this alternative system of ad hoc linkages.

The Historical Context and Stages of Development

The development of the linkage system through which the Christian Democratic party has been able to maintain itself in control of power can be broken down into four distinct stages. Each stage was charac-

4. Samuel P. Huntington, *Political Order in Changing Societies* (New Haven: Yale University Press, 1968), p. 399.

247

terized by a particular configuration of the internal party structure, the relationship between the party organization and external groups, and the methods used for the control of political power.

The first stage covers the founding of the party, the period from July 1943 to May 1946 when the DC was: (1) organizationally, an outgrowth of Catholic Action and other church-related organizations and (2) politically, one of three mass parties in government (the other two being the Socialists and Communists). During the first stage the DC did not have an autonomous organizational structure. It survived as a party of notables whose organizational needs were filled by Catholic Action and whose electoral campaigns were mostly staffed and financed through the civic committees organized by the church parishes. Thus, from the beginning the DC lacked an autonomous party structure. Catholic Action, the civic committees, and local notables provided the links to friendly societal subgroups that could be induced to vote for the party. The DC lacked any semblance of structural autonomy from the subgroups or parallel voluntary organizations that it sought to attract in support of its candidates for elections.

Given the bitter competition with the other two mass parties (which, on the whole, had stronger party organizations), the DC had to expand its potential clientele beyond the Catholic subculture and backward agrarian regions of the South. The largest potential pool of votes included the frightened elements of the middle classes who had become compromised in the Fascist experience and who were eagerly seeking an escape from the tide of revolution set in motion by the anti-Fascist resistance. The Christian Democrats succeeded in becoming this haven of safety for these classes and for all those elements in society who feared radical change at the hands of the Communists and Socialists. In support of this electoral strategy the DC undertook to prevent any extensive purge of the state bureaucracy and radical redistribution of the resources or responsibilities in society.[5]

The second stage of party development (May 1947 through June 1954) was characterized by the DC's assumption of predominant political power at both the national and local levels of policymaking. In May 1947 the Communists and Socialists were forced out of the govern-

5. For a well-balanced discussion of the early history of the Christian Democratic party see Leo Valiani, *L'avvento di DeGasperi* (Turin: Francesco De Silva Editore, 1949), and the more recent study by Giovanni Baget-Bozzo, *Il partito cristiano al potere* (Florence: Valecchi Editore, 1974).

ment by the Christian Democratic leaders and Prime Minister Alcide DeGasperi in return for United States aid, and a split was promoted in the Socialist party, which divided the Saragat Socialists (i.e., Social Democrats who formed the PSDI) from the Nenni Socialists, who remained on a maximalist track.[6] This left the DC as the only mass party in government with the responsibility of organizing the minor parties of the Center and Center-Left (Social Democrats, Republicans, and Liberals) into a viable governmental coalition. The effort was greatly enhanced by the results of the 1948 parliamentary elections, which gave the DC an absolute majority in Parliament. Nevertheless, DeGasperi decided to invite the other centrist parties to join the government so that the DC could more effectively establish its control over the center of the political spectrum.

After the 1948 elections the fate of the DC became increasingly identified with the perpetuation of the then existing state apparatus; it subordinated large elements of its initial party program—calling for a restructuring of the public sector (e.g., creation of the regions, reform of the bureaucracy, social control of industry, etc.)—to the interests of the economic and social status quo. Having gained predominant control of the political system as a result of the 1948 elections and being able to maintain on its side the entire gamut of church organizations, the DC leadership postponed the creation of a viable party organization.

Nevertheless, certain elements of the party, led by Giuseppe Dossetti and organized around the journal *Social Chronicles* (*Cronache Sociali*), undertook a struggle at the 1949 Party Congress to free the party organization from its dependence on external cadres and support.[7] Dossetti's forces succeeded in getting the congress to adopt a measure to limit the predominance of elected officials, especially parliamentarians and governmental ministers, in the determination of party policies. The purpose was to emphasize the role of the party organization as the primary linkage between the party's leadership and base so that internal decisions would remain with the party organs rather than be farmed out sector by sector to auxiliary extraparty organizations.[8] The victory, however, was only superficial. The party remained in the hands of De-

6. See Alan A. Platt and Robert Leonardi, "American Foreign Policy and the Postwar Italian Left," *Political Science Quarterly* 93 (Summer 1978): 197–215.

7. Baget-Bozzo, op. cit.

8. Franco Boiardi, *Dossetti e la crisi dei cattolici italiani* (Florence: Parenti, 1956).

Gasperi and the "antiparty" forces—that is, the moderate wing of the party.

The group of party leaders close to Dossetti had to wait until the following Party Congress in 1954 to implement their ideas on party organization. The moment of victory came in the defeat of DeGasperi's attempt to institutionalize the de facto role assumed in party affairs by the "notables" in representation of extraparty and local interests. In his introductory speech to the congress, DeGasperi clearly described the role that the notables had played in party affairs:

Now, I would like to bring to mind the dual function of the party. The function which is more specifically its own is to give political direction to the representatives and legislators who find their origin in the party. The party carries out this function democratically, that is, based on the decisions of its cadres in its public meetings and ruling organs. But at the same time, the party represents a much wider reality which is pertinent to its electoral base and, as a result, to the general public. Here, along with numerical strength must be considered experience, personal capabilities, and social position. It is in this light that enter into consideration the so-called notables, conceived as persons with certain capacities and conceived as representatives of important social or local groups. Political decision making must remain the responsiblity of the organs of the party in the manner foreseen by the statutes, but the need for elaborating legislative proposals or general lines of orientation—and above all when one is considering matters of great importance—requires one to also consult people with experience, technical expertise, or extensive cultural backgrounds and the representatives of general or local interests. One must contact all of them. This is why we should complete our organization in two ways: (1) to have a frequent and constant exchange of ideas at the center with professional, trade union, and cultural organizations and (2) in the regions and at the periphery to promote a continuous contact of the party organization with the authoritative and friendly notables in order to consult with them on the more important affairs and interests of the region and the nation.[9]

The followers of Dossetti were successful in defeating DeGasperi's proposals because of (1) DeGasperi's clear antiorganizational stance, which promised to perpetuate the subordination of the party's cadre structure to local notables and (2) the inability of the existing structure (or lack thereof) to ensure the DC's control of political power. First,

9. Alcide DeGasperi, "Nella lotta per la democrazia," *Dieci Congressi D.C., 1946–1967* (Rome: SPES, n.d.), pp. 203–04.

by 1954 the role assumed by the southern notables and external organizations during the 1948 elections had proved to be highly unstable.
In the 1953 parliamentary elections the DC and its centrist allies fell
from a high of 62 percent of the vote in 1948 to 49.2 percent. The distribution of the vote (precipitous decline of the DC and resurgence
of the radical Right represented by the Neo-Fascists and Monarchists)
seemed to suggest that many of the southern agricultural interests had
become disenchanted with the DC in its refusal in 1950 to stop the
agrarian-reform legislation pushed through Parliament by the parties
of the Left. Second, the church was beginning to have second thoughts
with regard to its unlimited support of the DC on the heels of the party's
refusal in 1952 to go along with Pius XII's proposal to form a conservative
coalition, extending from the DC to the Neo-Fascists, in an attempt
to prevent the Left from gaining control of the Rome city government.
The wavering loyalty and diminishing political efficacy of these two
crucial elements in the DC's system of social-political linkages with
its voting base forced the party to contemplate seriously the need to
begin a vigorous program to build up its long-neglected party organization. The defeat of the DeGasperi proposal and the victory of the
ex-Dossetti group, Democratic Initiative (Iniziativa Democratica),
now led by Amintore Fanfani, opened up a new stage in the history
of the party organization.

This third stage thus begins in June 1954 and extends through to
December 1963. During these nine years the Christian Democratic
leadership undertook to: (1) build an autonomous party organization
and reduce its dependence on external organizations and local notables
and (2) find an alternative coalition formula (Center-Left or Center-
Right in substitution for the traditional centrist coalition) that would
allow it to maintain its control over public policymaking.[10] Drives in
both areas were led by Amintore Fanfani, who had been elected to the
secretaryship of the party at the end of the 1954 Party Congress. He
immediately undertook an ambitious program to reinforce the existing
party apparatus, extend the presence of local party organizations in
sections of the country where up to then they had been absent, and increase the membership base of the party organization. During the five-
year span of his leadership, the number of local party organizations,
termed "sections," grew by 20 percent, from 10,560 to 12,672, and

10. Giorgio Galli, *Fanfani* (Milan: Feltrinelli Editore, 1975).

membership figures rose by 28 percent, having reached 1,602,929 in 1959 in comparison with the 1,254,732 in 1954.[11] By 1957 Fanfani had also begun to prepare the party for an eventual "opening to the Left," which implied the entrance of the Nenni Socialists (the PSI), into the government coalition. The alternative coalition—that is, "opening to the Right"—seemed to offer fewer guarantees of success because of the unstable voting base of the rightist parties and the danger that any alliance with the Neo-Fascists would split the DC along progressive-conservative lines and the even graver danger that such an alliance would permanently destabilize the socioeconomic fabric of the country.

In the long run the opening to the Left offered more guarantees to the existing socioeconomic order by allowing the DC to continue its predominance in the political sphere and avoid the instigation of a new civil war. The Center-Left formula promised greater political stability, assuming that the Nenni Socialists would effectively disassociate themselves from the Communists and join the Saragat Socialists (Social Democrats) in the re-creation of a unified Socialist party. A fusion of the two wings of the Socialist movement was seen as providing the necessary assurances to Italy's foreign allies and internal socioeconomic interests that the entrance of the Nenni Socialists into the government would not be followed by the institution of a series of radical reforms.[12] However, despite the initial guarantees, the PSI entered the government only in December 1963 and only after Fanfani had been forced out of the DC party leadership. It took four years under the tutelage of Aldo Moro to convince a majority of the party, the church, and major economic interests in the country that the only viable alternative for a national government was the Center-Left coalition. The ousting of Fanfani from the party secretaryship also brought a halt to the organization effort in the party and consolidated the trend toward the reinforcement of the party structure through the penetration of the growing public sector rather than through the building of an autonomous party organization.

The fourth and present stage of party development began with the first Aldo Moro government in December 1963. As the political price for collaboration of the Nenni Socialists in the government, the

11. Gianfranco Poggi, ed., *L'organizzazione partitica del PCI e della DC*. (Bologna: Il Mulino, 1968), p. 263.
12. Giuseppe Tamburrano, *Cronache e storia del centro-sinistra* (Milan: Feltrinelli Editore, 1973).

Center-Left coalition undertook to pass a series of reforms that began with the unification of the lower secondary educational system and the nationalization of the electrical power industry. These measures were to be followed by attempts to increase the potential impact of the public sector in the economy. Contrary to the expectation of many, by 1963 the DC had already changed its orientation on the public role in the economy. In fact, the DC began to exploit this innovation in the Italian economy for internal party advantages.[13]

In the middle and late sixties the DC was able to perfect its use of the control of key ministries (e.g., State Participations, Treasury, Finance, Industry, etc.) to reinforce the party structure. The dominant position of the DC in the governmental coalition and in the Italian political system as a whole has allowed it to enjoy considerable privilege in its relation to the public economic sector. As recently expressed by Giuseppe Tamburrano, the control of political power gives the DC the necessary leverage in bargaining with other forces to insert individuals faithful to its commands and receptive to its interests at the top rungs of the decision-making apparatus of these public enterprises:

The directors of the [state enterprises] need political power and the latter needs them. There is created a relationship of interpenetration between the DC as political power and the DC as economic power in which the common denominator is the DC. This is not only due to the fact that the directors of the state enterprises are in large part men of the DC, but it is also due to the "dependence" of the independent technicians on the financial system and nomination process which are controled by Christian Democracy.[14]

Thus, the public enterprises have been effectively transformed into supportive bodies of the Christian Democrats, providing the party leadership with the economic power to back up its political positions. Given the importance of the public sector in the Italian economy— estimated to account for approximately half the economic activity—

13. Prior to the nationalization of the electrical-power industry, only the *Base*, a leftist faction of the DC, had maintained an extensive relationship with the public sector. *Base* was to a great extent the creature of Enrico Mattei's National Hydrocarbon Agency (ENI), established in 1953 by Parliament to control the activities of a series of public enterprises active in the field of energy sources. See P. H. Franke., *Mattei: Oil and Power Politics* (New York: Praeger, 1966), p. 22.

14. Giuseppe Tamburrano, *L'iceberg democristiano* (Milan: Sugar Editore, 1974), p. 122. See also Eugenio Scalfari and Giuseppe Turani, *Razza padrona* (Milan: Feltrinelli Editore, 1974).

the potential economic base available to the DC for its political purposes is quite large. In much of the literature that has recently appeared on the DC there are numerous examples cited of how local and national leaders of the DC have used employment opportunities and capital resources available in the public sector to the advantage of the party organization and/or individual DC candidates for public office.[15] In this manner the DC has been able to maintain a large army of party cadres and capillary organizational structure without the need to resort to large contributions from its members, the creation of party-controlled economic enterprises, or appropriation of a part of the salaries given to its elected officials by the governmental organs in which they operate. In contrast, to maintain its large party organization, the Communists (the PCI) have had to charge more than twice the DC fee for a membership card, develop an extensive cooperative movement and economic ventures of various kinds that feed profits into the party coffers, and demand half the pay of all public officials elected on its electoral lists.[16]

An Attempt at Empirical Verification

The extent to which the DC has been able to penetrate the enterprises and agencies in the public sector has never been adequately established. However, this information is vital in evaluating the potential success and efficiency of the DC's attempt to create an alternative linkage system that bypasses constitutional linkages and that, in the final analysis, ensures its continued predominance in Italian political and economic affairs. Such an attempt will be made here, using data collected in 1967 in a national study of party leaders (i.e., members of the provincial and national councils of the various party organizations).[17] The analysis

15. See Giampaolo Pansa, *Bisaglia una carriera democristiana* (Milan: Sugar Editore, 1975), pp. 75–79; Massimo Caprara, *I Gava* (Milan: Feltrinelli Editore, 1975), pp. 50–86; Lidia Menapace, *La democrazia cristiana* (Milan: Mazzotta Editore, 1975), p. 51; and Gianfranco Pasquino, "Crisi della DC e evoluzione del sistema politico italiano," *Rivista Italiana di Scienza Politica* 5, no. 3 (December 1975): 443–72.

16. It should be remembered that a Communist party leader is in most cases a full-time politician (i.e., party employee) whether he is located at the national or the local level. For a full accounting of expenditures and sources of funds by the PCI see *L'Unità*, 11 April 1976.

17. The following is an elaboration of data initially presented in Giacomo Sani, "Profilo dei dirigenti di partito," *Rassegna Italiana di Sociologia* 13, no. 1 (January–March 1972): 117–48. The 1967 study was directed by Giovanni Sartori and financed by the Italian National Council for Research (CNR).

will be based primarily on a comparison of the declared occupations of Christian Democratic and Communist party leaders.[18] From this analysis there should emerge the answers to two basic questions: (1) Does there exist a relationship between employment in the public sector and the holding of leadership positions in the DC? If so, which way does the causal relationship go: Does the DC put its cadres into jobs in the public sector or do those employed in the public sector join the DC and become leaders in an attempt to promote their chances for upward mobility and job security? (2) What is the potential effect for the decision-making and policy implementation structure in Italy of such a close identification of the public sector with the Christian Democratic party organization in case of a government coalition in which the DC would be excluded or have only a subordinate role? Can the informal, ad hoc linkage system created by the Christian Democrats exist beyond their control of political power or is it a mere reflection of their predominance in the political system?

Looking in table 11.1 at the ten occupations most commonly declared by Christian Democratic and Communist party leaders, it is evident that a good portion, 60.5 percent, of the latter support themselves through their political activity as "professional" politicians, party functionaries, or trade-union leaders. In comparison, the Christian Democrats have more diversified professional backgrounds. White-collar employees top the list with 18.1 percent of the sample, followed by secondary-school teachers at 11.8 percent. Exclusively political careers were admitted to by a relatively small 11.2 percent of Christian Democrats, although this response was the third most frequent one to be registered. The actual nature of the DC "politician" is difficult to interpret, given the lack of any large-scale employment in the party organization. The DC functionaries that do exist (i.e., administrative secretaries at the provincial, regional, and national levels) are strictly forbidden to hold elected party offices. As a result, the self-identified DC "politician" must by necessity fit into one of the following categories: (1) be independently wealthy, (2) engage in politics as a primary concern but still have a "secondary" profession that provides the necessary economic support, or (3) be a member of Parliament or a Regional

18. As the second most powerful party in Italy, the PCI is used for purposes of comparison throughout this study. For a discussion of the 1976 elections, see Howard R. Penniman, ed., *Italy at the Polls: The Parliamentary Elections of 1976* (Washington: American Enterprise Institute, 1977).

TABLE 11.1. Top Ten Occupations of Italian National and Provincial Party Leaders (in percent)

Total Sample (N = 7,664)		DC Sample (N = 1,869)		PCI Sample (N = 1,055)	
Politicians	19.0	White-collar employees	18.1	Politicians	55.4
White-collar employees	12.4	Secondary-school teachers	11.8	White-collar employees	4.4
Lawyers	10.3	Politicians	11.2	Blue-collar workers	3.5
Secondary-school teachers	8.1	Lawyers	10.7	Skilled workers	3.4
Company directors	4.4	Public officials	7.3	Trade unionists	2.9
Public officials	4.1	Elementary-school teachers	6.2	Journalists	2.9
Elementary-school teachers	3.9	Company directors	6.2	Secondary-school teachers	2.8
Doctors	3.6	Doctors	4.2	Lawyers	2.7
Journalists	3.1	Journalists	2.8	Party functionaries	2.2
Shopkeepers	2.3	University professors	2.3	Elementary-school teachers	1.9
	75.2		80.8		82.1
Others	24.8	Others	19.2	Others	17.9

SOURCE: Italian National Research Council Study of Political Party Leaders, 1967.

Council with the stipend of a full-time legislator. The latter seems to be the most common characteristic of Christian Democrats who profess themselves politicians. Approximately half the DC national leadership in the 1967 study is made up of parliamentarians.

In the coding scheme used to classify the responses to the 1967 study no provision was made to distinguish between public and private employment. Appropriate attention was given to jobs clearly in the public sphere—for example, teaching professions, governmental administration, railroad and post-office services, and so on—but white-collar employees and company directors were not separated into those working in public enterprises and those operating in the private sector. Nevertheless, an estimate of the presence of public officials among the ranks of Christian Democratic party leaders can be arrived at by taking into consideration the evidence presented in table 11.2 and additional data from a 1972 study of DC provincial leaders in a north-central region of the country, Emilia-Romagna, which did focus on the interpenetration of the DC party organization with the public sector.[19] First, a comparison of the occupational patterns of national versus provincial party leaders surprisingly reveals that the largest component among DC provincial party leaders—that is, white-collar employment—practically disappears from the responses of national leaders. In the other categories the relevant percentages remain the same. It could be hypothesized that the white-collar employee category masks party leaders employed in public agencies. It would follow that as they move up to national leadership positions these activists (who at the. provincial level are in fact "semiprofessional" politicians, given the interconnection between the holding of party leadership positions and public employment) become "full-time" politicians by making the full transition to political activity as parliamentarians or regional councillors. A partial confirmation of this hypothesis is offered by the evidence from a 1972 study of Christian Democratic party leaders (members of the provincial and regional councils that comprise the party organization) in Emilia-Romagna.

Table 11.3 shows that 65.8 percent of all respondents were involved in jobs connected with the public sector. Thirty-three percent had jobs

19. For other aspects of the study see Robert Leonardi, "The Politics of Choice: An Inquiry into the Cause of Factionalism in the Italian Christian Democratic Party" (Ph.D. diss., University of Illinois, 1974).

TABLE 11.2. Top Ten Professions of Italian National Party Leaders (in percent)

Total Sample (N = 1,074)		DC Sample (N = 188)		PCI Sample (N = 139)	
Politicians	30.3	Politicians	39.4	Politicians	74.8
Lawyers	19.1	Lawyers	14.4	Journalists	7.9
Journalists	8.4	University professors	10.6	University professors	3.6
Secondary-school teachers	5.7	Journalists	8.5	Trade unionists	2.9
University professors	5.1	Secondary-school teachers	5.3	Specialized workers	2.2
Company directors	4.7	Company directors	4.3	Party functionaries	2.2
Public functionaries	3.0	Public functionaries	3.7	Lawyers	2.2
Trade unionists	2.9	Trade unionists	3.2	Blue-collar workers	1.4
White-collar employees	2.4	Commercialists	2.1		97.2
Doctors	2.3	Elementary teachers	1.6		
	83.9	White-collar employees	1.6		
			94.7		
Others	16.1	Others	5.3	Others	2.8

Top Ten Professions of Italian Provincial Party Leaders (in percent)

Total Sample (N = 6,590)		DC Sample (N = 1,681)		PCI Sample (N = 917)	
Politicians	17.2	White-collar employees	19.9	Politicians	52.5
White-collar employees	14.0	Secondary-school teachers	12.5	White-collar employees	5.0
Lawyers	8.8	Lawyers	10.3	Blue-collar workers	3.9
Secondary-school teachers	8.5	Politicians	8.0	Skilled workers	3.6
Elementary-school teachers	4.4	Public officials	7.7	Secondary-school teachers	3.2
Company directors	4.4	Elementary-school teachers	6.7	Trade unionists	2.9
Public officials	4.3	Company directors	6.4	Lawyers	2.8
Doctors	3.8	Doctors	4.6	Journalists	2.2
Surveyors	2.5	Journalists	2.2	Artisans	2.2
Journalists	2.2	Coop functionaries	2.0	Elementary-school teachers	2.2
	70.1		80.3		80.5
Others	29.9	Others	19.7	Others	19.5

SOURCE: Italian National Research Council Study of Political Party Leaders, 1967.

TABLE 11.3. Public Employment Among DC Provincial Party Leaders in Emilia-Romagna (N = 151)

	%
Government Employment	
Secondary-school teachers	13.9
Elementary-school teachers	11.3
Local town administrators	4.0
Local level national civil service	2.6
University professors	1.3
	33.3
State Social-Service Agencies	
Social-security agencies	9.3
Economic-development agencies	4.6
Post-office workers and officials	4.0
Provincial chambers of commerce	3.3
Hospital administrators	2.0
Provincial public-housing agencies	1.3
Regional chambers of commerce	0.7
Public tourist agencies	0.7
	25.9
State-Controlled Banks	
Directors	1.3
Administrators	1.3
Employees	1.3
	3.9
IRI and ENI Enterprises	
Administrators	2.0
White-collar employees	0.7
	2.7
Total for all four categories	65.8

SOURCE: 1972 study of Christian Democratic party leaders in Emilia-Romagna. See Robert Leonardi, "The Politics of Choice: An Inquiry into the Causes of Factionalism in the Italian Christian Democratic Party," Unpublished Ph.D. diss., University of Illinois, 1974, pp. 172–78.

260

in the types of professions that are traditionally connected with public employment: national civil service, local town administration, and various levels of the teaching profession, for example. This figure compares well with the national average for DC leaders of approximately 28 percent with public jobs registered in the 1967 study. However, what is of particular interest in table 11.3 is the almost equal number, 32.5 percent, of the respondents who were employed in what can be termed the new areas of public employment that have come to fruition during the past decade: state social-service agencies, state banking institutions, and public economic enterprises. This new group of "white-collar employees" and "company directors" are no longer part of autonomous private enterprises. On the contrary, they are a new type of public employee whose recruitment and eventual advancement on the job depend to a great extent on political connections.

An analysis of the career patterns of those employed in this new sector of public activity reveals that most of these individuals were members of the Christian Democratic party *prior* to finding employment in these agencies. It is generally pointed out by the respondents that their membership in the DC was motivated by prior activity in the social organizations directed by Catholic Action rather than to an impulse originating from any "on the job" experience. Thus, a Catholic socioreligious background was instrumental in bringing the respondents in contact with the party, but it was the party that opened the way to finding a job in the public sector. Most had been engaged in DC grassroots activity prior to finding this particular type of employment.

Once employed in the public sector the subsequent pattern in the careers of the respondents does not permit the drawing of a clear conclusion of whether advancement in the party brings about an automatic advancement in one's job or vice versa. The two career patterns seem to be interrelated, but it is impossible to establish which one is predominant over the other. Nevertheless, the extent of the phenomenon is quite important: in 1972 almost one-third of the DC party leaders interviewed in Emilia-Romagna worked for state social-service agencies, banks, and economic enterprises in a region where the party was almost entirely excluded from the control of local political power. This result points to the importance of political control at the national level as a requisite for providing access to national public agencies. It is also interesting to note that in the 1967 sample of party leaders in Emilia-Romagna the possible maximum number of respondents that could have fallen into this new area of public employment was around 20 percent. Thus, during the passage of time between the taking of the two samples it seems that the ability, or need, of the DC to penetrate the state apparatus may have increased rather than decreased in line with its electoral fortunes.[20]

Given the ability of the DC to use the public sector to reinforce its party organization, can the same be said to be true for other governmental parties such as the PSI, PSDI, and PRI? Is the interpenetration of the state structure a general characteristic of governing parties, or does it have a particular significance for the DC?[21] At the time of the coding the 1967 questionnaires, the PSDI and PSI were united as a single Socialist party, the PSU; therefore, with the available data it is not possible to clearly distinguish between the two wings of the Italian Socialist movement. Despite this inconvenience, figure 11.2 clearly illustrates how the Center-Left coalition (DC, PSU, and PRI), which has governed Italy since 1963, with only a brief parenthesis in 1972–73, has the highest percentage of government employees and of the categories of government employment hypothesized to exist in the 1967 sample behind the labels of white-collar employees and company directors. In contrast, the Italian parties traditionally associated with middle-class interests—PLI, MSI, and PDIUM—have a lower percentage of their party leaders at the provincial and national levels in all three categories. The PCI with its lower-class voting base and cadre system appropriately falls into last place in all three, in large part owing to its extensive system of party leaders who are also paid party functionaries.

From the above analysis it is clear that there is some sort of relationship between positions of leadership in governmental parties and jobs in the public sector, and the relationship seems to be most accentuated in the Christian Democratic party.[22] At present it is not

20. The two samples were drawn quite differently. The 1972 Emilia-Romagna study was based on a random sample of all of the regional and provincial party leaders who were directly contacted by the author and with whom a structured interview was conducted. The 1967 sample was based on those who returned a written questionnaire to the Istituto Carlo Cattaneo in Bologna, which conducted the research project. In the latter case, the respondents, in effect, "selected themselves" by returning the questionnaire. Therefore, there was no guarantee of randomness or representability.

21. A similar question is posed by Franco Cazzola in "Partiti e sottogoverno," *Rassegna Italiana di Sociologia* 15, no. 3 (July–September 1974): 351–85.

22. There is always the possibility that no relationship exists between the holding

FIGURE 11.2.   Selected Employment Patterns among Italian National Provincial Party Leaders

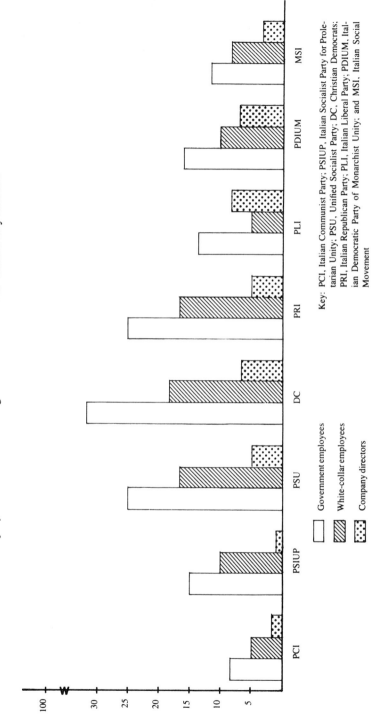

Key: PCI, Italian Communist Party; PSIUP, Italian Socialist Party for Proletarian Unity; PSU, Unified Socialist Party; DC, Christian Democrats; PRI, Italian Republican Party; PLI, Italian Liberal Party; PDIUM, Italian Democratic Party of Monarchist Unity; and MSI, Italian Social Movement

SOURCE: Calculated by the author from Italian National Research Council Study of Political Party Leaders, 1967.

possible to isolate all the ramifications of this relationship. In fact, empirical studies of this phenomenon are practically nonexistent from the point of view of both the party organization and the public enterprise and administrative structure. However, one can speculate on some of the political implications of an interpenetration of the party organization with the organizations operating in the public sector.

First, the Christian Democratic party seems to have been able to transform its dominant role in the Italian political system into a lever to gain access to the top as well as to intermediate and lower positions in the public sector. This access privilege has been transformed into a vehicle for placing party leaders in jobs in the public sector, thereby decreasing the economic burden on the party organization. Through such a placement, the party is able to call upon the services of an activist whose economic condition depends upon his relationship with the party, but it also provides the party with a direct link with the public sector. The party activist employed in the public sector is expected to perform two roles: as a part-time party worker and as a conduit for party policies and preferences in the administrative apparatus of the state. What does this imply for the decision-making process? It means an unequal influence among the parties in the political system on the upward or downward linkage structures. In fact, it may point to the existence of a completely separate linkage system that will respond only to the dictates and interests of one party.

Second, there is the problem of political change. Has the constitutional system for the transfer of power through the electoral process been short-circuited and can the public sector respond to other types of political leadership? A realistic test of this proposition may soon occur in the specific case of the Christian Democratic system of ad hoc linkages in the Italian political system. Such a test would probably require a drastic change in government coalition, structure, and direction of public policy over an extended period to render ineffective the informal linkage patterns thus created by the DC. Short of such drastic changes, this system of ad hoc linkages could assume a function in stabilizing the DC's control of the public-policy process that goes be-

---

of party office and being employed in the public sector, but a growing number of authors—for example, Pansa, Caprara, Galli, Menapace, Pasquino, and so on—maintain that the opposite is true and that any understanding of the working of the Italian political system is based on the ability to grasp the significance of this interpenetration of the dominant party, DC, with the public sector.

yond simple calculations of its electoral strength. Just as the Communist party's organizational network gives it a presence and influence beyond the effective numbers of its adherents, so the DC's strength in affecting the making and administration of public policies is multiplied by the existence of the informal linkage system. In recent years there have been numerous attempts by the parties of the Left to decentralize the state administrative apparatus to the regional level in an attempt to break the DC's national system of clientelism in support of the party organization and individual party leaders. However, these attempts have been met at every turn by political as well as procedural complications (e.g., reform of the health insurance and medical sector in general). Therefore, any change in the present situation would require not only a change in government coalition and policies but also a complete purge and restructuring of the state apparatus.

Such drastic changes happen infrequently in advanced industrialized societies in the Western Hemisphere. Thus, the existence of an ad hoc, informal linkage system, which provides the Christian Democrats with privileged access to the decision-implementation (if not decision-making) system, may be a long-range rather than only a temporary characteristic of the Italian political system.

12.

Patrons, Brokers, and Clients: Party Linkages in the Colombian System

STEFFEN SCHMIDT

The study of political linkages and of the role of political parties in this process is a relatively new theoretical framework. It grows out of concerns of other established areas of inquiry such as the study of elites, interest groups, policymaking, and the historical development of suffrage.

Linkage studies can focus on inter-elite relationships. They can also analyze the process of political mobilization of the polity and the role of parties in accomplishing this mobilization. Linkage is defined in the context of this study as the process of bringing individual members of a society into more or less stable aggregates that will interact to: (*a*) communicate political demands, (*b*) legitimize political leadership, and (*c*) generate affective ties with the system or part of the system. The links are, in part, *horizontal*, establishing the rules of interaction between elite sectors. Links also tie together members of the masses, again as a function of common interests pursued through political structures. But links may also be *vertical*, establishing patterns of association for individuals at different levels of the socioeconomic hierarchy. Vertical linkages are the points of connection between individuals (or groups) and the policymaking process, making popular participation possible and determining the degree of congruence between leaders' and followers' values and goals.

This analysis of political linkages in Colombia focuses on the Liberal and Conservative parties, which have dominated the political process since the mid-1800s. The link between the individual and regional and national party structures is stressed. It will be argued that this linkage has been accomplished in Colombia largely through what are called clientelist ties.

Clientelism is the process whereby individuals of unequal status relate to each other on the basis of reciprocity. The lower status individual (client) and the higher status person (patron) often rely on a third party (the broker) to mediate the exchange. In those cases the broker sometimes plays the functionally equivalent role of the patron vis-à-vis the lower status individual. Although the broker's resources are not his own, he can often create the illusion of controlling jobs, money, and other preferments and can on occasion divert resources from the patron for his own use.

The patron-broker-client model can be contrasted to a class-conflict (or -consciousness) model, which stresses the cohesiveness of individuals in the same socioeconomic level. The class model also stresses the conflict and incompatibility of interests between classes.

From a different perspective Nobutaka Ike has discussed clientelism in the context of "democratic models," among which he identifies a *rational-choice* model, a *civic-culture* model, and a *pluralist-democracy* model. The *patron-client* model, according to Ike, is an elitist type in which individuals "relate to the political system through their patrons, who typically are local notables, political bosses, union leaders, local politicians, and leaders of local organizations." He continues, "In this model, voters tend to trade their ballots for anticipated benefits that are particularistic in character—that is, for jobs and favors for themselves or their relatives; schools, roads, hospitals and other public works projects for the community."[1]

The literature on clientelism suggests five specific characteristics of clientelist linkage:

1. The *inequality* of participants
2. The *reciprocity* of exchange
3. The *proximity* of actors
4. The two-person (*dyadic*) basis of the relationship
5. The wide range of interactions that make up each patron-client tie (*multiplexity*)

---

1. Nobutaka Ike, *Japanese Politics*, 2nd ed. (New York: Knopf, 1972), pp. 19–20.

The purpose here will be both to establish the existence of clientelism in the Colombian party system by demonstrating the existence of these five characteristics and to make explicit the mechanisms and "exchange currencies" that have sustained Colombian clientelism.

The first section will review the ample but little-known historical literature on Colombia, which strongly suggests that political linkages in Colombia have been premised on clientelist ties for many years. The second section will present three case studies illustrating the process of party linkages and clientelism: (1) the 1904 presidential election and the "Register of Padilla"; (2) the 1930 election and the return of the Liberal party to power; (3) the case of guerrilla leader Dumar Aljure in the 1950s and late 1960s. Section three consists of contemporary accounts of clientelism derived from interviews with local-level political leaders and from interviews and correspondence with Colombian historians.

In the final section of the analysis the two objectives cited above will be reviewed in a concluding discussion. The purpose of the study is to generate insights and the outlines of a process that can be the basis for exploring party linkages in a rather wide range of empirical cases, using clientelism hypotheses to test political behavior. Although a description and analysis of the structure and functioning of political clientelism will be stressed, brief mention will also be made of the consequences of clientelism.

The Historical Roots of Clientelism in Colombia

The *cacique* is the mayor, or president of the *consejo*, or municipal treasurer, or judge invested in that office which best suits his purpose, or which best allows him to share his preeminence with the *cacique* of the other party. He does not disguise his satisfaction of feeling himself to be "the owner of all this." ... That conglomeration of men, who only euphemistically can be called citizens, vegetates in a total ignorance of the nation and the world. No one there knows of the preoccupations, anguishes and triumphs of the human spirit.[2]

This observation in 1925 by one of Colombia's former presidents, Laureano Gomez, reflects one view of the "patrons" in that nation's

---

2. Laureano Gomez, *El Caracter del General Ospina* (Bogotá: Ediciones Colombia, 1928), p. 11.

clientelist system. Gomez calls the cacique the "corrupting institution in Colombian politics."[3] But however corrupting, the caciques have in fact always been part of the larger society, not living "in total ignorance of the nation," and indeed existing only because they *are* linked to a larger system. Edwardo Santa calls the cacique "the distorted echo of the *caudillo*," the "boss of the public offices," giving and taking away jobs at will, obtaining scholarships and promotions for those who follow his political lead.[4] He is an appendage of a larger more prominent individual, the caudillo.

This description can be found in other references as well. One author describes traditional Colombian politics as taking place "in quiet, secret dialogues between the Departmental capitals and municipal *gamonales*."[5]
Fals Borda adds to this a more explicit description:

Gamonales were petty political leaders whose position in society permitted them to exert influence upon rural voters. Public officials, hacienda owners and overseers, and some priests were counted among them. The machine organized by these leaders was designed to perpetuate them and the higher ranking *caudillos* in power. They saw that their friends, employees, and followers went to the polls and voted "right," paid for the liquor consumed as a reward, and acted as protectors of the constituents.[6]

In 1938 President Alfonso Lopez acknowledged the importance of local politicians but denied they were still powerful in national party structures and leadership:

The *gamonal*, the peasant boss who mobilized his peons, the rural influential who controlled the conscience of hundreds of humble men ... now knows that he can no longer figure decisively in the Republic through falsification of votes.[7]

3. Ibid.
4. Eduardo Santa, *Sociologia Politica de Colombia* (Bogotá: Tercer Mundo, 1964), p. 77.
5. Hugo Escobar Sierra, "La Organizacion Interna de los Partidos," in *Los Partidos Politicos*, Coloquios de la Universidad Externado de Colombia (Bogotá, 1968), p. 38.
6. Orlando Fals Borda, *Peasant Society in the Colombian Andes* (Gainesville: University of Florida Press, 1962), p. 241. See also José M. Samper, *Los Partidos en Colombia* (Bogotá: Imprenta Echeverria, 1879).
7. Cited in Richard Weinert, "Political Modernization in Colombia" (Ph.D. diss., Columbia University, 1967), p. 134.

With the establishment of the secret vote, the national role of the cacique or gamonal became that of mobilizing voters, supervising the constituency, and setting the boundaries of its political choices.

In sum, in the nineteenth and early twentieth centuries Colombian politics revolved around the struggle of factional leaders of the Liberal and Conservative parties for influence. Their base of support was a network of people bound to them through instrumental and affective ties and mobilized at the local level by gamonales, or political brokers. In turn, young Colombians interested in achieving high political office, especially in the period 1900–50, needed "the nod of approval of the *cacique*" in order to fulfill their aspirations.[8]

The following cases illustrate the specifically political relevance of brokerage in the Colombian two-party system and the effects of its existence on national politics. Many of the factors that prove significant in these historical cases find an echo in the interview and questionnaire responses reported in the third section. They justify calling the linkages discussed here a clientelist, factional, two-party system.

Case Studies of Colombian Clientelism

JUANITO IGUARAN AND THE 1904 PRESIDENTIAL ELECTION

The province of Padilla, in the department of Magadalena, has as its capital the remote port of Riohacha, and over the comings and goings of that area, even today removed from the active centers of national life, General Juanito Iguaran exercised an unrivaled electoral *caciqueship*. Not a leaf or the sandy dust stirred from the ground without a prior order from Juanito. He therefore reigned tranquilly over a happy and ignorant people, which prematurely and perhaps unnecessarily had been granted the right of suffrage.[9]

People in Padilla province had always voted as Iguaran thought they should; after all, he knew which candidate would be in the best interest of the "glorious town of the province of Padilla."[10] However, in

8. Agustin Rodriquez Garavito, *Gabriel Turbay: Un Solitario de la Grandeza* (Bogotá: Internacional de Publicaciones, S.A., 1965), p. 78.
9. Eduardo Lemaitre, *Rafael Reyes: Biografia de un Gran Colombiano* (Bogotá: Ediciones Espira, 1967), p. 263.
10. Ibid.

the election of 1904, Iguaran himself was not sure which candidate to choose, General Rafael Reyes or Dr. Joaquin F. Velez. So he invited the electors to join him for drinks and persuaded them to sign, but leave blank, the voting register (*acta*), permitting him to fill in the name of the favored candidate later.

Thus prepared, General Iguaran arrived a few days later in the city of Barranquilla and on the same day attended the funeral of a prominent local merchant. There he entered into a conversation with his friend the Marquez de Mier, who was interested in the politics of Riohacha and was an associate of the governor of the region, José Francisco Insignares. Patting the folded document in the inside pocket of his suit, Iguaran said, "I have here the register of my district, signed and left blank. It is my responsibility to fill it in."[11]

There is no evidence of what kind of a pact was made. However, the next morning the voting register of the province of Padilla was filled, giving the votes to Rafael Reyes. Under normal conditions this voting arrangement would have passed unnoticed. However, in this case Reyes won the election to succeed President Marroquin by only twelve votes over his competitor, Dr. Joaquin F. Velez (both were Conservatives), and those twelve votes came from the province of Padilla.[12]

The Velistas, furious at the defeat of their candidate, began a heated public debate of the results, focused mostly on the famous "register of Padilla." This public debate led the electoral court to launch an investigation of the results, and a commission was formed and sent to Riohacha to carry out the investigation.

The commission arrived early one evening in Riohacha and installed itself in the local hotel. Iguaran, who knew all the comings and goings in his town, became annoyed at the idea of such an investigation. He talked a friend of his into shooting out all the lanterns in the hotel room of the investigating commission. The next morning the commission turned on its heels, the Padilla votes were declared legal, and Reyes became president of Colombia for a six-year term.

The Padilla incident is important because it defines so specifically the links connecting a traditional autocratic boss, Juanito Iguaran, a dependent community, and the regional (de Mier and Governor Insignares) as well as the national party system. The Liberals were not to

11. Ibid., p. 264.
12. Ibid., p. 265.

come to power for another twenty-six years. When they did, the mobilization of community leaders by them became an important, controversial, and often violent first order of business.

A division in the Conservative party opened the door for a Liberal presidential victory in 1930 after forty-five years of Conservative hegemony. The winner, Enrique Olaya Herrera, clearly recognized the precariousness of his victory (compounded by a two-thirds Conservative majority in Congress) and hastened to form a coalition government in which he appointed four Conservatives to cabinet positions and six to governorships.

In the months following the Liberal election victory, a movement to consolidate Liberal power throughout the country began to take shape. The struggle involved a series of conflicts over patronage control as well as the mobilization of Liberal partisans and the intimidation of Conservatives. In December 1933 a bitter struggle erupted in the city of Cartagena between the mayor and the city council over who would have the right of appointment to city jobs. In the town of Antioquia (Magdalena), the postal administrator and a member of his staff organized a disturbance protesting job appointments made by an opposing faction of Liberals; the incident became so violent that a number of city council members had to be herded into a nearby house and guarded by the police to protect them from bodily harm.[13]

In addition to creating tensions within the newly emerging Liberal party, the struggle over patronage was an important instrument in the development of Liberal party power vis-à-vis the Conservatives. A letter from the leader of the Liberal party in the city of Medellin to the president of the National Party Directory graphically illustrates the point:

To reach our objectives of winning the 1935 election we need the active support of both the political leadership and of the public officials, especially as it affects our chances of gaining access to positions in the telegraph office, post office, police forces, etc. We can already count on the cordial cooperation of the secretary of Government, the state revenue bureau, the superintendency of railroads and some help in the post

13. Abel Carbonell, *La Quincena Politica* (Bogotá: Ministerio de Educacion Nacional, 1952), p. 11.

office and telegraph departments; some municipal employees resist our advances, as they want to continue controlling positions to maintain secure their parochial role in the Liberal party.[14]

In another case a Liberal mayor who was appointed to administer the town of Itagui (Department of Antioquia), a community with an overwhelming Conservative majority, selected as the municipal secretary a competent, experienced Conservative. The mayor apparently felt he could create a more harmonious climate with this gesture and facilitate his administration of community affairs. However, four days after the appointment he was forced to dismiss the secretary on instructions from the Liberal Party Directory in Medellin, which said sternly:

You know that when the Governor's office names a Liberal mayor to administer a community with a Conservative majority it is for the exclusive purpose that he Liberalize said community.[15]

The successful application of this formula is described by *Organizacion Liberal*, a Liberal party paper in Medellin, in reference to the town of Sonson:

In the last year thanks to the efforts of the governorship to maintain at all costs Liberal mayors in that Conservative town, and thanks to the titanical efforts of Major Fidel Cuellar, the Liberal *sonsonites* have been steadily gaining valuable posts, filling positions and conquering the will of the masses.[16]

Thus to "Liberalize" meant to turn over patronage and appointed power to Liberals, even in the most Conservative areas of the country like Antioquia. But to what end? Carbonell and others suggest that it was primarily a strategy of strengthening Liberal gamonales, and thus building from the grass roots a Liberal electoral majority. Nor were the Liberals always content to use legal means to achieve their goal:

The Liberal party, from the first days of the new administration, studied the election map of the country and finding from their calculations that through the normal electoral process it was impossible for them to

14. This letter was published in *El Pais* and reported in Carbonell, Ibid., p. 46.
15. Ibid., p. 47.
16. Reproduced in ibid., p. 45.

win legislative majorities, decided instead to counterbalance the Conservative strength with violence, especially in Boyaca and Norte de Santander.[17]

The Liberal community brokers moved swiftly, destroying ballot urns where they couldn't marshal a Liberal majority (as in Guatavita and Gacheta), creating a climate of terror that kept the Conservatives away (as in Manta and Gacheta), or simply manufacturing election results in much the same way as Juanito Iguaran had done in the 1904 presidential election.

The election results were highly controversial and held no legitimacy among the Conservatives. The differences in Liberal votes between 1930 and 1934 were simply too enormous:[18]

Presidential Vote 1930, 1934

1930	
Enrique Olaya Herrera (Liberal)	369,934
Guillermo Valencia (Conservative)	240,360
Alfredo Vasques Cobo (Conservative)	213,493
1934	
Alfonso Lopez (Liberal, uncontested)	938,934

The brokers thrived and were carefully groomed in the early 1930s as instrumental to the return of the Liberal party to a position of dominant influence. No one was immune to their wishes. Dissident Liberal leader Jorge Eliecer Gaitan found this out when he tried in 1934 to hold a rally in Fusagasuga, only to find the mayor of the town creating an incident and suspending the right of assembly, "like a village mandarin protecting his constituency from the disturbing and possibly subversive influence of Gaitan's gospel."[19] Even more dramatic was the lynching of Marco Fajardo, a worker, in Villeta by a mob directed to do so on instructions from Tito Vega, one of the caciques of the town. Gaitan launched an investigation of the incident, "but the fact is that politics intervened. The urge to protect votes stood in the way of justice being carried out; for Mr. Vega and his companions are the electoral bosses [*jefes electorales*] of that town."[20]

17. Ibid., p. 31.
18. From the Archive of the Registra duria Nacional de Estedistica.
19. Carbonell, op. cit., p. 56.
20. Ibid., pp. 127–29.

This period thus quite intensely reflects the tensions and political dislocations created by national party turnover. The Liberals came to power in 1930 and in order to stay in power had to perforate the Conservative cocoon. This proved to be most traumatic and violent in the villages and rural settlements (*veredas*), so long dominated by Conservative gamonales. The "Liberalization" of Colombia precipitated electoral fraud and armed violence on a massive scale.

As an editorial in *El Diario Nacional* pointed out in a critique of election reforms in 1923, election fraud in Colombia has been supported by prevailing societal norms and structures.[21] The psychological and physically dependent status of so large a segment of the population inhibited reform efforts, however numerous and sincere. The importance of patronage in political competition tempted marginal men to struggle for its rewards without undue regard for legal procedures. *Gamonalismo*, the intertwining of human relationships on the basis of clientelistic connections, has allowed for a relatively systematic, and not always legitimate, penetration of the national political structures into the countryside.

Election controversies and conflicts have afflicted Colombian clientelist politics from the very start. In 1855 the settlement of Sabanilla with approximately one hundred eligible voters cast twenty thousand votes for the Liberal party presidential candidate, Dr. Manual Murillo Toro.[22] In the 1873 election for senators and representatives *all* the voting books from the *municipios*, scrutinized by the elections board (*jurado electoral*), were found to have fictitious signatures, all with the same handwriting.[23] (The investigation was inconclusive, however, as the majority group on the board explained that all the signatories had taken penmanship from the same professor!) It has been claimed that the 1885 civil war broke out in part because fraud prevented General Eustorgio Salgar from becoming president and gave the presidency to Francisco Ordoñez.[24]

It should be stressed that in the struggles for local preeminence, both the brokers and their national party allies often precipitated quasi-

---

21. Issue of 25 June 1923, in Jenaro Guerrero, *Prensa, Reforma Electoral* (Bogotá: Editorial Minerva, 1925), pp. 49–50.
22. Ibid., p. 60.
23. Ibid., p. 58.
24. Aurelio Acosta, *Memorias: Un sobreviviente del Glorioso Liberalismo Colombiano* (Bogotá: Editorial Cromos, 1940), p. 43.

insurgent conflicts. The leadership during this period of violence was at least in part congruent with the functions of brokers, that is, to mediate between a clientele and the outside world and to provide reciprocally beneficial resources covering a wide range of needs and situations. The following case study of such a contemporary gamonal guerrilla will serve to specify these interconnections.

THE CASE OF DUMAR ALJURE, 1951

Dumar Aljure was the son of a Lebanese shopkeeper. He was born into a nation about to be convulsed by civil war, and his desertion from the army in 1951 was so common for young Liberals at the time that it went unnoticed. The Liberals lost control of the government in 1946 after a bitter internal struggle in which two candidates ran for president on the party's ticket. This gave the Conservatives their election victory. The Conservative president, Mariano Ospina Perez, coming to power as a minority-party candidate, moved cautiously at first, just as had Olaya Herrera in 1930 when the Liberals returned to dominate national politics. And similarly, the Conservatives then moved rapidly to consolidate themselves locally, to replace the Liberal gamonales, to terrorize Liberal voters, and to win the next elections in 1949.

The army and the police were increasingly employed to terrorize Liberals, especially under the Laureano Gomez administration (1950 to 1953). Large sections of Colombia once more saw great numbers of people fleeing from their communities. Many of the Liberal refugees joined the irregular guerrillas, who were supported by the Liberal party as a counterbalance to the policies of the Conservative government. Aljure joined one such guerrilla group in the eastern Llanos (plains) of Colombia. He developed a reputation as a brave and ruthless man and soon dominated an important segment of the Liberal guerrillas in the Arari River area of Meta department. As Maullin indicates:

Aljure established himself as the regional political chief with virtual autonomy from the central government, protecting himself (against the army sweeps of the area) with the maintenance of an armed force given to occasional banditry. His domain extended over sixty thousand hectares, parts of which he exploited in the style of the early Texas cattle barons.[25]

25. This description and subsequent discussion of the Aljure case comes largely from Richard L. Maullin, "The Fall of Dumar Aljure," Rand Document 17010-1-ISA (27 June 1968), p. 3.

Aljure's life revolved around a network of rather delicately balanced relationships and served a number of distinct functions. Because he lived outside the law and because he represented a military threat to the government (especially after General Rojas Pinilla overthrew Gomez and became president in 1953), "he needed an element of protection from the local population, and he gained that support by playing lord and protector to a population itself subject to mistreatment by the army and police during the 1950's and suspicious of the government since then."[26] The reciprocity that existed in this leader-follower relationship was striking, each contributing something vital for the continuity of life in the area.

Aljure's political influence is in many ways similar to that described in other Colombian places at other periods of time:

He helped elect certain municipal council members by corraling the necessary votes, and he made sure that local party directorates included some of his friends. As years went by his attention focused on the role of the municipal *personero.* . . . Others whose services he often bought included local police chiefs . . . who passed on information to Aljure of police and army moves and who contributed to the formation of lists made up of people who complained about Aljure's operations.[27]

His power, based in part on a functional and paternalistic relationship that he maintained with his client subjects, also included the use of terrorism. A private cemetery in the heart of his territory at Rincon de Bolivar contained more than one hundred bodies of executed victims of his rule.

Aljure was linked to the national party system by a close connection to several Liberal leaders, especially Senator Hernando Duran Dussan, whom he supported electorally for many years. In return, Aljure was assured a tie to influential people and an embarrassing hold on prominent Liberal leaders like Duran Dussan, should these relationships ever become public. This was in a sense a guarantee that he would be politically protected as much as possible (especially after General Rojas Pinilla was ousted and the Liberal-Conservative coalition arrangement was established in 1957) and protected as well from serious military threats. As Maullin suggests:

26. Ibid., p. 4.
27. Ibid., p. 10.

Aljure's fifteen years of domination of his local region owed much to his Robin Hood and mafioso techniques, and they included an essential tie-in with the forces of respectability in the national capital.[28]

Why then was Dumar Aljure killed, along with wife, twelve men, and six soldiers in an army ambush? What finally happened to break the delicate balance that had allowed him to rule the lives of nearly thirty-five thousand people?

Three factors converge to explain his demise and all point to a tearing of the links that strengthen patron-broker-client relations. First, under incentives from the national government through its agrarian reform program,

some parts of the Arari region of Meta department ... attracted new settlers and some investment from people without any relationships to Aljure in his partisan days. These people, with an interest in agronomy rather than old political styles, may have helped to cultivate the anti-Aljure climate.[29]

This climate was enhanced by a tour of the region by Colonel Elevio Ramirez Palacio, commander of the Seventh Brigade, Twenty-first Component (the Vargas Battalion), which was responsible for the section of Meta run by Aljure. The tour itself seems to have been precipitated by a second rupture in the chain of linkages on which the guerrilla leader's power depended. In January 1968 Aljure murdered a bartender as he, Aljure, was drinking in the company of an army sergeant. Maullin suggests that this incident gravely violated a modus vivendi worked out between the army and Aljure.

Committing a crime in the presence of the army may have been an act so intolerable to the army's leaders that there could be no more sufferance of Aljure.[30]

Finally, and critically, Aljure appears to have violated his electoral commitment to Duran, who lost in the winner-take-all congressional election of 1968. Duran, infuriated, indicated in a tempestuous speech

28. Ibid.
29. Ibid., p. 14.
30. Ibid., p. 13.

in the capital of Meta, Villviencio, that "some heads would roll" as a result.[31]

Aljure's ties to Duran and other prominent Liberals served as a lever that he could use to discourage the army from moving against him and in the process bringing to light embarrassing arrangements that both sides wanted to conceal. Thus, breaking the political links was probably the most serious cause for his demise.

Maullin sums up Aljure's career with a comment that makes clear the guerrilla leader's brokerage function:

Aljure had a well-developed role in Meta department as a political, economic, and social figure. Politically he represented an element of and was visibly connected with one of the two traditional and popularly sanctioned political party labels in Colombia. Economically he served a local and perhaps national function, supplying some of the needed grease for a society faced with the sacrifices of economic development and the precariousness of life in frontier areas. Socially he was a hardy symbol of resistance and resilience in the harshness of the Llanos as well as a shield against the vagaries of national governments psychologically and physically centered high in the Andes. To the old-time Llaneros at least, Aljure was part of the larger family making up the region's subculture.[32]

Aljure's career is better documented than that of the hundreds of other insurgent leaders whose lives and deaths during the 1950s and 1960s passed in relative anonymity. However, one can assume at least that many of them were functioning in the context of local and local-regional-national networks very similar to those described above. Their cases, like Dumar Aljure's, are illustrative of the continuity and elasticity that characterizes patron-broker-client relations, a continuity stretching from the quiet abandon of nineteenth-century villages like Sabanilla, which with a hundred voters delivered twenty thousand votes for the candidacy of Manuel Murillo Toro, to the mid-twentieth-century guerrilla terrorism of a Dumar Aljure.

Contemporary Accounts of Colombian Clientelism

In the following discussion gamonales and small-town politics are described in the words and images of contemporary participants in that

31. Ibid., p. 9.
32. Ibid., p. 17.

process. It is largely on the basis of subjective perceptions that political actors are likely to respond to political situations. Therefore, an understanding of the language, preconceptions, constraints, anxieties, and compensations as well as losses perceived by political actors may provide important clues about their behavior.

The major themes of Colombian politics reflected in the historical record are duplicated in the opinions of Colombian participants in local politics and in the comments of contemporary scholars. For example, there is a strong tendency to identify patronage as an important incentive in the political process. A state election supervisor says:

In the district of Darien the following jobs are open. Mayor, *consejales municipales*, *personero*, secretary, janitor, *tesorero*, teachers, janitor of school, about ten positions for road building and building maintenance, secretary of the political parties. That is about thirty or forty positions which mean economic sustenance for those who hold them. If there are five hundred municipios in Colombia there are about twenty thousand people who care about politics only at the level of the municipios like the one I talk about. Naturally they vary in size and therefore in the number of people for positions. For each of these people there are, what should I say, from three to five people who depend on and benefit by the receiving of positions, so that means one hundred thousand people interested in these positions and therefore in politics. Let's say that for every position there is one Liberal and one Conservative. That means two hundred thousand people interested.[33]

A member of a municipal council described the electoral process as significant in two stages. Winning national elections and securing the presidency for his party's candidate was important because the president would appoint a governor and a town mayor of the same political affiliation. This in turn assured that

people who work hard for us get positions, and it is good for a party to have many public jobs filled with its own members. Here in Caldas thousands of people hope to get a public job when the party comes to power.[34]

As historian Francisco Ramos Hidalgo said, "Local leaders attain that

33. Cali, July 1969. Location, month, and year for subsequent interviews will be given. In most cases informants were interviewed more than once.
34. Manizales, June 1971.

rank by being loyal party members and because they support and promote public works such as aqueducts, hospitals, electric plants."[35]

A longtime newspaper correspondent in a small town gave a slightly different interpretation to the matter of patronage by suggesting in effect that the gamonal differentiates between a number of different groups of people in his use of patronage resources.

Jobs are distributed by the gamonal or gamonales to family and friends. Sure, these usually are party loyals too, but let's be frank that the family always comes first.[36]

These incentives are often public funds that are secured from the local, state, and national government and disbursed with political (or family) criteria in mind. However, gamonales often are personally affluent and use their private resources to accomplish the same end. For example, a cattle rancher whose political influence in a municipio was reputedly very important indicated that his hacienda contributes

to many religious fiestas; I have a doctor come once a month and allow people besides my workers to see him. We have a Christmas fiesta for the children.[37]

A small-town politician remembers that in one election he bought votes for ten pesos each.[38] Still a different form of trade-off took place in a coffee-growing district in which the coffee buyer could inflate or depress prices and use this power to influence people's political choices.[39] On the other hand, Guillermo Uribe, a librarian, tells of a gamonal who owns a large general store in town and extends credit "to those he needs to win over."[40] Two of the people interviewed indicated that the giving of parties at which roast pig or barbecued veal and large quantities of free alcoholic beverage would be served to anyone in the community was an important political event.[41]

35. Cali, July 1969.
36. Palmira, June 1969.
37. Popayán, February 1969.
38. Bogotá, February 1969.
39. Pereira, June 1971.
40. Salado, June 1971.
41. Bogotá, February 1969.

STEFFEN SCHMIDT

Elections and voting are also a central medium for exchange in the hands of the clients. The landowner mentioned earlier suggests that his position in the community has an impact on the way people behave politically:

My political power comes from the fact that I always vote Conservative as did my father. The people then feel that it will please me to have them vote the same way. In fact I am not politically active. Naturally it is pleasing to have my party win but I personally have never made an effort to organize the voters in our municipio.[42]

However, Jorge Isaza, election supervisor, indicated that winning elections was a crucial part of the gamonales' role:

The gamonal ... who distributed the forty jobs had an interest in his party winning [it is essential for his prestige in the party and his power]; the following had an interest personally because they are interested in the job for themselves or for a relative; the national elite and departmental politicians are interested in their party winning because they are interested personally in winning. So the election is very important to those people all the way from the janitor to the president.[43]

Uribe suggested that "many voted only so the gamonal would see them and continue to do favors for them." On the other hand, Salustro Lopez disclaims any pressure on the people to vote one way or another but indicates that most people vote in a way that pleases the leaders because they "have been good men who look after people."[44]

An underlying thread to the description of voting as trade-offs for patronage suggests that extensive use of coercion and fraud are common features of this process. The most subtle hint of this comes from Julian Zambrano, the cattle rancher, who indicates that although he himself is not interested in influencing votes, there are those who pretend to speak for him and by doing so get people to vote. A more straightforward description is offered by Uribe:

Fraud was committed: minors with forged cards were allowed to vote, partisans with cards in the names of dead people voted; blank votes

42. Popayán, February 1969.
43. Cali, July 1969.
44. Salado, June 1971.

282

were put in the box when the opposition was ahead in votes [when the total votes are more than the names on the lists, a number of ballots equal to the excess is taken at random and burned. If the Conservatives had many more votes, usually the burned ones disfavored them]. Often one of ours would even come back for a second vote—the revolver in his belt was his permit and the guarantee that the Conservative member of the election table shut up.[45]

Incentives to vote in Colombian clientelism are proffered within a well-defined historical confrontation between Liberals and Conservatives. Factionalism inside the national political parties is felt at the local level as in the division of the Conservatives between Vasquistas and Valencistas in the late 1920s and Gaitan's challenge in the 1940s.

You know when Gaitan and Turbay ran for president it was very bad. A Gaitanista came from Manizales and organized a group here. They were very violent. Don Samuel [the patron] finally stopped this and we worked for Turbay because he was the candidate of the party. Naturally many people voted for Gaitan because he was a very good man, one who represented the poor people. The gamonal for the Gaitanistas was Pedro Azevedo who was one of the *exaltados* [violent ones]. He is now in Bogotá and working for Lopez Michelsen.[46]

One suspects that Azevedo first supported Gaitan and then switched to Lopez Michelsen because there was no room for additional gamonales in the dominant stream of the Liberal party. Factions may serve as political bases for individuals who are interested in entering politics but unable to do so under normal conditions.

Interparty competition is most violent where the parties are divided and less so where one has established hegemony. In some cases there is acknowledgment that municipios tend to be prominently dominated by one party or the other:

The Liberals and Conservatives have lived apart. Expecially after Olaya where politics heated up. I remember some people here voted for Gaitan. The leaders in the town [*jefes politicos*] found out who they were; you know one cannot lie to a *campesino*; and these people went south because they were mistreated.[47]

45. Salado, June 1971.
46. Ibid.
47. Popayán, February 1969.

In another case recounted by Isaza, the gamonal forged a majority in his area by refusing credit to Liberals, thereby making it impossible for them to finance their seasonal agricultural production. The Liberals were said to have eventually moved out, and the area (Salta) is now almost exclusively Conservative. Another man said, "We are Liberals and proud of it; you won't find too many people except out in the rural townships up on the hill who vote for Conservatives." His reason for this was that the leaders in the community were Liberals and good people, and thus everyone voted that way. He further indicated that it is fortunate that the people vote Liberal and that the patron, who owns the sugarcane fields on which the community depends for employment, is also a Liberal.

Summary and Conclusion

In Colombian small-town and rural society political and economic forces converge to create an institution called gamonalismo or cacicazgo. It consists of a network of individuals who have access to scarce resources like jobs, money, or goods as well as more diffuse qualities such as the ability to sponsor events that entertain and provide moments of pleasure and leisure (a religious fiesta, a roasted calf, liquor for the men, etc.) or connections with important institutions like the police. These individuals (called gamonales, caciques, patrones, jefes politicos, or *caudillos*) are plugged into the national political party system. The incentive for them to be active, to use their resources and influence in the community and to work as politically relevant individuals, is varied. In some cases the gamonal is in the service (paid or not) of a nationally prominent patron who needs help in mobilizing local votes and thereby retaining political power. Such gamonales assume the day-to-day responsibilities of politics in the community and carry out the routine tasks of supervising the constituency. Others are more independent and can "play the field" politically speaking, searching for state or national leaders who can be supported in exchange for preferments (and it appears sometimes for just the satisfaction and prestige that the role confers).

Whichever role they play, gamonales are generally regarded as negative elements in the Colombian political process. It is not uncommon to hear it asserted that the institution of the gamonal is disappearing from Colombian life. Meanwhile, however, brokerage politics persists in Colombia and continues to manifest all the characteristics of clientelist linkage described at the outset of this study.

The inequality of participants. Gamonales rely on widespread *inequality* in the socioeconomic structure of the country for their function. If resources were more evenly accessible to everyone, the patronage aspects of the system would be far less attractive to the clients. The cost of interchanging items might rise to a level where it would no longer be possible for the patron or gamonal to supply them. It should be added that this aspect of clientelism is perhaps the one that most negatively affects the entire image of the broker. It defines the client as poor or peasant, the broker and the patron as rich.

Reciprocity of exchange. As is true in all clientelist systems, there is an element of barter in Colombian politics. The peasant would not receive his payoff if he did not have his vote and his more generalized support in politics to offer to the patron; the patron on the other hand would not have access to peasant votes if he could not provide the desired goods and/or services.

Proximity of actors. A third area of similarity between clientelism elsewhere and Colombian clientelism is the *proximity* of the participants in the relationship. The term "small municipios" was used by one commentator to describe the setting in which gamonalismo takes place. A similar description is given by others who indicated that small-town municipio politics is an intimate process, one in which distance between actors (as when the patron lives in a faraway city) is bridged by intermediary roles (a gamonal who works on the patron's land in the municipio, for instance). This proximity is of course fundamental to the relationship for a number of reasons. The nature of the exchanges requires rather carefully constructed relationships in which needs are known. Frequent contacts reinforce the partnership, and "strangers" cannot effectively operate in the context of small towns. Clientelism also relies on rather extensive socialization experiences in which the ties that bind a Liberal gamonal to his Liberal following, for example, must be frequently renewed through contacts. The political role of the broker is a delicate boundary-maintenance operation. In situations where traditional ascriptive authority performs important brokerage functions (such as where a family has dominated the scene for generations) the need for proximity is even more self-evident.

Two-person relationships. The *dyadic nature* of clientelism, which Scott and others have identified, emerges in the Colombian case as well. Each gamonal must build a delicate spider web of two-person relationships based on the media of exchange (which may well vary from one dyad to the next). That dyadic network becomes politically important only when it is large enough and sufficiently politicized to carry weight in the political process. The distinction between the word "gamonal" and the word "caudillo" lies in the greater extensiveness of the networks of the second. This is significant because it reinforces the earlier suggestion that unequal status is vital for the link to take place, not only between citizen and gamonal, but also between gamonal and national leader. The gamonal needs extraordinary resources (i.e., more than the average person has) to achieve his position. Such resources need not be exclusively financial; a clever man, well connected and with personality characteristics that set him apart, can build the necessary network of relationships to interest national party leadership. This interest can in turn ensure him the control of public moneys, which when allocated to his village or municipio become the basis of his continued political legitimacy in the eyes of the citizens.

The multiplexity of clientelist ties. Colombian clientelist relationships cover an extremely wide range of situations, political and non-political. There is more to gamonalismo than simply the exchange of a vote for a job or a ten-peso bill. Gamonalismo is a cultural and economic phenomenon as well as a political tie that binds. It is, in other words, a *multiplex* relationship.

Having established that Colombian brokerage politics manifests the characteristics of clientelist systems everywhere, a more direct consideration of the role gamonalismo plays in the functioning of Colombian political parties as linkage agencies between the local populace and national politics can be undertaken.

When viewed from a linkage perspective, the key quality of the system of gamonalismo is a seemingly paradoxical blend of loyalty and flexibility. Clientelism evolves from a series of socioeconomic exchanges that create binding ties between client and patron. So long as these exchanges continue, such ties are not easily broken, and enduring political loyalties are consequently formed. On the other hand, precisely because the basic ties are socioeconomic rather than political, gamonalismo affords a framework for local politics in which adjustment to changing national political patterns can be made. Motivated by economic need rather than by political passion, the clientelist link depends on the continued supply of material rewards, however minimal. If ensuring this supply requires shifting with one's gamonal from faction to faction, or even from party to party, the shift will be made. If the gamonal himself will not or cannot shift with prevailing national tides, he may well find his clientele shifting without him, following a new gamonal linked to a more powerful faction or party. Thus during the Gaitan period in the 1940s serious problems arose over the matter of insulating communities from Gaitanista organizers. When such threats develop from "outside" gamonales, the local patron must fight rigorously to insulate his clients. Four developments are possible. First, the gamonal may be able to maintain his group intact and continue to relate to that sector of his national political party with which he has influence or contact. Second, part of his constituency may break away and attach itself to a "new" gamonal (if the penalty to them is not too high and the gains seem worth it) with a consequent division of the community around two clientelist networks. Third, a gamonal may entirely lose his constituency as it is absorbed into a new network of association. Finally, the gamonal himself may shift to a new political faction—Gaitan and Lopez Michelsen showed great strength because they became national faction patrons over local networks.

Whichever of these directions a given situation takes, the likelihood of some tension is clear. Indeed, one of the consequences of clientelism in Colombia, especially in the rural areas, has been a rather high level of violence and coercion. This tendency toward violent revolution is compounded when the quest for converts crosses party boundaries, as during the "Liberalization" of Colombia in the 1930s or its "Conservatization" in the early 1950s.

Another result of the flexibility of Colombian clientelism is the tendency for political loyalties to vary from community to community. Colombian parties are strong in communities, not in regions, with each party working through a network of gamonales whose constituencies are small and frequently noncontiguous. In communities existing side by side, the population of one votes more than 80 percent Liberal and that of the other more than 80 percent Conservative. Such checkered voting patterns among communities that share regionwide social and economic problems necessarily reduces regional solidarity in the pursuit of national political solutions to those problems. The very strength of community-clientelist links to national parties is thus an impediment to the effective communication of local needs to Colombian policymakers. As a consequence, Colombian parties have greater legitimacy in the eyes of Colombian citizens than does the national political system. The party at least represents a flow of material payoffs via the gamonal. But ultimately, legitimacy rests not on the party or the system but on the success-ful gamonal. Defeat of the party need not mean loss of the services essential to an improverished and isolated population if it is blessed with a local leader capable of shifting his loyalties, or if it can join itself to a new leader, with better national credentials. In sum, however reassuring and materially useful the clientelist link is to the client, it is not an effective means of ensuring popular influence over Colombian party politics nor, in turn, over Colombian national policy.

13.

Linkage without Parties: Legislators and Constituents in Kenya

JOEL D. BARKAN AND
JOHN J. OKUMU

Central-Local Relationships and Linkage in Africa

Concern with central-local relationships and political linkage in new states has become a recurrent theme in the literature as an increasing number of scholars have defined political development in terms of the capacity of central (i.e., national) political institutions to extend and maintain their authority over the resident populations in these societies.[1] Viewed in this manner, political development can be partially measured in terms of the degree to which the members of these societies participate in, and/or indirectly influence, the making of public policy and the degree to which they comply with public policy decisions. As such, political development is also a *spatial* phenomenon involving both the expansion of the national political system from one or more

This article is the initial report of field research conducted by the authors in 1974 and a revision of a paper presented at the Seventieth Annual Meeting of the American Political Science Association in September of the same year. The discussion presented here is part of a larger comparative study on the relationships between citizens, local elites, and legislators in Kenya, Korea, and Turkey sponsored by the Comparative Legislative Research Center of the University of Iowa.

1. Samuel P. Huntington, *Political Order in Changing Societies* (New Haven: Yale University Press, 1968), pp. 8, 12.

central locations and the expansion of local political arenas from the periphery to the point where the boundaries between central and local political institutions overlap and are progressively dissolved until all members of society are incorporated into a single domain for the resolution of disputes. It is, consequently, a process dependent on the creation and maintenance of linkages, or networks for communication and/or the exchange of resources, between the center of the national political system and the periphery.

Explanations of how and under what conditions political development occurs must therefore consider the conditions under which different types of linkages between the center and periphery are created and maintained. This is especially true when examining the process of political development in sub-Saharan Africa where the degree of vertical integration between the center and the periphery is low and political parties are weak.

Systematic examinations of "linkage development" in Africa have been few, although a number of interesting case studies of central-local relationships have appeared in the literature.[2] Most studies of central-local relationships in the context of black Africa, however, have suffered from one or more of the following problems: (1) They consider these relationships from the perspective of either the actors at the center or those on the periphery but rarely both at the same time. Studies of the former variety have focused mainly on aspects of development administration, a process almost exclusively concerned with the penetration of the periphery by agents of the center, whereas studies of the latter type have focused on the nature and function of micropolitical (i.e., subnational) systems. (2) They have frequently ignored the linkage functions performed by elected politicians, particularly legislators. Given the decline or demise in Africa of parliamentary institutions, on the one hand, and political parties, on the other, little attention has been paid to the linkage roles played by those political brokers who continue to exist. (3) These studies have rarely involved any systematic

---

2. To cite but a few examples: Goran Hyden, *Political Development in Rural Tanzania* (Nairobi: East African Publishing House, 1969); Maxwell Owusu, *Uses and Abuses of Political Power: A Case Study of Continuity and Change in the Politics of Ghana* (Chicago: University of Chicago Press, 1970); Audrey C. Smock and David R. Smock, *Cultural and Political Aspects of Rural Transformation: A Case Study of Eastern Nigeria* (New York: Praeger, 1972); and Joan Vincent, *African Elite: The Big Men of a Small Town* (Teso, Uganda) (New York: Columbia University Press, 1971).

attempt to trace, particularly in spatial terms, the extent, variation, and proliferation of linkage networks between individual agents of central political institutions and citizens in the society at large. Rather than focusing on the patterns of communication and exchange between individuals, most studies of central-local relationships in Africa have concentrated on larger units of analysis, the central institutions and rural localities to be linked.[3] As a result, the policies and activities of groups and institutions at the center vis-à-vis the periphery and vice versa have often been described in detail, whereas the linkage networks connecting the two realms have been ignored. Consideration of central-local relationships at this level, moreover, makes it all but impossible to determine how far down political linkages actually extend from the center toward the periphery of society, and conversely, how far upward they extend from the grass roots. As a result, the boundaries of the national political system are also difficult to discern. A given community acting as an aggregate through its leaders may or may not make demands on the center and receive resource allocations in return, but this is not indicative of *the degree to which individual members of that community have been incorporated into the national political system, in short, the degree to which they have become "citizens" of the nation.*

Given these considerations, this study shall address itself to three questions: (1) What are the spatial patterns of central-local linkages in Kenya in respect to the networks Kenyan citizens utilize to make demands on their central political institutions? How far down do these linkages extend from the central institutions to the grass roots of Kenyan society? How far up do the linkages initiated by those on the periphery extend to the center? (2) What are the factors that bear on the creation, institutionalization, and decay of these linkages? (3) What are the prospects for further linkage development in Kenya, and what does this, in turn, suggest for the pattern of politics in that society and in others on the African continent where political parties play a minor role in political life?

Efforts to answer these questions have been guided by two underlying hypotheses. In the first hypothesis linkage development has been

---

3. Notable exceptions to this trend have been studies of patron-client relations. See René Lemarchand and Keith Legg, "Political Clientelism and Ethnicity in Tropical Africa: Competing Solidarities in Nation-Building," *American Political Science Review* 66 (March 1972): 68–90, and James C. Scott, "Patron-Client Politics and Political Change in South-East Asia," *American Political Science Review* 66 (March 1972): 91–113.

conceived to be a multidimensional process involving the creation of increasingly specialized sets of linkage chains manned by different, albeit sometimes overlapping, groups of political actors. In posing this hypothesis, Huntington's argument that the creation of political order depends on the establishment of autonomous, coherent, stable, and valued organizations for the purpose of responding to increasing levels of political participation by society's members[4] has been extended to include the argument that the establishment of autonomous, coherent, stable, and valued linkages is an integral part of this process. As such, separate linkage chains are likely to emerge for the purpose of representing local interests at the center, penetrating the periphery by the center, and mediating between the interests of the two.

The second hypothesis suggests that in political systems such as those found in sub-Saharan Africa, where executive and administrative institutions dominate and political parties are weak, legislators, given favorable conditions, may play important and unique linkage roles between the center and periphery even though they exercise little influence on the making of national policy. In this regard, African legislators seek both to create and to maintain linkage chains for the purpose of connecting their localities to the administrative state in a manner that civil servants, as agents of the center, do not.

To test these hypotheses and answer the questions raised above, the process of linkage development in Kenya has been observed by exploring the creation of linkage chains from three points in Kenyan society—at the grass-roots level through a series of surveys of approximately three hundred Kenyan citizens in each of fourteen parliamentary constituencies; at the level of the local power structure through a series of surveys involving twenty-one to forty-five notables in each of these same constituencies; and at the center through interviews of the M.P.'s who represent these constituencies, a group that included one minister and three assistant ministers. By simultaneously cutting into the Kenyan political system at three levels and by focusing on individuals as the primary unit of analysis, some of the problems of earlier explorations of central-local relationships have been avoided. Before presenting an overview of the findings, however, it will be useful to consider the historical factors that have affected the process of development in Kenya.

4. Huntington, op. cit., pp. 8–24.

Historical Factors: Administration and the Rise of Political Machines

Administratively, Kenya is divided into eight provinces, each headed by a provincial commissioner who is responsible for law and order and the coordination of all development activities in the province. Each province is divided into a number of districts (forty-one districts in the country as a whole), each headed by a district commissioner. The district commissioner is a very important link in the chain of command because he is much closer to the people than the provincial commissioner and chairs all development committees in the district. The provincial commissioners and the district commissioners are personal representatives of the president in the field and report to him. Each district is further divided into divisions headed by a district or divisional officer subordinate to the district commissioner. Each division is, in turn, divided into locations and sublocations headed by chiefs and subchiefs respectively. The chiefs[5] are important elements in this chain of command because they are in closest contact with the mass population.

This administrative structure was erected by the British during the colonial period and was the colonial governor's main instrument of control. Between 1945 and 1955, the bureaucracy grew from fourteen thousand to forty-five thousand[6] as the British developed a closer system of administration to defeat the Mau Mau insurrection and to implement the Swynnerton Plan.[7] By 1969, six years after independence, the bureaucracy numbered seventy-seven thousand.[8]

During the period after World War II, however, when the Provincial Administration began to expand rapidly, there was no corresponding development of African political life. By 1952 there were only six African members of the Legislative Council (the colonial parliament), all of whom were appointed by the colonial governor. With the rise of the Mau Mau insurgency in the same year, top African political

5. In Kenya "chiefs" are not men of high traditional status but civil servants. Unlike other members of the Provincial Administration, however, "chiefs" are long-term residents of the communities in which they work.

6. Goran Hyden, Robert Jackson, and John Okumu, eds., *Development Administration: The Kenyan Experience* (Nairobi: Oxford University Press, 1970), p. 8.

7. The Swynnerton Plan was the first attempt by the colonial government to consolidate landholdings among African farmers. The objective of the plan was to create a rural middle class to thwart further discontent of the type that gave rise to Mau Mau. The plan, initially financed by a £5 million grant from the British government, has been the model for Kenyan government land policy for more than twenty years.

8. Hyden, Jackson, and Okumu, op cit., p. 8.

leaders, including Jomo Kenyatta, were detained and their political organizations banned. Except for tribal (local) welfare associations, which mushroomed all over the country, political associations in the formal sense were forbidden until June 1955 when an act of the Legislative Council was passed to enable Africans to form political associations. The activities of these associations, however, were confined to administrative districts whose boundaries largely coincided with those of tribal groups. Political associations on a nationwide basis were not allowed.

Since 1922 it had been colonial policy to confine African political activities within ethnic boundaries. The main arenas for such activities were the Local Native Councils, which were viewed as appropriate training grounds for the development of African political life. The emphasis on local government was based on the premise that future African leaders should develop a strong *interest*, usually economic, in district and in tribal affairs. In the future, so argued the colonial authority, the Local Native Councils would form the constituency basis for future national political activity. The act of June 1955 was thus intended to reinforce this practice.

With the promulgation of the act, tribal voluntary associations, where they existed, were immediately converted into district political associations by educated Africans who saw them as vehicles to national political leadership in the future. These district political associations played a major role in the 1957 elections when Africans were for the first time elected to the Legislative Council on a common roll. To prepare for this election, constituency boundaries were drawn to coincide with district boundaries. This enabled the district political associations to become the first organizational expression of constituency parties.

In 1960, as Kenya commenced its transition to independent rule, political parties were permitted to organize on a nationwide basis in preparation for national elections the following year in which an African majority would be elected to the Legislative Council for the first time. By this time, however, the district political associations were already established as the most viable units of local party organization. In most districts there was a strong sense of local participation built around a single local leader or boss who used the organization as a personal political machine.[9] Thus when the Kenya African National Union

9. Perhaps the best known of these was Oginga Odinga's African Political Association in Central Nyanza in western Kenya, which was grafted onto the Luo Union, a powerful voluntary association in that area.

(KANU) and the Kenya African Democratic Union (KADU) were formed in 1960 as the first nationwide parties, the district political associations were converted into district (and often ethnically homogeneous) branches of the KANU and the KADU. This enabled them to retain a good measure of autonomy within the larger organizations to which they were now affiliated. Right from the start, therefore, the KANU and the KADU were cartels composed of autonomous district political associations over which the national party leadership had little influence. Most of the original leaders of the district associations, moreover, continued in office as branch officers of the new parties. Their first loyalty was to other local notables in their areas rather than to the executive leaders at the national level. To get access to the party's grass roots, the national leaders had to pass through the district bosses, a process that depended almost entirely on the kind of personal relationships existing between the two groups. Kenya thus approached independence in 1963 with an extremely fragile and faction-ridden party system, which could not provide a viable structure of linkages between the center and the grass roots.

This decentralized pattern of political organization became more pronounced with the advent of universal suffrage for the elections of 1961. To broaden the franchise and to create a more representative legislature, the old constituencies based on the administrative districts were subdivided, usually into three or more new constituencies. This opened new opportunities for a younger and essentially urban-based generation of leaders to enter politics. The 1961 elections in which the KANU won a majority of the seats in the Legislative Council, produced many new faces who were not members of the old political machines and not indebted to the district bosses.

This phenomenon did not affect all districts equally. In some, like Central Nyanza, whose powerful boss, Oginga Odinga, had a well-organized machine, candidates had to get a public endorsement from the district boss before they could be elected.[10] In other districts, however, districtwide political machines declined in significance and were replaced by constituency machines operated by sitting members of Parliament. These new machines exist and operate independently of the party organization that remains at the district level. Through them, a member

10. By the elections of 1974, however, three candidates on whose behalf Odinga campaigned were defeated, and his influence was falling.

295

of Parliament can work out direct links with the center for himself and his constituency.[11] Their alternative route to the center is through the provincial administration. This route can be equally beneficial for an M.P., because provincial administrators and their technical staff control and distribute most of the resources and equipment available in the rural areas.

The developments described above had a significant cumulative effect on the Kenyan political system. The KANU became the ruling party at independence in 1963. By the end of 1964, Kenya had become a de facto one-party state after the KADU M.P.'s joined the ruling party and dissolved their own. The factional nature of the KANU, however, spread beyond the control of the party's national leaders, and the party, which had little internal coherence to begin with, became progressively weak. Given this organizational vacuum, President Jomo Kenyatta quickly emerged as a strong executive and took advantage of the situation by asserting his personal power. Following independence, Kenyatta reestablished the Provincial Administration as the only dependable link between the central government and the grass roots.[12]

By putting greater and greater emphasis on the administrative infrastructure as a vehicle for control and development, the president soon became more dependent on it than on any other institution. Kenyatta deflated the status of the KANU, the National Assembly, and the legislators as well. The latter responded by criticizing the administration, which they thought still evinced all the characteristics of its colonial heritage as a vehicle of control.[13] Many went to the extent of suggesting that the provincial commissioners be made subordinate to elected representatives at the provincial level. The schism between administrators and M.P.'s continued throughout the life of the First Parliament from 1963 to 1969. The M.P.'s wanted it understood that civil servants were merely an instrument of the president to implement policy and should, therefore, be subordinate, not superior, to Parliament. The M.P.'s wanted to assert the superiority of the party and Parliament

11. So far the best model for a constituency-based political machine is that led by Arthur Magugu, a young M.P. from Githunguri division of Kiambu district. In recognition of his base of power, Magugu was appointed assistant minister after the election of 1974 and minister after the election of 1979.

12. In seizing the Provincial Administration as his main instrument for control, Kenyatta was simply following the example of colonial governors before him.

13. Cherry Gertzel, *The Politics of Independent Kenya* (London: Heinemann, 1970), pp. 29–31.

in order to gain access to the inner circles of government around Kenyatta and thus influence major policy decisions.

The M.P.'s also wanted the ruling party and its representatives in the National Assembly to become the vital link between the periphery and the central government, but the power of the presidency continued to grow and soon preempted the influence and status of Parliament. This was a significant development because it reflected a fundamental struggle between the backbenchers and the government for control of policy decisions. During this period the legislators devoted most of their time to national issues and very little time to their own constituencies. It was a conflict of roles, and most members of Parliament had not learned how to balance their contribution to national debate in Parliament with the satisfaction of demands from constituents. Further, many civil servants, who were convinced that the stability of the system depended on their ability to respond to public demand, were prone to separate a little too sharply the purely political roles from administrative rules. As a result, the role and activities of M.P.'s tended to be completely ignored by civil servants, as if the M.P.'s role ceased to be important the moment they stepped outside of the parliamentary buildings. This attitude led to constant and often crippling conflicts between the two wings of the governmental process.

Toward the end of the 1960s, this pattern began to change. The role of the legislator took on a new meaning as President Kenyatta began to emphasize the principle of self-help, or *Harambee*,[14] as the means for achieving rural development. To the president, self-help development projects, in which members of the local community built their own schools, roads, irrigation works, and so on, provided good opportunities for direct involvement by legislators in the day-to-day development of their constituencies. It gave M.P.'s access to resources hitherto solely controlled by administrators, enabled them to stay in closer proximity to problems of rural transformation and administration, and made it possible for them to work hand in hand with members of the provincial administration to solve local problems. Most important, self-help put some limitations on the extent to which civil servants could effectively exercise their authority without regard to the wishes of the M.P.'s representing the areas in which they served.

14. Harambee is a Swahili idiom that means "let us pull together." It is also Kenya's official motto and the word applied to all community-development projects in which self-help plays a part.

By spending more time in their constituencies, the more enterprising M.P.'s soon discovered that self-help development projects were activities that could also be used to build and/or sustain constituency political machines. These M.P.'s quickly forged links with senior administrators and with the president through personal networks and succeeded in diverting money and other resources to their constituencies. Thus, as the role of the legislator began to change, so did the emphasis on self-help. To the president, a legislator's status was directly related to his popularity in his constituency and the degree of loyalty and support he generated for the government. On the other hand, the popularity of the legislator in his constituency usually depended on his ability to attract new projects to the constituency and to support those already in existence. This requirement became more noticeable during and after the first postindependence election in 1969.

When the activities of the members of the First Parliament (1963 –69) are compared with the activities of the members of the Second (1969–74), the linkage role of Kenyan legislators independent of party becomes more apparent. Prior to the president's emphasis on self-help, the majority of legislators in the First Parliament were primarily concerned with personal image building through public utterances in the National Assembly and in the press. On the one hand, they sought to reassert the role of the party and Parliament and outflank the civil service. On the other, the relatively free atmosphere of debate that existed in the assembly permitted backbenchers to criticize the government on major issues, engaging in the kind of debate that would have presumably taken place within the KANU had the ruling party developed into a centralized forum. As one observer put it, the members felt that "their own future was dependent to a large extent on the kind of reputations they created for themselves *in* Parliament as the representatives of the people."[15] For the bulk of the Kenyan population, however, who are peasants residing in the rural areas, the central question was not the quality of the representative's performance in the National Assembly but whether he contributed to the economic development of his constituency.

The extent of the discrepancy between these different perceptions of the M.P.'s proper role was dramatically illustrated by the election of 1969 in which more than half the members of the First Parliament

15. Gertzel, op. cit., p. 138; our italics.

failed to win reelection to the Second. Debate preceding the election was dominated by local issues, and the results underscored the terms by which constituents evaluated their M.P.'s. Hyden and Leys, in their study of the election, state that reelection was largely a function of the amount of benefits individual M.P.'s extracted from the government for their districts during their terms in office. Their jobs as lawmakers, as explainers of government policies to the electorate, and as devoted party supporters seemed to be unimportant.[16] The same pattern of constituent evaluation of M.P.'s was observed by the authors of this report in their study of the election of 1974.[17]

The historical factors discussed above, particularly the structural decentralization and decline of the KANU, the emergence of self-help, and the elections of 1969, significantly altered the role of the M.P. in Kenyan society. Given these developments, what kind of relationships now exist between M.P.'s and their constituents, and what does this signify for the process of linkage development and politics in Kenya today?

Linkage Development in Kenya: An Overview of Research Findings

If linkage development is a multidimensional process involving the reciprocal penetration of the center and the periphery by their respective agents, the structural evolution of Kenyan politics and administration since the 1950s and especially since 1969 suggests that the linkage networks forged by M.P.'s are an important aspect of this process. The extent to which such linkage networks actually exist, and their prospects for becoming institutionalized across the Kenyan political system largely depend on the existence of two conditions: (1) Congruent sets of role expectations by members of the Kenyan National Assembly and the constituents they purport to represent (especially local elites), which specify a set of desired relations that is functionally

16. Goran Hyden and Colin T. Leys, "Elections and Politics in Single-Party Systems: The Case of Kenya and Tanzania," *British Journal of Political Science* 2, no. 4 (October 1972): 401.
17. See Joel D. Barkan with John J. Okumu, "'Semi-Competitive' Elections, Clientelism and Political Recruitment in a No-Party State: The Kenyan Experience," in *Elections Without Choice*, ed. Guy Hermet et al., eds. (New York: Wiley Interscience, 1978), pp. 88–107, and Joel D. Barkan, "Further Reassessment of the 'Conventional Wisdom': Political Knowledge and Voting Behavior in Rural Kenya," *American Political Science Review* 70, no. 2 (June 1976): 452–55.

different from that existing between constituents and agents of the Provincial Administration, and (2) a series of activities (including the distribution of resources) and sanctions through which these congruent sets of role expectations are both substantively and symbolically fulfilled and maintained.

To determine the presence or absence of these conditions in Kenya, a series of surveys were conducted in fourteen parliamentary constituencies in the country between April and June 1974. As noted above, these surveys were designed to observe simultaneously the process of linkage development at three points along the potential linkage chains between each constituency and the center by considering the attitudes and behavior of citizens, local elites, and the M.P. for the district. Because of the near impossibility of listing dwelling units in rural Africa, members of the citizen sample in each constituency were drawn on a quota, rather than a random, basis according to their age and sex. Quotas for age/sex combinations (which were limited to adults over twenty years old) were based on the results of the Kenyan National Census of 1969.[18]

The samples of local elites interviewed for the study were determined by a combination of positional and reputational criteria. Included in these samples were all chiefs, subchiefs, district councillors, headmasters of secondary schools, senior officials of the KANU, chairmen of all cooperative societies and other associations in the constituency, and any other individuals who were considered to be important citizens by at least five respondents of the citizen sample.[19]

18. To increase the prospects of obtaining a representative sample in each constituency, the quotas for each age/sex combination to be included in the sample were randomly allocated across thirty sampling plots of approximately a quarter mile in diameter. These plots were in turn randomly distributed across the constituency on the basis of aerial photographic maps of the area. The procedure substantially reduced the bias normally inherent in quota samples by ensuring that all areas of the constituency were represented in the survey. Given the authors' concern with the linkage patterns, this consideration was especially important as citizens living in highly developed sections of the constituency and along lines of communication would obviously be more likely to be linked into the national political system than those who did not.

19. There was a considerable overlap between the leaders included in the local elite by virtue of their formal positions and those selected according to reputational criteria. Approximately 90 percent of the latter held formal positions in the local power structure, the major exception being approximately from two to four prominent businessmen and farmers in each district. Conversely, from 50 percent to 70 percent of those included in the elite sample because of their positions were regarded as influential by at least five members of the citizen sample.

The fourteen constituencies chosen as research sites were also selected on a stratified basis, as this was the most efficient way to obtain a representative and logistically feasible sample of Kenya's 158 parliamentary constituencies.[20] In selecting these constituencies, controls were introduced to account for variations in ethnic composition, geographic location and accessibility to the capital city of Nairobi, level of economic development, and whether the constituency was represented in the National Assembly by a backbencher, assistant minister, or cabinet member.[21]

As the initial report of the study, this essay will consider citizen and elite responses from only six constituencies: Starehe, an urban district of mixed ethnic composition located in Nairobi; Githunguri, a prosperous coffee-growing area twenty miles north of Nairobi inhabited by members of Kenya's largest and most important ethnic group, the Kikuyu; Kilifi-South, a relatively poor area twenty miles west of the port city of Mombasa; Kajiado-North, the home of roughly a fifth of Kenya's nomadic Masai and the largest district in the sample, covering more than five thousand square miles from Nairobi to the Tanzanian border; Ikolomani, an area of high population density in Western Province, the home of the Abaluhya people; and Nyakach, a rice-growing area in Nyanza Province, the home of the Luo. Given the small sample, no claim is made here regarding the representative nature of this group of constituencies. In respect to ethnicity and geographic location, however, they are typical of most constituencies in the country.

The interviews of citizens and local elites were conducted in the appropriate vernacular language or Kiswahili, and interviews with M.P.'s were conducted in English. Given the low number of the latter sample, an additional thirty-two M.P.'s were randomly selected to augment the original group. Fourteen of the latter group were ultimately interviewed. This report, therefore, will examine the responses of the fourteen representatives of the six constituencies that were the research

20. For example, constituencies in Northeastern Province and the Turkana and Marsabit districts were excluded as possible research sites because of the inability of the authors to supervise interviewing in those areas because of weather and road conditions.
21. Constituencies included in the study were as follows: Kilifi-South (Coast Province), Embu-South and Mbooni (Eastern Province), Githunguri and Kirinyaga-West (Central Province), Kajiado-North, Laikipia-West, and Kericho (Rift Valley Province), Kitutu-East, Mbita, and Nyakach (Nyanza Province), Busia-East and Ikolomani (Western Province), and Starehe (Nairobi).

JOEL D. BARKAN AND JOHN J. OKUMU

sites for the citizen and local-elite surveys, plus those of the fourteen M.P.'s interviewed in the supplemental survey.

ROLE EXPECTATIONS

Perhaps the first requisite for the development of institutionalized linkage between the center and the periphery of a political system is the emergence of congruent and mutually reinforcing sets of role expectations on the part of those on the periphery, those at the center, and those attempting to link the two. Although the existence of congruent sets of role expectations in itself does not constitute linkage between center and periphery, congruent role expectations are a necessary condition for such linkage to exist.

As noted in the preceding section, electoral politics in Kenya evolved along highly parochial lines based on personal machines in which local interests were repeatedly stressed and the articulation of national goals was of secondary importance. Despite this local orientation, the role of the M.P. as a link between his constituents and Kenya's central political institutions did not fully manifest itself until after the elections of 1969. Whereas prior to the elections most M.P.'s saw themselves as parliamentarians whose first duty was to deliberate and legislate national policy, members of the Second Parliament primarily defined their jobs in terms of constituency service.

Although longitudinal data to measure the extent to which members of the National Assembly have redefined their roles is not available, their current thoughts on the matter are quite clear and are highly consistent with the expectations of their constituents. When asked what types of problems occupied most of their time, 82 percent of the M.P.'s reported that problems in their constituency were their main concern. Only 7 percent reported that general problems of a national scope drew most of their attention, and 11 percent said they divided their time about equally between local and national issues. As might be expected, frontbenchers (ministers and assistant ministers in the Kenyan government) were more inclined (25 percent) than backbenchers (15 percent) to devote from half to almost all their time to national issues. But only slightly so. Indeed, each of the frontbenchers noted that he could better serve his constituency because of his ministerial status and that he regularly took steps to ensure that a "fair" share of his ministry's resources reached his constituency. Backbenchers and members of the government thus share a common local perspective of their duties.

302

The local orientation of M.P.'s is further revealed by their answers to the question of what specific activities occupy most of their time. When asked to rank six activities that are widely considered to constitute the legislative role in Kenya, the mean ranks accorded each activity by backbenchers and members of the government were as follows:

TABLE 13.1.   Activities Occupying Time of M.P.'s (mean ranks)

Backbenchers (N = 20)		Frontbenchers (N = 8)	
Rank	Activity	Rank	Activity
1.7	Obtaining resources and projects for constituency	1.7	Obtaining resources and projects for constituency
		2.5	Formulating government policy
3.1	Expressing views of constituents	3.0	Expressing views of constituents
3.1	Interceding with civil servants on behalf of constituents	3.3	Explaining policies to voters
3.1	Formulating government policy	3.8	Interceding with civil servants on behalf of constituents
4.1	Explaining policies to voters		
5.7	Resolving conflicts in constituency	5.8	Resolving conflicts in constituency

As indicated in table 13.1, frontbenchers and backbenchers allocate their time to similar activities. Although ministers and assistant ministers are more inclined than backbenchers to spend time formulating and explaining government policy and less likely to intercede with civil servants on their constituents' behalf, *both* are primarily concerned with obtaining government resources and projects for their districts. Indeed, securing government expenditures for schools, roads, agricultural projects, and so on in one's district was *the* criterion on which virtually all members of the M.P. sample expected to be judged in the parliamentary elections in October 1974, five months after the survey.[22] When probed as to whether they should spend more or less time on each of these same six activities, 83 percent said they hoped to do more

22. The expectations of the M.P.'s interviewed proved to be an accurate prediction of the way Kenyan voters arrive at their voting decisions. For a discussion of voting behavior in the elections of 1974, see Barkan with Okumu, op. cit.

to obtain government projects for their district, and another 54 percent felt they should be more active in pressing the civil service to respond to constituent demands. No other activities were mentioned as deserving more attention by more than a quarter of the sample.

With one exception, constituents' role expectations of Kenyan M.P.'s and the expectations held by local elites are highly congruent with the role definitions M.P.'s set for themselves, although the conceptions most citizens hold of what a member of the Kenya National Assembly actually does are often diffuse and frequently emphasize symbolic as well as substantive aspects of the job. Role expectations held by citizens and local elites were probed by two sets of questions, a series of open-ended queries that asked the respondents to describe how legislators handled community problems in contrast to civil servants, party leaders, and judges and a series that asked respondents to specify the relative importance of seven activities in which legislators are most frequently engaged. Responses to the former series indicate that most citizens do not perceive their representative as performing any specialized functions other than that he is a person whose first duty is to serve the community and that, unlike senior officials of the Provincial Administration, he is a long-term resident of the community. More than half the respondents could not formulate more precise answers to these questions other than noting that M.P.'s participate in making laws. These diffuse conceptions of a legislator's duties can pose difficulties for an M.P. When asked whether their constituents perceived the job of M.P. in the same manner as they themselves defined it, 82 percent of the M.P.'s stated that their constituents expected them to deliver far more than was possible in terms of attending to their constituents' personal (as contrasted with community)[23] problems and that they did not appreciate the limits of an M.P.'s power.

When presented with a list of specific activities with which M.P.'s are concerned, members of the citizen sample were more precise and consistent in their pattern of response. As indicated in table 13.2, citizens and local elites alike perceive their M.P.'s as a means to communicate the needs of their community to the national government and as an agent for obtaining resources from the center for community development. Particularly significant is the low emphasis citizens and

23. Typical of the personal problems constituents expected their M.P.'s to solve were assistance in obtaining employment, land titles, and places for one's children in school.

local elites place on the explicitly legislative duties of deliberating and passing bills in the National Assembly and on the explanation of government policy to constituents, an activity repeatedly stressed by President Kenyatta. Put differently, both M.P.'s and their constituents primarily define the M.P.'s role as an agent of the periphery whose main duty is to penetrate the center. Legislative roles as conventionally defined are decidedly viewed as less important than linkage roles. On the other hand, the linkage roles expected of M.P.'s are qualitatively different from those expected from civil servants in the Provincial Administration.

This view of the M.P. as an instructed delegate whose primary duty is to labor on his constituents' behalf is supported further by responses to a series of questions regarding the opinions M.P.'s should follow when trying to determine their positions on important issues. When asked whether "your M.P. should do what the people of this district want no matter what his own opinion is," and whether "your M.P. should follow his own judgment because he knows more about what is best for you," a large majority of all the constituent and all but two of the elite samples responded affirmatively to the first statement and negatively to the second in every constituency except Ikolomani. These attitudes, which are reported in tables 13.3 and 13.4, are buttressed by those reported in table 13.5. When asked whose views an M.P. should follow when faced with a decision on a controversial issue in the National Assembly, both constituents and local elites contended that the views of constituents should take priority, especially over those of the M.P. The responses reported in table 13.5 are also interesting in respect to the relative saliency of the KANU as a source of public policy in the minds of local elites. Although the party's organization at the local level has been moribund since the late 1960s in all but a handful of constituencies, the government continues to refer to itself as "the KANU government," a concept that still strikes a responsive chord among a significant proportion of the local leadership groups.

Although constituents, local elites, and M.P.'s all stressed constituency service in their expectations of the latter's role, the concept of the M.P. as a mere agent of local opinion does not fully describe the role M.P.'s feel they play. While Kenyan legislators certainly regard themselves as accountable to their constituents, most members of the M.P. sample felt they were better equipped (usually because of their superior education and experience) to articulate and define the interests

TABLE 13.2. Role Expectations: Activities on Which M.P.'s Should Spend Most of Their Time (in percent)

				Constituents' Expectations			
	Starehe	Kilifi	Githunguri	Kajiado	Ikolomani	Nyakach
Linkage Activities						
Explain government policies to constituents	3	10	10	9	9	6
Tell government what people in district want	35	36	27	38	29	25
Obtain projects and benefits for the district	39	31	25	19	20	34
Visit district frequently	13	8	4	10	20	13
Nonlinkage Activities						
Take active part in the debates of the National Assembly and pass bills	4	9	27	4	7	9
Help constituents with their personal problems	4	3	6	15	10	10
Help solve conflicts in the community	2	3	—	6	4	4
Total Linkage	90	85	66	75	78	78
Total Nonlinkage	10	15	33	25	21	23
N =	(270)	(269)	(49)	(284)	(277)	(282)

Local Elites' Expectations

	Starehe	Kilifi	Githunguri	Kajiado	Ikolomani	Nyakach
Linkage Activities						
Explain government policies to constituents	24	32	6	17	—	12
Tell government what people in district want	6	55	12	54	11	74
Obtain projects and benefits for the district	41	5	53	13	53	7
Visit district frequently	18	—	9	9	32	—
Nonlinkage Activities						
Take active part in the debates of the National Assembly and pass bills	—	9	21	—	5	7
Help constituents with their personal problems	—	—	—	4	—	—
Help solve the conflicts in the community	12	—	9	4	—	—
Total Linkage	88	91	70	92	95	93
Total Nonlinkage	12	9	30	8	5	7
N =	(17)	(22)	(34)	(24)	(19)	(42)

TABLE 13.3. "Should Your M.P. Do What the People of This District Want No Matter What His Own Opinion Is?"

	Starehe	Kilifi	Githunguri	Kajiado	Ikolomani	Nyakach
Continuents						
% responding YES	78	90	93	83	87	95
N =	(292)	(289)	(284)	(298)	(285)	(293)
Local Elites						
% responding YES	41	91	100	96	37	98
N =	(17)	(22)	(35)	(23)	(17)	(45)

TABLE 13.4. "Should Your M.P. Follow His Own Judgment Because He Knows More About What Is Best for You?"

	Starehe	Kilifi	Githunguri	Kajiado	Ikolomani	Nyakach
Constituents						
% responding NO	69	86	97	63	46	66
N =	(291)	(288)	(284)	(297)	(287)	(295)
Local Elites						
% responding NO	53	68	100	61	53	69
N =	(17)	(22)	(34)	(23)	(19)	(45)

TABLE 13.5. "When an M.P. Faces a Controversial Issue in the National Assembly, Whose Views Should He Follow?"

	Constituents (in percent)					
	Starehe	Kilifi	Githunguri	Kajiado	Ikolomani	Nyakach
Constituents	70	88	37	50	64	65
KANU	9	7	19	9	10	12
Views of civil service	3	2	15	11	6	2
Interest groups	1	—	18	10	4	5
Advisers and friends	6	1	1	6	2	2
Own beliefs	11	3	1	13	13	10
Other	—	—	9	2	1	2
N =	(276)	(264)	(74)	(281)	(281)	(286)

	Local Elites (in percent)					
	Starehe	Kilifi	Githunguri	Kajiado	Ikolomani	Nyakach
Constituents	86	59	47	79	52	69
KANU	14	9	17	13	33	21
Views of civil service	—	14	12	—	10	—
Interest groups	—	9	12	8	—	—
Advisers and friends	—	—	3	—	—	3
Own beliefs	—	9	6	—	4	8
Other	—	—	3	—	—	—
N =	(21)	(22)	(34)	(24)	(21)	(39)

of their constituents than the people themselves and considered this to be one of their main tasks as leaders. All saw themselves as opinion leaders who, though bound to represent the general wishes of their constituents, played a role in determining what the specific content of those wishes were. Thus, although 56 percent of the M.P.'s *strongly* disagreed with the statement that "society is better run by a few enlightened and experienced leaders than by the will of the masses," only 39 percent agreed or strongly agreed with the proposition that "most citizens generally know enough about public affairs." An M.P.'s constituents might, therefore, repeatedly express a general demand for better health or educational facilities, but it is the M.P. who specifies what type of schools or health centers are feasible and takes the initiative in organizing the members of the community to realize their goals. As a result, most M.P.'s also define their roles vis-à-vis their constituents, on the one hand, and the central government, on the other, in entrepreneurial terms. Both present the M.P. with a set of demands and resources that, if properly combined, result in service to his constituents, enhanced political stature for himself, and the further development of linkage networks between the center and the periphery. The role of the M.P. as an entrepreneur for his constituents will be discussed further in the next section.

ACTIVITIES AND RESOURCES

Although the first requisite for linkage development is the existence of congruent sets of role expectations on the part of those on the periphery and those at the center of the political system, the second most important requirement is the existence of behavioral patterns and a method of distribution of resources through which these role expectations find expression. Turning first to the activities of actors on the periphery, most constituents and virtually all members of the local elites are highly aware of the problems facing their communities and discuss these problems on a regular basis. A similar finding was obtained in respect to national issues as shown by table 13.6 which suggests that at a minimum, most Kenyans are at least subjectively members of a national political system.[24] Voting turnout among members of the samples was

24. No data are presented here for the nomadic peoples living in remote areas of northern Kenya and Masailand. The level of political discourse in such areas, particularly

also high: 45 percent of the constituents in Starehe, 73 percent in Kilifi, 67 percent in Githunguri, 53 percent in Kajiado, 68 percent in Ikolomani, and 83 percent in Nyakach reported that they had voted in the parliamentary elections in 1969.[25] Respective figures for the elite samples were 86, 96, 100, 100, 100, and 94 percent. If minimal membership in the political system is thus defined in terms of regularly discussing public affairs on a weekly basis and participating in national elections, roughly half to two-thirds of the adult population make the grade. Such a definition of the boundaries of the political system is, of course, arbitrary and includes no measures of popular support for the system's major institutions or the degree of consensus on the system's rules of the game, two conditions that must be fulfilled if the system is to persist. These figures, however, are highly suggestive of the parameters within which linkage networks forged by legislators can develop. The data also suggest that residents of the rural areas, most of whom are peasants, are far more aware of political issues and events than most politicians (and social scientists!) have heretofore supposed.[26]

Although a majority discussed issues of public policy on a regular basis and sought, at least indirectly, to influence the making of public policy via the electoral process, the number who have sought to develop more extensive linkages to the central arenas of decision making was substantially less. When asked whether they had ever talked to a government official about the problem they had previously named as the most significant in their community, only a sixth or less of the respondents in each constituency said "yes" except in Nyakach. As might be expected, the corresponding figures for the local-elite samples were substantially higher, as indicated in table 13.7. The relative magnitude of these figures is not surprising, though it is significant to note that the lowest level of communication between citizens and officials (but not between local elites and officials) was in Starehe, the only urban constituency

in respect to national issues, is undoubtedly lower than that reported here. People residing in such areas, however, account for less than 12 percent of Kenya's population.

25. The relatively low figure for Starehe is a reflection of the fact that many people residing in the area vote in a rural constituency from which they have migrated to Nairobi, and others, because of their transient existence, do not vote at all.

26. For more extensive discussion of the relatively high level of political knowledge among African peasants see Fred M. Hayward, "A Reassessment of Conventional Wisdom About the Informed Public: National Political Information in Ghana," *American Political Science Review* 70 (June 1976): 433–51.

TABLE 13.6. Frequency of Discussion of Local and National Problems (in percent)

			Constituents			
	Starehe	Kilifi	Githunguri	Kajiado	Ikolomani	Nyakach
Local Issues						
One or more times per week	62	30	67	36	65	49
Once a fortnight	14	3	7	41	19	18
Less than once a fortnight	18	19	17	13	10	23
Never	5	48	9	11	6	10
N =	(290)	(263)	(280)	(297)	(265)	(289)
National Issues						
One or more times per week	65	13	72	62	69	55
Once a fortnight	12	4	5	11	15	14
Less than once a fortnight	15	14	12	11	8	23
Never	8	70	10	16	7	8
N =	(294)	(191)	(271)	(292)	(241)	(278)

Local Elites

	Starehe	Kilifi	Githunguri	Kajiado	Ikolomani	Nyakach
Local Issues						
One or more times per week	100	68	89	92	91	81
Once a fortnight	—	27	8	8	9	12
Less than once a fortnight	—	5	—	—	—	2
Never	—	—	3	—	—	5
N =	(22)	(22)	(37)	(25)	(22)	(42)
National Issues						
One or more times per week	91	55	66	82	85	88
Once a fortnight	5	32	21	4	15	7
Less than once a fortnight	5	9	13	14	—	—
Never	—	5	—	—	—	5
N =	(21)	(22)	(38)	(22)	(20)	(43)

TABLE 13.7. Discussion with Officials About Most Important Problem Facing Community (in percent)

	Constituents					
	Starehe[b]	Kilifi	Githunguri	Kajiado	Ikolomani	Nyakach
Has discussed problem with official?						
Yes	7	6	16	10	16	36
No	93	94	84	90	84	64
N =	(271)	(265)	(265)	(295)	(278)	(282)
Official with whom respondent has discussed problem[a]						
Subchief	—	6	40	17	32	65
Location chief	6	56	51	47	45	85
D.C. or D.O.	22	38	33	33	20	47
Other official at district level	22	—	14	33	16	37
Provincial officer	11	—	—	7	—	6
Official in Nairobi	22	6	—	3	—	—
M.P.	—	13	47	10	—	16
Cabinet minister	—	6	—	—	—	—
Other	11	19	2	—	2	10
N =	(18)	(16)	(43)	(30)	(44)	(81)

Local Elites

	Starehe[b]	Kilifi	Githunguri	Kajiado	Ikolomani	Nyakach
Has discussed problem with official?						
Yes	62	95	43	87	60	79
No	38	5	57	13	40	21
N =	(21)	(21)	(37)	(24)	(15)	(43)
Official with whom respondent has discussed problem[a]						
Subchief	—	—	—	10	—	—
Location chief	—	70	56	76	22	38
D.C. or D.O.	8	55	19	71	56	100
Other official at district level	—	5	44	86	44	18
Provincial officer	15	—	—	—	—	21
Official in Nairobi	—	—	6	10	—	—
M.P.	15	15	19	14	—	24
Cabinet minister	15	—	—	5	—	—
Other	46	—	—	10	—	6
N =	(13)	(20)	(16)	(21)	(9)	(34)

[a] Percentages total to more than 100 because the respondents who discussed problems with government officials often talked to more than one.

[b] In Nairobi there are no chiefs, and the Provincial Administration and District Administration are combined under the Provincial Commissioner.

included in the survey.[27] Of greater significance is the type of official contacted by citizens and local elites respectively, for a clear pattern emerges as to the nature of political linkages at the grass roots of Kenyan society. This pattern, however, is also affected by the behavior of the M.P. vis-à-vis his constituents.

As suggested by table 13.7, contact between citizens and government officials is most likely to occur with the lowest members of the district administration, chiefs and subchiefs. The pattern is present in all constituencies except Starehe, where chiefs are not part of the urban administration (but where most contacts are with officials of the city administration), and underscores the highly parochial orientation farmers in the rural areas have toward their government. In contrast, local elites rarely deal with subchiefs and approach location chiefs less frequently than the average citizen. Local elites are far more inclined to press their demands on senior officials of the district administration, the district commissioner and district officer. Neither citizens nor local elites, however, are likely to contact administrative officials at the provincial level, and the extent of their approaches to their M.P.'s is highly variable.[28]

The variable rate of contact between constituents and M.P.'s and between local leaders and M.P.'s suggests that linkage development via M.P.'s is not nearly as uniform as that involving members of the Provincial Administration at the district and local level. However, the perceived utility of such linkages, where they do exist, as in Githunguri where the M.P. holds public meetings every week, can be quite high.

Linkage development via M.P.'s is a function of how the M.P. is perceived by his constituents, which in turn is a function of his frequency of contact with his constituents and the other activities he undertakes in his district, in short, his performance. Although most citizens in the samples did not approach their M.P. about community problems, most are nevertheless aware of who he is (an average of 80 percent of the citizen samples could correctly identify him by name), what he

27. The low level of communication in Starehe is probably explained in terms of the highly transient nature of the population and the nonvisibility of government officials to the general public in urban areas as compared with rural areas where such officials do not compete with a host of other leaders for the public's attention.

28. It should also be noted that people who contact officials usually do so on their own without the use of intermediaries. Less than 5 percent of the respondents in each of the citizen samples reported using intermediaries, and none of the local-elite respondents reported such contacts.

TABLE 13.8. Number of Times Respondent Has Seen His M.P. Within the Last Six Months, November 1973 –April 1974 (in percent)

	Constituents					
	Starehe	Kilifi	Githunguri	Kajiado	Ikolomani	Nyakach
None	72	39	16	44	60	64
Once	4	28	20	11	14	21
Twice	10	19	22	17	10	10
Three or four	7	10	20	20	9	2
Five or more	5	3	21	7	3	—
Few	1	—	—	—	3	2
"Many"	1	—	1	—	1	1
N =	(244)	(227)	(288)	(241)	(261)	(274)

	Local Elites					
	Starehe	Kilifi	Githunguri	Kajiado	Ikolomani	Nyakach
None	5	—	—	4	5	76
Once	5	—	—	—	—	17
Twice	—	—	—	4	—	5
Three or four	—	9	4	8	—	—
Five or more	20	86	21	71	—	—
Few	—	—	—	—	—	—
"Many"	70	5	75	13	95	2
N =	(20)	(22)	(24)	(24)	(20)	(41)

does, and, as suggested above, what he should do. However, when asked how many times they had seen their representative within the last six months, considerable variation was again reported across the six samples, as indicated in table 13.8.

As expected, members of the local power structure were far more likely to see their M.P. than the average citizen, a pattern present in all constituencies except Nyakach, which reflects the conscious decision by most M.P.'s to contact as many local leaders as possible each time they return to their constituencies. More interesting is the correlation between the number of times an M.P. has been seen in his constituency and the extent to which both members of the general public and local leaders attempt to talk to him about their personal problems and those of their community. As suggested by table 13.9, M.P.'s who make themselves more accessible to their constituents are approached more frequently, particularly by members of the local elite. This relationship, which is present in all but one of the sample constituencies, again suggests that the residents of rural Africa are predisposed toward being members of a national political system and can be linked to that system, at least insofar as they seek contact with their representatives to national political institutions.

Citizens who regularly see their M.P. are also more likely to evaluate favorably his performance in his job. When asked whether they felt their M.P. was "active," "somewhat active," or "not active" in respect to each of the seven activities considered in table 13.2, both constituents and local elites who had seen their M.P. most frequently were those who gave their representatives the highest marks as indicated

TABLE 13.9. Whether Respondent Has Ever Discussed a Problem with His/Her M.P. by Number of Times Respondent Saw M.P. Within Last Six Months (in percent)

| | Frequency of Contact | | | | | |
| | Constituents | | | Local Elites | | |
	0	1–2	3+	0	1–2	3+
Ever talked with M.P.?						
Yes	5	8	18	17	13	61
No	95	92	82	83	87	39
N =	(1298)	(979)	(803)	(47)	(47)	(233)

TABLE 13.10. Mean Evaluation Respondent Accorded M.P. by Number of Times Respondent Saw M.P. Within Last Six Months (in percent)

| | Frequency of Contact | | | | | |
| | Constituents | | | Local Elites | | |
	0	*1–2*	*3+*	*0*	*1–2*	*3+*
Evaluation of M.P.						
"Active"	19	25	42	—	19	45
"Somewhat Active"	28	34	36	33	27	35
"Not Active"	53	42	23	67	54	20
N=	(1055)	(942)	(909)	(54)	(52)	(287)

by table 13.10, which presents the mean percentages for all seven activities. The relationship was found in all six constituencies.

The correlations between the number of times constituents see their M.P.'s, their propensity to approach him about community problems, and their general evaluation of his performance suggest several conclusions about the prospects for linkage development along this dimension. First, linkage development, whether by the Provincial Administration or by the M.P., depends on the *physical* presence of a linking agent in the rural areas. In these areas, where facilities for mass communication are nonexistent or poor, there are no substitutes, and it is for this reason that the Provincial Administration in Kenya, especially through its network of chiefs, has been so effective in penetrating and controlling those on the periphery.[29] M.P.'s, therefore, must circulate among their constituents on a regular basis if they are to maintain their support and create parallel linkage structures of their own. Given the difficulties of this task and the demise of local party organizations, M.P.'s must also attach themselves to the chiefs' networks and/or create their own personal machines composed of prominent local leaders.

29. The authority of the chiefs should not be underestimated. Although this network s a remnant of the colonial state, and was consequently viewed with great suspicion by politicians preceding Kenya's independence, it is nevertheless an important institution that, as the data suggest, has been too frequently ignored by observers of contemporary Kenyan politics.

Linkage development by M.P.'s in Kenya thus requires a two-pronged effort involving the establishment of downward linkages into one's constituency and upward linkages to the center. Most M.P.'s seek to achieve the former through frequent visits to their districts and participation in self-help projects. They establish ties with the center by lobbying with agencies of the central administration for support for local development projects and by attaching themselves as clients to nationally prominent leaders who control the purse strings (both officially and unofficially) to the resources an M.P. needs. Lawmaking and participation in parliamentary debates are increasingly treated as low priorities, a fact underscored by low attendance in the House.[30] There is considerable variation, however, in the way individual members approach these activities and the degree of success achieved.

Although 96 percent of the M.P. sample reported that they visited their constituency at least once a week, these visits varied greatly both in quality and in the number and type of people each legislator saw. About a third of those interviewed indicated that they were content to make themselves available to their constituents at their homes, whereas two-thirds made systematic attempts to canvass members of the local elite, especially the chiefs. About half attended public meetings once or twice a month, but only 11 percent reported doing so on a weekly basis. Only 8 percent maintained offices in their constituency, although another 8 percent had done so in the past. Of the M.P.'s representing the six constituencies considered in this study, only one, the M.P. for Githunguri, held regular weekly meetings with his constituents.

Perhaps the most important activity contributing to linkage development is the organization and active participation in self-help projects.[31] Harambee projects present M.P.'s with a wide range of opportunities

---

30. During the course of field research in Kenya, attendance in the House varied between 20 and 30 percent of the membership, a situation that led President Kenyatta to publically castigate the members as "lazy" public servants who were not doing their jobs. As tempting as it is to conclude that members stayed away to do their constituents' bidding in other locales, it should also be noted that many M.P.'s run businesses of various types in addition to tending to their legislative duties. Attendance during this period was also a bit lower than normal as many M.P.'s had already returned to their constituencies to mend the fences prior to the forthcoming election campaign.

31. For a more detailed analysis of the political significance of self-help in Kenya see E. M. Godfrey and G. C. M. Mutiso, "The Political Economy of Self-Help: Kenya's Institutes of Technology," *Canadian Journal of African Studies* 8, no. 1 (1974): 109–33, and Frank Holmquist, "Toward a Political Theory of Self-Help Development in Africa," *Rural Africana*, no. 18 (Winter 1972).

for organizing support at the grass roots and extracting resources from the center on their constituents' behalf. It is not surprising, therefore, that 96 percent of the M.P. sample claimed to be involved in such projects. These projects are officially sanctioned by the government and thus provide a legitimate vehicle through which an M.P. can simultaneously respond to his constituents' demands, press for resources from central authorities, and create a personal patronage system for himself. The "rules of the game" that govern these projects, moreover, have become sufficiently well defined that in many cases the government ministry under whose jurisdiction a project falls will promise to take over the project or provide matching funds if a specified minimum standard is reached. For example, if a community builds a secondary school and hires enough teachers to provide four years of education for its students, the Ministry of Education may absorb the school into its system. Government assistance is not automatic, and in some areas, such as education, has even declined. The prospect of such assistance, however, is a powerful incentive both to a community considering a Harambee project and to its M.P.[32] In this regard it should also be noted that the displacement of the KANU by constituency machines created by M.P.'s has been hastened by the fact that M.P.'s have always obtained the resources they need to maintain such patronage operations through direct contacts with government agencies and *not* via the party. As the party had neither a national organization nor financial resources to put at the disposal of faithful M.P.'s, it is little wonder that Kenya has evolved into a "no-party" state.

A final and important stimulus to linkage development by M.P.'s is the existence in Kenya of periodic elections through which constituents can remove those M.P.'s who fail to perform. As suggested above, the results of the 1969 elections, in which 54 percent of the incumbents were turned out of office, redefined the roles to which M.P.'s are supposed to conform. The necessity for M.P.'s to play linkage roles in order to remain in office was further underscored by the elections of

---

32. A case in point is the M.P. for Githunguri, Arthur Magugu. In addition to systematically contacting his constituents each week, this man's high performance rating can be directly attributed to his entrepreneurial abilities at organizing self-help projects, particularly the building of feeder roads and cattle dips in his constituency. In his mid-thirties, and head of a construction firm in Nairobi, he in many ways represents the Kenyan model of what an M.P. as a linkage agent should be. First elected in 1969 with only a 31 percent plurality in a seven-man race, he was reelected in 1974 with 76 percent of the vote. Following his re-election, he was appointed Assistant Minister.

October 1974, which resulted in the defeat of 51 percent of the incumbents standing for reelection. In each of these elections, defeated M.P.'s were those with mediocre records in obtaining government resources for community development projects and were perceived by their constituents as "inactive" in this task. In both elections, backbenchers, who have considerably less access to such resources than ministers or assistant ministers, suffered disproportionately: 63 percent went down to defeat in 1969, and 65 percent in 1974, compared with 33 percent and 31 percent of the frontbenchers. In each election, defeated M.P.'s were usually replaced by younger and better educated challengers who convinced voters that they would do more for the district. It might therefore be speculated that as time goes by the electoral process will further institutionalize the role of the Kenyan M.P. as a development entrepreneur, with the result that the linkages M.P.'s forge between the center and the periphery will become institutionalized as well.

Summary and Conclusion

This study began with the premise that if political development involves the establishment of autonomous, stable, and valued organizations for the purpose of responding to increasing levels of political participation, the establishment and maintenance of autonomous, stable, and valued linkages between a society's central political institutions and its people is an essential component of the process. It was further hypothesized that in nations where the dominance of executive and administrative institutions has weakened parties beyond usefulness as linkage agencies, legislators might play a unique role in the linkage process by creating contacts between the center and the periphery that are functionally different from those already established by agents of the Provincial Administration. Having presented an overview of the findings, can the conclusion that this is so be made?

In respect to this question, the conclusion must be tentative, given the limited data considered herein and the high variability in the performance of linkage activities by M.P.'s that this data suggests. It can nevertheless be contended that M.P.'s do constitute a unique set of political actors in the Kenyan political system in respect to the process of linkage development in that they have the *capability* of establishing linkages between the center and the periphery that are autonomous from those established by the Provincial Administration (with the possible exception of those networks established by the chiefs). Whether most Kenyan legislators will ultimately exercise this capability is an empirical question. Clearly it is in their own interests to do so if they wish to maintain themselves in office.

As indicated by the data, the first prerequisite to linkage development by M.P.'s, a well-defined set of role expectations that is mutually shared by the potential members of the linkage chain, is widely fulfilled. Citizens, local elites, and M.P.'s all define the latter's role in terms of constituency service and see linkage as the mechanism through which the M.P. obtains resources from the center to facilitate and achieve this end. These expectations not only define the duties of the M.P. as a link between the center and the periphery but also recognize the sanctions that will be applied to those M.P.'s who fail to carry out their assigned role.

That many M.P.'s do not fulfill this model is due mainly to a lack of entrepreneurial skills on their part and a failure to recognize the magnitude, if not the nature, of the task. As has been indicated, some M.P.'s clearly work harder and are more systematic than others when it comes to establishing contact with both the local elite and the public at large. Others, quite obviously, have superior access to those who dispense resources at the center. This study has not explored, however, the degree to which an M.P.'s success in establishing downward and upward linkages is contingent on other factors beyond his control, such as the topography, level of development, and communications infrastructure of his district, his ethnic background, the presence or absence of rival leaders in his district, and so on. Nor has the study considered in any precise manner the actual amount of resources available to M.P.'s as a group, except to contend that present resources are sufficient to stimulate linkage development by M.P.'s and that an increasingly specific set of rules has evolved regarding the conditions under which they are dispensed.

This study thus concludes with the contention that the development of valued and autonomous linkage systems between M.P.'s and their constituents in Kenya, without benefit of party, is a reality if not the rule. The links established are based on the proficiency of M.P.'s in securing material assistance for their communities and not on the representation of others' wishes regarding national policy. Although this form of linkage may be seen as qualitatively inferior, it nevertheless has two undeniable advantages: (1) it is the only kind of linkage legislators *can* provide, excluded as they are from the policymaking processes dominated by the executive and the administration and (2) it is the kind of linkage Kenya constituents expect and demand at this stage of national development. Kenya thus maintains close connections between citizens and state via development-oriented legislators. Whether such links will endure and will continue to be found satisfactory substitutes for the broader, more issue-oriented linkage that political parties are able to provide in other systems are questions to be answered only by close observation of Kenya's political development in the coming years.

PART V

Directive Linkage

14.

Linkage as Manipulation: The Partido Revolucionario Institucional in Mexico

JOHN G. CORBETT

"Modernization," writes Myron Weiner, "generates pressures for political participation."[1] In any search for confirming cases, Weiner would do well to look in Mexico. One of the outstanding political phenomena of modern Mexican history has been the dramatic and vigorous increase in political participation that has transformed politics from the province of a handful of elite leaders to a concern involving millions of common citizens. Conflict over political participation helped to trigger the Mexican Revolution, and the struggle to share in decision making and the allocation of the fruits of the Revolution has been a major focus of Mexican politics for the last half century. In this regard, Mexico is like many other modernizing countries, for the "crisis of participation" presents one of the most difficult and persistent challenges to political development.

Some observers believe Mexico to be well on the way to meeting this challenge, citing the strong party system, increased national integration, and the heritage of the Revolution as positive factors. Others,

Funds for support of the research from which this study is drawn were supplied by the Fulbright-Hays Graduate Overseas Fellowship Program, the Stanford University Center for International Studies, and the Vanderbilt University Research Council. Their assistance is gratefully acknowledged.

1. Myron Weiner, "Political Participation: Crisis of the Political Process," in Leonard Binder et al., eds., *Crises and Sequences in Political Development* (Princeton: Princeton University Press, 1971), p. 159.

327

however, question the nature of participation and the depth of commitment to participation by dominant groups in the polity. A number of studies, ranging from voting behavior to political recruitment, suggest that access to power and influence on policy formation remains quite limited, despite the apparent development of numerous institutional linkages between elites and masses.[2] There is a growing disposition to see the political system as more oriented toward mobilization than toward participation. Evelyn Stevens writes:

Mexico thus provides a clear example of the distinction between *participation*, understood as action taken with the conscious intent of increasing the share of benefits from the system, and *mobilization*, seen as support for the existing distribution of benefits.[3]

The growing support for the "mobilization, not participation" interpretation of Mexican politics raises serious questions about the role and nature of the party system. Perhaps the most critical question relates to the direction of linkage interaction, with "linkage" following Rosenau's conceptualization, that is, "any recurrent sequence of behavior that originates in one system and is reacted to in another."[4] The specific concern here is with the party as a mechanism or structure linking local subsystems and actors with higher (more inclusive or superordinate) systems and actors, particularly in terms of communication and control. There is a strong tendency in the conceptual literature on political parties to emphasize linkage upward through the system, from masses to elites or from the grass roots to upper echelons. Such a notion is implicit in the idea of parties as "specialized aggregation structures"[5] or sometimes explicit as "the organization called the party is expected to organize public opinion and to communicate de-

2. For a summary of the contending perspectives, see Wilfried Gruber, "Career Patterns of Mexico's Political Elite," *Western Political Quarterly* 24, no. 3 (September 1971): 469–71.

3. Evelyn P. Stevens, "Mexico's PRI: The Institutionalization of Corporatism" (Paper delivered at the 1974 American Political Science Association Annual Meeting, Chicago, Ill.), p. 18.

4. James N. Rosenau, "Toward the Study of National-International Linkages," in James N. Rosenau, ed., *Linkage Politics* (New York: The Free Press, 1969), p. 45.

5. Gabriel Almond and G. Bingham Powell, *Comparative Government: A Developmental Approach* (Boston: Little, Brown, 1966), p. 102.

mands to the center of governmental power and decision."[6] But in the Mexican context the emphasis on mobilizing support for the status quo suggests that attention should be directed to the downward linkages or to those aspects of the party system that facilitate communications and control from the top down. As Hansen, Johnson, Stevens, and numerous other analysts point out,[7] the distribution of benefits is so sharply skewed to the elite that there are either serious constraints on mass participation (as defined by Stevens) or a substantial majority of Mexicans are voluntarily forgoing the improved living conditions and mobility that could be theirs through political participation. Realistically, then, any discussion of Mexican parties should include attention to their potential for mass manipulation and mobilization.

The control, manipulation, and mobilization capabilities of the Mexican party system are not accidental or secondary by-products of political development; they have been the central focus of party activity for nearly fifty years. In 1929 the postrevolutionary Mexican elites recognized that great strains were being placed on the existing system by the growing pressures for mass participation in national politics, the need to mobilize the population in support of the goals of the Mexican Revolution, and the lack of any institutionalized means for coping with intense political competition. The failure of the Porfirio Díaz regime to resolve the "participation crisis" in the early twentieth century sparked the Revolution in 1910, yet after nearly a generation of struggle and conflict a solution had not been found. To forestall further violence and consolidate their position, the new elites organized the Partido Nacional Revolucionario, precursor to the current Partido Revolucionario Institucional. What is noteworthy is, first, that the elites created a political party as a structure within which to resolve conflict and pursue revolutionary goals; and second, that the party was created from the top down with the explicit expectation that it would serve as a control and restraint on political competition. In other words, the elites created a

6. Joseph LaPalombara and Myron Weiner, "The Origin and Development of Political Parties," in Joseph LaPalombara and Myron Weiner, eds., *Political Parties and Political Development* (Princeton: Princeton University Press, 1966), p. 3.

7. Roger D. Hansen, *The Politics of Mexican Development* (Baltimore: Johns Hopkins University Press, 1971); Kenneth F. Johnson, *Mexican Democracy: A Critical View* (Boston: Allyn and Bacon, 1971); Stevens, op. cit.; John Womack, Jr., "The Spoils of the Mexican Revolution," *Foreign Affairs* 48, no. 4 (July 1970): 677–87.

party emphasizing downward linkages with the intent of manipulating participation to ensure popular acquiescence in elite-determined policies. Although there have been variations in party name and organization, this pattern has remained virtually unchanged to the present.

The PRI and System Dominance

Mexican and foreign observers agree that the Partido Revolucionario Institucional, more commonly known as the PRI, plays a central role in the Mexican political system. Some students of political parties consider the PRI to be among the most dynamic and successful parties in the Third World. Robert J. Alexander sees the PRI as "in many ways . . . unique in Latin America."[8] Ronald McDonald comments: "Nowhere in Latin America and rarely in the world has a political party achieved and maintained the sophisticated integration of organizations, financial resources, leadership skill, ideological fervor, regularized channels for communication and recruitment, and overall stability of the PRI in Mexico."[9] Melvin Croan suggests the PRI as a possible model for party development in Eastern Europe.[10]

Even a brief review of the PRI's performance will reveal the extent to which it dominates Mexican politics. Since its inception, no other party has won the presidency, a governorship, or a senate seat. Opposition parties have won only a handful of mayoralties and a few seats in the Chamber of Deputies, the latter largely on the basis of a limited proportional-representation scheme regulating election to the Chamber. Returns in presidential elections usually show PRI candidates polling approximately 90 percent of the vote nationwide, with more than 95 percent in some states. The party claims several million members and a broad base of support among the middle class, urban workers, and peasants. It maintains an extensive research and information-gathering apparatus and a continuing exchange of talented executives and leaders

8. Robert J. Alexander, *Latin American Political Parties* (New York: Praeger, 1973), p. 278.

9. Ronald H. MacDonald, *Party Systems and Elections in Latin America* (Chicago: Markham, 1971), p. 259.

10. Melvin Croan, "Is Mexico the Future of East Europe: Institutional Adaptability and Political Change in Comparative Perspective," in Samuel P. Huntington and Clement H. Moore, eds., *Authoritarian Politics in Modern Society* (New York: Basic Books, 1970), pp. 451–83.

between the party bureaucracy and government agencies. In comparison, opposition parties are poorly developed and offer only limited, largely symbolic, opportunities for participation.[11]

Yet the foregoing reveals little about the nature and operations of downward linkages, or how the party converts its organizational capacity and resource base into overwhelming margins at the polls and a virtual monopoly on non-elite access to political influence. Party linkages at the grass roots have received little attention for two reasons: (1) the centralized nature of the regime stimulates a focus on upper-echelon decision making, recruitment, career mobility, and leadership behavior; and (2) the masses are assumed to be apathetic and parochial with little interest in public policy issues or are treated as under the sway of co-opted leaders and political bosses. Some scholars, members of the opposition, and dissident groups attribute the continued dominance of the PRI to fraud and coercion.[12] Others emphasize the importance of co-optation as a means of neutralizing potential competition.[13] These explanations have merit in some cases but appear inadequate in others. Although demonstration effects and historical memory should not be discounted, overt violence in support of the PRI appears to have diminished over the last generation. Co-optation assumes that labor officials, agrarian leaders, rural *caciques* (self-imposed political bosses), or other brokers possess sufficient sanctions to impose their will on their respective clienteles, yet millions of Mexicans live outside, and hence are not subject to, the institutional frameworks that make such sanctions effective. The PRI recognizes the limitations of coercion and co-optation,

11. The opposition parties are, in order of importance, the Partido Acción Nacional, Partido Popular Socialista, and Partido Autentico de la Revolución Mexicana. Only the first mounts any consistent opposition to the PRI, and even that is generally brushed aside. The best scholarly study of the PAN is Donald J. Mabry, *Mexico's Acción Nacional: A Catholic Alternative to Revolution* (Syracuse: Syracuse University Press, 1973).

12. See commentaries in Johnson, op. cit., pp. 130–46; Mabry, op cit., pp. 77–85; Jorge Capriata, "The Political Culture of Marginal Elites" (Ph.D. thesis, Stanford University, 1972), pp. 115; and *La Nación*, monthly journal of the PAN, which cites alleged cases of fraud and violation of voting rights in almost every issue.

13. The most widely cited discussion of co-optation is Bo Anderson and James D. Cockcroft, "Control and Cooptation in Mexican Politics," *International Journal of Comparative Sociology* 7, no. 1 (March 1966): 2–28. Many others have since picked up the concept, including Antonio Ugalde, *Power and Conflict in a Mexican Community* (Albuquerque: University of New Mexico Press, 1970), pp. 171–75; and Hansen, op cit., pp. 114–16.

and for this reason has developed additional linkage mechanisms to facilitate access to and manipulate otherwise independent segments of the population. This study will explore these mechanisms.

Research Background

Drawing upon materials gathered in the course of continuing research on political change in rural Mexico, this study focuses primarily on the state of Oaxaca. One aspect of the project treats the penetration and integration of hitherto autonomous, self-contained community political systems, tracing the tensions and opportunities arising as traditional political structures and culture undergo modification. Community residents must learn to cope with the intrusion of new elements and must see themselves as part of a nation, not just a small community. Political parties constitute such a foreign element, for they have no analogous counterparts in the traditional system and are little understood by the people whom they seek to influence. In turn, the absence of easily coerced or co-opted brokers requires the PRI to find new ways to reach and mobilize people unaccustomed to, and sometimes skeptical of, party activities.

Although anthropologists have written extensively on Mexican communities, they have for the most part ignored or treated in cursory fashion the issues of political transformation noted above.[14] At the time research began there was little systematic information on the nature of community politics and practically no discussion of party behavior or organization at the village level.[15] Consequently, much of the research on parties and participation in this project has been exploratory, isolating and identifying linkage points, studying party-citizen interaction, and attempting to specify how parties relate to a complex political setting that includes elements of "traditional," "transitional," and "modern"

14. Anthropological studies of Mexican communities have reached a sizable number. Among the best known are Oscar Lewis, *Life in a Mexican Village* (Urbana: University of Illinois Press, 1951); George Foster, *Tzintzuntzan* (Boston: Little, Brown, 1967); and Frank Cancian, *Economics and Prestige in a Maya Community* (Stanford: Stanford University Press, 1965).

15. At an early stage in the research I thought it might be useful to use portions of Gabriel Almond and Sidney Verba's *Civic Culture* survey. When I tried to implement this, however, I found it had grave limitations in peasant villages. When I asked one interviewee several times which political party he thought best for Mexico, he pondered and finally said, "Maybe I can tell you that if you will tell me what is a political party."

political cultures, a policy network linking municipal, state, and national governments, new issue areas, and the prospect of continuing change. The following comments on downward linkage mechanisms within the PRI reflect research by several scholars, but fieldwork in Oaxaca clarified PRI grass-roots operations.

Although party attempts to penetrate and control the state's *municipios* date from the 1940s, recent signs of deterioration in the party's former near-monopoly position have stimulated more aggressive efforts, including image building and limiting access to municipal office. Only limited written and documentary sources were available, so data collection depended heavily upon formal and informal interviews with party and civil officials, discussions with former officeholders and other community residents, attendance at party and municipal meetings, and observation of electoral campaigns and elections. Although functionaries in the state PRI headquarters were quite reluctant to discuss party activities, many community and local party officials were open and frank about their relationships with the PRI. Close contact with campaigns and elections proved especially useful for understanding party linkage behavior and dynamics, because it is during electoral periods that such phenomena are most visible and meaningful. Field research coincided with the Mexican presidential election of 1970 and the Oaxaca gubernatorial election in 1974, providing excellent opportunities for direct field observation and research.

The PRI and Local Politics in Oaxaca

With infrequent exceptions, the PRI has little electoral competition for local offices in most small and medium-size Mexican communities. Opposition parties are generally poorly organized and rarely gain power in municipal elections. In November 1974 the Partido Acción Nacional took only 5 of 572 *ayuntamientos* (municipal councils) elected throughout the state of Oaxaca.[16] More to the point, however, is the fact that in municipios of less than ten thousand residents, or approximately 95 percent of those in Oaxaca, political-party identification means little in the contest for community political offices. Communities tend to elect those individuals who satisfy local recruitment criteria, regardless of party membership. Many reported PRI "victories" in local elections

16. *El Imparcial*, Oaxaca, 24 December 1974, p. 1.

are nothing more than a postelection conferral of party membership on a winner who has no ties at all to the party.[17]

If party affiliation is irrelevant for most local elections, why does the PRI expend considerable effort and resources to extend its influence at the local level? The answer is to be found in the dynamics of Mexican national politics, a point that underscores the importance of the party in linking multiple levels of political organization. At least five factors enter into consideration at this point:

1. An effective local presence helps the PRI pile up overwhelming majorities in national elections, which dilute opposition votes acquired in more sophisticated and less manipulable urban areas. In some areas of the state the PRI reported 500-to-1 margins in the 1970 presidential elections. The concern is not to forestall opposition victories but to legitimize the PRI's continued hold on the presidency.
2. Local organization also facilites the mobilization of other forms of legitimizing support, such as supplying participants for campaign rallies or inaugural celebrations.
3. Local party members offer a lever for putting pressure on ayunta-mientos to conform to and support national policy decisions, thereby circumventing the idea of the "free municipio" enshrined in the Mexican Constitution. Ayuntamientos tend to be more vulnerable and responsive to pressures generated within the community than they are to bureaucratic directives from Mexico City.
4. A strong PRI presence in the community limits the freedom of oppo-sition parties to mobilize votes or to gain access to local power. Localized opposition success means little to PRI control of national government but may provide the opposition with encouragement and leverage or may prove embarrassing to middle-level PRI func-tionaries.
5. Party activity at the local level promotes political socialization and the development of a national identity. The PRI, as the "institution-alized revolution," contributes to political stability through the propagation of the legitimizing values of the Mexican Revolution and the apparent implementation of the notion of effective suffrage.

17. The presidente municipal in Santa Clara told me that shortly after his election at a public meeting in which parties played no part whatsoever, he received a letter from the president of the state committee congratulating him as a PRI activist for his recent victory, offering the advisory services of the party, and reminding him that the party needed his support.

Linkage Techniques

Central to any mobilization strategy of the PRI are the needs to establish the party as a legitimate and respected actor in Mexican politics and to minimize potential embarrassment or opposition to the party or to government policy. In addition to the common strategy of co-optation or, in moments of necessity, coercion, the PRI may turn to three additional techniques for mobilizing support: (1) symbol saturation; (2) organizational penetration; and (3) recruitment centralization. These techniques are intended to secure public acceptance of, or at least acquiescence to, PRI domination of political life and to ensure that all centers of decision making are subject to PRI influence. Symbol saturation refers to practices intended to create a desirable and readily recognizable image in the public eye by linking the party with the Mexican Revolution, democratic values, and popular programs such as agrarian reform. Organizational penetration reflects continued efforts to create party committees at the level of the municipio (the smallest formal political unit, roughly analogous to the U.S. county but often much smaller in size and pupulation) many of which have experienced a high degree of autonomy for centuries. Recruitment centralization involves the attempted concentration of ayuntamiento selection in the state and local party machinery, thereby ensuring the election of council members sympathetic to the PRI. Although these techniques are not inherently sequential and may be applied randomly or simultaneously, in practice there does appear to be a progression from the first to the third for reasons that will be discussed later in this study.

SYMBOL SATURATION

In a general sense symbol saturation is exactly that, the saturation of communities with the symbols and slogans of the PRI in an attempt to build citizen recognition and acceptance. Prior to state and national elections, party activists paint the party's initials on walls, utility poles, rocks, and almost anything else to which paint will adhere. Coverage is so complete that one may find the party insignia miles from any inhabited place. Other promotional materials include posters, T-shirts, notebooks, and plastic shopping bags imprinted with candidates' names and party initials. Informants claimed that during the 1970 presidential election the PRI headquaters in Oaxaca offered prizes to those most active in promoting the party and its candidates. One indicator of the volume of PRI efforts, and of the disparity between its resources and those of opposition parties, is a count taken in several villages during the 1970 campaign that revealed the PRI outpainted and outpostered other parties by ratios from 35 to 1 and 132 to 1, respectively. In 1974 a typical village campaign stop by the PRI candidate, Manuel Zarate Aquino, would find him making a brief speech beneath a large party banner while aides moved through the crowd passing out shopping bags and notebooks: the emphasis was clearly on the party, not the man.

Such saturation efforts are important in areas of low functional literacy, where recognition of party labels is essential when the voter is confronted with a ballot listing several parties and names. Furthermore, the notion of selecting national leaders by ballot and the typical functions of a political party are only dimly understood by many Mexicans. The PRI portrays voting as a means of ratifying its actions and candidates, not as an opportunity to select among competing candidates, and interviews with voters just after they cast their ballots in the 1970 election bear this out. When asked why they voted for the PRI, answers ranged from "it is the party of Zapata and the agrarian reform" to "it has the colors of the national flag" and even "are there other parties?"

The use of symbol saturation provides a useful downward linkage in that it allows the party to bombard citizens with a continuing flow of images and simple messages that, in the absence of information to the contrary, conveys the impression that the PRI and the Mexican government are one and that support for the PRI means support for the continuation of the Revolution. It is easily managed and maintained by functionaries with access to white paint and a budget sufficient to turn out an enormous volume of posters, banners, and *regalitos de la gira* ("little campaign gifts"). The weakness of symbol saturation is that it is primarily no more than a device to foster party identification, which serves the PRI only when the voter is marking a ballot. It has limited utility for influencing other dimensions of political behavior, such as turning out for a rally or pressuring local officials. As voters become more sophisticated, or as opposition parties such as the PAN increase their symbol distribution efforts, the prospects that symbol saturation by itself will hold political support for the PRI begin to diminish.

ORGANIZATIONAL PENETRATION

Election totals in Mexico consistently award the PRI in excess of 90 percent of the vote, but this figure obscures abstentions, intrastate variations, and the PRI's ability to "adjust" the reported vote through control of the state election commission. Although the PRI routinely claims from 97 to 99 percent of the vote in rural areas, in urban centers it does not do as well; the PAN candidate polled almost 25 percent of the reported vote in the state capital during the 1974 election.[18] Furthermore, limited evidence suggests erosion in PRI voting strength in its traditional rural strongholds. For example, data from the municipio of Santa Clara show the PRI slipping from 71 to 61 percent of the vote from 1958 to 1974, despite some PRI-oriented manipulation at the polling place.[19] Abstention reached 80 percent in the 1974 election, challenging the notion of strong popular approval.[20] In the face of trends (urbanization, improved education and communication) that elsewhere in Mexico correlate with a decline in its share of the vote,[21] it is not surprising to find the PRI turning to more aggressive techniques to mobilize support.

Organizational penetration, the direct fostering of community committees by the central party bureaucracy, represents the principal party response to the problem of diminishing support. Organizational penetration provides two critical access points to local residents. First, the municipio committees constitute a cadre of adherents that may be mobilized to paint walls, distribute literature, act as polling-place representatives, and carry out a myriad of other services, thereby freeing central headquarters from onerous logistical problems. Second, the local committee provides an organizational base from which to lobby the ayuntamiento in favor of policies acceptable to the PRI and to act on behalf of the PRI. In Ejutla de Crespo during the 1974 campaign for governor a group of forty men, reportedly accompanied and assisted by the local police, removed posters and banners put up by the PAN. The use of public employees and police for such activity is common and is one reason why the PRI wants access to, or control over, ayuntamientos.

Almost without exception, PRI local committees come into existence through the efforts of state party headquarters, not as an outgrowth of local interest or commitment to the party. These committees have a standard structure, which is imposed on new branches by state headquarters. A cursory investigation would suggest extensive organiza-

18. *Oaxaca Gráfico*, Oaxaca, 19 August 1974, p. 1.
19. Calculations based upon my review of data in the municipal archives.
20. *Oaxaca Gráfico*, Oaxaca, 19 August 1974, p. 3.
21. José Luis Reyna, "An Empirical Analysis of Political Mobilization: The Case of Mexico" (Ph.D. diss., Cornell University, 1971), pp. 119–20.

337

tion, but in fact most offices and components exist only on paper or are held by individuals whose sole purpose is to fill a space on the organization chart. For example, most of the small farming municipios of the Oaxaca valley have committees with agrarian, labor, and popular (professional and business) sectors, plus special units for women and youth, even though many of these categories are applicable only in complex urban settings. In San Alfredo the committee chairman's wife and teenage son head the women and youth wings of the local organization because, as he put it, "they [state party officials] tell me someone must do it, but no one else here has any interest." Most committees draw their initial membership from community residents who have personal ties with activists in the state organization or who perceive advantages for themselves in alliance with the dominant party. The committee in Santa Clara was founded by an individual who turned to a PRI lawyer for assistance in a legal dispute; allegedly he recruited additional members by facilitating access to legal and social services provided by the state organization.[22] In Diaz Ordaz the PRI exploited local factional strife to gain a foothold.[23]

One of the principal responsibilities of the municipio committee is to ensure a massive vote for the PRI in state and national elections.[24] This reflects party concern with overwhelming electoral margins as a source of legitimacy for its policies and to delegitimize protest and charges of fraud. High levels of voter participation give the appearance of a meaningful implementation of the revolutionary slogan "effective suffrage." Peasant endorsement of the PRI is especially important, for the rural population has received fewer benefits from the Revolution than any other sector, and a decline in peasant support would remove one of the principal ideological and organizational props of the regime. Local committees offer a means of manipulating voting outcomes. If done carefully, it preserves the facade of democracy and participation and at the same time ensures a substantial PRI victory; if bungled, the

22. I have a circular distributed by the PRI in various municipios in 1969 calling attention to services and programs offered free to party members. Legal assistance and part-time education programs are popular attractions.

23. Antonio Ugalde, "From Hacienda to PRI: Political Leadership in a Zapotec Village," in Robert Kern, ed., *The Caciques: Oligarchic Politics in the Luso-Hispanic World* (Albuquerque: University of New Mexico Press, 1973).

24. Based on memoranda from the state PRI headquarters in April and June 1970, urging their local committees to work for "triumph with the highest possible vote."

party can always shift responsibility for abuses from itself to "over-zealous" local committees.

Beyond involvement in the symbol-saturation efforts discussed earlier, the local committee may attempt to manipulate the balloting itself. Although election laws specify secret ballots, observation revealed that in some communities balloting is anything but secret. Voters mark their ballots at a table in plain sight of dozens of bystanders and polling officials, handing the ballots to others to place in ballot boxes. In one community subject to extensive observation in the 1970 election, voters were required to sign or place thumbprints on their ballots. Observation by PRI pollwatchers may have influenced some voters. Others may have been influenced more directly by the practice of one PRI representative who, in the process of giving "advice" to voters uncertain about voting procedures, simply indicated the PRI candidate as the place to mark the ballot. This directed voting accounted for from 15 to 20 percent of the total vote cast; there is no way of knowing, of course, whether voters would have selected other parties had they cast their ballots without intervention. In theory other parties should have had pollwatchers present to object to such practices, but in many municipios it is impossible to find someone willing to act in this capacity for the opposition. The PAN estimated that it would be able to find pollwatchers for no more than one-third of the polling stations in Oaxaca for the 1974 gubernatorial election.[25] Under such conditions, direct manipulation of the voting process may go unchallenged.

Securing only a favorable share of the vote for the PRI is insufficient; the local committee must turn out a high percentage of registered voters, lest a high abstention rate betray popular disenchantment with the entire electoral process. In 1970 PRI candidate Luis Echeverría frequently claimed "we prefer a vote against us rather than an abstention" in an effort to ensure ample participation. To avoid embarrassingly low turnouts, the committees pressure ayuntamientos to get out the vote.[26] For example, in the community cited in the preceding paragraph barely a quarter of the registered voters had come to the polls by the official

25. Eugenio Ortiz Walls, PAN candidate for governor, personal interview, July 1974.

26. The 1973 congressional elections were seen as a test of public support for President Echeverría's policies, and some observers felt the 35 to 40 percent abstention rate reflected low voter enthusiasm. See *Latin America* 7, no. 27 (6 July 1973): 209, and 7, no. 30 (27 July 1973): 239.

closing time. The PRI representatives argued that without a good turn-out, and a turnout supporting the PRI, it would be difficult to obtain government services and community development support. Reluctant to report poor participation for a national election, the *presidente muni-cipal* kept the polls open three more hours to allow the police to bring in people who had not yet voted.

Although the municipio committee's activities are most obvious in the weeks before a major election, in all communities save the smallest and most poorly organized the committee maintains continuing liaison with the ayuntamiento and other municipal officials. The party wants not only to influence decision making regarding acceptance of, or sup-port for, government policies but also to receive the legitimacy that the traditional political structure can confer upon a new and unknown body. The tradition of community autonomy and a deeply ingrained suspicion of outsiders condition residents of many Oaxaca communities to regard PRI activities within the community as potentially divisive and threaten-ing (activities outside the community are regarded as probably less threatening and beyond the control of local people). There is a wide-spread belief that political parties, the PRI included, are instruments of outsiders who desire to introduce dissension and conflict into the community for their own nefarious purposes. Informants and inter-viewees commonly commented "here we have nothing to do with par-ties" or "the PRI belongs to Mexico [meaning Mexico City], not here." Consequently, the PRI committee often attempts to work through municipal officials, using their legitimacy and authority for party pur-poses.[27] Although the local political culture would appear to inhibit this effort, the complex personal relations found in such communities means the approach is based on a cousin-to-cousin or neighbor-to-neighbor appeal rather than through positional roles of the presidente municipal and the party delegate. Personal ties, face-to-face contact, and an intimate knowledge of local conditions give the local party com-mittee access and leverage not available to strangers from state head-quarters.

Perhaps a good example of the way this works in practice is to be found in a case observed during the 1970 presidential campaign. The

27. All presidentes municipales in Oaxaca received letters from the PRI candidate Luis Echeverria asking them to serve as his personal representatives in their municipios during the 1970 presidential election.

PRI candidate, Luis Echeverria, planned a visit and rally in the state capital, and the state organization accordingly directed each committee in central Oaxaca to send a delegation of twenty or thirty representatives. Few committees could muster delegations of this size, especially since attendance meant losing a day's work and incurring the costs of a round trip to the state capital, and they had no means of convincing or compelling others to spend the day waving flags and acclaiming the PRI. In Santa Clara, and reportedly in other communities, the presidente of the PRI committee appealed to the ayuntamiento to name a community delegation. He couched his appeal not as party official but as an interested community resident addressing a council, which included several relatives and neighbors, arguing it would be good for the community to have a large delegation appear before the next president. Through the use of moral suasion, arm twisting, and appeals to a sense of service to the community, the ayuntamiento was able to assemble a delegation, drawing upon norms imbedded in the local political culture in ways that were not available to the PRI. In this way municipio authorities were converted into temporary agents of the PRI.

RECRUITMENT CENTRALIZATION

Despite the clear utility of having ayuntamientos responsive to the PRI, until the early 1960s the party directed most of its mobilization efforts toward ensuring massive electoral victories in state and national elections. Except for the larger towns and cities, the PRI limited its involvement in local elections to conferring ex post facto party membership on newly elected officials, trading access to party services for a modicum of loyalty and support.[28] Reasons for the change toward a more interventionist stance are not entirely clear: some observers attributed it to factional conflict and change within the state organization itself, whereas others believed state party leaders were troubled by the prospects of more independent behavior by restive, dissatisfied voters and local officials. By the mid-sixties the PRI was pressing ayuntamientos to accept a new electoral system whereby the outgoing council nominated its successor and the subsequent vote was a formality, a major departure from the previous practice of voting for public officials in open

28. It should be noted that the PRI has long had effective control over most of the larger population centers in the state, although the PPS continues to challenge it in Juchitan and the PAN is very strong in Huajuapan de Leon, both major regional centers.

community assemblies. Fajerstein records the response to the new system in Soledad Etla: "The public was surprised by the new system.... An attitude of non-cooperation with the authorities developed. The intention was not to attend meetings nor support new projects."[29]

During the 1974 municipal elections the PRI appeared ready to extend its control over recruitment to the ayuntamiento even further. In some cases all pretext of popular participation disappeared, with the PRI committees (using the power of the state organization) simply carrying off the ballot boxes, stuffing them, and then proclaiming the PRI candidates elected. *El Imparcial* carried a brief report of one such case:

The elections were set for the 17th of November, but both the presidente municipal, Antonio Avendaño, and the presidente of the municipal committee of the PRI considered it was not necessary to install the voting booths.

In this way these and other functionaries took it upon themselves to mark ballots and vote for the slate of José Ortega, whom they were trying to impose, putting democracy to the side and impeding the public's right to vote.

There are witnesses that the aforementioned marked ballots, signed documents, and closed the proceedings of balloting in the home of the PRI functionary.[30]

The article then notes that the great majority of the voters preferred another candidate, and that there was fear of violence. Only a few days before the inauguration of the new governor on 1 December, 1974, peasants from several Oaxaca valley municipios demonstrated outside the state capitol to protest PRI efforts to impose its candidates upon local ayuntamientos. When asked the reason for the rally one participant responded, "We want authorities who serve us, not the PRI."[31]

In a sense this response returns to the notions of coercion and co-optation mentioned earlier in this study. There is a clear presumption that council members or other community officials entering office with the approbation and assistance of the PRI will be manipulable through pressure and persuasion, and there is ample evidence to confirm the

29. Abraham I. Fajerstein, "Soledad Etla: Estudio de un Proceso de Modernización" (M.A. thesis, Escuela de Antropologia e Historia, Mexico, 1969), p. 131, my translation.

30. *El Imparcial*, Oaxaca, 24 December, p. 1.

31. As an eyewitness, I talked with approximately a dozen participants, all of whom expressed the same general sentiments.

presumption. Thus the end result of organizational penetration and recruitment centralization will be to bring those millions of rural and small-town Mexicans, previously difficult to reach except through the limited technique of symbol saturation, more completely into the orbit of the PRI. It would be a mistake to overstate the PRI's capacity for control, as community residents see party affiliation as irrelevant for local affairs, and as an unwarranted intrusion of an external body into the community for the benefit of outsiders. Nevertheless, the linkage of local political recruitment to events in the national political arena is merely a specific manifestation of a much more complex process of national integration, a process that includes improved communications, the increased use of Spanish, participation in a national market, and the creation of a national identity. It is in this sense that symbol saturation, organizational penetration, and recruitment centralization may be seen as sequential techniques, moving from a sporadic linkage with little responsiveness to an improved linkage with greater responsiveness, and finally to direct control by the party.

The PRI and the Nature of Political Linkages in Mexico

The response "We want authorities who serve us, not the PRI," also reflects the prevailing skepticism among lower-class Mexicans as to whose interests are served by the PRI and their own capacities for influencing party decisions. There are neither norms, structures, nor processes facilitating the aggregation of interests or their articulation upward to decision makers. Problems or requests may be dealt with on an ad hoc, personalistic basis, but broad-gauge solutions are avoided. Local committees represent the party to the community and carry out directives from state party headquarters but lack the institutionalized means for articulating community interests or effectively influencing party policy or candidate selection. When asked about opportunities for input or consultation with higher levels, the most common reactions among committee presidents were puzzlement or cynical amusement. One stated bluntly, "The role of the PRI is to direct, not to discuss," and another inquired, "What can poor *campesinos* say to the PRI?" Among those charged with party responsibilities at the bottom, therefore, there is little doubt as to the downward thrust of linkage orientations. In this context improvements in the operating effectiveness of party linkage mechanisms must be viewed not as facilitating the communication of public opinion to "the center of governmental power and decision," as LaPalombara and Weiner put it, but as enhancing central manipulation of individual and subsector choices.

It is difficult to assess the prospects for major change in the direction and nature of linkage patterns within the PRI. Extension of PRI influence into domains hitherto beyond its control through continuing organizational penetration and recruitment centralization would appear to enhance the party's position in the Mexican political system. Graham, Turner, and others argue that the trend toward consultation and co-optation, forgoing earlier patterns of open imposition of leadership and policy, represents a gradual opening of linkage channels upward.[32] It must be remembered, however, that attempts in the mid-sixties to open the party to rank-and-file input via local primaries, an experiment of then PRI president Carlos Madrazo, foundered on upper-echelon concerns of losing control.[33] Since assuming the presidency in 1976, José Lopez Portillo has announced a series of political reforms nominally intended to enhance citizen participation and increase competition for the PRI, reforms expected to make the PRI more responsive to popular input. It is premature to assess the effectiveness of these reforms, but observation of the November 1977 municipal elections in Oaxaca and of the early manuvering for nominations in the 1978 elections to the federal Chamber of Deputies revealed little evidence of change in party operations at state and local levels. Mexico's continuing economic problems and political conflicts within the PRI and the higher levels of the administration constrain Lopez Portillo's ability to pursue party reform, particularly when confronted by noncooperation from the PRI hierarchy.[34] Under these circumstances the likelihood of significant modification in the prevailing linkage system in the direction of improved two-way flow and greater input into party policy and operations from below, thereby reducing the capacity for manipulation, appears remote.

32. Lawrence Graham, *Politics in a Mexican Community* (Gainesville: University of Florida Press, 1968), pp. 51–52; and Frederick C. Turner, "Mexican Politics: The Direction of Development," in William P. Glade and Stanley R. Ross, eds., *Criticas Constructivas del Sistema Político Mexicano* (Austin: Institute of Latin American Studies, 1973).

33. See W. V. D'Antonio and Richard Suter, "Elecciones preliminares en un municipio mexicano: nuevas tendencias en la lucha de Mexico hacia la democracia," *Revista Mexicana de Sociologia* 29, no. 1 (January–March 1967): 93–108; and Richard R. Fagen and William S. Tuohy, *Politics and Privilege in a Mexican City* (Stanford: Stanford University Press, 1972), pp. 18–41.

34. See Carlos Pereyra's short but insightful essay on the need to reform the PRI, "El desgaste de 49 años obliga a reformar al PRI," *Proceso*, no. 70 (6 March 1978): 34–35.

15.

Party Linkage in a Communist One-Party State: The Case of the CPSU

RONALD J. HILL

This study examines the role of the Communist Party of the Soviet Union (CPSU) as a link between society and the political decision makers in the USSR and explores various facets of society-party-state relations. Two fundamental questions will be asked: How extensive is the CPSU linkage role in the political system? and What are the mechanisms by which it plays such a role? In seeking to answer these two questions, the special position of the party in this system will be elucidated and the concept of linkage illuminated.

Soviet views of the party and its relations with society and political decision making will be examined first, giving special emphasis to the ideological dimension. The interests in Soviet society and how the party may directly accommodate them will be explored. The nature and forms of the linkage relationship in Soviet society will be considered next, paying particular attention to relations between the party and state institutions. The forms that party-state linkage may take will be analyzed, and the effects of linkage on the processing of demands will be assessed. The discussion will be based largely on the writings of Soviet scholars,

Some of the material for this chapter was gathered in the course of a research trip to Moscow in the summer of 1975; data from my Tiraspol study are based on a similar trip to Kishinev and Tiraspol in 1967–68. These visits were made under the auspices of the Anglo-Soviet Cultural Exchange Agreement; I am grateful to the British Council for their sponsorship on both occasions.

345

illustrated by reference to my study of the political elite in the town and rural district of Tiraspol in Soviet Moldavia.[1]

The definition of the term "linkage" used here is a commonsense one: the notion of a *connection* between society and the political decision makers, involving such concepts as socialization, communication, and recruitment. In its linkage function, the party acts, in Kirchheimer's words, as a "transmission belt" or "relay" between the population at large and the governmental structure, although for reasons that will be made clear, in this study the phrase "political decision makers" has been substituted for "governmental structure." Moreover, whereas in his description of the "catch-all" party Kirchheimer stressed the uni-directional nature of linkage ("taking up grievances, ideas, and problems developed in a more searching and systematic fashion elsewhere in the body politic" and transmitting these to the political decision-making unit[2]), here the contention is that, as a link in any chain serves its purpose when viewed from either end, the CPSU in its linkage role provides channels for both "upward" and "downward" communication—from society to the political decision makers and from them back to society. Hence, the terms used here are "input linkage" and "output linkage."

The basic question that must be faced, however, is the nature of the single party and its relationship to ideology. This study, in accordance with Soviet political scientists and many contemporary Western scholars, rejects the notion that a party can be said to exist only in a competitive situation.[3] Nevertheless, it would be absurd to maintain that a single

1. "Tiraspol: A Study of a Soviet Town's Political Elite" (Ph.D. diss., University of Essex, England, 1973); a revised version of this study is *Soviet Political Elites: The Case of Tiraspol* (London and New York: Martin Robertson and St. Martin's Press, respectively, 1977). Information on Tiraspol rural district is here presented for the first time; statistical and other data on both town and district were derived from materials published in the local newspapers, principally *Dnestrovskaya pravda* and *Znamya pobedy* or their Moldavian-language counterparts, *Adeverul Nistryan* and *Drapelul Biruintsei*.

2. Otto Kirchheimer, "The Transformation of Western European Party Systems," in Joseph LaPalombara and Myron Winer, eds., *Political Parties and Political Development* (Princeton: Princeton University Press, 1966), pp. 177–200, esp. pp. 177, 189.

3. This idea was expressed most forcefully by Sigmund Neumann in his celebrated phrase, "A one-party system is a contradiction in itself," in Sigmund Neumann, "Toward a Comparative Study of Political Parties," reprinted in Harry Eckstein and David E. Apter, eds., *Comparative Politics: A Reader* (New York: The Free Press, 1963), p. 351. The emergence of nondictatorial single parties in developing countries has led political scientists to drop this qualification: see Peter H. Merkl, *Modern Comparative Politics* (New York: Holt, Rinehart and Winston, 1970), pp. 271–72. For a Soviet view of Neumann's assertion (which is seen as deliberately anti-Soviet as well as unscientific) see M. Kh. Farukshin,

party is identical in its role and functioning to parties in pluralist systems, especially when the party in question has the strong ideological commitment that the CPSU possesses. Indeed, the particular nature of the ideology of Marxism-Leninism and the special relationship that exists between it and the party can be seen as the fundamental features that determine the party's position and role in Soviet society. It is instructive to examine the CPSU's view of itself and its relationship to the population.

Soviet Views of the CPSU

In the past decade or so, Soviet writers have paid considerable attention to analyzing the party's position, often coupled with critiques of Western analyses. In one such book, M. Kh. Farukshin stresses two basic points about the CPSU and its relations with society: first, its class basis, relating (in the Marxist tradition) to ownership of the means of production; and second, its special position with respect to the Marxist-Leninist ideology. Farukshin's basic point, to which he returns time and time again, is that "a party not only represents a class, but is a part of it." For instance, in discussing the political recruitment function, he says that the fundamental question to be asked is, In the interest of which *class* is this function performed? Political socialization—a concept that Soviet social psychologists have found valuable—must also be examined in terms of the class in whose interests parties perform the function. Then, coming near to the concept of linkage, Farukshin discusses parties as communications channels between society and government. Bourgeois political science, he says, suffers from a formalistic approach, which ignores the class content of the function: the point, he says, is that parties channel the demands and interests of *particular* classes and social groups; moreover, he argues, reverse communication (from government to society) is not carried out by opposition parties, hence his conclusion (erroneous, in my opinion) that "the function of political communication cannot be considered a general function of parties."[4]

Partiya v politicheskoi sisteme Sovetskogo obshchestva (protiv kontseptsii sovremennogo antikommunizma) (Kazan: Izdatel'stvo Kazanskogo universiteta, 1973), p. 50; Farukshin points out that this approach is essentially linguistic.

4. Farukshin, op. cit. The initial point is made on p. 39; the recruitment function is discussed on pp. 58–61; on socialization, see pp. 61–68; on communication, pp. 71–72. It is interesting that Soviet writers are obliged to invent the word *rekrutirovanie* to express

RONALD J. HILL

THE CPSU AND CLASS

If (as Farukshin says) Western views of political parties are "unscientific" in their failure to incorporate class as the basic defining factor, Soviet scholars have reversed the emphasis and are more preoccupied with the question of class in their writings, particularly in evaluating the CPSU. Originally, the class in question was, of course, the proletariat; however, there has been a development in the theory since the days when the CPSU was seen as the vanguard of the working class alone. Although the importance of the proletariat as the "basic productive force of society" is still stressed, considerable attention is now paid to other social classes— the collective farm peasantry and the intelligentsia—which are linked with the proletariat in a system of "socialist social relations." The official argument is that class relations underwent a transformation in the period of "socialist construction," and in the current phase of "developed socialism" a novel entity exists, the *Soviet people*, characterized by "new, harmonious relations among classes and social groups, nations and nationalities—relations of friendship and collaboration."[5] In this situation, the position of the party too is radically altered: it no longer serves as the vanguard of the proletariat in exercising its dictatorship, but, in the words of its own rule book: "The Communist Party, the party of the working class, has today become the party of the whole Soviet people."[6] Moreover, this change took place not because the party subjectively desired it but, according to Mikhail Suslov, ideologist of the Politburo, "because the aims and ideals of the working class became the aims and ideals of all classes and strata of the people which had built socialism."[7]

Hence, because the basic aims and interests of the nonproletarian classes are now seen to be identical with those of the proletariat (namely, building up a communist society as quickly and smoothly as possible),

the concept of recruitment: Farukshin clearly feels much more comfortable with the Communist party concept of "selection and placement of cadres" (*podbor i rasstanovka kadrov*). He uses two words for "communication": the Russian word *svyaz'* (which could also be translated as "linkage") and the borrowed word *kommunikatsiya*; here he appears to employ a very restricted view of the concept.

5. Leonid Brezhnev's report to the Twenty-fourth CPSU Congress (1971) in *XXIV s"ezd Kommunisticheskoi partii Sovetskogo Soyuza: Stenograficheskii otchet* (Moscow: Politizdat, 1971), 1: 97–101.

6. *Ustav KPSS* (Moscow: Politizdat, 1967), pp. 3–4.

7. Quoted in I. N. Yudin, *Sotsial'naya baza rosta KPSS* (Moscow: Politizdat, 1973), p. 245.

the party that first embraced the cause of the proletariat can now logically and easily accommodate other classes and groups.

THE CPSU AND IDEOLOGY

A further identifying feature of the CPSU is its relationship with the ideology. It sees itself as the party of scientific communism; it claims to be "unswervingly guided by the science of Marxism-Leninism, the most advanced and revolutionary science of the present day," and to do everything for the further development of that science.[8] Two basic assertions make Marxism-Leninism a powerful legitimizing tool: first, that this ideology embraces eternal scientific truths about human and social development, and second, that the party has a unique appreciation of it. To quote party leader Leonid Brezhnev:

[Marxism-Leninism's] theoretical comprehension of the phenomena of social life and [the latter's] main tendencies permits the party to foresee the course of social processes, to work out the true political course, and to avoid errors and subjective decisions. . . . We have been and remain true to the fundamental principles of Marxism-Leninism, and will never allow any compromise on ideological questions.[9]

The Soviet picture of the party's position, as put forward in statements by its leaders and in interpretations by committed scholars, is now clear: the CPSU began its existence as the party of the proletariat, acting on behalf of that class's real interests; but the basic interests of all other classes now coincide with those of the proletariat, so the CPSU can and does act in conformity with the interests of all sections of the Soviet people; in its actions in leading the people toward a communist society, the party is guided by Marxism-Leninism, whose scientific laws of social development the party uniquely comprehends and applies. In other words, the party knows what is in the best interests of the people and always acts in this light.

If this argument were extended, it might be concluded that the CPSU would reject a view of its role as one of providing linkage between various social groups and the political decision makers and of transmitting demands from the one to the other. It sees itself as *part* of society, but

8. *XXIV s"ezd*, op. cit., p. 127.
9. Ibid., pp. 127, 128.

also as a *vanguard* that appreciates better than the individual members of society what society's true interests are. As one writer on the subject has expressed it, there still remains under socialism a difference between the level of consciousness of the party and that of the masses.[10] Indeed, the party sees itself as somehow above class, because, "unlike other organizations, the party is not linked with any professional, departmental or national interests."[11]

The CPSU and the Representation of Interests: Forms of Linkage

The tone of Soviet comment cited so far has been to suggest that the question of group and interest representation in the party is largely irrelevant. If all groups have the same interests, then any group can represent the interests of any other group. For some writers, the simple fact that a socialist revolution has taken place means that "a political system of a new type expresses and defends the deepest interests of the working class and all other strata of the toilers."[12] However, is it correct to accept official CPSU views of itself and the assumptions of Soviet political scientists such as Farukshin? Their point that many Western writings on the Soviet political system, particularly on the CPSU, have a hostile bias may be conceded. But the assertion that *class*, in the simplest Marxist (one might even say Stalinist[13]) definition, is the only form of social differentiation of real significance certainly need not be accepted without challenge, nor the bland claim that there are no conflicts of interest in Soviet society: indeed, there is ample evidence that such conflicts do exist, as a number of Western scholars have documented.[14]

Soviet social scientists too have challenged the assumption of monolithic unity in society. Beginning with a highly influential article in 1955 by the philosopher G. M. Gak, an increasing number of Soviet authors

10. M. Imashev, writing in A. Aimbetov, M. Baimakhanov, and M. Imashev, *Problemy sovershenstvovaniya organizatsii i deyatel'nosti mestnykh Sovetov* (Alma-Ata: Nauka, 1967), p. 82.

11. V. M. Lesnyi and N. V. Chernogolovkin, eds., *Politicheskaya organizatsiya razvitogo sotsialisticheskogo obshchestva: struktura i funktsii* (Moscow: Izdatel'stvo Moskovskogo universiteta, 1976), p. 39.

12. Farukshin, op. cit., p. 67.

13. David Lane, *Politics and Society in the USSR* (London: Weidenfeld & Nicolson, 1970), p. 388.

14. See in particular the work of H. Gordon Skilling, especially *Interest Groups in Soviet Politics*, edited, with Franklyn Griffiths (Princeton: Princeton University Press, 1971).

have analyzed the forms of social differentiation and the concomitant different interests that do exist, including differences in type of work (manual or mental), income, and rural-urban distinctions, as well as the basic class differences between workers and peasants.[15] Georgi Shakhnazarov, for example, has stated that "the absence of antagonisms does not signify an identity of the needs of the different social groups. Along with the complete and permanent coincidence of the fundamental interests of all classes and social groups, there may arise, and does arise, a lack of coincidence of specific interests.... No political organization can function efficiently without being constantly informed about the aspirations and requirements of all classes and sections of society and without reacting to them in some form or another."[16] An analysis of linkage therefore leads to the questions: How does the CPSU serve to channel these "nonfundamental," "specific" interests from society to the political decision makers, and in what ways does it do so?

The first and most obvious factor is representation within the ranks of the party: To what extent does the party draw its membership from all social classes and groups? As has been noted, the party now sees itself as a party of the whole people, and figures indicating its social composition can be used in support of this claim. Thus, in a booklet produced for Western readers, one writer cites figures on the composition of the party purporting to show that "the link between the ruling Communist Party and the working people is ensured first of all by the widely representative composition of the Party itself."[17] The latest published set of full figures, which appeared in November 1977,[18] show a total membership of 16,203,446 (out of a population of almost 260 million) and give a detailed breakdown according to a range of variables (table 15.1). In his report to the Twenty-Fifth Party Congress, in February 1976, Leonid Brezhnev stated that 41.6 percent of party members were

15. G. M. Gak, "Obshchestvennye i lichnye interesy i ikh sochetanie pri sotsializme," *Voprosy filosofii*, no. 4 (April 1955), pp. 17–28; more recent developments in Soviet thought on the subject are contained in, for example, G. Glezerman, "Interes kak sotsiologicheskaya kategoriya," *Voprosy filosofii*, no. 10 (October 1966), pp. 14–26; V. P. Gribanov, "Interes v grazhdanskom prave," *Sovetskoe gosudarstvo i pravo*, no. 1 (January 1967), pp. 49–56; V. A. Patyulin, "Interesy gosudarstva i grazhdan pri sotsializme," *Sovetskoe gosudarstvo i pravo*, no. 5 (May 1974), pp. 20–29.

16. Georgi Shakhnazarov, *The Role of the Communist Party in Socialist Society* (Moscow: Novosti, 1974), pp. 29, 42.

17. Ibid., pp. 42–45.

18. "KPSS v tsifrakh," *Partiinaya zhizn'*, no. 21 (November 1977), pp. 20–43.

TABLE 15.1. Social Composition of the CPSU (in percent)

Variable	Percentage of Total Party Membership (N = 16,203,446)
Occupational-Social Group	
Workers	42.0
Collective-farm peasants	13.6
Employees and others	44.4
Sex	
Women	24.7
Men*	75.3
Nationality	
Russians	60.5
Ukrainians	16.0
Belorussians	3.6
Other major nationalities*	11.5
Other national groups*	8.4
Age	
Under 25	5.8
Under 40*	42.5
Over 50*	31.1
Education	
Primary only	13.6
Secondary and incomplete secondary*	58.9
Higher and incomplete higher*	27.5

SOURCE: "KPSS v tsifrakh," *Partiinaya zhizn'*, no. 21 (November 1977), pp. 20–43.
*Calculated by author from published figures.

workers, 13.9 percent collective farmers, about 20 percent "representatives of the technical intelligentsia," and more than 24 percent "scientists, literary figures, artists, workers in education, health, the administrative apparatus, and military comrades."[19] It can thus be seen that there is, indeed, a wide representation of various social categories within the party.

However, Western scholars have pointed out that the social balance within the party does not correspond to the distribution of the various categories in the population at large.[20] Indeed, this is not difficult to

19. *Pravda*, 25 February 1976, p. 7.
20. T. H. Rigby, *Communist Party Membership in the USSR, 1917–1967* (Princeton: Princeton University Press, 1968), chap. 14, esp. pp. 449–53; Vernon V. Aspaturian, "The Soviet Union," in Roy C. Macridis and Robert E. Ward, eds., *Modern Political Systems:*

demonstrate: official statistics reveal, for instance, that the population in 1977 consisted of 53.5 percent women, 61.6 percent workers, 15.7 percent collective farmers, to name only the more basic classifications.[21] The discrepancy is clear when these figures are compared with those given by Brezhnev for most of the same variables (above). In this sense, the party is not truly "representative." The Soviet rejoinder is that such imbalance does *not* affect the issue of representation. Interests are seen to be represented through "formal corporative representation" in certain organs or institutions by "major associational interest groups,"[22] hence the presence of members of a group within the party's ranks ensures that its special interests can be articulated in the party's policymaking procedures. Even so, party recruitment policies have aimed in the post-Stalin period to make the party more reflective of the social and occupational patterns in society, and there have been attempts—endorsed by Soviet scholars—to recruit more women, young people, and members of the non-Russian nationalities.[23] How the disproportionate representation affects policymaking is difficult to determine; however, one might speculate that the inadequate agricultural policy over the years may be, at least in part, a reflection of the weakness of rural representation in the party membership.[24]

In this connection, one should note that membership in the CPSU is not open to all. Joining the party entails an involved process of application, with supporting references, careful screening, and a year's probation before full membership is granted. Selection is on an individual basis, and after rapid expansion in numbers during the Khrushchev era, the party is now said to be "by no means oriented towards forcing ad-

Europe, 3rd ed. (Englewood Cliffs, N.J.: Prentice-Hall, 1972), pp. 585–97; David Lane, *The End of Inequality? Stratification Under State Socialism* (Harmondsworth, Eng.: Penguin Books, 1971), p. 122.

21. *Narodnoe khozyaistvo SSSR za 60 let* (Moscow: Statistika, 1977), pp. 8, 40.

22. Philip D. Stewart, *Political Power in the Soviet Union: A Study of Decision-Making in Stalingrad* (Indianapolis and New York: Bobbs-Merrill, 1968), p. 38.

23. See, for example, I. N. Yudin et al., eds., *Nekotorye voprosy organizatsionno-partiinoi raboty* (Moscow: Politizdat, 1973), pp. 57–67; V. A. Kadeikin, *Problemy nauchnogo podkhoda v partiinoi rabote* (Moscow: Mysl', 1974), pp. 60–61; V. A. Kadeikin et al., eds., *Voprosy vnutripartiinoi zhizni i rukovodyashchei deyatel'nosti KPSS na sovremennom etape* (Moscow: Mysl', 1974), pp. 172–75.

24. A particular reason for the rather inept agricultural policy is the urban-industrial bias of the ideology, which also explains in part why the party has not paid attention to involving the rural population in its membership: see Aspaturian, op. cit., pp. 586–87; Rigby, op. cit., pp. 486–92.

missions into its ranks, but towards raising demands on both new entrants and all communists, so that quantitative growth of party ranks should not lower their quality."[25] The party is thus an exclusive body; it follows specific recruitment policies and expels members who fail to live up to the high demands placed on them: explusions of "passive" members stood at 13,600 in 1962, 14,400 in 1963, 17,200 in 1966, and 12,000 in 1967. The exchange of party membership cards initiated in 1971 and completed in the spring of 1975 involved the expulsion of about 347,000 members (from 2.2 to 2.3 percent), amounting to what Western commentators had predicted to be a "well-controlled, undramatic weeding out of members."[26]

In view of the exclusive recruitment practices, party membership is not a form of linkage open to most Soviet citizens. However, an interesting question is whether those outside the party can have any influence over selection processes. In principle, the answer would be in the negative, because recruitment policies are established at the higher levels of the party and implemented in the localities. However, a handbook for primary party organization secretaries hints that such influence is desirable and may be achieved by discussing applications for membership in an *open* party meeting, that is, one which nonmembers may attend, because "for a party organization it is very important to know the opinion of non-party people."[27] If this practice were the rule rather than the exception (indeed, if open party meetings were regularly held and well attended by both members and outsiders), this could then be one significant form of linkage between the society at large and the party hierarchy.

But for most purposes, nonmembers have no direct access to the party, and linkage is indirect. It operates through party members in other social groups and institutions, from workers' collectives to trade-union branches and local government organs. Because of their distri-

25. Yudin, op. cit., p. 273.

26. Robert J. Osborn, *The Evolution of Soviet Politics* (Homewood, Ill.: Dorsey Press, 1974), p. 233. Figures for expulsions, 1962–67, from Yudin, op. cit., p. 80. For a comment on expulsions in the period 1962–67, see Darrell P. Hammer, "The Dilemma of Party Growth," *Problems of Communism* 20, no. 4 (July–August 1971): 19–21; the figure for expulsions during the 1971–75 operation was given by Leonid Brezhnev at the Twenty-fifth Congress (*Pravda*, 25 February 1976), p. 7.

27. *Spravochnik sekretarya pervichnoi partiinoi organizatsii* (Moscow: Politizdat, 1967), p. 137; also *Organizatsionno-ustavnye voprosy KPSS* (Moscow: Politizdat, 1973), p. 80.

bution in Soviet society, party members are in a position to observe and gather "valuable information about the aspirations and requirements of all the different sections of society," [28] which can then be fed into the system via party meetings proper or through any other institutions to which the individual party member may belong. This includes practically any institution in the country, such as the soviets, the trade unions, the Komsomol (Young Communist League), and other "public" or "voluntary" organizations, and the practice is justified by the argument that the party is "a superior type of social organization, which serves as the leading nucleus in all other workers' organizations, including those of the state." [29] Among such organizations, the soviets occupy a special position as "organs of state power" and as the main instrument though which the party plays its directing role in Soviet society. [30] The discussion here, therefore, will concentrate on this aspect of linkage, the party and the soviets. However, it should be kept in mind that similar linkage patterns connect the party with other institutions in the sociopolitical system of the USSR.

The Mechanics of Party-State Linkage

In political terms, the state apparatus—which includes both local soviets and their executive (administrative) organs and also what is officially referred to as the "government" of the USSR (the Council of Ministers) —is subordinated to the party and works under its leadership and guidance. The relationship between the two structures is complex.

First, the party has effective control over the initial selection of representatives: the 1977 Constitution (Article 100) accords to party organizations the right to nominate candidates for election, and the electoral law gives them the right to representation on the electoral commissions, which are responsible for registering candidates and for supervising the conduct of the elections. All candidates are endorsed, if not specifically nominated, by the party: they are at least strong supporters of the party line, acceptable to the local party authorities at the

28. Shakhnazarov, op. cit., p. 45.
29. A. I. Luk'yanov and B. M. Lazarev, *Sovetskoe gosudarstvo i obshchestvennye organizatsii*, 2nd ed. (Moscow: Yuridicheskaya literatura, 1961), p. 212.
30. S. S. Kravchuk, ed., *Gosudarstvennoe pravo SSSR* (Moscow: Yuridicheskaya literatura, 1967), p. 153. In my usage, the noun "soviets" is restricted to refer to the organs of government; it does not refer to "the Soviet people" or "the Soviet government," as is common in American and journalistic usage.

TABLE 15.2. Party Representation in Tiraspol Town Soviet, 1950–67 (in percent)

	Date of Election								
	1950	1953	1955	1957	1959	1961	1963	1965	1967
Nonparty	30.8	21.0	15.8	26.8	25.0	25.7	29.1	29.3	34.8
CPSU full members	52.3	53.6	56.4	64.5	68.1	62.4	55.3	51.8	58.8
CPSU candidate members	3.8	0.0	0.0	2.2	1.6	2.5	3.1	4.4	0.0
Komsomol members	3.8	1.4	0.0	6.6	5.3	9.4	12.6	14.0	6.4
Not available	9.2	23.9	27.9	0.0	0.0	0.0	0.0	0.4	0.0
N =	130	138	165	183	188	202	223	249	250

SOURCE: Compiled by author from information published in the local newspapers, *Dnestrovskaya pravda*, *Stalinskii put'*, and *Drapelul Leninist*. Only partial details of the soviets elected in 1950, 1953, and 1955 were published.

time of their nomination. It is also clear that the social composition of the body of deputies is influenced by central party directives, issued ultimately to local district party committees (*raikoms*), which are responsible for coordinating all aspects of a Soviet election campaign.[31]

In local soviets, party members are frequently in a minority; however, the careful selection and screening of all potential deputies removes any real likelihood that opposition to party-approved policy would arise within the soviets. Moreover, the party is in a minority only at the relatively unimportant village level: at all levels of any real significance, party members are normally in a safe majority, reinforced by party candidate (probationary) members and Komsomol members, whose commitment is likely to be as firm as that of full party members. The example of Tiraspol illustrates this point. The figures in tables 15.2 and 15.3 identify a clear majority of full members in all years for which data are available, even including those cases with substantial missing data; when the candidate members are added, the majority is overwhelming,

31. See Everett M. Jacobs, "The Composition of Local Soviets, 1959–69," *Government and Opposition* 7, no. 4 (Autumn 1972): esp. 506; Ronald J. Hill, "Patterns of Deputy Selection to Local Soviets," *Soviet Studies* 25, no. 2 (October 1973): 196–212; and especially Yu. V. Shabanov, *Partiinoe rukovodstvo Sovetami deputatov trudyashchikhsya* (Minsk: Belarus', 1969), discussed in Ronald J. Hill, "The CPSU in a Soviet Election Campaign," *Soviet Studies* 28, no. 4 (October 1976): 590–98.

TABLE 15.3. Party Representation in Tiraspol Rural District Soviet, 1950–67 (in percent)

	Date of Election								
	1950	*1953*	*1955*	*1957*	*1959*	*1961*	*1963*	*1965*	*1967*
Nonparty	28.6	20.5	28.3	20.0	—	22.5	27.7	26.2	32.1
CPSU full members	66.7	63.6	60.9	66.7	—	62.5	58.1	58.5	59.0
CPSU candidate members	0.0	6.8	2.2	2.2	—	0.0	0.0	0.8	0.0
Komsomol members	2.4	4.5	8.7	8.9	—	13.8	13.5	14.6	9.0
Not available	2.4	4.5	0.0	2.2	100.0	1.3	0.7	0.0	0.0
N =	42	44	46	45	80	80	148	130	134

SOURCE: Compiled by author from information published in the local newspapers, *Znamya pobedy, Drapelul Biruintsei, Dnestrovskaya pravda, Leninskoe znamya* and *Drapelul Leninist*. Full details of the soviet elected in 1959 were not published.

and Komsomol-member deputies boost the strength of the formally "committed" deputies still further.

The party-affiliated deputies thus form a leading core among the deputies, and they meet separately as a party *group* to discuss the work of the soviet. Such groups are directly subordinated to the local party committee and work under its direction in checking on the efficiency with which the party deputies fulfill their obligations as deputies. They also provide an important instrument for implementing party policy through the soviets. Decisions of party committees are automatically binding on all party members, including those who serve as deputies. Therefore, insofar as party committees discuss issues that need implementation by the soviets, the party-group members are obligated to strive for their execution. Decisions adopted by the party group (which normally meets immediately before a session of the soviet) are likewise binding on members, and frequently these groups prepare draft resolutions on questions to be debated in the soviet and agree on their position in advance.[32] This practice is followed not only in the soviets but in all other institutions as well and obviously places the party in an extremely strong position.

32. *Raionnyi komitet partii* (Moscow: Politizdat, 1972), p. 100; also "Partiinye gruppy v mestnykh Sovetakh," *Partiinaya zhizn'*, no. 8 (April 1973), p. 51.

357

Another important aspect of party control or influence over the work of other institutions lies in the selection, placement, and training of personnel, a concept that is not entirely analogous with that of political recruitment.[33] The system of *nomenklatura*—a list of appointments for which a particular party committee has responsibility—plays a key role here, giving to the party bodies effective control over staffing. The appointments include positions in the party apparatus itself (secretaryships at lower levels, for example) and also in the state and other structures, as Soviet sources occasionally reveal. The system operates in two ways: first, appointments to such positions are made "only after a review of the candidatures by the corresponding party organs," and second, the party organs create reserves of workers whom they train for appointment to such party or other positions.[34] The party groups within nonparty institutions also have a role to play here, discussing the merits of available candidates and making recommendations to the relevant party authorities.[35] All appointees to such positions of responsibility are thus, at the time of their appointment, regarded as reliable and competent, willing to strive for the implementation of party policy.

A further form of party-state linkage is the system of overlapping or interlocking membership between, on the one hand, the party structure and, on the other, state and other bodies. This question has been little studied by Western scholars, and Soviet writers virtually ignore it. It is, of course, well known that there is overlapping among the top organs: thus, Alexei Kosygin, chairman of the Council of Ministers, or prime minister, is also on the party Central Committee and its Politburo; Leonid Brezhnev, party secretary-general, is a deputy of the Supreme Soviet and chairman (or president) of the Supreme Soviet Presidium; other members of the Politburo hold important positions in the state apparatus, such as Yuri Andropov, head of the KGB, the State Security Committee; Andrei Gromyko, foreign minister; and Dmitri Ustinov, defense minister; and all are deputies of the Supreme Soviet. Similar interlocking can be observed among the top positions at any level: the

33. Farukshin, op. cit., pp. 58–61.
34. Shabanov, op. cit., p. 17. The most thorough recent study of the phenomenon is by Bohdan Harasymiw, in his article "*Nomenklatura*: the Soviet Communist Party's Leadership Recruitment System," *Canadian Journal of Political Science* 2, no. 4 (December 1969): 493–512. One Soviet source states quite explicitly that the post of prime minister is filled on the recommendation of the party Central Committee (Kravchuk, op. cit., p. 469).
35. "Partiinye gruppy v mestnykh Sovetakh," op. cit., p. 51.

TABLE 15.4. Membership Linkage Between Tiraspol Town Soviet and Party Committee, 1950–67

	Date of Election of Soviet							
	1950	*1955*	*1957*	*1959*	*1961*	*1963*	*1965*	*1967*
Number of deputies	130	165	183	188	202	223	249	250
Percent of deputies also on party committee	29.2	33.3	32.2	29.8	30.7	15.2	16.9	24.0
Number of party committee members	66	68	81	92	98	104	108	112
Percent of party committee also deputies	57.6	80.9	72.8	60.9	63.3	32.7	38.9	53.6

SOURCE: As in table 15.2. No details are available of the party committee incumbent at the time of the 1953 soviet elections.

first secretary of the party committee is normally a deputy of the local soviet, and the soviet executive committee chairman is invariably a party committee member (and usually a member of its bureau).

However, another important dimension is the overlapping among the ordinary membership of party committees and state organs. Data compiled in the study of Tiraspol institutions permit a degree of quantification of this phenomenon (tables 15.4 and 15.5). The dates chosen for analysis here encompass the election of a new soviet, and reference is made to the incumbent party committee.

Two points merit comment: the contrast between the patterns of the town and of the rural district; and the tendency toward a decline in the overlap in the 1960s. The proportion of rural-district soviet deputies accounted for by party committee members was much higher than in the town in the early years. This probably reflects the general weakness of the party in the countryside, necessitating relatively more intensive deployment of the elite in the task of guiding the work of other institutions, including the soviets. Party-committee members who also serve on soviets not only possess prestige that others do not but also enjoy a level of familiarity with party policy and its interpretation that enables them to play the required leading role in determining the direction of the soviet's work and in ensuring that it is in line with party policies.

Explaining the declining overlap in the 1960s is a little more diffi-

TABLE 15.5. Membership Linkage Between Tiraspol Rural District
Soviet and Party Committee, 1955–67

	Date of Election of Soviet						
	1955	*1957*	*1959*	*1961*	*1963*	*1965*	*1967*
Number of deputies	46	45	80	80	148	130	134
Percent of deputies also on party committee	45.7	53.3	43.8	37.5	25.7	23.8	23.9
Number of party committee members	48	64	92	92	100	102	108
Percent of party committee also deputies	43.8	37.5	38.0	32.6	38.0	30.4	29.6

SOURCE: As in table 15.3.

cult. One might suggest that it reflects a growing maturity of the party organizations, which no longer needed to deploy their elite in this way. That is plausible, but there is a further set of interpretations with a strong bearing on linkage. The trend might reflect growing confidence in the capacity of the soviets, somewhat revitalized since 1957, to act without close party-committee supervision. However, a number of scholars have pointed out that there was in fact a significant *reduction* in the role of the soviets in the period 1960–64, during Khrushchev's attempts to force the pace of the state's "withering away," precisely when the declining overlap between the party committee and the soviet in Tiraspol is identified.[36] What this probably indicates, therefore, is that the party authorities did not regard the soviets as of sufficient importance to place their most prestigious and influential personnel in them as deputies and instead used other means of implementing policy.

In this connection, the party's role in *interpreting* policy is relevant. Much of the party's activity concerns the economy in one form or another, and this is reflected both in the content of central committee resolutions

36. Jerry Hough, "Reforms in Government and Administration," in Alexander Dallin and Thomas B. Larson, eds., *Soviet Politics Since Khrushchev* (Englewood Cliffs, N.J.: Prentice-Hall, 1968), p. 24; L. G. Churchward, "Soviet Local Government Today," *Soviet Studies* 17, no. 4 (April 1966): 433–38; and especially George A. Brinkley, "Khrushchev Remembered: On the Theory of Soviet Statehood," *Soviet Studies* 24, no. 3 (January 1973): 398.

and in the business of lower party-committee meetings. In his study of the Stalingrad provincial party committee, Philip D. Stewart points out that the function of these meetings is to decide not policy but how best to implement policy: a resolution of the central organs is taken as a basis for debate, and agriculture and industry figure prominently among the topics discussed at party-committee meetings.[37] In Tiraspol, too, a similar pattern can be identified: in the years 1964–67, the town party committee held sixteen plenary meetings, at seven of which the committee discussed matters arising from a recent Central Committee resolution; in the district committee during the same period, the published record shows that seventeen meetings were held, at nine of which the "results" of a plenum, or party congress, held at the all-union, or the republican, level were analyzed and the lessons for the district party organization discussed.

The channels of output linkage can be clearly seen in the example of the Tiraspol District Committee Plenum of June 1966. The committee met in the House of Culture in the Kotovsky collective farm, and the first secretary, I. L. Durnop'yanov, read a report entitled "The Tasks of the District Party Organization in Fulfilling the Decree of the May Plenum of the CPSU Central Committee and the June Plenum of the Moldavian Central Committee 'On the Widespread Development of Land Improvement for Obtaining High and Stable Harvests of Grain and Other Agricultural Crops.'" This question had been debated in the CPSU Central Committee on May 27, was taken up and interpreted for Moldavia by the republican Central Committee on June 17, and was broken down into further detail for the district on June 27. In performing this interpretative function, the committee was assisted by the fact that its first secretary had participated in the republican Central Committee Plenum (indeed, had spoken at it) and was thus aware of the emphases in the argument and could speak with enhanced authority.[38] Presumably the district committee members similarly returned to the party organizations on their farms and led the debate on how specifically to implement the decree on the ground. The point is that local party bodies—and indirectly all party members—are involved in transmitting, interpreting,

37. Stewart, op. cit., pp. 55–64; note esp. p. 59, table 10.
38. This plenum was reported in *Dnestrovskaya pravda*, 29 June and 2 July 1966; the original decree of 27 May 1966 appears in *Spravochnik partiinogo rabotnika: Vypusk 7* (Moscow: Politizdat, 1967), pp. 104–18; a report of the Moldavian Central Committee Plenum that discussed this topic appeared in *Sovetskaya Moldaviya*, 18 June 1966.

and subsequently implementing Central Committee resolutions; this implementation may be direct or indirect, through the state and other institutions.

Central Committee decisions are also transferred to other institutions at the top level: party directives are interpreted and turned into practical arrangements in the Council of Ministers; they are then formalized in legislation by the Supreme Soviet, and eventually passed down the chains from the ministry to the local administrative department and from the Supreme Soviet to the local soviets. The process can be seen by examining the chronology of legislative acts, including even the five-year economic plans.[39] First details of the contents of the tenth plan (1976–80) were given by Leonid Brezhnev, as head of the party, to the Twenty-fifth Party Congress; a full report to the congress was later given by the prime minister, Alexei Kosygin, outlining the congress's draft directives on the plan; these directives were later adopted by the congress, together with instructions to the Council of Ministers and individual ministries to work out the detailed implications for each sector of the economy and at each administrative level, taking into account comments received from various party meetings around the country, and to submit this detailed plan to the USSR Supreme Soviet. This was approved by the party Central Committee in October and formally adopted by the Supreme Soviet a few days later. Individual plans for republics, cities, and other administrative units were subsequently discussed in party and state institutions.[40] Thus, the plan originated in the party, was formalized by the state apparatus and subsequently executed by the state under party supervision. Other examples also reveal that political initiatives come from the party: thus, Brezhnev's suggestion for drafting a new statute to define the legal position of Soviet deputies was made at the Twenty-fourth Congress (April 1971) and eventually became law in September 1972.[41]

39. G. Kh. Shakhnazarov, *Sotsialisticheskaya demokratiya: nekotorye voprosy teorii* (Moscow: Politizdat, 1972), p. 86.

40. This timetable is chronicled in the following sources: *XXV s"ezd Kommunisticheskoi partii Sovetskogo Soyuza: Stenograficheskii otchet* (Moscow: Politizdat, 1976), 1:63–86; 2:3–51, 226–307 (note esp. 226); *Pravda*, 26–30 October 1976; *Sovetskaya Moldaviya*, 24–27 November 1976.

41. *XXIV s"ezd*, op. cit., pp. 102–03; *Pravda*, 22 September 1972. The party may have taken this initiative in response to pressure from outside and specifically from within the state apparatus or legal profession. For example, in an article published in 1967 (originally a conference paper), A. Ye. Lunev, deputy director of the Institute of State and Law

These examples indicate the party's fundamental role as policy-maker, and it is easy to appreciate the predominance in Western literature of the view of a state apparatus dominated or controlled by the party. John Armstrong, for example, has written of the Soviet state as a facade behind which "the real power of Communist control is exercised"; David Lane refers to the party's "monopoly of authoritative political power."[42] The relationship, however, is considerably more complex and subtle.

The Communist Party of the Soviet Union certainly does claim the right to decide the appropriate course for that country to take, and it has the political power to enforce its view. Yet the sheer technical complexity of issues arising in political life today demands reliance on the advice of experts outside the political hierarchy.[43] Party policies are clearly not produced in a vacuum; nor are they wholly dervied from the ideology of Marxism-Leninism, which has nothing specific to say about running a wealthy, consumer-oriented, high-technology society of ever better educated citizens. The range of interests arising in this society is of an order that could not have been envisaged at the outset of the regime; yet, as Soviet writers have acknowledged, if policies are to have any relevance, these interests and opinions must be taken into account by the policymakers. In the next section, the channels of *input* linkage, through which interests are articulated and brought to the attention of the political decision makers, will be outlined.

Party-State Linkage and the Processing of Demands

The overlap between party committees and soviets, discussed above, also has implications for the effectiveness of *input linkage*. The greater the

of the USSR Academy of Sciences, urged the legal regulation of "a number of questions connected with the activity of deputies"; these questions have in large measure been covered by subsequent legislation; see his "Konkretno-sotsiologicheskie issledovaniya i ikh znachenie dlya razvitiya pravovoi nauki," in L. A. Petrov, ed., *Nekotorye voprosy sotsiologii i prava* (Irkutsk: Publisher unidentified, 1967), pp. 103–04. There can be no doubt, however, that the initiative for raising this question as a *political* issue lay with the party.

42. John A. Armstrong, *Ideology, Politics, and Government in the Soviet Union: An Introduction*, 3rd ed. (London: Nelson, 1974), p. 157; Lane, *Politics*, op. cit., p. 128.

43. Henry W. Morton, "The Structure of Decision-Making in the USSR: A Comparative Introduction," in Peter H. Juviler and Henry W. Morton, eds., *Soviet Policy-Making: Studies of Communism in Transition* (London: Pall Mall, 1967), p. 9. For a discussion of Soviet views on the role of experts in government, see Donald V. Schwartz, "Information and Administration in the Soviet Union: Some Theoretical Considerations," *Canadian Journal of Political Science* 7, no. 2 (June 1974), pp. 240–44.

overlap in membership, the greater are the chances that demands and interests channeled into the soviet via the deputies (including nonparty members) will be absorbed by the local party authorities and passed upward; any reduction in the level of overlap would imply that the soviet was in a weakened position to influence the debates in the party committees on issues relevant to its own role as the body with legal responsibility for administration and to reflect, and respond to, the interests and needs of citizens. Party committee members on the soviets help to ensure that party policies are effectively implemented, and in the reverse direction, deputies on the party committee contribute the administrators' and constituents' viewpoint to the policy debates within the party committee. The fact that, in Tiraspol, the overlap diminished at a time when the soviets were of reduced significance in the political system lends support to this interpretation, and a precisely similar view of the role of soviets and public organizations has been put forward by the Soviet Union's leading student of the role of public opinion, R. A. Safarov.[44]

The deputy is well placed to perform the role of articulator of his constituents' interests. For example, through the standing commissions (which operate on a more regular and permanent basis than the whole soviet), the deputy can "serve as a channel for criticism and suggestions from constituents whose interests and background are not very different from his own."[45] Here the so-called electors' mandate (*nakaz*) can play a key role. It is the nakaz that, essentially, forms the deputy's electoral program. A Western political party aggregates perceived demands into a program, which it then puts before the electorate for endorsement: Kirchheimer's "catch-all party" is based on such a view. In the Soviet context, by contrast, a deputy is supposed to receive "mandates" from his electors—specific requests of public or social relevance, with which he is charged at a public meeting during the election campaign and which it is his duty to try and fulfill during his term of office. Some Soviet writers see these mandates as *demands* fed into the political system by the population.[46] Such demands may be introduced into the system at any level in the administrative hierarchy (although usually at the local level),

44. R. A. Safarov, "Vyyavlenie obshchestvennogo mneniya v gosudarstvenno-pravovoi praktike," *Sovetskoe gosudarstvo i pravo*, no. 10 (October 1967), pp. 50–51.

45. Armstrong, op. cit., p. 165.

46. A. V. Moshak, "Nakazy izbiratelei i status deputata Soveta." *Sovetskoe gosudarstvo i pravo*, no. 2 (February 1971), p. 93.

discussed in the full soviet, and then implemented, with appropriate reference to higher authorities via the planning mechanism and, as often as not, the party structure.[47]

These demands may also be discussed separately by the party group, which has the duty to investigate what happens to constituents' complaints once raised by party deputies and the right to bring issues to the attention of the party committee to which it is subordinated.[48] Here is a second form of indirect linkage: demands articulated by the population as individual mandates are aggregated in the state apparatus, whence they may pass into the party for further processing.

A more direct form of linkage is provided by letters from the population to party committees and other organs. Such letters are seen as "one of the manifestations of the party's link with the masses" and "an important form of the expression of public opinion, an inexhaustible source of information on the state of affairs in different branches of production and public life."[49] The point was further stressed at the Twenty-fifth Congress, by Leonid Brezhnev, who referred to such letters as "one of the important points of linkage [between] our party and its central committee and the masses." He told delegates that the number of such letters is increasing and assured them that the Central Committee "systematically informs itself about everything deserving attention in workers' letters. The most important proposals and opinions," he added, "are reviewed by the Politburo and the central committee secretariat, and are taken into account in working out edicts and statutes." As to the scale of this form of linkage, the Moldavian Central Committee first secretary, Ivan Bodyul, reported to the Fourteenth Congress of his

47. Soviet political scientists have identified as a problem the difficulty of coordinating these unplanned or spontaneous mandates with the economic plan, a question that has apparently been partially resolved by switching the election campaign, during which mandates are given, from the traditional March to June: on this question, see N. Ye. Sukhanov, "Rabota mestnykh Sovetov s nakazami izbiratelei," *Sovetskoe gosudarstvo i pravo*, no. 6 (June 1969), p. 79; also Yu. A. Tikhomirov and K. F. Sheremet, eds., *Pravovye voprosy raboty mestnykh Sovetov (Organizatsiya deyatel'nosti)* (Moscow: Yuridicheskaya literatura, 1974), chap. 4. The party's role in the planning process can be seen in B. Michael Frolic's description in "Decision Making in Soviet Cities," *American Political Science Review* 66, no. 1 (March 1972): 38–52.

48. B. N. Gabrichidze, *Gorodskie Sovety deputatov trudyashchikhsya* (Moscow: Yuridicheskaya literatura, 1968), p. 40; *Organizatsionno-ustavnye voprosy KPSS*, op. cit., pp. 72–73.

49. *Sovetskaya Moldaviya*, 16 February 1972, p. 2; 22 July 1972, p. 1; 18 March 1975, p. 1; the point is also stressed by Safarov op. cit., pp. 51–52.

party in January 1976 that 22,147 letters from the public had been received by the republic's central party apparatus since the previous congress, held in 1971.[50]

The question that must now be asked is what is at the other end of the link? To whom is the party passing these demands received either directly from the population or indirectly via the state apparatus or other institutions? Why stress that the *party* receives demands via the *state*? The answer is again connected with the party's special position with regard to the ideology: because it is the *party* that claims to know what is best for society in the long term and the state that is the main instrument for carrying out party policy, the state (soviets, government) is capable of responding directly to popular demands only insofar as these can be accommodated within the overall guidelines of the ideologically inspired party policy. Although there is room for argument among observers as to how far ideology does influence decision making,[51] the theory is quite clear.

Putting this theory into practice means that there is a severe limitation on the freedom of action enjoyed by the state machine. It may be able to influence policy formulation—perhaps by feeding in information on popular demands, perhaps too by advising on the technical or administrative implications of potential policy decisions. But policy decisions are made not within the state apparatus but within the party. At the local level, where the soviets are governed by a whole range of ministries and other republican and central state institutions, it appears that there is less direct supervision by the corresponding party committees: even there, however, the town and district party committees review all major questions (including the local budgets, which make the financial allocations necessary for responding to public demands) and sometimes formally debate issues that have been tabled for discussion at a session of the soviet.[52] Thus a February 1967 session of the Tiraspol town soviet, which formalized several major personnel changes, was accompanied by a

50. Brezhnev's speech, *Pravda*, 25 February 1976, p. 7; Bodyul's figures, *Sovetskaya Moldaviya*, 30 January 1976, p. 7; the scale of this phenomenon is indicated by the fact that the population of the republic stood at 3,568,873 in 1970 (*Itogi Vsesoyuznoi perepisi naseleniya 1970 goda*, 1:7). Jerry Hough has argued that such communications may be a significant form of political participation: see his "Political Participation in the Soviet Union," *Soviet Studies* 28, no. 1 (January 1976): 14–15.

51. See, for example, A. H. Brown's comments in his review article "Policy-Making in the Soviet Union," *Soviet Studies* 23, no. 1 (July 1971): 127–29.

52. Shabanov, op. cit., p. 64.

plenary session of the town party committee at which the changes were decided in principle.[53]

At the level of broad policy innovations, the ultimate decision-making power lies with the Politburo: there can be little doubt about this. Despite constitutional arguments about the soviets as organs of state power and the subordination of the Politburo to the Central Committee and party congress, real policymaking power is held by the Politburo members. In the words of one experienced student of Soviet affairs, the Politburo "brings together most of the men with great personal influence in the Soviet elite, . . . [It] can and does act as a day-to-day decision-making body. . . . [A]ll major domestic policy innovations receive the stamp of approval of the Politburo . . . [whose] members jealously maintain their right to scrutinize every proposal."[54]

Hence it may be concluded that linkage through the party is between society and the party hierarchy. Input linkage is direct, via letters and similar channels, or indirect, through the medium of the state institutions or other organizations, which are more closely connected with the population than are the party committees. Demands communicated to the party either directly or through a further link are assessed and processed at the level where they are received or passed upward for evaluation by a party committee of an appropriate level of competence. Once policy decisions have been taken, at whatever level, in relation to a demand or set of demands, and guidelines issued, output linkage follows similar channels in the reverse direction.

This output linkage is the form of linkage stressed in much Western writing, in which the CPSU is seen as a structure engaging in mobilization, and the overall aim of the regime is assessed as the replacement of one complete set of values (culture) by another, defined by the ideology.[55] This aim is clearly contained in the CPSU's picture of the "new Soviet man," whose formation is seen as "one of the main tasks of the party in building communism."[56] The party rules stress this aspect of the party's role, requiring the party member to fight for creating the material basis for communism; to serve as an example of the communist attitude

53. *Dnestrovskaya pravda*, 21 February 1967; this example shows the principle of *nomenklatura* in operation.

54. Armstrong, op. cit., p. 88.

55. Robert C. Tucker, "Culture, Political Culture, and Communist Society," *Political Science Quarterly* 88, no. 2 (June 1973): 173–90.

56. *XXIV s"ezd*, op. cit., pp. 107–16.

toward work; to raise labor productivity; to stand out as an example of all that is new and progressive; to play an active part in the country's political life; and to fight decisively against any manifestations of bourgeois ideology.[57]

In this aspect of the party's work, a leading position is occupied by agitators and propagandists, working under the aegis of the local party committee's agitprop department. This work brings party members into face-to-face contact with the broader public. But the ultimate way in which the party members play the role of leading and guiding Soviet society is through participation in the work of other institutions, including those of the state. In other words, the agent of party linkage is the party member.

Conclusions

By focusing on linkage, attention has been drawn not only to the means whereby the party transmits central decisions downward for implementation by the state and the population but also to the channels of upward communication, from population to policymakers. The importance of indirect linkage through other institutions was stressed, but it was also pointed out that more direct channels of upward communication or input linkage are gradually becoming more effective and also that the party itself is aware of the need for effective linkage. The theme of party responsiveness to critical materials appearing in the press and to letters and proposals emanating directly from the public has been aired frequently in the official literature over the past decade, indicating an intention on the part of at least the top leaders to develop direct party linkage with the population.

It remains true nevertheless that input linkage is less well established than output linkage. Demands emanating from the population—which play such an important part in some Western models of the political process—are still given relatively low significance in Soviet analyses and Soviet political practice, where they are duly balanced against the "real needs" of the people as revealed in the ideology and perceived by the party. Whatever the ideal toward which some Soviet social scientists may be striving, political *practice* still seems to approximate to the view that demands are "a resource which must be used and structured by the

57. *Ustav KPSS*, op. cit., Rule 2.

political leadership in order to achieve the goals which it has set for society."[58] Linkage between party, state, and population is therefore of a different order and takes different forms from similar linkage in other types of systems: the concept itself helps to identify the peculiarities of the Soviet system.

58. Schwartz, op. cit., p. 235.

16.

Chiefs, Bureaucrats, and the MPR of Zaire

THOMAS TURNER

Linkage Policy and the Structure of Power

According to regime spokesmen, the central African state of Zaire is presently engaged in a radical transformation of its political and administrative structures. The primary instrument and object of this transformation is the Popular Revolutionary Movement (MPR), to which the entire state apparatus is to be subordinated. The MPR is said to be a "mass party," an organ for the enlarged participation of the population, and a "national party," or "the nation organized politically."

A key step in this transformation was to be the abolition of hereditary chiefship and the incorporation of the chiefs into the administration. Inasmuch as the administration has itself been incorporated into the MPR, the chief as redefined was to be the principal link between the party and the people. However, the elimination of hereditary chiefship ran into difficulties and was abandoned. The failure of this policy is thus inextricably linked to the role of the MPR as an agency of linkage between populace and state. This paper will seek to understand the reasons for the failure and thereby reach a conclusion regarding the structure of power in Zaire in general and the linkage role of the single party, the MPR, in particular.

This paper is based upon two years of fieldwork in Zaire, 1973–75, including interviews, archival research, and (not least important) participant observation at the Lubumbashi campus of the National University of Zaire. Neither the Rockefeller Foundation (on whose field staff I served) nor the National University of Zaire bears any responsibility for the observations contained in this study.

A possible explanation of the failure of the policy is offered by Zolberg, for whom the overriding characteristic of the African party-states is not authoritarianism but lack of authority. For Zolberg, such systems have two sectors, one "modern" and one "residual," which authoritatively allocate "modern" and "residual" sets of values. The central authorities are weak in part because a large part of the process of the authoritative allocation of values is beyond their control.[1]

Zolberg's argument that the central authorities are weak is complemented by that of Miller, according to whom the chiefs are strong because of their position on the border between the "modern" and the "traditional" (or "residual") sectors.[2] For Zolberg and Miller, the failure of the Zairian regime to transform the chiefs into disciplined linkage agents between party and people is comprehensible, given the coexistence of the two sectors.

An alternative explanation of the apparent inability of the regime to implement its policies will be suggested here. Rather than accept the Zolberg-Miller argument, or the tautological attribution of this inability to low capability,[3] this study will proceed from a detailed examination of the pattern of policy formulation and application and the consequences thereof to a consideration of the distribution of power. In the following section what the Zairian government actually has done with regard to the problem of chiefs and the consequences of government action for the people will be examined, and in the third section the ideological justification of these outcomes—what values, assumptions, and goals are apparent in the policies and their effects—will be explored. In the fourth section, the process of policy formulation and application as regards chiefs, and the consequences thereof, will be compared to the pattern of policy and consequences regarding other aspects of linkage. "Where we know what the long-term patterns of benefit and burden from government policies have been—who consistently wins and loses—and we find that the beneficiaries have the apparent power to shape decisions as they

1. Aristide Zolberg, *Creating Political Order* (Chicago: Rand McNally, 1966), pp. 130–31.

2. Norman Miller, "The Political Survival of Traditional Leadership," *Journal of Modern African Studies* 6, no. 2 (1968): 183–201.

3. Colin Leys points out in his review of M. Lofchie, ed., *The State of the Nations* (Berkeley: University of California Press, 1971), in *Journal of Modern African Studies* 11, no. 2 (1973): 315–17, that the concepts of capabilities and obstacles assume that a genuine effort was made to accomplish a given goal but failed because the obstacle was greater than the capability; the assumption of a genuine effort often is unwarranted.

wish, we have a solid basis for inferring that they do so for their own benefit."[4]

"Linkage" is used here to mean "any recurrent sequence of behavior that originates in one [sector of the political system] and is reacted to in another." The sectors being considered are the center and the periphery, conceived of in geographic terms rather than (as Zolberg does) in terms of distinctive types of values. The concentration here is on penetrative linkage, in which the members of one sector serve as the participants in the political processes of the other, to the exclusion of reactive linkage, in which there is no sharing of authority.[5]

Linkage will be classified according to outcome, of which four types are possible: (1) stalemate, (2) coercion, (3) mutual adjustment, and (4) "administration."[6] Types two and four involve essentially top-down, or one-way, communication, and one and three involve two-way communication.

It will be argued here that incoherence in the area of linkage policy is more apparent than real, that the regime has a general policy of establishing one-way communications linkage with the rural population because such a policy is in the interest of the central decision makers. When faced with the possibility that removal of the hereditary chiefs would open up two-way communications linkage, the decision makers backtracked; this, rather than the weakness of the center or the strength of the chiefs, seems to be the best explanation of the policy outcome in the linkage area.

The Effort to Abolish Hereditary Chiefship

Under colonial rule, Zaire (then the Belgian Congo) was divided into eight hundred "native circumscriptions." Of these, the majority were

4. This approach has been borrowed from the innovative study by Kenneth Dolbeare and Murray Edelman, *American Politics*, 2nd ed. (Lexington, Mass.: D. C. Heath, 1974). As the authors explain, such an approach "will avoid many of the fruitless arguments between political scientists about who actually made or influenced particular decisions. Such arguments normally cannot be resolved, because the necessary evidence about a specific decision cannot be obtained by analysts, and because that decision can only really be understood in a context of many other decisions" (Introduction, n. p.). In a subsequent study I plan to analyze policy in other areas according to the same approach, thereby verifying the provisional conclusions reached in this study regarding the structure of power in Zaire.

5. James Rosenau, "Toward the Study of National-International Linkages," in James Rosenau, ed., *Linkage Politics* (New York: The Free Press, 1969), pp. 44–46.

6. Theodore J. Lowi, *The End of Liberalism* (New York: Norton, 1969), pp. 51–53.

traditional units with African chiefs chosen according to customary law and recognized by the state. Other circumscriptions, referred to as "sectors," were created by fusing several small traditional units together, and still others, known first as "extracustomary centers" and later as "cités," were small towns composed of people not living in a traditional setting.

Although this distinction is maintained today, it should be stressed that the present situation represents restoration of, rather than continuity with, the colonial setup. Because many of the chiefs were considered by the nationalist parties and the population to have been collaborators with the colonial administration, efforts were made in many parts of the country to elect new chiefs or even to eliminate the position of chief.[7]

Following his seizure of power in 1965, President Mobutu initially assumed a legalistic position regarding the chiefs. As part of his campaign to depoliticize the country following the coup, he restored to office all chiefs who had been deposed for "political" reasons during the first years of independence and all administrative boundaries to their 1960 position, which had the effect of reuniting a number of chiefdoms and sectors that had been divided in response to popular pressure.

Even during the first years of the single party, Mobutu continued to court the chiefs. In 1968 a decision to eliminate the duality between the party and the territorial administration enhanced the position of the collectivity chiefs. Henceforward the chiefs were the presidents of the subsections of the MPR. Modern (party) and traditional (chiefs) authorities were thus made one on the local level. Mobutu's positive orientation toward the chiefs was also expressed in March 1969 when a law was passed calling for popular election of the chiefs of sectors and cités.[8]

However, sometime in 1970–72 Mobutu changed his orientation toward the chiefs. In January 1973 a new law was passed repudiating the earlier reforms in almost every respect. Collectivities lost all autonomy and became simple territorial subdivisions. The distinction between chiefdoms, sectors, and cités was abolished. Collectivity chiefs were

7. In Sankuru, a region dominated by the MNC-Lumumba, new elections were held in 1961 even though the chiefs' terms of office had not expired; in Kongo Central, dominated by the ABAKO party, the position of chief was replaced by that of burgomaster.

8. Following review by the Interior Ministry, almost all the chiefs elected were confirmed for a five-year term. In the chiefdoms (35 percent of rural collectivities), chiefs continued to be chosen according to "custom."

integrated into the administration. A circular issued a week later made it clear that the change was designed to eliminate hereditary chiefship.[9]

Later the same year, yet another decree specified that collectivity chiefs were to have completed two years of postprimary school, to be physically and mentally competent, and to be "militant" in party terms. The state commissioner for political affairs ruled that all incumbent chiefs were considered to have resigned and would have to file candidacy-papers like anyone else. The regional commissioners initiated the process of candidate selection on the zone level, and in the course of screening by the zone, subregional and regional officials and a number of incumbent chiefs were eliminated on grounds of unsatisfactory health, eduction, or militancy. In a number of areas the process of collecting candidatures reportedly led to "effervescence" on the part of the population; by "effervescence" the administration meant stirring up conflict between supporters and opponents of the incumbent chief. Apparently alarmed by this renaissance of politics on the local levels, the central authorities abruptly suspended the process of screening candidate chiefs in mid-1974 and adopted a totally new policy: now the state commissioner ordered the regional authorities to retain all incumbent chiefs but to switch them to new collectivities. The only possible exceptions were to be certain *grands chefs* (major chiefs); no mention was made of other criteria such as age, health, education, or the chiefdom-sector distinction.[10]

Even before the first of the transferred chiefs had left for his new post, however, the state commissioner backpedaled; in a telegram of 18 October 1974 he informed the regional commissioners that the transfer of chiefs applied not to "customary chiefs" (those of ex-chiefdoms) but only to the "administrative chiefs" (of the ex-sectors and cités). Chiefs of former chiefdoms might be transferred at an unspecified later date.

With the October message, the original objective of moving against hereditary chiefship had been completely set aside. But in March 1975 the state commissioner sent yet another telegram, ordering that chiefs who were "broken by age" or "amortized" be replaced. Chiefs of former

9. Commissaire d'Etat aux Affaires politiques, "Note aux Citoyens Commissaires de Région (tous) relative à la Réforme sur l'organisation territoriale et administrative," 22 January 1973.

10. Commissaire d'Etat aux Affaires politiques, Telegram No. 0162 of 17 June 1974 to all zone commissioners; Commissaire d'Etat aux Affaires politiques, Instruction No. CAB/25/00/0280 aux Commissaires de Region (tous), 8 August 1974.

sectors and of cités could be replaced by members of the territorial administration, but in the case of the ex-chiefdoms, research would have to be carried out to find an heir who was eligible under both customary law and the new decree.[11]

Finally, in 1976, the remaining chiefs of the cités and ex-sectors were returned to their original collectivities. The reform policy of making the chiefs into administrators of the party-state had been totally abandoned.

Throughout these twists and turns of chieftancy policy, two sets of actors, the regional commissioners and the chiefs themselves, played key roles, the former in determining how each new policy was to be implemented, the latter in resisting its implementation. A review of these patterns of action in the period 1974–76 will not only demonstrate their significance for the eventual outcome of the state's efforts but will also permit analysis of that outcome in terms of its meaning for linkage politics.

In mid-1974 when the state commissioner ordered the suspension of candidate selection and the transfer of all incumbent chiefs, the response of the chiefs was immediate. Chiefs flew to the capital from all over the nation or contacted relatives living there in order to seek exemption from this measure. The difficulties of the regional commissioners in implementing the unpopular new policy were exacerbated by the fact that the state commissioner had provided no guidance as to how the moves were to be effected and no clear criteria as to which chiefs did in fact have to be moved. They resolved this problem by establishing their own systems for exchanges and their own criteria as to which chiefs to move.[12]

In Shaba, where there are ninety-nine rural collectivities, only fifty-two chiefs were switched in response to the new decree. Shaba is a "strong chief" area, that is, one where precolonial states were relatively large and strong, where the colonial administration displayed a certain deference toward the chiefs, and where a number of chiefs were active in politics during decolonization and the First Republic (1960–65). Some of those

11. Interviews with personnel of Regional Divisions of Political Affairs, Lubumbashi and Bukavu, 1974–75.

12. I cannot exclude the possibility that the regional commissioners received more detailed instructions orally; in my interviews I was unable to get beyond generalities as to why certain chiefs were switched and others not, so I have been forced to induce criteria from the patterns of switching.

not transferred were grands chefs, such as the Mwant Yav (Emperor of the Lunda), but these are too few to account for more than a minority of the exceptions.

In any case, a variable with greater power to explain why some chiefs were not moved is the old distinction between chiefdoms, sectors, and cités, even though the distinction no longer had a basis in law and had not been mentioned in the new order. Only 30 percent of the chiefs of former chiefdoms were moved, as against 77 percent for chiefs of former sectors and 86 percent for those of cités. Those chiefs of ex-chiefdoms who were switched tended to be younger than those who remained in place.[13]

In East Kasai, a "weak chief" area where sectors predominate, the authorities decided to switch everyone, with the exception of one elderly grand chef. As to the pattern followed (which chief to send where), authorities of Sankuru Subregion mentioned two guiding principles: (1) the necessity of avoiding "tribalism" or ethnic favoritism, apparently considered inevitable when an administrator remained in his home area, and (2) the desirability of revitalizing "nonviable" collectivities by placing dynamic chiefs in charge. Analysis of the pattern of switching confirms that two principles were followed almost without exception, first to switch chiefs between rather than within zones, and second, to avoid "tribalism" by switching chiefs between ethnic groups or sub-groups, even at the risk of setting off overt conflict by naming a chief from a group with which the population of the collectivity had fought during the First Republic.

Following the October message stipulating that only chiefs of cités and ex-sectors were to be switched, the regional authorities were faced with a difficult decision, to follow the instructions to the letter or to temporize. In Shaba, the authorities decided to follow the instructions almost to the letter (table 16.1). All the chiefs of the former chiefdoms who had been switched were sent back to their original collectivities. Almost all the chiefs of former sectors and of cités now were switched, including five who had been spared during the first round. After the December changes, only twenty-five chiefs of Shaba remained assigned

13. Because seven of thirteen Lunda chiefs and both minority chiefs were not switched, whereas all three Cokwe chiefs were switched, I hypothesized that ethnic favoritism might have been involved; however, this seems to have been a coincidence, because the variable of age is sufficient to account for the result.

TABLE 16.1. Switching of Chiefs in Shaba and East Kasai Regions: Situation After Second Wave of Switches

Action Taken	No Switch	Switched, Then Restored	New Chief Named	Left Vacant
Region & Subregion				
Shaba				
("strong chief" area)				
Lualaba	8	10	6	2
Tanganika	17	0	15	1
Upper Lomami	6	5	7	1
Upper Shaba	5	3	12	1
Total	36	18	40	5
East Kasai				
("weak chief" area)				
Kabinda	1	5	21	0
Sankuru	0	0	41*	2
Total	1	5	62	2

*This figure includes nine civil servants who had not previously served as chief.

to collectivities other than their own, twenty of them from the first wave in September.

In East Kasai, in contrast, one can scarcely speak of a second wave of switches, because most of the collectivities are ex-sectors. In several cases, however, chiefs of ex-chiefdoms did return, and new assignments had to be found for their ephemeral successors.

On the collectivity level reactions to the various measures and countermeasures varied. In Shaba, several chiefs refused to be switched. One justified his refusal by saying, "My wife has just had an operation and my child is sick, which obliges me to remain here to see to their state of health." His replacement had a difficult time, however, because of the presence of the ex-chief, to whom the villagers continued to submit problems. In several other cases, chiefs who had been transferred and were then allowed to return took their revenge against those who had collaborated with the temporary replacement.

In Sankuru Subregion (East Kasai), the switching of chiefs was readily accomplished and seems to have worked well. Tax receipts rose in some collectivities, because the new chiefs obliged almost everyone to pay, whereas their predecessors had exempted relatives and friends. The policy of sending effective chiefs into "nonviable" collectivities worked to some extent; in several such cases, the new chiefs were able to put the population to work repairing the roads. Likewise, the policy of eliminating "tribalism" by switching chiefs between cultural categories was partly successful. The people of Ngandu-Wuma Collectivity, savanna Tetela, accepted their new forest Tetela chief; apparently, they felt that earlier savanna-forest hostilities were outweighed by the fact that the chief spoke their language and descended from the same ancestor. In contrast, the locality chiefs of the Basonge Collectivity of Lubefu refused to collaborate with their new chief, a Tetela, on the grounds that a legitimate chief must belong to their ethnic group.

The different reactions can be explained by the fact that the term "chief" does not correspond neatly to Miller's "traditional leader." In Sankuru, as in many other parts of Zaire, many collectivity chiefs were "administrative chiefs," lacking legitimacy at any level. Their linkage with each of the localities was of the same type. Switching such people presented little difficulty. After the switch, as before, the "modern" and "residual" sectors met not in the person of the chief but in his relations with his subordinates, the chiefs of the localities (former *groupements*).

Most of the remaining chiefs in Sankuru had traditional status in their own groupement, or subunit, but no legitimacy on the collectivity level. Such a chief had a much better linkage, in terms of complementarity of communication and shared interest, with his own groupement than with the others. It could be expected that switching such a chief would produce a divided reaction, with his own groupement upset over losing its privileged position and the others pleased to see him go. This may have been the case, but several such chiefs seemed pleased to be transferred to a collectivity where they would keep the authority of chief but be freed from the pressures of such a conflict-laden situation.

The fact that all chiefs were returned to their original collectivity, including those who lacked legitimacy at the collectivity level, often led to an exacerbation of conflict within the collectivity. In the past, such chiefs had tended to favor their own groupements; now, in reaction to the behavior of the other groupements, they often took their revenge. The prestige of chiefs who were not switched or who were restored after having been transferred has been reinforced, and because the territorial administration had to back down, its prestige has diminished.

Ideology, Party, and Chiefship

From the analysis in the preceding section, it is possible to answer the first of the two questions posed earlier: Who gets what from action and inaction of the party-state in the area of linkage? The masses were winners, temporarily, in those cases where unpopular chiefs were transferred; they lost where unpopular chiefs were maintained and above all where unpopular chiefs were transferred, then reinstated. In any case, the masses were losers in that their possibilities for political participation (two-way linkage) were restricted. The chiefs, and especially the hereditary chiefs whose position was under attack in 1972–73, emerged with an acceptable compromise. The administrators, who at one point seemed on their way to a victory over the chiefs, were forced to back down. For the central decision makers, the result was ambiguous. It could be considered unsuccessful in that the objective of eliminating hereditary chiefship was not achieved; however, if the main objective was to bring the administrators, the chiefs, and the population under direct control of the party-state, then the objective was partially achieved and the central authorities can be satisfied.

In order to answer the second question—why such a pattern exists—one must take into account both the structure of power in Zairian society and the role of ideology, "those beliefs about how government does and should work that are held by the members of a society." To a great extent, contemporary Zairian politics can be viewed as the struggle of a particular group not only to stay in power and reap the benefits of doing so but also to impose an ideology. Like all ideologies, that ideology would affect the perception of social problems, explain and justify the form of social policies, and provide people with "a coherent sense of the relationship between themselves, their values, and the workings of their government."[14] The developing Zairian ideology seems to have influenced the decision makers themselves, to a degree; more important, propagation of that ideology became a principal policy goal.

Mobutu seized power in Kinshasa at a time when the country (and his own position) was threatened in a triple sense. The first threat was territorial fragmentation, expressed and justified in terms of particularistic ideologies, often strongly neotraditional. The second and third threats

14. Dolbeare and Edelman, op. cit., pp. 137–39.

379

were the "rebellion," or popular insurgency, and the disaffection of many intellectuals, both of which expressed themselves in variants of "scientific socialism."[15]

As of the take-over, the legitimacy of the state apparatus was at its nadir. The authority of that state apparatus had had a "legal-rational" basis, deriving from continuity with the colonial state and expressed in a constitution copied blindly from that of the kingdom of Belgium. Mobutu himself had a modicum of legitimacy in his role as head of the armed forces; beyond that, he and his colleagues of the so-called Binza group had had considerable influence, prior to the coup, but no legitimacy. Thus, a major concern of the new regime was to achieve a new basis for legitimate authority.

The legitimacy of the new regime reposed to a great extent on its ability to offer a contrast to the 1960–65 situation: unity in place of territorial fragmentation and order in place of conflict. In addition, however, Mobutu attempted to reconcile contradictory patterns of legitimacy and sets of symbols in the state apparatus and in particular in his own person. One such set of symbols was neotraditional. Thus, the stylistic resemblance between the Mobutu regime and the "presidential monarchy" of Nkrumah reflects not so much borrowing, though that may have occurred, as response to a common situation:

It seems to me that Ghana politics makes little sense unless one appreciates that what has occurred is a new relationship between traditional and secular politics in the *form* of the mobilization system. At the top of this system is a Presidential monarch—a kind of chief. . . . One view is that of society as a continuation of the clan and the chief. The position of Nkrumah is that of chief. The entire society is composed of clans. The local party figures are related to the clans, and thus the web of association between community and chieftaincy is maintained on a national level. The concept of chieftaincy is the essence of the African personality. The leader is duty bound to serve the state because the state is the ensemble of clans, and the leader himself derives from the clan. Hence the principle of legitimacy is a traditional one.[16]

15. On insurgent ideology see Renée C. Fox, Willy De Craemer, and Jean-Marie Ribeaucourt, "'The Second Independence': A Case-Study of the Kwilu Rebellion in the Congo," *Comparative Studies in Society and History* 8 (1965–66): 78–110; on the ideology of the student opponents of the regime, see Jules Gérard-Libois et al., *Congo 1967* (Brussels: Centre de Recherche et d'Information Socio-Politique, 1969), pp. 137–66.

16. David E. Apter, *Ghana in Transition* (New York: Atheneum, 1963), p. 365, cited in Zolberg, op. cit., pp. 143–44.

Like Nkrumah, Mobutu also has made himself into a chief; in the place of *kente* cloth, Mobutu wears the leopard skin, which is the symbol of chiefship throughout the Zaire basin.

Apter's description of the situation in Ghana under Nkrumah is exaggerated; there, as in Zaire, "tradition" was only one of several contradictory principles of legitimacy to be invoked.[17] Nonetheless, at certain moments during the early years of his rule, Mobutu did behave as though his objective was, quite literally, to place himself as chief of the chiefs. Such an objective is implied by his declaration, in 1967–68, that the chiefs were "the veritable cornerstones of our society, unanimously known and esteemed for their wisdom, their moderation and their uncontestable authority."[18]

Yet for a personalistic politician such as Mobutu, the use of tradition has its dangers; the symbols are the property of others, the chiefs, who can use them against the leader. It is widely believed that Mobutu abandoned his earlier policy of wooing the chiefs and turned to the policy reflected in the decree of 1973 because Chief Kasongo Nyembo of the Luba-Shaba, then a member of the Political Bureau of the MPR, argued against the idea that Mobutu be named president for life, declaring, "Not even the Emperor of the Luba is chosen for life." The shift in policy was expressed in democratic, constitutional symbols, the state commissioner for political affairs stigmatizing "the procedure of hereditary investiture that made of some citizens born into families called royal or dominant, men superior to others by virtue of their ancestry, and this, in flagrant contempt of democratic principles and our revolutionary constitution."[19]

A second set of symbols bolstered the legitimacy of the regime by stressing continuity with the colonial state. This form of legitimacy would seem (not surprisingly) to be particularly strong among members of the territorial administration; the use (until recently) of colonial-style uniforms was an important effort to restore the morale of the administrators and, of course, to intimidate the population by evoking

17. Zolberg, op. cit., p. 143.
18. J. D. Mobutu, *Paroles du Président* (Kinshasa: Editions du Leopard, 1968), p. 19. During this same period, he had himself invested as a chief of the Tetela (Lumumba's ethnic group).
19. Commissaire d'Etat aux Affaires politiques, "Note aux Citoyens Commissaires de Région (tous) relative à la Réforme sur l'organisation territoriale et administrative," 22 January 1973.

colonial coercion. In the training given the administrators, "science," that is, proper technique, was stressed as opposed to political or human-relations skills; principles dear to people who have undergone such training include "unity of command" and "going through channels."

Probably the most important ideological strand corresponds to what Zolberg calls the "one-party ideology." The justification of single-party dominance in Zaire closely parallels that advanced by Sékou Touré around 1960 (as summarized by Zolberg):

(1) There is a natural trend toward "unity"; (2) African societies *are* divided; (3) these divisions are not to be viewed as an American thinker might, as a healthy "pluralism," but rather in a negative way as "internal contradictions" (a Marxist borrowing); (4) unity is manifested in support for the dominant party ... (5) the failure of unity can only stem from The actions of men who willfully interfere with the natural course of history.[20]

Of course, Guinea and the other west African states studied by Zolberg differ from Zaire in that in those states the party existed, as an organization and as a symbol of anticolonial struggle, prior to the elaboration of the five-point "one-party ideology." In the west African cases, the ideology justified the restriction of participation to the single channel of the government party. In Zaire, on the other hand, the current regime emerged from a military coup d'état. Mobutu and other spokesmen initially advanced the equivalent of points 1, 2, 3, and 5, arguing that the natural trend toward unity was being sabotaged by politicians, who often had links to outside forces. In order to complete the paradigm, a party was needed, so that unity could be manifested in support for that party. Regardless of the intercountry influences at work, "the concepts were reinvented autonomously" in Zaire as in the west African states, "because they corresponded to a common situation."[21]

Formed in order to express national unity but not particularism or even competition, the party is led by the internal logic of its one-party ideology to socialize the population into a "subject-participatory" orientation in which compliance with directives from the politico-administrative hierarchy would be automatic because the sanctions would be internalized.[22] At some moments, the party-state does in fact seem

20. Zolberg, op. cit., pp. 45–46.

21. Ibid., pp. 47–48.

22. Gabriel Almond and Sidney Verba, *The Civic Culture* (Princeton.: Princeton University Press, 1963); Lowi, op. cit., p. 52.

to be promoting such socialization; at other moments there is an improvisational quality about public policy contrary to such socialization efforts. At some points, the position of the chiefs is enhanced, at others, that of the administrators. Each of these tactics can be justified by one strand or another of Zairian ideology; their alternation can best be understood as a defense of the interests of the decision makers, which will be discussed in the following section.

The Zairian Party-State

The highly centralized Zairian party-state of the 1970s bears little resemblance to the regime that Mobutu overthrew in 1965. Under that regime, power was shared between the central and provincial governments. The characteristic form of linkage was the patrimonial faction, composed of a politician and his collaborators and followers, the latter being tied to the former by kinship, ethnic or regional solidarity, and especially personal interest.[23] Where power was once shared by the central and provincial governments, it is now monopolized by the center. Within the central government, power is concentrated in the presidency. Autonomous groups within the system—first the largely discredited politicians and their factions and parties, later the companies and the church—have been neutralized. A consequence of all these changes has been to vastly increase the patronage dispensed by the president and to limit severely such opportunities not under his control.

Mobutu first depoliticized the Zairian system, then formed the MPR. The N'Sele Manifesto, the charter of the party, made it clear that democracy and order would have to be balanced. The MPR was to ensure "the active participation, direct or indirect, of everyone, men and women, in public discussion of the problems of everyday life" and "the permanent confrontation of the interests, the needs, the economic or political necessities ... [but] the authority of the State cannot be contested.... The Power does not draw back from groups, whether of interests or of opinions."

The manifesto also affirms (correctly) that the administration "lives with the heritage of the structures of colonial times" and "no longer

---

23. On patrimonial linkage during the period 1960–65, see Jean-Claude Willame, *Patrimonialism and Political Change in the Congo* (Stanford, Calif.: Stanford University Press, 1972), chaps. 2–6.

corresponds to the necessities of reconstruction of the state." It would have to be reorganized and new personnel brought in. It would have to be "detribalized" and "depoliticized." [24] Nothing was said as to how either of these objectives—orderly participation of the population in politics and freeing the administration from its colonial heritage—was to be achieved. In fact, political participation was severely limited. Administrative personnel were upgraded but no major reorganization took place. Rather than being "depoliticized," the administration was merged with the MPR.

At first the MPR was set up with a separate structure on all levels below that of the president. Then, following a series of disputes between state and party officials on the same level, for example, regional commissioner and regional president of the MPR, the duality was eliminated; the regional commissioner became head of the MPR on the regional level, the collectivity chief, head of the party in his own collectivity, and so on. The MPR has decided that it is the "sole institution" of the Republic; because the National Executive Council is a party organ and the territorial administration is an emanation of the NEC, the administration is an integral part of the party.[25]

Politics still exists, but in the hands of the administrators. There are committees of the party at each level of the administrative structure, but the composition of these committees makes it clear that the party has little separate existence. In a typical rural zone, the MPR committee comprises the zone commissioner and his two assistant commissioners, the director of the party youth wing, the commander of the gendarmerie, the secretary of the single trade union (UNTZA), and the chiefs of the collectivities that compose the zone. The preoccupations of the committee are overwhelmingly administrative.[26]

Communication within the MPR mostly passes down the administrative chain of command, from the founder-president to the Political Bureau (over which Mobutu presides) to the state commissioner for political affairs (former interior minister) to the regions, subregions,

24. *Manifeste de la N'Sele* (n.p., n.d.), pp. 4, 14, 15.
25. Lissanga Egala, "L'impact du Mouvement Populaire de la Révolution 'M.P.R.' sur l'administration publique zairoise," *mémoire de licence*, Political and Administrative Science, National University of Zaire, 1975.
26. Mouvement Populaire de la Révolution, Zone de Lodja, *Rapport Annuel*, 1974. The eight-page report contains just fifteen lines on "desiderata of the population," citing inadequate medical services, two unpopular locality chiefs, and the mismanagement of the local soccer association.

zones, collectivities, and localities. Officials at each of these levels address themselves directly to the population, in the form of *causeries morales*, or sermons, but the population's role on such occasion is limited to applause, the reciting of slogans, and the occasional voicing of grievances. As Nzongola explains:

Instead of being able to articulate clear-cut demands in defense of their rightful interests, they may only voice *doléances*, or grievances, in the hope that the benevolent governor who receives them will act expeditiously to correct the wrongs visited upon his/her children by some unfortunate circumstances beyond their control or by the folly of some administrative official. This recourse to the traditional concept of the role of a chief, and the traditional political symbols it seeks to evoke, may at times be beneficial to individual members of the dominated classes. But in the last analysis, it provides a convenient distraction from the reality of the depolitization of the masses, and it has a negative effect on administrative performance.[27]

There is an ad hoc quality to such receptivity; no stable linkage is established.

Nor do the legislators, who act as linkmen in other countries, perform such a role in Zaire to a large extent. The population is asked to approve a single list of candidates for the post of people's commissioner or member of the National Legislative Council; voting is obligatory, voting "no" almost impossible. The National Legislative Council, formally a representative body, is almost powerless in practice, because it meets only a few weeks a year and debates only such measures as are submitted to it by the Political Bureau. It can be counted upon not to introduce unnecessary complications. The people's commissioners may serve as linkmen in an individual capacity, representing elements of their constituency in dealings with central government services. However, their main significance would seem to be as symbolic representatives of their areas or ethnic communities.[28]

27. Nzongola-Ntalaja, "Urban Administration in Zaire: A Study of Kananga, 1971–73" (Ph.D. diss., University of Wisconsin–Madison, 1975), p. 44.

28. This passage was written prior to the elections of November 1977, in which multiple candidacies were permitted within the MPR framework. Mobutu apparently accepted this "reform" under pressure from the United States, the International Monetary Fund, and other outside forces. The resultant legislature is somewhat less of a rubber stamp than the preceding one, suggesting that two-way communication has been enchanced; however, it remains to be seen whether the outcome will be a stalemate or mutual adjustment.

Policy regarding the chiefs fits into the same pattern of centralization and personalization of power. The 1973 law integrating chiefs into
the administration was the principal statement of the hypothesized
policy of establishing hierarchical relations with the rural population
(thereby eliminating or at least restricting Zolberg's "residual sector").
This law differed from the 1969 law on chieftaincy in several respects,
but of particular importance was the fact that elections were eliminated,
thus preventing the people from choosing their linkmen.

As has been seen, major shifts occurred as to how this law was to
be applied. These shifts, which contributed to the impression of confusion, are in fact very revealing as to the priorities of the regime. For
example, the 1973 law initially was justified in advocating the abolition
of hereditary chiefship on the constitutional grounds that all Zairians
are equal; however, the desire to promote equality was clearly not a
priority in the eyes of the decision makers, as the focus on hereditary
privilege was jettisoned early on.

The first attempt to apply the 1973 law on the collectivity level
was the soliciting of candidatures for the post of chief; this procedure
would have permitted the naming of new, more qualified chiefs, especially
as regards educational level. Although no explanation was advanced as
to why the collecting of candidatures was suspended, it is reasonable to
assume that the "effervescence" stirred up by the process was a factor in
the suspension. In other words, maintaining order and preventing the
population from politicking over the choice of its linkmen were deemed
more important than choosing new, more qualified chiefs.

Had the measures of transferring chiefs been carried out as initially
announced, a great many unqualified chiefs would have been retained in
office (in another collectivity). However, hereditary chiefship would have
been abolished; no chief would have had any legitimacy in the eyes of
the population of his collecitivity, other than the legitimacy conferred
upon him as local representative of the party-state. In the event, of
course, transferring the chiefs met with resistance. The demands of the
chiefs and their relatives for a change in policy were listened to. The
opinion of the population, in many cases favorable to the switching of
the chiefs, was ignored. The central authorities fell back on a colonial
legalism—the distinction between so-called traditional and artificial
collectivities—thereby abandoning all pretense of abolishing hereditary
chiefship. This responsiveness to pressures articulated at the central level,
bypassing the zone, subregional, and regional levels, would seem to be

an indication not merely of weak "regulatory capability" on the part of the Mobutu regime but of a desire to dispense goods, service, and status from the center.

The most recent modification of the instructions, permitting replacement of old chiefs, preserves the distinction between "traditional" and "artificial" collectivities but makes it possible to take into account the concern with competence. Throughout all the shifts in instructions, a consistent factor has been the avoidance of the popular election of chiefs as in 1970 and, indeed, of taking into account public opinion.

If the modalities of application of the 1973 chieftaincy laws had been established after consultation with the regional, subregional, and zone officials, who would have had to implement them, and had been applied consistently, these measures probably would have worked.[29] However, such consultation would have meant sacrificing some of the omnipotence of the central organs of the party-state, that is, the granting of a certain autonomy to the middle levels of the structure. This was as carefully avoided as was concession to public opinion, which suggests that the success of the measures was less highly valued than the monopoly of decision making in the hands of the central authorities. As things worked out, the regional administration emerged somewhat demoralized by having to back down to the chiefs.

In another sense, the middle echelons of the administration were allowed or forced to take a measure of initiative. As has been shown, important instructions regarding the implementation of linkage policy were transmitted in the form of telegrams; such telegrams typically were laconic, forcing the regional authorities to work out details for themselves or to pass the responsibility farther down the line to the subregions. Such a practice has the advantage, from the perspective of the central authorities, of making it easier to repudiate decisions that prove unpopular or unworkable.

Thus, neither the chiefs nor the legislators nor the administrators were able to serve as important linkages for communication upward from the masses. Articulation of demands goes on continuously, to be sure, but less through the MPR than around it. Letters and petitions, visits to an authority by a mutual relative (broadly defined), payment of

29. This is the opinion of a regional director of political affairs, highest-ranking career civil servant in the Political Affairs Department on the regional level (my interview, December 1974).

bribes, these and other procedures enable individuals and groups to express their interests and especially to request that they be exempted from one measure or another. Aggregation of demands, as through committees or demonstrations, is strongly discouraged.[30]

Conclusion

This study began by setting forth an apparent contradiction. The Zairian regime had shown itself capable of breaking up autonomous centers of power in the society and centralizing power in its own hands, yet seemingly was unable to implement a policy touching the chiefs of the approximately eight hundred rural collectivities. One possible explanation was presented, that of Zolberg, according to which the African party-states are not powerful but weak and the chiefs are situated partly in the "residual sector" within which the party-state does not yet allocate values authoritatively. Miller's point of view is consistent with this; some chiefs have been "so strong that the local authorities have been forced to deal with them directly as spokesmen for their areas." In brief, these authors maintain that the party-state is weak, whereas the chiefs are relatively strong; if this point of view is valid, the attempt to eliminate hereditary chiefship was bound to fail, because the chiefs remain indispensable linkmen.

The Zolberg-Miller position, though plausible, is not supported by the Zairian case study. Some of the chiefs feigned illness and thereby thwarted the zone and subregion authorities who were trying to transfer them; this would seem to demonstrate that the chiefs were stronger than the administrators, their nominal superiors. Yet the chiefs, or many of them, were not strong in the sense that Miller would suggest, that is, in retaining authority in the eyes of the population; on the contrary, in many cases public opinion was unfavorable to them and could have been used against them but was kept muzzled. The chiefs were strong in this instance because the government needed their support and because distributing favors to chiefs was one way both to increase that support and to strengthen the government's control over those to whom the favors had been granted. It would seem to be clear that the central

30. The population is required or urged (depending on the circumstances) to participate in various "spontaneous" manifestations, such as *marches de soutien* or marches supporting various decisions of Mobutu. Most of those I observed were failures, able to mobilize only a small percentage of those called to participate.

decision makers decided it was preferable to keep the chiefs rather than open up a two-way linkage, or channel for "mutual adjustment," between the center and the masses on the periphery of the system. The administrators, weaker than the chiefs in this instance, were weak because the central authorities chose not to back them up.

It could be argued that the chiefs demonstrated their strength by flying to Kinshasa and arranging to have transfer orders rescinded; I would argue instead that such a procedure and outcome reflect a predisposition on the part of the regime to dispense favors from the center on an ad hoc basis. Like the masses attending a causerie morale, the chiefs also were "voic[ing] *doleances*, or grievances, in the hope that the benevolent governor who receives them will act expeditiously to correct the wrongs visited upon his/her children by some unfortunate circumstances beyond their control or by the folly of some administrative official."[31] It appears that each chief pleaded only to be made an exception, and the central organs aggregated these individual demands into a collective position requiring that the means of applying the law be changed.

Policy formulation and application in unrelated areas have tended to follow a pattern strikingly similar to that regarding the chiefs. For example, in 1973 Mobutu announced "Zairianization" of many foreign-owned businesses. No detailed instructions were made public as to how the "Zairianization" was to take place; many of the businesses went to political figures, including the regional and subregional commissioners charged with distributing them. At the end of 1974, after the failure of the *acquéreurs* (new owners) to pay taxes or import duties had severely damaged this financial position of the Zairian state, the president announced measures of "Radicalization," according to which many of the "Zairianized" businesses were put in the hands of the state, Finally, at the end of 1975, still another major change was announced; this was "Retrocession," under which many of the confiscated businesses would be returned to the former foreign owners.[32]

Further examples could be cited from almost any sector of public life in Zaire in support of the proposition that policies typically are

31. Nzongola, op. cit., p. 44.

32. On "Zairianization," "Radicalization," and "Retrocession," see the Kinshasa newspaper *Salongo*, 1973–75. Comprehensive treatment of this policy area, unlike that of the chiefs, would require treatment of the position of Zaire in the world economy and the constraints upon choice deriving from that position.

adopted on the basis of little reflection and little or no consultation with those who will have to apply them. Instructions typically are laconic, the president dissociating himself from the process of application of the measures, then intervening again when the initiative has run into difficulty.

It seems clear that these patterns are more than a matter of style, or at least that style in this case is an important indicator of the nature of authority in the Zairian system. Common to the examples of the chiefs, of other potential linkmen such as the people's commissioners, and of Zairianization, is a desire to distribute rewards directly from the center.

That the Popular Revolutionary Movement (MPR) has not become a force for the transformation of Zairian society is not attributable simply to the fusion of the party with the administration. Rather, the fusion of the party with the administration represents the resolution of contradictory imperatives flowing from the one-party ideology and the interests of the decision-making elite, which are justified by that ideology, first, to incorporate the population into a political party and, second, to minimize upward communication. The result of fusion is linkage limited to the top-down forms of coercion and administration. Similarly, it is no accident that the people's commissioners or legislators are able to play only a very restricted linking role.

It can be argued that the essential characteristic of the political party is that it brings together individuals "who seek, in the name of that organization, electoral authorization from the public for specified members of that organization to exercise the political power of particular government offices."[33] The MPR clearly is a political party according to this minimalist definition, in that it and only it makes such a claim within Zairian society. However, such a definition implies a relationship between public opinion and public policy, in which the party is the intervening variable. As has been shown, such a relationship scarcely exists in Zairian society, where public policy reflects the interests of the central decision makers rather than public opinion.

Linkage development, defined as involving "the creation of increasingly specialized sets of linkage chains," is not being promoted.[34] And

33. Kay Lawson, *The Comparative Study of Political Parties* (New York: St. Martin's Press, 1976).

34. Joel Barkan and John Okumu, "Political Linkage in Kenya" (Paper presented at Seventieth Annual Meeting of the American Political Science Association, Chicago, 29 August–2 September 1974).

it is not being promoted because the institutionalization of linkage is contrary to the interests of the central authorities. The evidence strongly suggests that the party-state is in reality a huge patrimonial network, headed by the president, who monopolizes or attempts to monopolize the distribution of rewards within the society; institutionalization of two-way linkages would be incompatible with the continued existence of such a network.

Contributors

Joel D. Barkan, Associate Professor of Political Science at the University of Iowa, has taught and conducted research in Africa on three occasions, working in Ghana, Tanzania, Uganda, and Kenya. He is the author of *An African Dilemma: University Students, Development and Politics in Ghana, Tanzania and Uganda* and the editor and co-author of *Politics and Public Policy in Kenya and Tanzania.*

Roland Cayrol is a Research Associate at the Fondation Nationale des Sciences Politiques in Paris and scientific adviser for Louis Harris France. His comments on French political life are regularly broadcast on that nation's radio and television. His most recent publications include *Le député français, Les élections législatives de 1967, La presse écrite et audiovisuelle* and *La télévision fait-elle l'élection?* His articles on French political parties and political communication have appeared in *Revue française de science politique* and *Projet.*

John G. Corbett is Assistant Professor of Public Administration at Florida International University. His special interests are community and urban politics. He has spent three years in Latin America conducting research on dimensions of decision making, political recruitment, and resource mobilization. The author of several papers and articles, he is currently working on a manuscript dealing with conflict and change at the community level in southern Mexico.

Samuel J. Eldersveld is Professor of Political Science at the University of Michigan, where he was Department Chairman from 1964 to 1970. From 1957 to 1959 he served as mayor of Ann Arbor. He has authored numerous works on the subject of parties, including *Political Parties: A Behavioral Analysis*, which won the Woodrow Wilson Foundation award for 1965, and *Mass Political Behavior in Democratic India.* He is currently working on a study of party elites in the Netherlands and the United States.

Frances Hill, Assistant Professor at the University of Texas in Austin, has done field research in Tanzania and published articles on agrarian political economy. She is the author of *Ujamaa: Mobilization and Participation in Tanzania,* and is presently focussing on American agrarian questions; her next book will be *American Women on the Family Farm: Kinship and Capitalism in the Middle West.*

Ronald J. Hill, Lecturer in Political Science and Fellow of Trinity College, Dublin (Ireland), has visited and conducted research in the Soviet Union and Eastern Europe on several occasions. He is the author of *Soviet Political Elites: The Case of Tiraspol,* and a forthcoming monograph on Soviet political science. He has contributed articles and reviews to a number of scholarly journals and is currently writing a text, *Soviet Politics, Political Science and Reform.*

Karen Hopkins, Assistant Professor of Sociology at the State University of New York at Brockport, has worked and traveled in Scandinavia, Finland, and the Soviet Union. She is the author of *Sweden: Focus on Post-Industrialism,* and her articles have appeared in *Journal of Intergroup Relations, Georgia Journal of Corrections,* and *Criminal Justice Review.*

Jérôme Jaffré is director of political studies at SOFRES (Société française d'enquêtes par sondages). He edited *L'opinion française en 1977.* His analyses of French political life and voting behavior have appeared in *Revue française de science politique, Projet* and *Pouvoir.* He regularly comments on French opinion polls and electoral results on *Radio-France.*

Young Whan Kihl, Professor of Political Science at Iowa State University, has published numerous articles on parties and politics in Korea and is the author, with C. I. Eugene Kim, of *Party Politics and Elections in Korea.* He is currently working on the reunification politics of Korea, as well as on a comparative study of the politics of North and South Korea.

Kay Lawson, Professor of Political Science at San Francisco State University, has lived and conducted research in France and Nigeria. Her articles and reviews have appeared in numerous journals, and she is the author of *Political Parties and Democracy in the United States* and *The Comparative Study of Political Parties.* She is currently working on a study of the Rally for the Republic, the Gaullist party in France.

Robert Leonardi is Associate Professor of Political Science at DePaul University in Chicago. He has conducted field research in Italy on a number of topics, most recently on Parliament and the institutionalization of regional governments. He has contributed articles to the *American Journal of Political Science, Political Science Quarterly, European Journal of Political Research, Legislative Studies Quarterly, Urban Law and Policy* and to the Italian journals *Il Mulino* and *Rivista Italiana di Scienza Politica.*

Michael Marsh is a member of the faculty of Trinity College, University of Dublin (Ireland). His doctoral dissertation was a study of variations in European socialism. He is presently interested in Irish political recruitment and the relationship between violence and social change.

William C. Martin is Associate Professor of Sociology at Georgia State University. He has worked and traveled in Finland, Scandinavia and the Soviet Union. His published works include two chapters (with Karen Hopkins) in *Management and Complex Organizations in Comparative Perspective* and articles in the *Journal of Intergroup Relations,* the *Journal of Social and Behavioral Sciences,* and the *International Journal of Contemporary Sociology.*

Dwaine Marvick is Professor of Political Science at the University of California at Los Angeles. He is the author of *Competitive Pressures and Democratic Consent* (with Morris Janowitz) and the editor of *Political Decision Markers: Recruitment and Performance.* His numerous articles on parties and political recruitment have appeared in a broad range of scholarly journals and anthologies.

John J. Okumu is Director of the East African Management Institute, Arusha, Tanzania, and has been a member of the Departments of Political Science at Grinnel College, the University of Khartoum, the University of Dar es Salaam, the University of Nairobi and Yale University. He is the co-editor and co-author of *Development Administration: The Kenyan Experience,* and the co-author of *Politics and Public Policy in Kenya and Tanzania.*

Steffen Schmidt is Associate Professor of Political Science at Iowa State University. His books include *Soldiers in Politics* (coeditor), *Latin America: Rural Life and Agrarian Problems,* and *Friends, Followers and Factions* (coauthor). His articles have appeared in *Comparative Politics,*

395

the *Journal of Latin America Studies*, the *Journal of Inter-American Studies*, *World Affairs*, the *Iowa Journal of Research*, and the *Third World Review*.

A. H. Somjee is Professor of Political Science at Simon Fraser University in British Columbia. He has done extensive fieldwork in rural and urban India and has contributed to the growing field of ethnopolitical studies. His published works include *Democracy and Political Change in Village India* as well as articles in the *American Political Science Review*, *Political Studies*, *Asian Survey*, and other journals. His next book will be entitled *Political Capacity: Complexities of its Evolution in Developing Societies*.

Tom Truman is Professor of Political Science at McMaster University, Hamilton, Ontario. He is the author of *Catholic Action and Politics*, *Ideological Groups in the Australian Labor Party*, and several articles on Australian and Canadian politics. His current interests are in the linkages between political attitudes and personality traits (attitudes), specifically correlations between anti-Quebec attitudes and anti-American attitudes and the personality traits of conservatism and authoritarianism among English Canadians.

Thomas Turner, Assistant Professor of Political Science at Wheeling College, Wheeling, West Virginia, has served as a member of the Rockefeller Foundation field staff and taught at the National University of Zaire in Lubumbashi. His numerous articles on Zaire politics have appeared in *Etudes Congolaises* and the *Pan African Journal*, and he is contributor to V. A. Olorunsola's *The Politics of Cultural Sub-Nationalism in Africa*. He is coauthor, with Crawford Young, of a forthcoming book on authoritarian politics in Zaire.

Index

ABAKO party (Zaire), 373n7
Abaluhya, 301
Accommodation: across-party, 16, 20; and linkage, 212T. *See also* Strife accommodation
Accommodationist model, 161, 162, 163, 164, 168–70, 177, 180, 182
Ad hoc linkage. *See* Linkage, informal
Administration, the: control of policy by, 17; Kenya, 293–99, 322; Zaire, 370, 379, 380, 383–84, 386, 387, 389, 390
Administrative functions (of a society), 246–47
AFL-CIO, 136
Africa: central-local relationships and political linkage in, 289–92; parliaments in, 18; party politics in, 222, 223–29
African party-states, 17; authority in, 371; linkage perspective on, 222–40; modern and residual sectors and values in, 371, 378
African Political Association, 294n9
Agitators and propagandists (USSR), 368
Agrarian party (Finland), 194, 195–98, 202
Ahmedabad, India, 213, 214
Alexander, Robert J., 330
Alford, Robert A., 132
Aljure, Dumar, 268, 276–79
Almond, Gabriel, 158, 332n15
Amalgamated Metal Workers' Union (Australia), 138n12
American Politics (Dolbeare and Edelman), 372n4
Amul Dairy, 216–17, 219
Anand, India, 16, 205; party politics in, 211–15; strife accommodation in, 215–20
Anand Congress party, 213, 215
Anand Milk Consumers Union, 216

Andropov, Yuri, 358
Anti-government demonstrations (South Korea), 85, 86, 87n35
Antioquia, Colombia, 272, 273
Apter, David, 221, 226, 381
Aquino, Manuel Zarate, 336
Armstrong, John, 363
Ashanti, 233
Australia: Commonwealth Electoral Office, 146; House of Representatives, 135T, 151T, 154T; Industrial Arbitration Court, 146; party system of, 132–35; percent of population in trade unions of, 135; politics in, 15–16, 130–32, 134, 141–54; Trades and Labor Councils, 136
Australian Communist party, 130, 141–44
Australian Council of Trade Unions (ACTU), 135–36, 142: dominated by ALP Industrial Groups, 146–47
Australian Country party-National party, 134
Australian Labor party (ALP), 15; background of, 132–35; campaign funds for, 140; federal conference, 137, 138–39, 149, 150, 153; federal executive, 137, 138–39, 143, 147, 149, 150, 152–53; Industrial Group, 131, 145–47, 147–51; organization of, 136–37; and trade unions, 129–54
Australian Security Intelligence Organization, 148
Australian Workers' Union, 138n12, 140, 147
Australia party, 134
Austrian Social Democratic party, 50–59, 64–70
Authority: in African party-states, 371; Zaire, 390

Autonomy: of political parties, 80; local (Mexico), 340
Avendaño, Antonio, 342
Ayuntamientos (Mexico), 334, 335, 337, 339, 340, 341
Azevedo, Pedro, 283

Barkan, Joel, 18, 20, 21; article by, 289–324
Barranquilla, Colombia, 271
Base, 253n*13*
Basonge Collectivity of Lubefu (Zaire), 378
Bauman, Z., 57
Bebel, August, 57n*15*
Belgium, 159, 380
Benefits, distribution of (Mexico), 329
Beria. Lavrenti, 131, 147–51
Bhavan's College (India), 217
Binza group (Zaire), 380
Blake, J. D., 142
Bodyul, Ivan, 365–66
Borda, Fals, 269
Borg, Olavi, 193n*28*
Brezhnev, Leonid, 349, 351, 353, 358, 362, 365
British Labour Party, 45, 133, 142; class breakdown of parliamentary group of, 50–59, 64–70
British Trade Union Congress, 135–36
Brokerage (Colombia), 270–79, 284
Brokers, political, 17–18, 103, 290; Colombia, 266–68; party activists as, 116–19, 128
Bureaucracies, 77, 158, 231; Kenya, 293
Bureaucracy, Dutch: contacts/communications of, 173–82; elite perspective of, 175–80; linkage function of parliamentary leaders with, 157, 164, 170; party and religious affiliations of, 166–68; social backgrounds of, 164–66; systems orientations of, 168–73; theoretical expectations re, 162–63
Bureaucrats (Zaire), 370–91
Butler-Stokes Survey Data on British Elections in the 1960s, 71n*46*

Caciques: Colombia, 268–69, 270–72, 274, 284–88; Mexico, 331
Cadre parties, 83, 226, 262; Finland, 192, 193
Caldas, Colombia, 280
Cambodia, 85n*32*

Campaign resources (Los Angeles), 112–15
Canada: class voting in, 132
Canadian New Democratic party, 133n7
Capabilities and obstacles, concept of 371n*3*
Carbonell, Abel, 273
"Catch-all party," 27, 63, 346, 364
Catholic Action, 144–45, 147; Australia, 130; Italy, 248, 261
Catholic organizations: influence of, in Australian Labor party, 130, 131, 132, 144–47
Catholic Social Movement (Australia), 130, 147, 149, 150
Caudillo (Colombia), 269, 284, 286
Causeries morales (Zaire), 385, 389
Cayrol, Roland, 13, 19; article by, 27–46
Center, the: in Australian politics, 134, 143, 153; in Italian politics, 249, 251–53
Center-Left coalition (Italy), 262
Center party (Finland), 194, 195
Central-local relationships: and linkage (Africa), 289–92
Central Nyanza, Kenya, 294n9, 295
Centralism (South Korea), 94–97, 98, 99
Chad, 233
Chamberlain, F. E. (Joe), 136
Chang Myon, 86
Charotar Vidya Mandal, 217–18
Charutar Educational Society, 219
Chicanos, 113
Chief (term) (Zaire), 378
Chiefdoms (Zaire), 376–77
Chiefs: Kenya, 293, 300, 316, 319; Zaire, 370–91
Chiefship: abolition of hereditary (Zaire), 19, 370–78, 386, 388–89; relationship with ideology and party (Zaire), 379–83; symbol of, 381
Choi Kyu-ha, 98
Christian Democratic party (Italy), 17, 56n*10*, 243–65; leaders of, 255–56; stages of development of power, 247–54
Christian Workers' party (Finland), 194, 195–98, 202
Citizen consent, 230, 231
Citizens: Africa, 222–40; cleavage crystallization and, 184–85; interaction with leaders, 7; as linking unit, 7, 8, 9, 12; as members of national political system (Kenya), 310–12, 314, 316; role expectations of legislators (Kenya), 304–10,

Political actors, 48, 222–23; in linkage perspective (Africa), 229–35, 240
Political associations (Kenya), 294–95
Political change: and ad hoc linkage, 264–65
Political development, 184, 289–90, 322. *See also* Modernization
Political loyalties (Colombia), 287–88
Political machines (Kenya), 293–99, 301, 321
Political norms (India), 207
Political participation, 8–9, 13; Mexico, 327–30, 342; Zaire, 384–85, 386–88
Political parties: African, 229, 232, 234–35, 292, 322; as agencies of democracy, 21–22; as agencies of manipulation and control, 18–19, 75–76; autonomy of, 80; as brokerage organizations, 116–19; campaigns of, 23, 112–15; cadre, 83, 192, 193, 226, 262; central offices of, 23; competitive, 20; as creators of political systems, 224–25; elite (Africa), 226–27, 228, 229; essential characteristics of, 390; European, 27–28; factionalism in, 83, 283; functional centrality of, 158; functions of, 3, 184; governing, 235; institutionalization of, 247; and linkage, 3–24, 76–79, 222–40; as linking agents, 3–4, 13–14, 22–23, 110, 184, 194–95, 222–23, 234, 244, 286–88, 328–29, 346; majority, 27, 33; mass, 83, 226–28, 233, 370; minority, 27; national, 370; necessity of, 247; objectives of, 27; "out," 104–05; policy stances of, 19; relationship with ideology and chiefship (Zaire), 379–83; rival, 100–28; ruling, 81–89, 96–99; splitting and merging in (South Korea), 84; symbolic, 235; US, 116–19; used as instrument of coercion (South Korea), 86. *See also* Opposition parties
Political Parties (Michels), 234
Political systems, 222; Kenyans as members of, 310–11; Mexican, 330–32; in USSR, 345–69
Politicians, professional (Italy), 255, 257, 262
Politics, 101; defined, 77; "high-risk," 80–81, 82, 86, 87, 88–99; local (Mexico), 332–33; multi-party, 16
Popular Revolutionary Movement (MPR) (Zaire), 370–91
Portillo, José Lopez, 344

Power, 27; concept, 102n4; centralized, 79, 82, 87; decentralization of, 79; in Finland, 186n7, 187–88; "hire and fire," of electorate, 113–15; local systems of, 233
Power and Society (Lasswell and Kaplan), 102n4
Power structure: Kenya, 292, 300, 318; Zaire, 370–72, 379–81, 383, 387, 388–89
Preferential linkage, 14, 28, 29, 30–34; intrapartisan linkage and, 35–46; societal linkage and, 30–34
Presidency: Zaire, 383, 391; power of (Kenya), 296–97, 298
"Presidential monarchy," 380
Prewitt, Kenneth, 8, 9, 14n26, 100, 105–08, 109, 128
Process (term), 10n19
Professional background: of party activists (Los Angeles), 113
Professionalization (of politics), 56–57, 70–71, 255, 257, 262
Proletariat (USSR), 348–49; membership of, in CPSU, 351–52
Proportionality (Dutch system), 160, 162, 166–68
Protestants: Australia, 132; in Republican party (US), 113
Public economic sector (Italy), 253–65
Public opinion, 108, 109, 119, 128, 206, 328; government responsiveness to, 101–06
PVDA (Dutch Labor party), 172

Queensland, Australia, 135, 150; ALP Industrial Groups in, 145; Labour-in-Politics Convention, 138; State Executive, 147; Trades and Labour Council, 136, 146

Radicalism (Socialist parties), 61–62, 64–70, 71
Radicaux de Gauche (Movement of the Left Radicals) (MRG), 29, 30, 32
Rank-and-file/leadership contradictions (France), 35–46
Rational-choice model, 267
Recruitment, 346; centralized, 18, 21, 335, 341–43, 344; in CPSU, 353–54, 358; in high-risk politics countries, 81–82; and interest representation, 48–50; and party leaders and working class (Europe), 47–74; social, 63; and support, 48–50; USSR, 348n4